Connell Ward and Lucas

Connell Ward and Lucas

Modern movement architects in England 1929–1939

Dennis Sharp | Sally Rendel

F

FRANCES LINCOLN LIMITED

Frances Lincoln Ltd
4 Torriano Mews
Torriano Avenue
London NW5 2RZ
www.franceslincoln.com

Connell Ward and Lucas
Copyright © Dennis Sharp 2008

First Frances Lincoln edition: 2008

A catalogue record for this book is available from the
British Library.

ISBN 13: 978-0-7112-2768-2

Printed and bound in China

9 8 7 6 5 4 3 2 1

Commissioned and edited by Jane Crawley
Design and graphic production by Malcolm Frost
and Graeme Martin

Previous page: Staircase at Temple Gardens.

This page:
Entrance staircase of New Farm.

Contents

Preface

Above: An early impression of High and Over.

'Connell, Ward and Lucas introduced a new language into British Architecture at a time when there were hardly any British Architects thinking in an uncompromising contemporary vernacular.' Arthur Korn

The architectural work of Connell Ward and Lucas of the 1930s has been internationally acclaimed and its influence widely acknowledged. However, little has been published in detail on their buildings, ideas and projects, despite the fact that architectural and art students have dedicated dissertations and theses to the position the practice held in Britain during that decade. Even less has been written about the work of each of the trio after the practice closed in 1939.

This book is the culmination of my own long-term interest in Connell Ward and Lucas and recent detailed work carried out with Sally Rendel. It has taken many years to prepare and is the result of fundamental first-hand research which has included site visits and interviews and discussions with a wide range of people including the architects themselves, clients, house owners, colleagues and historians of the period, building controllers, planning officials and fellow critics. It is the first dedicated monograph to illustrate the depth and breadth of their ground-breaking projects. These range from a predominant number of modern private houses, for which they are best known, to social housing, film studios, preventoria and sanatoria, as well as competition entries and designs for a Vitamin Café. The partners also made appearances on film and were interviewed on radio.

Our aim is to set the work in context and to chart the changing shape of the practice over ten years, with names that ranged from Connell and Thomson to Connell and Ward and from Lucas Lloyd and Co. to the final Connell Ward and Lucas partnership in 1934. It follows on from a slender catalogue that was prepared in 1994 for the exhibition on Connell Ward and Lucas. This was initially held at the Building Centre in London and then travelled extensively in the UK to schools of architecture, the new gallery at the De La Warr pavilion in Bexhill, the Volume Gallery in London and to the Brighton Festival as a featured exhibit.

The first part of the monograph sets out the social, political and intellectual framework of the Britain of the 1930s in which Connell, Ward and Lucas lived and worked. The book then focuses on each of their major projects – built and unbuilt – concentrating on the technical, structural, aesthetic and constructional innovations central to their work, but also giving some insight into their relationships with like-minded clients and their involvement with interior fittings and furniture. Much unpublished original material, including working drawings, has been assembled from a variety of sources. Contemporary photographs, sketches, original texts and recent illustrations indicate the changing and current conditions of some of the buildings and the text also describes major refurbishments, renovations, alterations and even full-scale destruction. At Wentworth one of the best iconic (and listed) houses of the decade was destroyed through a misinterpretation of the European Human Rights Act.

The postscript traces the diaspora of their ideas in the post-war period after the partnership was dissolved in 1939. Each went their separate way: Connell to East Africa, Ward into practice with New Zealand colleagues Murray and White, and briefly into academe as the first Lethaby Professor of Architecture at the Royal College of Art, and Lucas to the housing group of the London County Council.

The contribution of Connell Ward and Lucas to the development of modernism in England in the 1930s was exceptional, even though the main proponents of the 'New Architecture' were widely recognised as those émigré architects, settlers and visitors who came from various European countries threatened by the conditions in Nazi Germany and Austria. Among these Mendelsohn, Gropius, Samuely, Korn and Breuer were to make an impact, as were Goldfinger and Lubetkin from Paris. This book celebrates the generally less well recognised roles of those émigrés who came from the dominions and the colonies and the native English modern architects.

The survey also draws out some interesting connections between a committed modernist practice and its involvement with bureaucratic England, with local authorities, planners and planning committees, as well as the RIBA, the building industry and several architectural journalists during the 1930s. In a decade of practice apart and then five years in partnership, the trio produced some of the most innovative, yet consistently controversial modern buildings of their time. They also contributed actively to the contemporary debates about the role and place of modern architecture in what they saw as a resistant, traditional and at times xenophobic England.

The two New Zealanders – always the closest of friends – were quite unlike in character. Connell was patriarchal, tall, slim and bearded, while Ward was much shorter, stockier and given to sporting a heavy cavalry moustache. Connell and Ward took a different line from the other émigré architects who arrived in Britain in the thirties and their 're-appraisal of technique' was, as Ward recalled, to prove fundamental in establishing a unique body of work in an 'uncompromising contemporary vernacular'. It included flat roofs, transparent staircases and thin wall reinforced concrete.

Connell Ward and Lucas scored some important goals. They revolutionised the appearance of the modern house; they produced what were probably the two most interesting Constructivist interpretations with their designs for preventoria and they built the most progressive film studio in the country. Had their St John's Wood flats scheme been completed, it would undoubtedly have set a precedent in apartment design, perhaps as significant as that of Tecton and Lubetkin's High Point flats, One and Two in Highgate. The drawings (only rediscovered in 1994) indicate that the St John's Wood flats were exploring an organic approach to design, with clever, curved, somewhat expressionist, balconies to enliven what was fundamentally a slab block.

Connell's High and Over was widely acknowledged as the first authentically designed modern house in England. It was one of the first of the Connell houses to stir up open opposition from the local authority and the general public. The case against modern architecture was to continue throughout the decades, prejudicially at Ruislip, ignorantly at Wentworth and epically at Hampstead, where the house at 66 Frognal, now an icon, listed and renewed, received virulent verbal abuse from local establishment architects and an LCC chairman who called it 'one of the greatest pieces of vandalism ever perpetuated in London' – a comment that was duly noted by the trio in their invitation to their guests for its opening.

Dennis Sharp
Epping Green, Hertford   December 2007

Early years of Connell, Ward and Lucas

Two utterly exhausted, bedraggled and bewildered student architects arrived by ship at Tilbury Dock at 4am on a cold and frosty spring morning in March 1924. They had come through the tropics and found Tilbury something of 'an anticlimax'. Their hands were so damaged by their work on board that neither could draw for a long period after they disembarked.

Amyas Douglas Connell and Basil Robert Ward had journeyed together from New Zealand, where they had met as articled pupils, to the 'Mother Country' arriving at Tilbury on the cargo ship SS *Karamea* via Montevideo. Their 56-day carriage was paid for in back-breaking toil, heaving heaps of coal into place for the stokers. Ward remembered that it taught him 'a very great deal about humanity'. For Connell, the memory of the horrendous voyage conjured up pictures of Dante's *Inferno*.

Basil Ward (1902–1976)
Basil Ward, born on 22 July, was one of three children who had been brought up in a musical and literary family in Hawkes Bay on the New Zealand North Island. His father Louis Ernest Ward (died 1938) and mother Agnes Theresa Kilgour sent him to Napier Boys High School and then decided to article him to James Augustus Louis Hay of Napier, Hawkes Bay.[1] Here he stayed from 1918 to 1923. According to Ward, his principal was a colourful character with 'rather bohemian habits' for the small town environment he inhabited. He was 'partly German, was unashamedly fond of beer and played the flute with professional ability'.

Despite only having travelled once outside New Zealand to Sydney in 1908, Louis Hay had been influenced by Louis Sullivan, Frank Lloyd Wright and also the Austrian art nouveau architects through the books and periodicals that lined his office. Hay's library included a bound collection of large architectural images from the 1902 International Exhibition of Decorative Art held at Turin, which included work by Josef Maria Olbrich and Raimondo D'Aronco; the Studio magazine; American bungalow design published in the US between 1901 and 1916 in Gustav Stickley's magazine *The Craftsman* (readily available in Australia by 1908), along with other books. The Wasmuth folios on Frank Lloyd Wright of 1910–11 seem to have had a great influence on him, particularly that on Wright's Susan Lawrence Dana House at Springfield, Illinois (1901–4). 'Hay's interest in Wright was unusual at the time, indeed it was not until the mid 1930s that the American architect's work was discussed with any great enthusiasm in New Zealand's architectural schools and not until after the Second World War that some of his more adventurous ideas about planning were to be adopted by young architects.'[2]

Hay's senior assistant was an American.[3] RA Lippincott worked in New Zealand from 1921–39 on Auckland

University College. He had supervised Wright's Robie House construction. But this was not the only Wright connection. Walter Burley Griffin, a former assistant of Wright's from the Oak Park years who had won the competition for the new Australian capital at Canberra in 1912, lectured on 'Art and economics in town planning' to the New Zealand Institute of Architects in July 1924.

The Hay practice is perhaps best remembered for a number of municipal buildings in Napier. During Ward's time these included the Soldiers' Club (1919), the temporary dias for the Prince of Wales' visit in May 1920 and the Central Fire Station in 1921 for a city which, ironically, was a few years later to be burned to the ground and rebuilt in the art deco manner. Louis Hay had also shown an interest in the single-family houses going up in California and opportunities arose to design houses in New Zealand with which he could experiment with this architectural language. The first of these was at Hatuma, a house called 'Hinerangi'.

Amyas Connell (1901–1980)
Amyas Connell was born in Eltham, New Zealand, on 23 June and attended Strafford High School until 1916. He was meant to have a career as an artist under the tutelage of his father. It soon became obvious that this was a poor choice and he was articled to the English architect Stanley W Fearn ARIBA in Wellington from 1919–24.

A published paper given by Stanley Fearn, 23 November 1926, entitled 'The aesthetic use of building materials' provides an insight into Fearn's architectural philosophy. He extolled the virtues of 'constant study of the work, both past and present, of the recognised leaders of the profession throughout the world' in order to 'reach a high level of excellence in our own work'.[4] He had recently travelled to San Francisco to see exhibition buildings there and one may assume that in his five year experience at Fearn's office Connell became well versed in the master architects from history and was encouraged to keep up with news of the worldwide emerging architectures.

Fearn's views on concrete are also interesting in the light of Connell's future work. The erection of a large concrete church in Wellington had been considered by many of the architects who saw it under construction to be more beautiful in its naked state than when coated with stucco. To Fearn this begged an interesting question: 'Is there one of us who having the opportunity has had the temerity to leave the building in its rough state and thus save the client's pocket and educate the public to the fact that rough, unassuming concrete is not a material to be despised?' He explains that this might only be suitable if building in a gothic style or a vernacular character, but his pupil was to take this idea much further.[5]

Two competition entry house designs appear in the *NZIA Journal* of December 1933 illustrating the work of

THE VILLA OF TIBERIUS
ON THE ISLAND OF CAPRI
PLAN OF THE ACTUAL STATE

Above:
Amyas Connell's plan for the restoration of the Villa of
Tiberius made in his second year at the British School in
Rome, 1928.

Opposite:
A Survey photograph of the Capri coastline.
Connell's winning entry for the NZIA war memorial
student competition, 1921.
Connell's competition entry for a Greek theatre.
Louis Hay's temporary Dias built in Nelson Park for the
Prince of Wales' visit, May 1920.

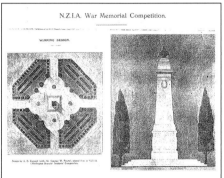

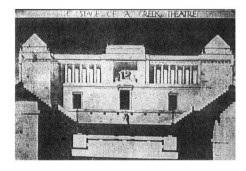

the practice at that time as very much in the arts and crafts vein in brick and render. Quite independently Connell took part in student competitions in Wellington during his time with Stanley Fearn and appears for the first time in the press with his winning entry to the NZIA Wellington branch war memorial students' competition in 1921.

Basil Ward moved to work in Wellington for Messrs Crichton, McKay and Haughton for a short time. The two talented students studied for their intermediate examination of the NZIA and vied for recognition in the same competitions. It was this 'friendly rivalry' that led them to join forces in seeking greater scope for their talents. They believed that their future lay abroad, specifically in England. It was the 'conventional way for young men to come Home to study'[6] and this view was supported by their architectural mentors, if not by their parents.[7] Louis Hay particularly prompted the journey to England, 'emphatic about the need to pass the essential examinations in architecture ... to study classical architecture and the "styles", but in practice to follow the teaching of men whose illustrations filled his bookshelves'.[8]

Life in London
Arriving in London, Connell and Ward initially found digs together in Torrington Square. The examinations they had taken in New Zealand under the New Zealand Institute of Architects were not integrated with the RIBA examination system and hence it was necessary for the two New Zealanders to complete their training in line with the RIBA before practising in England.

Only relatively recently had architectural education been formalised in England. In the late nineteenth-century connections and social class traditionally shaped an architect's career more than competitive architectural education (as in France). Independent private practitioners were respected over architects in official employment. As the RIBA attempted to close the profession to unqualified outsiders, the systematisation of architectural education became inevitable and really began in 1892 with Banister Fletcher's full-time course at King's College, London. Courses were devised to prepare for the RIBA qualifying examinations and also aimed to correct the perceived tendency for English students of architecture to detail a building before conceiving its totality. Three to four year courses were created at the Architectural Association (1900), Bartlett School of Architecture, Birmingham and Liverpool (1904).

In 1924 Professors Reilly (in Liverpool) and Richardson (at the Bartlett) were 'outstanding figures in architectural education, though the AA, having got over its Neo-Grec phase, was being, as usual, adventurous, if somewhat romantic, under the beneficial influences of Howard Robertson and Robert Atkinson, and Frank

Yerbury, one of the most enlivening British laymen in the architectural history of our times'.[9] The first London atelier was founded by Arthur Davis in 1913 and some institutions began to run evening courses for the benefit of articled pupils and assistants. Howard Robertson started one at the AA school and Hector Corfiato another at the Bartlett with his colleague Albert Richardson. Ward tried to enrol at the Royal Academy School but his 'probationary scheme' was considered untraditional and he was refused full admission. Eventually he applied to join Connell at the Bartlett atelier to undertake architectural studies at evening classes. Studies were supplemented by work as architectural draughtsmen. Connell spent the greater part of his working time at Messrs William and Edward Hunt's office and Ward with FW Troup FRIBA.

Connell, Ward and the Beaux Arts
Professor Hector Corfiato, or 'Corfy' as he was known, became a very good friend of the two New Zealanders. Ward remembered that his 'Latin Greek logic and Mediterranean taste, combined with his Beaux Arts training, helped to broaden our somewhat colonial outlook'. They had several disagreements with the other professor, Albert Richardson, but enjoyed his 'splendid lectures on Georgian architecture'.[10]

The NZ Building Trade Journal of 20 April 1925 reported that Connell had won an architectural competition held by the London University to 'solve the problem of shopping in the congested areas of London', especially on New Oxford Street. The programme was drawn up by Professor Richardson, and the starting point of the competition was the principle of zonal planning in built-up areas. Shopping ways were provided on ground, first and roof level in Connell's scheme, intersecting streets spanned by light bridges, lifts, glazed pathways, and the roof gallery converted to a loggia in summer with a bird's eye view of London. He makes reference to the Rows at Chester and Florentine streets, but 'the general affect of the scheme would be modern'.

Connell and Ward used London as their base from which to travel in Europe. Off to Paris the architects made a 'pilgrimage' to the Rue Franklin to see Auguste Perret's 1902 apartment building. 'But above all', Ward recalled 'Le Corbusier's "Pavillon de l'Esprit Nouveau" was a revelation in its classic purity amongst the predominant Art Deco designs and a ragbag of eclecticism and of leftovers from the past, in the Exposition des Arts Décoratifs, held from April to October 1925'.[11] 'This was our first contact in reality with the man whose influence upon us was and remained profound. His work stirred us greatly, so clear was it in its intention and so uncompromising in its execution.... I believe the Russian Pavilion ... gave us this sense of an understanding, and a feeling for the Cubism and for the Constructivism which was beginning to play a very important part.'[12] The young architects soaked up the

art and cultural ambience in Paris, not concentrating solely on architecture. Ward remembers Picasso's work, early cubism and surrealism. They bought what they could of the books on contemporary architecture and art available in Paris, but not yet in London – including Le Corbusier's publications and Tony Garnier's design for Lyons, *Grandes Constructions* in the Albert Morance edition.[13] Although they did not understand the French, 'the drawings were, in themselves, quite sufficient for us to understand'.[14]

'Thenceforward', said Ward, they were 'part of the Modern Movement, though in spirit they were perhaps before that.'[15] Besides Le Corbusier, Ward lists as influences Bruno Taut (*Modern Architecture*, 1929), Perret, Lurçat, Roux-Spitz, Mies van der Rohe, Gropius, Scharoun (particularly the Schminke house), Brinkman, van der Vlugt, Rietveld, Bijvoet, Duiker, Oud (these Dutch moderns most caught his fancy). He was enchanted too by the lyrical symbolism of the Russian Constructivists of the early twenties and, not wowed by the romantics, he became more interested in functional forms and in architectural discipline.

Winning the Rome Prize

Despite their germinating interest in the modern movement, Ward recalled: 'Architecture was for us a whole subject, not just a modern movement', a notion reinforced by their time in Rome.[16] The two young students had more on their minds than just completing the RIBA requirements when they arrived in England, an underlying ambition for them both was to attain the Rome Prize and they took the challenge very seriously. 'When Connell and I left New Zealand our first aim was the Rome Scholarship,' Basil Ward wrote in the *AAJ* in 1956.

Just as the new courses in architectural education were based on the French model of the Ecole des Beaux Arts, so were the architectural prizes. Sir Reginald Blomfield had tried from 1909 to set up an English version of the French Grand Prix at the Royal Academy. The French scholarship was awarded to the best student at the Beaux Arts entitling them to four to fove years study at the French Academy in Rome and the emerging scholar would then be provided with a career in public service. The Royal Academy idea failed. Blomfield became chairman of the British School in Rome in 1911 (until 1939) and an English Rome Prize was set up there. The school had been in existence from the late nineteenth century and, in the wake of the Grand Tour and later more pointed professional study, catered mainly for archaeologists. The school had a broad vision from early on and letters were sent to the RIBA offering to enrol their students. The first architect at the school, Bernard Webb, was admitted in 1901. Students were admitted under the rules of a committee in London and worked in museums, galleries, libraries and churches, just as Inigo Jones

and Sir John Soane had done, measuring buildings and making studies. There were 80 students in 1913–14, but enlistment dramatically reduced numbers. The director, Dr Ashby, went to Australia in 1914 on a lecture tour and spread the word of the Rome School and it is likely that Fearn, Hay and the younger generations of architects may have heard of it.

In 1912 a change in the constitution at the school provided three Rome scholarships, each tenable for three years: decorative painting, sculpture and architecture. Each subject was overseen by a faculty and that of architecture included CH Reilly from Liverpool, Lethaby from Central School, Sir Reginald Blomfield from the Royal Academy, Lutyens, who designed the new Rome school, and Aston Webb. The scholarship in architecture was tenable for three years and open to students under the age of thirty. The RIBA funded the Henry Jarvis two year travelling scholarship and there was a shorter Bernard Webb award given for six months of study in Rome.[17] The prize aimed to provide full-time training leading to professional qualification, as opposed to the alternative of pupillage in an architect's office, and provided an annual stipend, board and lodging but meant postponing professional practice.[18]

It was seen as the most notable achievement in architecture, the top of four main prizes of the period: the Tite prize, Soane medallion, Victory scholarship and the Rome prize. It also involved the most gruelling examination. Again, modelled on the French system, two stages included *en loge* designs followed by long periods of 'drawing up', the whole taking about four months to complete. By 1924 the Tite, Soane and Victory prizes had adopted similar *en loge* examinations but each lasted only twelve hours with a period after for design development. Connell was limbering up for Rome when he became the Soane medallion finalist in 1925.

Connell and Ward's long examination for the Rome scholarship started at the beginning of January 1926 with a twelve hour sketch design *en loge* for a memorial hall for Lord Nelson with 31 subsequent days for each of the 23 entrants to complete their design. Ten students were then selected to proceed to the final competition for a Royal Naval College which was 36 hours *en loge* followed by twelve weeks to complete the design. They worked through the great General Strike in May 1926. In June 1926 it was announced that Connell was the new Rome scholar and Basil Ward a special grantee of the RIBA from the Henry Jarvis funds for a single year's study in Rome. Although he had won second place in the competition, Ward was neither a student nor associate of the institute and therefore could not be awarded the second place Henry Jarvis travelling studentship. The Jarvis was instead awarded to Herbert Thearle who, as it happened, had been a student of Professor Reilly's at Liverpool University.

Right:
A typical collective meal at the British School in Rome in the late 1920s.

Opposite:
Reginald Brill's portrait of Bernard Ashmole in the Director's apartments in the British School in Rome, 1928. Brill was a contemporary and friend of Amyas Connell at the Rome School.
Dorothy and Bernard Ashmole photographed among the Rome scholars including Connell.

Connell later joked that he had won because he had the most columns in his scheme but this belies the seriousness with which they approached the prestigious award. Both students had invested a great deal in the application and even given up their jobs to complete the examination.[19] Corfiato was delighted that they made it to Rome, not least because his old friend and rival CH Reilly had been regularly sending his students there from Liverpool. The New Zealand press proudly covered their success.

They had both exhibited a good understanding of the orders and studious regard for the finer principles of the Beaux Arts *en loge*, but seemed to have been blithely unaware of Le Corbusier's warning in *Vers une Architecture* that 'Rome is the damnation of the half-educated. To send architectural students to Rome is to cripple them for life.'[20]

For Connell and Ward it did the very opposite. These scholarships were one of the few ways to travel and study in Europe at that time without incurring ridiculous expense. In the first year, illness prevented Connell from travelling south with Ward but he travelled later to Sicily with other members of other faculties to study Greek remains. He visited Greece and northern Italy in the summer of 1927. In the second year he travelled extensively in southern Italy and studied hill towns, also seeing Genoa, Florence, Lucca, Pisa, Siena and Venice in the north. He went to Paris and London and saw Dijon, Lyons, Marseilles and the Riviera. In travelling between Rome and England the pair were also able to see new work by Le Corbusier such as the Salvation Army shelter in Paris, as well as new buildings by André Lurçat and Perret.

Amyas Connell did not take his place up at the school until January 1927 due to a three month trip to New Zealand. Bernard Ashmole, himself a former student at the Rome school in 1921, had taken over the directorship from Dr Ashby in the autumn of 1925. He arrived in the city with his wife Dorothy (née De Peyer) and three-year-old daughter and soon shook up the school so that by the time of Connell's arrival many of the inherited problems had been addressed. The school appears to have flourished creatively under his liberal directorship. Connell, Thearle and Ward arrived just as John Skeaping, Rome scholar in sculpture from 1924, left with his new young wife Barbara Hepworth.[21]

In his first year Connell studied the Campidoglio and the Palazzi Cancellera, Massimi and Farnese producing superb measured drawings. The school encouraged imaginative restorations of important monuments rather than just measured drawings which could be taken from books. Connell worked to create a restoration of the Villa of Tiberius at Capri for the second year because of his particular interest in the great villas of ancient Rome. The architecture students

worked with archaeologists and historians, and also artists and sculptors on these restorations. Rex Whistler reportedly helped Connell paint trees on his drawings of the Villa of Tiberius, although it does not appear that he was a Rome scholar at the time (Whistler also associated with Ashmole).[22] The completion of the drawings of his restoration of the Villa Tiberius was planned to take up most of Connell's third year. From 1922 original design projects were permitted with sculptural and mural decorations from collaborations with other scholars. Connell had become a close friend of the artist Reginald Brill, Rome scholar for decorative painting 1927–29, and he proposed to collaborate with him on the design of a booking hall for a large tourist office. This was never realised although a later architecture student, Thornton White, was heavily criticised by the faculty in 1930 for his design for a travel agency and bank. They claimed it was modern and bore no relation to what the school was set up for. The design work of the architectural scholars at Rome thus reveals few clues about the diaspora of views and influences debated within the school by this crowd of talented individuals.

Basil Ward, also studied the Palazzo Massimo and the Farnese Palace in Rome as well as Salerno Cathedral and the Porta Dila in Genoa in his year at Rome. He tried to renew his scholarship at the end of his year of studies but was unable to do so. For him, Rome was a ball. He did little work. Here they were 'being more "English than the English" but tasting the heady wine of cosmopolitanism. Rome in the twenties was wholly Italian, also, to us, an architectural revelation.'[23]

Connell agreed that the experience in Rome opened his eyes. 'I won the Rome Scholarship with a vast classical essay involving Corinthian Columns ... but the atmosphere in Rome – Greek, Roman and Renaissance made me reassess architecture, particularly the social aspect.'[24]

The Ashmoles encouraged the students and often enjoyed their work, particularly admiring the more modern of the architects, sculptors and artists. Bernard Ashmole himself commissioned Skeaping to carve the reliefs on a new fountain at the school in 1926 and particularly admired the work of Amyas Connell reporting him to be 'Excellent in every way' at the end of his second year studies.

Connell's first year special study of the Campidoglio in Rome struck Ashmole as 'a series of exquisite drawings'. He felt that Connell had 'understood their subtleties perhaps more thoroughly than anyone before, except their creator'.[25] Ashmole also said that he had 'soon recognised Amyas Connell's exceptional abilities, He was not only an exquisite draughtsman, but had a wonderful appreciation of ancient and Renaissance architecture, and was a remarkably clear thinker.'

Above:
Campidoglio in Rome, executed while in his first year at the British School, 1927.

Opposite:
Detail of Connell's study of the Campidoglio.

Colin Lucas (1906–1984)

At the same time that Connell and Ward arrived in England, their younger future partner, Colin Lucas was preparing to undertake his architectural training at one of the most traditional educational establishments in England: Cambridge University. From 1925 to 1928 at Trinity College he attended the relatively new architecture school. Rather than offering a rigorous architectural education, the school operated under the faculty of fine arts and intended to deliver a 'practical, though not deliberately vocational training' providing 'a valuable field of study for students who wish to study art but who are undetermined in their choice of career'. The reality Lucas found 'rather dull'.[26]

The architecture school at Cambridge had opened in October 1912 when three pupils presented themselves to Professor Edward Prior, the newly appointed Slade Professor of Fine Arts, for tuition. Prior, a pupil of Norman Shaw and devoted to crafts, was also an authority on mediaeval art and architecture. One of the pupils of 1913, Graham Dawbarn, architect of Heston, Birmingham and Jersey airports, remembers that 'he had a horror of the machine and of commercialism in architecture'. A young Beaux Arts trained architect from London, Matthew Dawson, would visit three days a week during term to teach 'architectural studies', elemental construction from *Mitchell's Building Construction* and history through measured drawings of buildings such as the Wren Library at Trinity.

At the time Lucas arrived, the school still encouraged a practical grounding in the vernacular tradition of Norman Shaw and WR Lethaby as well as in the English grand manner and the classical orders. The head of school in 1925, Professor Theodore Fyffe, was an expert in Mycenean civilisation and firmly rooted in the aesthetic teaching of the traditional. He was, said Lucas, 'not very interested in what we did architecturally'. History and theory of art, essay writing, building materials and mechanics were on the agenda. Drawing (freehand and constructional) was compulsory, design surveying and planning was optional. The students were encouraged to study the unique buildings of Cambridge by measurement and survey. Lucas says, 'I didn't know what I was doing much. It was mainly traditional – learning how to draw, doing beautifully rendered drawings of sculptural vases – and a good deal of the theory, engineering.'[27] The nearby engineering department was open for opportunities to test materials although the school had not yet introduced theory of structures in 1928.

This experience was mirrored by that of Hugh Casson a few years later in 1929 and 1930:

> In those days, architecture was regarded with suspicion by the dons. It did not, in their view, warrant a chair and Fyffe was primarily an archaeologist.

Not surprisingly the school's flavour was at first glance firmly academic. Pinned to our boards that first day was our design problem – a structure involving a classical shelter for an urn to be placed in Trinity Great Court ... The school was small – only one girl student – and therefore cosy, the work was light – not much done after lunch – but the yearly examinations demanding.[28]

Undoubtedly, Lucas' most important early inspiration and training came from his creative background at home. He was born in 1906 which made him five and six years junior to Ward and Connell respectively. His mother was the modern composer Mary Anderson Juler (who composed orchestral and chamber works, and the ballet 'Sawdust', 1941). His father, Ralph Lucas, came from an avant-garde and innovative family and was a man of considerable talent.

Ralph Lucas' father, Colin's grandfather, was the managing director of a telephone construction and maintenance company and had been involved with laying the first telecommunications cables under the Atlantic, and his grandfather and great-grandfather were both astronomers. It was fitting, then, that Ralph Lucas trained as an engineer at Cambridge University, which was seen to be 'the crucible of engineering talent' from the 1880s until 1914. He made a living as an entrepreneur businessman and an inventor and was involved in building, furniture removals and operating barges on the Thames.[29] From his house in Blackheath, large-scale experiments were conducted to produce a series of pioneering cars driven by valveless engines, the first in 1901.[30] In 1919 he created a home-made Lucas cycle-car and in the early 1920s he collaborated with the chief designer at Scammell, Oliver North, to invent the North-Lucas Radial which was constructed at the Robin Hood engineering works on Kingston Hill. With a top speed of 55 mph and an engine at the rear of its narrowing boat-shaped body, the North-Lucas' cyclops front headlight and port-hole ventilators emerged to cause a stir in 1922. Although cramped as an intended four-seater, the car was praised for its lightness and airiness – helped by a roof of translucent canvas. It was hoped that manufacturing rights could be sold but the car industry did not bite. Ralph did 65,000 miles in the NLR before 1928 when it was sent to Scammell and later broken up. The Lucas family made a trip across Europe to Russia in the NLR and on the way visited the Citroen factory in Paris.[31] Undoubtedly this was an inspiration for the young Colin.

At Cambridge, Colin Lucas said that he was only 'half interested in modern architecture'. It was a subject of discussion even if it was not strictly on the curriculum, although he remembered that tutor George Checkley, who arrived the same year as himself, if he did not encourage at least, 'didn't have fits' if the students brought modern elements into their work.[32]

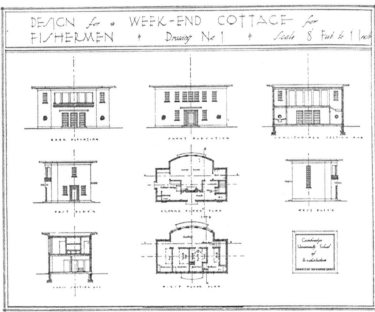

DESIGN for a WEEK-END COTTAGE for FISHERMEN + Drawing No 1 + Scale 8 Feet to 1 Inch

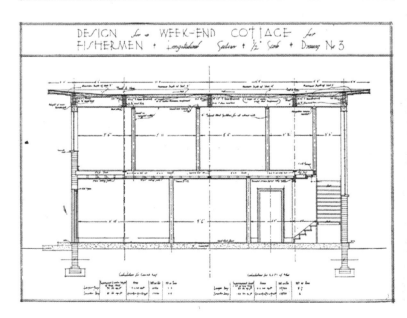

DESIGN for a WEEK-END COTTAGE for FISHERMEN + Longitudinal Section + ½ Scale + Drawing No 3

Checkley (1893–1960), a New Zealander like Connell and Ward, had been articled to Cecil Wood in Christchurch, and after the war had come to England to attend Liverpool School of Architecture from 1919–22. He had then gone to the British School in Rome having been awarded the Henry Jarvis scholarship in 1922. The year 1925 was also his first year at Cambridge, and the first of his career in teaching which would take him to the Regent Street Polytechnic in 1934 and eventually to become head of Nottingham University School of Architecture, 1937–48. Checkley was remembered by Hugh Casson as 'the tongue-tied but dedicated modernist with some highly influential houses to prove it'.[33] The most important of these were in Cambridge: the White House on Madingley Road, 1930–31 and Thurso House, Conduit Head Road, 1932. Lucas later exhibited with him at the RIBA centenary exhibition in 1934.[34]

The students would have been aware of what was happening on the continent through the architectural press coverage of contemporary projects in France, Germany and Holland. Mansfield Forbes, member of the faculty of fine arts and architecture and great arbiter of modern taste in Cambridge at this time, made his newly designed house, Finella, a focal point for discussion on contemporary issues, design and architecture.[35] The house was itself a testament to his convictions and had been refurbished extensively by the young Australian Raymond McGrath, who held an early research post at Clare College from 1927–29. University men such as tutor Harold Tomlinson and Raymond McGrath met with other architects and potential clients there.[36] This was a close network. Kit Nicholson (1904–48), brother of Ben Nicholson, was another exhibitor at the MOMA exhibition in 1937 and a highly competent modernist. He was also a Cambridge graduate from Jesus College (1923–26) who overlapped with Lucas for a year.

Colin Lucas' final year scheme for a Fisherman's Weekend Cottage of 1928, appeared in the *RIBA Journal*. It was a flat roofed, symmetrical, quiet scheme but showed evidence of simpler contemporary forms within the classical symmetry.

Opposite:
Silver Birches, Lucas' sketch from memory of his first private house commission of 1927 for Miss Madge Porter at Burghclere.
Photograph of Colin Lucas, featured in his section in the *Unit One* book, at the Blackheath offices of Lucas, Lloyd and Co.

Left:
The North-Lucas Radial car with its designer, Ralph Lucas, at the wheel.
Lucas' final year design for a fisherman's weekend cottage, 1928.

Architecture of the Devil's Decade

'There could be no revolution without a total reappraisal of technique.'[1]

The 1930s in Britain have been described as the 'Devil's Decade' in which a sweet and sour drama was played out against a background of horrendous poverty, huge unemployment (3.75 million in 1932) and an obsessive search for speed and commercial success. The beauty of bravery was extolled throughout the horrors of the Spanish Civil War, a flirtation with communism became for many a serious affair and the spectre and finally the reality of a hideous European war appeared before the end of the decade.

WH Auden, from the Left, described the 1930s as a 'low dishonest decade' which hugely advanced the transformation of British society into a consumerist one – the mass market, the emergence of advertising, hire purchase, credit, all the intrinsic components of our contemporary state. Society witnessed the introduction of mass media, the rise of supermarkets and the decline of northern industries, the emergence of new automobiles and electronics and the development of the service industry. The last steel section tower of the national grid was put into place near Fordingbridge in 1933 (begun in 1927) and it made possible a massive technical revolution, introducing new comforts such as lighting in the average house and the possibility of new household appliances. Wireless sets brought entertainment home and cinema conquered the world.

The publicising of the railways built up the hopes of travellers and new services to ports were advertised. London Underground linked the Piccadilly Line extensions and employed good design in new stations by Charles Holden and others promoted by Frank Pick. Local authorities with any sense of opportunism soon had their own local airports (often in the modern style) and aeroplanes were opening up a new dimension of travel to the public. The key to independent travel was becoming more affordable as motor cars were widely manufactured. In 1930 there were 700,000 motorcycles and nearly 1,000,000 licensed cars; by 1939 car ownership had almost doubled. Britain embraced the idea of travelling for pleasure. Easy access saw the growth of new leisure buildings in seaside resorts and major tourist centres, among them the magnificent new pleasure beach and casino by Joseph Emberton at Blackpool and Brian O'Rorke's designs for the floating hotel ship RMS Orion. Swimming in the sea or in newly completed lidos (for example; Saltdean Lido near Brighton) was just one activity in a spectrum originating from a nationwide interest in physical activities and the pursuit of healthy outdoor living, which predicated in a rather innocent English way the continental obsession with 'sun, light and air'.

In politics, the Labour party was torn over ambiguous allegiances with communism. At the other extreme

fascist rallies were held in Britain, most notably at Olympia with the involvement of Mosley's black shirts in 1934 and 23 arrests. The monarchy played musical chairs: George V celebrated his Silver Jubilee in 1935 and died a year later; Edward VIII succeeded briefly before he was caught in an amorous web and abdicated in December, to be succeeded by George VI.

Three young architects
The 1930s was a groundbreaking period for art and architecture. The so-called modern movement in the arts, which had firmly established itself throughout Europe, was to invade these reticent islands throughout the decade. Exceptional young artists and architects were emerging on the British scene and they were joined from the turn of the decade by scores of talented émigrés from the continent, the colonies and the dominions. This diverse fusion brought about a rich harvest of talent and many a new direction, fuelled by opportunities for growth and invention.

The practice of Connell Ward and Lucas epitomises this relationship, a coming together of three young architects: two from New Zealand, Amyas Connell and Basil Ward, and one from England, Colin Lucas. They were recognised at the time as exceptional talents, while years later, in the mid-1950s, with percipient hindsight, Peter Smithson was to claim that 'Connell, Ward and Lucas were the nearest we had in England to first generation modern architects'.[2]

Arthur Korn, a major architect of the Berlin of the twenties, but in the post-war period a long term unit master at the Architectural Association School of Architecture in London, wrote in the Architectural Association's 1956 Journal which was a special issue on Connell Ward and Lucas:

> Connell, Ward and Lucas introduced a new language into British architecture at a time when there were hardly any British architects thinking in an uncompromisingly contemporary vernacular. Of their work two aspects now seem important: the great courage with which they exploited new materials (concrete, glass and metal windows) and the artistic vigour in which they achieved a new way of life in building form. The classic purity, influenced perhaps by Lissitzky or van Doesburg, achieves this with extraordinary richness of forms and voids, and they obtained such qualities without resorting to rich materials like tiles, faience or mosaic. The flat planes, pierced by long windows like slots, and the large sheets of glass exposing the inner constructivist staircases, make a delightful, yet strong impression.[3]

In the 1930s what was called the International Style soon gained a strong foothold throughout the world. In an after dinner speech to the AA in 1946

Opposite:
Progress chart of 1901–1934 designed by John Gloag and Raymond McGrath for the *Architectural Review*, May 1934.

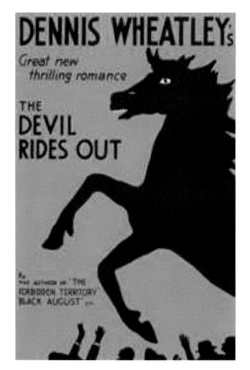

Henry-Russell Hitchcock made it clear that style was a straitjacket and that in the context of modernism it proved to be only a working hypothesis. However, '…considered as style', he said, 'the new architecture was necessarily international from the first, because its sources were obviously not all found in one place…'[4]

By the end of the decade most countries had a few International Style buildings, clearly influenced by the work of Le Corbusier and other architect members of CIAM (Congrès internationaux d'architecture moderne). This organisation was founded at the castle of Madame Hélène de Mandrot at La Sarraz in Switzerland in June 1928 to act as a mouthpiece for the new architecture – an aim that was reaffirmed in the Bridgwater Statement of 1947, when the first post-war CIAM congress was held in Britain. With the wide dissemination of the tenets of the new architecture, derivative modern buildings emerged bearing the unmistakable stamp of modernity – flat roofs, plain white wall surfaces, concrete structures and cubic exteriors. National groups – some attached firmly, others tenuously to the parent CIAM – developed and propaganda increased for a movement that had finally caught fire. Reactionaries were everywhere to be found, attempting to pour cold water on the efforts of those who were convinced that a new era and a new set of criteria had begun for architecture.

Almost simultaneously with its world-wide expansion a systematic subversion of modern movement ideas occurred in the Soviet Union and in Germany. A new kind of grotesquely monumental nationalistic architecture in these countries replaced the experimental and innovatory work of the previous decade. Only in fascist Italy was any real attempt made to attract the new art and architecture into the political arena.

Another brand of modernism had also grown out of the designs that had been displayed at the Paris Exposition of Decorative Arts in 1925. This had little connection with the current of modern architecture that pulsated within avant-garde circles. It did however reflect some of the characteristics of the work of the hard-core modernists and is now variously described as 'moderne', 'Art Deco' or 'Jazz Age' design. It was an important element at the time and incorporated architectural features such as zigzag surface patterns, reflecting mirror surfaces, rounded arches, corner details and ship-prow details, but it did not have the same lasting influence on design, nor did it have the wide commitment to social and aesthetic programmes that the modern architects themselves had.

The 1920s were indisputably the most important years in the formation of the principles which were to control the modern movement in architecture up to the beginning of the Second World War. The individualism and experimentation of the previous two decades led to an eventual consolidation of viewpoints on what constituted 'new' architecture.

The growth of modernism in England
England's performance on the world stage of modernism can quite generally be understood through its representation in the American publications of Henry-Russell Hitchcock and Philip Johnson. In their book *The International Style: Architecture since 1922*, published by the Museum of Modern Art of New York in 1932, England had a minor, fragmentary role. The country – and not the United Kingdom as a whole – was represented by a single building: the Royal Corinthian Yacht Club at Burnham-on-Crouch by Joseph Emberton, opened in 1931.

The Modern Architecture International Exhibition held at the Museum of Modern Art in New York from 10 February to 23 March 1932 saw an increase by one of English buildings. It was the house at Amersham, Buckinghamshire, by Amyas Connell (1929–31), but, like Emberton's Royal Corinthian Yacht Club, it was not featured in the catalogue. In their contribution to the catalogue Hitchcock and Johnson claimed in the last paragraph of a section called 'The extent of Modern Architecture' that 'Emberton, Etchells, Connell and Tait have done the most thoroughgoing modern work in England'.[5] And that was all.

By 1937, Henry-Russell Hitchcock was introducing a catalogue to another exhibition held at MOMA entitled 'Modern Architecture in England'. In this catalogue he recognised that the exhibition may have come as a surprise to the American audience as 'the generally conservative nature of the arts in Great Britain during the last generation is so well known as to be exaggerated'.[6] It is 'all the more remarkable', then, that the pages of the catalogue are illustrated by the modern offerings of 25 separate practices, Connell Ward and Lucas among them.[7] 'Today', said Hitchcock, 'it is not altogether an exaggeration to say that England leads the world in modern architectural activity'.[8]

Moving away from tradition
Two years after the Modern Architecture International Exhibition at MOMA, the Royal Institute of British Architects in London celebrated its centenary (1834–1934) with a move to new headquarters in Portland Place, won in competition and designed by Grey Wornum in a style that may be described as 'Scandinavian moderne'.

This elegant, spacious and well-planned building provided the showplace for a monumental exhibition covering the work of colonial, dominion and foreign architects arranged around categories ranging from 'planning the dwelling' (curated by Raymond McGrath) and 'the idea of planning' (Maxwell Fry) to 'building for worship' (organised by NF Cachemaille-Day). The

sectional category on dwelling included houses by Goodhart-Rendel, Guy Dawber and Baillie Scott as well as Oliver Hill with his Joldwynds, George Checkley's Thurso House at Cambridge, Tecton's reinforced concrete house at Gidea Park and Noah's House by Colin Lucas, attributed here to Connell Ward and Lucas. Connell's house at Grayswood was included and also attributed to the new firm. Neither example was shown in the catalogue of the exhibition but both appeared again in the same year in Raymond McGrath's book *Twentieth Century Houses* (Faber, 1934) alongside a selection of other international examples that were shown at the RIBA. McGrath's book was the most succinct statement of received architectural wisdom about continental modernism published in the UK at that time and was written in 'basic English'.

It was Art Deco, however, that for most people epitomised the early 1930s in England. It was found in the typically Art Deco-ish surroundings of the mermaid's grotto auditorium of the New Victoria Theatre (by E Walmsley Lewis) or the houses chosen to form the backdrop for Agatha Christie's Belgian detective Hercule Poirot. Shiny, brash, angular and spiky but slick, the style took its name from the Paris Exposition of Decorative Arts of 1925, which smacked of optimism and tasted of decadence. It was streamlined and modernistic and used to celebrate the new typologies of pleasure and leisure: cinemas, night-clubs and casinos, seaside showplaces, service stations, aerodromes and underground stations and transport depots. It was related too to rich interiors and design, to their finishes and style as well as to the burgeoning expansion and development of services in the post-depression period.

'This is the England', JB Priestley wrote in his travel book of 1934 *English Journey*, 'of arterial and bypass roads, of filling stations and factories that look like exhibition buildings, of giant cinemas and dance halls and cafes, of bungalows with tiny gardens, cocktail bars, Woolworths, motor coaches, wireless, hiking, factory girls looking like actresses, greyhound racing and dirt tracks, swimming pools....'[9] It could hardly be argued that for such buildings there was the need for a new aesthetic. Indeed the superficiality of the forms of such buildings clearly spelled the death of the genre. For the general public they were probably more characteristic of the times than the 'high art' or Museum of Modern Art architecture of the period more closely associated with the aspirations of the common weal than the didactic internationalist images of the avant-garde. The influences on the Art Deco structures stem from a popular bank of images ranging from the streamlined modern designs of the United States to the delicate work of the craftsmen and glass-makers of France. It was an all-purpose aesthetic, unlike modernism which was struggling for years for an identifiable aesthetic that suited the socialistic and functionalist causes espoused by its progenitors.

The more specifically 'modern' ideas current in the architecture of the period were concerned with more serious issues, which for some appeared to be scientifically based and for others demonstrated a desire for a move away from tradition. One has only to compare the Art Deco designs of, say, Andrew Mather or Oliver Hill with those of Connell Ward and Lucas, Lubetkin, Maxwell Fry and Wells Coates to see how far apart were ideology and metaphor. The two attitudes collided violently in the mid-1930s. Those with strong convictions about the nature and relevance of the modern movement in art, architecture, design, music and the theatre became more formally purist as the decade went on. Architects of this persuasion had little truck with the middle-of-the-road British architects and designers (e.g. Thomas Tait) who seemed to applaud the partial modernism of Dutchmen like WM Dudok (1884–1974) (incidentally the first international 'modern' architect to be awarded an RIBA Royal Gold Medal in 1935) with his cubistic, flat-surfaced, brick-faced buildings. Dudok's influence can be seen in many parts of the country in buildings ranging from pit-head baths and town halls to cinemas and hospitals. Less talented designers chose to delve into the storehouse of Englishness for their ideas and wallow in the glory of the Empire, late Edwardianism, bankers' monumentalism or the trusty details of neo-Georgianism.

Juxtaposed with curve-top display towers advertising the advantages of trading with Henleys, using the new Hoover, or shaving with Gillette were endless rows of new houses, mainly speculative estates with bow windows and kick back roofs lining the arterials and contributing greatly to a new suburban sprawl. Civic and leisure buildings were built to serve the major players in the construction game of the thirties – the speculative builders and their houses.

George Orwell's *Keep the Aspidistra Flying* of 1936 describes the English social normality as an environment of conformity, monotony and constraint. His main protagonist tussles with the pressing confines of expectation until his eventual and not altogether gloomy surrender to existence in his allotted groove. This would undoubtedly have taken him to live in the suburbs with his new family to claim a house with a garden. Speculative builders, usually without architects, were creating what the public wanted in a cacophony of styles including those featured in many an Osbert Lancaster cartoon as 'Tudor-be than', or the less seminal 'By-pass Tudor'.

Connell and Ward to England

When they arrived in the 1920s, our young pair of aspiring modernists did not see much to inspire them architecturally in England. The New Zealanders had been taught to have great respect for English architecture and Basil Ward was disappointed, when he arrived in England in 1924, that there was 'hardly a sign of the

Opposite:
The Devil's Decade saw vast unemployment in the UK, the rise of Fascism in Europe and the publication of books on satanism and black magic such as *The Devil Rides Out* by Dennis Wheatley which bucked the trend.

Above:
La Sarraz Castle, Lausanne, Switzerland, where CIAM was launched.
Catalogue cover for the International Architecture Exhibition held at the RIBA as part of the opening of the new HQ, Portland Place, London, designed by Grey Wornum, 1935.

revolutionary movements of a bare twenty-five years before'. Rennie Mackintosh was 'a tragic figure', Voysey 'a prophet without honour in his own land' and Lethaby's teachings had got lost in the upheavals of the Great War and his message mistakenly reinterpreted as a rage against the machine. Basil Ward quoted Lethaby in a speech of 19 December 1956: 'If I were again learning to be a modern architect I'd eschew taste and design ... and learn engineering with plenty of mathematics and hard building experience. Hardness, facts, experiments – that should be architecture, not taste.' Thus Ward identified himself with an architect to whom he frequently referred with admiration.

The lessons of English architects such as Lethaby had been exported to the continent and their influences remained strong in Europe, forming a springboard to new movements which underpinned the Modern Movement in the twenties and thirties. Not until the 1920s was the reformatted message of modernism ready to be re-imported to England.

Things modern had been stirring in the mid-1920s but England was still out in the cold as far as modernism was concerned until the early 1930s. Bassett-Lowke, a model railway manufacturer and a keen enthusiast for things modern (he had previously commissioned Charles Rennie Mackintosh to decorate his flat in London) had to go to Germany in the early 1920s to find himself a suitable architect.

The Berlin-based architect Peter Behrens (1868–1940) built New Ways (1924–5) for him in Northampton. Behrens, one of the founding fathers of modern architecture, had commenced his career as an architect with a rather English-looking house for his family at the Künstler Colony of the Grand Duke of Hessen at Darmstadt in 1901. Without setting foot on English soil he single-handedly built in England's green and pleasant land a modest cubic expressionist stucco and brick tribute to the modernist tendencies so long fostered in Berlin and Hesse. The house was, in fact, somewhat disappointing: a rectangular building with white stuccoed brick walls; although freed of all historical ornamentation, it was adorned with currently fashionable Art Deco motifs. The planning and structural principles were entirely traditional, and it is difficult to understand why Henry-Russell Hitchcock claimed it as 'one of his [Behrens's] most advanced non-industrial works and genuinely prophetic'.[10]

The *Architectural Review* featured New Ways in 1926 and later included it in a survey of British domestic design many years before Behrens' earnest fellow-countryman Nikolaus Pevsner discovered it. Pevsner referred to it as a 'most important [modern] house' in his *Buildings of England* volume *Northamptonshire*, but he was careful to differentiate between its expressionist road facade and the garden side, which was prophetic

Above: Peter Behrens' *New Ways* designed – in absentia – for Bassett-Lowke. This is often described as the first modern house in England, 1924. It caused considerable interest as these illustrations show.

Opposite:
Evelyn Waugh's Professor Silenus in a sketch by the author from his novel *Decline and Fall*.
Owen Williams DIO Factory building for Boots, Beeston, Notts, 1929-32 and his Daily Express Building, Manchester. Harry Weedon and Partners, Odeon Theatre, Colwyn Bay, 1936, a typical cinema design by Cecil Clavering who was later to work with Connell at the War Ministry.

of the future, 'the accepted style of the mid C20'.[11] It heralded a new sensibility.[12]

Evelyn Waugh introduced Dr Silenus, a distinctively Germanic architect, into his first novel *Decline and Fall* (1928) to restore and largely reconstruct the family house, King's Thursday, for the main female protagonist. It has often been said that the witty, reactionary Waugh based this character on Professor Dr Peter Behrens. The commentary is wry and pertinent to the contemporary view of modern architects:

> 'The problem of architecture as I see it', he [Silenus] told a journalist who had come to report of his surprising creations of ferro-concrete and aluminium, 'is the problem of all art – the elimination of the human element from the consideration of form. The only perfect building must be the factory, because that is built to house machines, not men. I do not think it is possible for domestic architecture to be beautiful, but I am doing my best.'[13]

Houses for the Silver End Estate at Braintree in Essex, designed by Thomas Tait of Sir John Burnet and Partners from 1927, were similarly middle-of-the-road, and even more confused in their expression. They were designed for Mr Crittall (later the first Lord Braintree), the manufacturer of windows with slim steel frames that were popular among young modern architects. This group of houses – 'the earliest in England in the International Modern style', as Nikolaus Pevsner put it – was added to the wide survey of modern architecture written by Sheldon Cheney and published under the title *The New World Architecture* in New York in 1929 to provide at least one example of new architecture in Britain.[14] Years later Basil Ward recalled:

> We dismissed the semi-detached houses at Silver End, Essex, by Sir Thomas Tait because they were of wall-loadbearing, conventional structure and design. We could not accept as modern, Peter Behrens house at Northampton for Mr Bassett-Lowke. There could be no compromise for us. Beauty in architecture was manifest only when a unity of formal and spatial relations based on the function of a building and rightness of its structure was achieved. This was modern architecture in which 'every stylistic reminiscence' was to be removed 'from the vocabulary of form'.[15]

It was obvious that the real revolutionary spirit could not embrace anything so compromising. Howard Robertson, having set up in practice with John Murray Easton, made his position clear when he designed an exhibition hall for the Royal Horticultural Society in 1929, whose interior, greatly influenced by German examples and the Gothenburg industrial exhibition of 1923, was bold and functional with a simply expressed structure. However, it conflicted inexcusably with an eclectic exterior with its elements of pseudo-Georgian and Art Deco detail; it was another well publicised compromise.

According to Henry-Russell Hitchcock, English interest in modernism was focused on Holland and Scandinavia in the 1920s, fostered by a sequence of photographic books illustrated by FR Yerbury, the Architectural Association's erstwhile secretary, that covered the work of the Amsterdam School in *Dutch Architecture of the Twentieth-Century* and the twentieth-century work in Sweden and Denmark in 1925.[16]

There was clearly an admiration for the technological miracle of Manhattan as well as a palpable sympathy for the new Scandinavian design, including somewhat paradoxically the National Romantic architecture of Östberg and Asplund. The manifestations of an Anglo/Scandinavian style were not to mature, however, until the mid-thirties with the aforementioned RIBA building in Portland Place and such curiosities as Lanchester and Lodge's palace for the Maharajah of Jodhpur – a Moghul monster of devastating size – underlining the desire then current for eclectic authenticity. In a cautionary contemporary statement, the leading architectural writer JM Richards said that the architect was inevitably 'tied to his patron', a comment as true for the modernists as it was for the vacillating traditionalists. Illustrating the underlying confusion of tastes at the time, the statement implied a lack of conviction and direction among those who were prepared to commission buildings. There is an apocryphal story of the period – echoing the theme of Adolf Loos' essay on the 'Poor Little Rich Man' – about an architect who would say to his client before carrying out a new commission: 'Tell me what your graven image is. Then I will build it.' Oliver Hill was probably the architect prepared to do this. It was true that there were some clients who were clear in their search for a mercurial meaning for their buildings and had a 'style' in mind. Others would quite justifiably leave the new problems of the modern age to the architect. The results were often inventive.

Sir Owen Williams emerged as one of the few non-aligned designers of the time with his brilliant, clear-minded projects for the Daily Express offices in Manchester, Glasgow and Fleet Street, his pioneering building for the Peckham Health Centre (1935) and, above all, the sheer structural and spatial inventiveness of his Boots warehouse and factory at Beeston, Nottinghamshire (1932), surely one of the great buildings of the century, let alone the decade. It was much admired by Connell and Ward and applauded abroad by no less a modernist than the Swiss architect and author Alfred Roth, a pioneer of the 'new school' in more ways than one. Williams, the engineer, had however little time for the much debated merits of modernism and fulfilled his task of designing a functional architecture based firmly on economic and structural principles.

As they emerged in the early thirties, Hitchcock took note of young English architects like Connell, Ward and Lucas, more clearly aligned with a purer modern architecture; Chermayeff (English educated), Wells Coates, Christopher Nicholson and Marshall Sisson, later also Gibberd, W Crabtree, FRS Yorke and A Pilochowski. He also recognised 1935 as the year that émigrés such as Mendelsohn began making a mark with their buildings in England.[17]

After the first manifestations of modern architecture on the continent in the 1920s, a number of factors compelled talented architects to spend time in England: political problems in Germany and Russia; the decline in Dutch architecture because of Oud's illness and Reitveld's less explorative later work; the French economic crisis. Their influence improved the presentation of modern architecture and gave it a new importance. Quantitively their work was not notable, but the English buildings they were associated with during their (sometimes brief) stays raised design standards all round. Berthold Lubetkin, the founding father of Tecton in 1930, came to Hampstead from Paris in 1929 after he had been refused entry into his Russian homeland. Others were Eric (pace Erich) Mendelsohn, the Bauhaus director Walter Gropius and Marcel Breuer, who came from Germany, Peter Moro and the engineer Felix Samuely as well as others who fled from Austria, and Arthur Korn, who came from Berlin via Yugoslavia. All of them practised for a while with RIBA members, most of whom belonged to the MARS Group.[18] The fruits of collaborations between the émigrés and English architects, such as those of Gropius and Fry (individual houses and Impington Village College) and FRS Yorke and Marcel Breuer's strangely elongated seaside house at Angmering-on-Sea, are relatively well known. All of this, it could be argued, was for wealthy and enlightened clients or, as in the case of Impington Village College, rare projects which were the inspiration of social revolutionaries such as Henry Morris. The guarantee of hospitality was provided by entrepreneurs such as Jack and Molly Pritchard and Edward 'Bobby' Carter (then the RIBA Librarian), who benefited by their contact with their continental colleagues and their admiration for the functionalist cause.

In part through the presence of these pioneering individuals from abroad, in part because of the talent of the English crop, according to Hitchcock 'it soon became evident that it was, unexpectedly, in England … that the new architecture was thriving' around 1931–35.[19] This was short-lived, however; he pronounced it 'all but over' in 1938.

Above:
Thomas Tait, early houses at Silver End, Essex for the workers of the Crittall window manufacturing company. A Punch cartoon, 'Owner: Do please say you loathe it', alludes to Connell's High and Over at Amersham.

Opposite:
Modernism in England was at its height in the late 1930s: House by Marshall Sisson, Carlyon Bay, Cornwall, 1936. Tecton and Lubetkin, Highpoint II, Highgate.
Fry and Gropius, Impington College, Cambridgeshire, 1939 Chermayeff and Mendelsohn, De la Warr Pavilion, Bexhill on Sea, 1935.

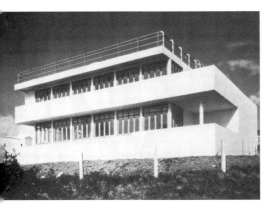

The dog-fight

Ward said that the young New Zealanders 'were impatient then with that strange mixture of matter-of-factness and lyricism, with the worship of history and literature, that goes in part to make up the character of the native Englishman'.[20] The giants in the profession, Sir Edwin Lutyens, MH Baillie Scott and Sir Reginald Blomfield, enshrined the national love for romantic historicism and 'somewhat snobbish taste'.[21] He recognised their passionate protection of historicism and 'good manners', 'scholarly use of local materials' and 'good taste', but said, 'I do not see architecture as a matter of taste, certainly not of purely personal and individual taste; and I do not see it as taste sanctioned by a select and specially informed few, a few who came to see themselves as self-appointed guardians of taste.' John Summerson remembers that the expatriates had a sharper focus and outlook than the average English architect, and 'also, of course, they hadn't got the Englishman's acute and sterilising sense of class'.[22]

There was a generation gap precipitated by the First World War that created a strange inertia in the creative world (among others). The war had interrupted the English development and left behind it a 'massive psychological resistance to innovation' which in turn fuelled a kind of militancy in the protagonists of modernism. Basil Ward in 1968 described this as 'a fortiori' a 'British distrust of new ideas' that was made worse by being 'combined with a strong preference for the traditional'.[23]

Sir Reginald Blomfield's damning dismissal of the modern design language in his book *Modernismus* of 1934 exemplified this attitude. He described a style invented to shock the establishment that was at its core reactionary and without substance. 'Modernismus', he said, 'is a vicious movement which threatens the literature and art which is our last refuge from a world that is becoming more and more mechanised every day'.[24] MH Baillie Scott agreed saying, 'Modern architecture ... attempts to get a transitory cheap notoriety by aiming at novelty for its own sake.' The attacks were clearly personal, as Ward suggested; here is Baillie Scott again: 'I have never met a functionalist, but imagine that believers in such a narrow creed must be rather dull and tiresome people of strictly limited intelligence'.[25] And when Blomfield referred to modern architecture as the 'German epidemic' with 'insidious and far-reaching repercussions', the criticism was also xenophobic. It was felt that this was a style for the continentals which could not be translated across the Channel. Such criticism ignored the fact that many other styles historically came to Britain's shores in this sinister way, not least classicism, which is widely deemed so traditional today.

The publicity given to Connell's first house High and Over at the turn of the decade ignited a wider debate on the authenticity of modern architecture in Britain, particularly in the domestic realm. Work had begun on the design for High and Over a year or so after Mies van der Rohe's Weissenhofsiedlung exhibition in Stuttgart, where for the first time a cohesive modern aesthetic was displayed.

High and Over was not quite that. Although essentially a modern building with minimal decoration, it was a pre-modern structure organised around a symmetrically or classically modelled plan that lacked the free flow of spaces shown in early continental houses by Le Corbusier. Clearly its image was the message. The Germans were quick to feature the house, referring to it as *Ein englisches Landhaus* (an English country house) in an issue of *Wasmuths Monatshefte für Baukunst u. Städtebau* in 1931–26 It was the first truly modern example from England featured by the editor Werner Hegemann in this influential organ of the new architecture, although earlier the journal had featured New Ways, the proto-modern house designed by Peter Behrens. Connell's house thrilled younger British architects and caused consternation among older members of the profession. In the BBC's broadcast in November 1934 'For and Against Modern Architecture' (also printed in *The Listener*), Amyas Connell was given a chance to respond to Blomfield's angst head to head. The antagonism shown in the broadcast between the elderly and increasingly cantankerous Reginald Blomfield and the young modernist had something to do with the generation gap, but one can sense also that Blomfield felt that Connell was getting too big for his boots and that the colonial boy needed to be kept in his place.

The BBC asked them to consider six loaded questions:
1. Is the engineer making the architect unnecessary today?
2. Has functionalism in building gone too far?
3. Can the English town and city ever properly assimilate the new architecture?
4. Is the new architecture ugly?
5. What will the next generation think of the ultra-modern style of present-day buildings, including the ultra-modern home?
6. Are we likely to evolve in the near future a new style of architectural ornament?

Sir Reginald perhaps represented the majority when he stated: 'This new architecture ... is essentially continental in its origin and inspiration, and it claims as a merit that it is cosmopolitan: I detest and despise cosmopolitanism.' He also accused modern architects of creating an anarchic situation where 'anything goes' and anything answering the purpose for which it is made is, *ipso facto*, beautiful.

Connell's refutation of these arguments was skilful, if a little narrowly based, his platform having been set by

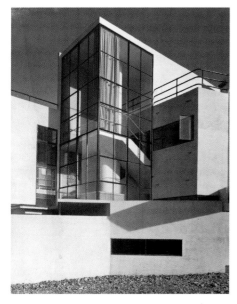

the biased and prejudiced remarks of Blomfield. He likened Sir Reginald to Sancho Panza in Don Quixote who greeted every fresh surprise in life with the remark 'I come from my own vineyard, I know nothing'. But he points out the difference, that in Sancho Panza's case it was 'an honesty of incomprehension which he never sought to cloud with abuse of what was new'. Connell took an interesting line on Sir Reginald's vociferous attack on cosmopolitanism. It has been a constant complaint by critics of the modern movement that in this decade a recognisable 'English' style was never developed. Whether this was the chief aim of those architects is very doubtful, for the principles on which the movement was based had nothing to do with national characteristics. Yet Connell stated: 'This cosmopolitanism, however, is – as was the cosmopolitan classicism of the eighteenth century – not an end in itself. Whereas Modernism was! It was an ideology – scientifically based!' A point later to be emphasised in the title MARS (Modern Architectural Research Group).

This ongoing public dog-fight is well documented but often denies the subtleties and individual interpretations that characterise the emerging modern architecture in this country. The language of bravado used to describe the young, innovative architects as 'pioneers' and 'young Turks' and their defensive retorts to their ridiculing by the traditionalists rides roughshod over the shades of opinion in both camps. Within the press, a few such as P Morton Shand and Geoffrey Boumphrey reported the creation of modern buildings sensibly and with open minds. Blomfield, a clever architect and writer, never lost his contempt for modern architecture and even in his last book, *Richard Norman Shaw*, of 1940 he idealised and romanticised 'English' architecture:[27] 'out of this chaotic welter of experiment', he predicted, 'our English tradition will again emerge.'[28]

Early practice

Amyas Connell was to come back to England in 1929, a calamitous year that saw the beginning of the Depression and for many people a fight for survival. John Summerson remembered architectural practice as being 'pretty flat' in the late twenties and early thirties. This was, at least partly, due to the severe recession between 1928 and 1932, which killed off the old style of practice. The recognised course for a young architect in England at this time was to set up by obtaining commissions from family, rent an office and get on by working on country houses and perhaps offices. Salaried architects working for the local authorities were generally looked down on by the profession.[29]

Architects revered at the time, such as Lutyens and Giles Gilbert Scott, were in another league that held little relevance for the up-and-coming 'post-war' architects in their early careers. Traditionalists such as

Blomfield were dismissed by the young, including the critic John Summerson, as 'utterly boring'. The emerging architecture students talked endlessly about the meaning of the word 'modern', a discussion that came to a head in 1939 in the pages of the AA student magazine Focus.[30]

But traditional views were disappointingly allied with general public taste, and reaction to modern architecture was particularly vehement when it pertained to the home. This, along with the reaction of the planning department, would have an enormously limiting effect on the output of the Connell Ward and Lucas office. To this subject we will return later when we discuss individual projects. Some of the young blood resented the atmosphere in England and escaped to the continent, to Stockholm and Berlin. Often the émigré architects did not stay long either. Oliver Hill epitomises the eclectic architect par excellence of the era: he was capable of producing nice buildings for charming clients, meeting the programme requirement for the modern (or partially modern), the traditional or the simply 'bright' scheme. He was not blatantly 'commercial' in his approach and was still making artistic choices.

Lucas, Lloyd and Co.

Colin Lucas' creative family interests, in particular his father's, were, as we have seen, a catalyst to his career. In 1928, when he left Cambridge aged 22, Lucas joined forces with a builder and his father's construction operation to create Lucas, Lloyd and Co., Architects and Builders, in London. Ralph Lucas was the general manager and Colin involved himself with the practical and technical side of the construction process from this early point.

It was in the technical side of construction that his basic interest lay throughout his career, his work with Connell and Ward, his research during the war and later his work at the LCC and GLC. He read *Scientific American* and was one of the architects who regularly responded to the Building Research Station's published notes.

In these early days, Colin Lucas nurtured a passion for concrete as a material 'one could model'. He became attracted to concrete mainly through his father, who wanted to build a house on the banks of the River Thames. 'We put our heads together', Colin Lucas remembered, 'and decided that the right thing to use was Thames ballast, cheap and delivered locally by barges.'[31] Economically it was a good solution and Noah's House was built on the river bank. This first adventure in concrete was designed in 1929 as a weekend cottage at Bourne End. It was heralded by the magazine *Architect and Building News* in 1932 as the first monolithic concrete house to be built in England. For a sum of £1,300 Lucas, Lucas and Co. constructed a bungalow with separate boiler house, and at the water's edge a boathouse for the inventive waterborne engineering experiments of Ralph Lucas, with a music room above for his wife. Years later the bungalow was roofed over with a pitched thatch roof but the Boat House has been Grade II listed by English Heritage.

The popularity of this weekend house typology and commissions from his family kept Lucas' early career buoyant in the depressed early 1930s, when he spent much of the rest of his time working from his office at East Greenwich 'putting up shop fronts in the Old Kent Road'. Two extensions to Noah's House, a weekend cottage for his grandfather in Sussex (Sunlight House) and one for himself at Wrotham in Kent (The Hopfield) kept the concrete experiment fluid under Lucas, Lloyd and Co. and Lucas felt comfortable in his role as architect-builder, likening himself to Auguste Perret. His passion for concrete only increased with time.[32] In 1930, Colin Lucas married Dione Wilson, the daughter of Henry Wilson, arts and crafts architect and jeweller and the first editor of the *Architectural Review*.

The last and the largest project Lucas started before he officially teamed up with Connell and Ward was the Flat Roof House at Little Frieth, near Henley in Buckinghamshire. This was for a friend of his wife. It was not constructed by Lucas, Lloyd and Co. but was fully supervised by Colin Lucas during its construction. It was completed in early 1935 after he joined with Connell and Ward, and it brought together elements of the classical symmetry of his student fisherman's cottage scheme, the sculptural playfulness of the Hopfield at Wrotham and the technical advances he had achieved since Noah's House.

Unit One

In 1933 Colin Lucas was invited by Wells Coates to become the second architect member of the avant-garde artist association Unit One, a group committed to exploring the nature of the contemporary spirit in design. Lucas saw the group as 'a sort of advertising campaign', with an objective 'to familiarise the British public with Modern art' as 'nobody would have anything to do with it in those days'.[33] It did this first through an exhibition at the Mayor Gallery, London, in 1933, and then through a travelling exhibition of members' work from 1934 on. Lucas' work was shown alongside that of Wells Coates, Ben Nicholson, Paul Nash and Henry Moore.

The group was formed by the artist Paul Nash with the architect Wells Coates, the sculptor Henry Moore and the painter Edward Wadsworth.[34] In his announcement of the group Nash stated: 'The formation of Unit One is a method of concentrating certain individual forces, a hard defence, a compact wall against the tide, behind which development can proceed and experiment continue.'[35] A unit, he felt, would be more capable than an individual of making an impression in the face of adversity to modernism in England at the time, giving

members a common identity and a means of acting together while registering their individual responses to the question of modernity.[36]

There was protracted correspondence about the choice of a second architect for the group. Frederick Etchells, Rodney Thomas and David Pleydell-Bouverie were all discussed. Amyas Connell came up as a recommendation, Coates describing him as a 'young and vigorous' man, 'who is a bit flighty, but would benefit enormously by association with artists like yourself'.[37] However, by June 1933 they had agreed on Colin Lucas, who became the youngest member of the group. Hence, Lucas' own house at Wrotham appeared in the exhibitions and publications among works by the other cutting-edge artist members, the sculptors Henry Moore and Barbara Hepworth, the painters Edward Wadsworth, Ben Nicholson, Paul Nash, Frances Hodgkins,[38] Edward Burra, John Bigge and John Armstrong.[39]

Herbert Read collected the voices of the group in his publication to accompany the travelling exhibition as a series of short pieces.[40] In Colin Lucas' statement, a rare glimpse of his thoughts, he said, 'I find arguments on aesthetics as meaningless as they are endless.' For him the contemporary trend to base critical analysis in the opposing dualities 'structure-economy-efficiency' on one side and 'appearance-style-art' on the other was senseless. He extolled the achievement of fitness for purpose in design as a thing that is inherently beautiful. 'A clean looking job', he said, 'is the engineer's aesthetic and an extremely successful one too.'[41] Lucas describes his belief in the beauty of functional form, honesty to materials and his commitment to explore the limits of a modern scientific approach to design, eschewing the precedents of previous styles. A general leanness and simplicity in Lucas' designs supports his Unit One manifesto but there is an additional playfulness in his aesthetic compositions (most evident in the Hopfield) that is not entirely contained by this logic.

After their first exhibition the members of Unit One found it hard to consolidate a way forward. Nash, supported by Herbert Read, became increasingly interested in setting up a 'functional unit' on the lines of the Bauhaus and in February 1935 Unit One was effectively disbanded. In its short life it had attained its objective.

Connell and Ward

A year after leaving Rome, in 1928, Ward married Connell's sister Beatrix Connell. They moved to Rangoon that year, where they lived until late 1930. Here Ward gained experience in the design of earthquake-resistant buildings and made a special study of their construction.[42] He later said that this was a very valuable time 'from the point of view of experience'.[43] He became the managing partner of Foster and Ward Architects with TO Foster FRIBA and he supervised

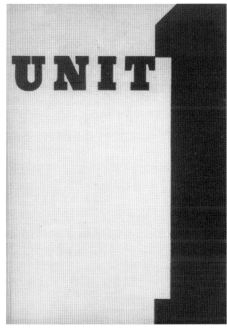

the new offices of the port trust, new magistrates' courts, the National Bank of India and the chief buildings of the new Rangoon University. A report of his address to the Rangoon Rotary Club where his 'Candid Expression of opinion regarding architecture and city planning caused a good deal of stir' hints at the less conventional spirit of Ward.[44]

Connell had begun to establish his architectural career while still at Rome. In the summer vacation of 1928 he obtained studio space in central London with his fellow scholar Herbert Thearle. Here he began work on the first of his built commissions. His client was his admiring Head of School, Professor Ashmole. An elaborate farewell party marked Ashmole's exit from the Rome School in 1928 and he returned to England to take up the Yates Chair of Archaeology.

Connell was approached to be the architect for the Ashmoles' new house on a site in Amersham. Ashmole remembered in his biography that Connell 'was deeply interested in modern architecture, and clearly had a talent for planning. Dorothy and I agreed that we would employ him on his return from Rome to build us a house in the modern style'.[45] Connell could not wait to begin his commission. He tendered his resignation to the scholarship programme just two months into the first term of his final year. The school's dismay was compounded by the fact that it had gone to great lengths to secure funding for Connell's last year in a particularly financially tight climate. When Connell gave the school a month's notice the faculty members, although they did not stand in his way, made it clear how strongly they felt about him breaching his declaration to complete the course. In particular, Sir Reginald Blomfield denounced Connell's premature departure. As we have seen, this was not the last time that these two architects would clash over a difference in priorities.

The revolutionary scheme for High and Over caused a stir at the Rome school as did modern designs at Cambridge by George Checkley (Henry Jarvis Scholar) and Marshall Sisson (Jarvis Scholar, 1924) for an archaeologist who had attended the British School. Blomfield again found it hard to reconcile these schemes with the classical grounding the architects received in Rome.

Connell, Ashmole and Howard Robertson went to some lengths to express their views that modern and classical did not have to be polarities, rather that great architecture could be created through an understanding of both. For Connell, Le Corbusier's classical influence was an important case in point. What he admired in Le Corbusier was his ability to encapsulate the traditional within the radically modern, which essentially was what Connell did at High and Over. 'His [Le Corbusier's] analysis of traditional architectural form is very evident in his adoption of proportional formulae and their aesthetic application into building.'[46]

To help keep the wolf from the door in his early practice when times were especially hard, Connell took up small commissions. Sir Philip Sassoon MP, a wealthy connoisseur and also a member of the executive committee of the British School at Rome in 1928, commissioned Connell to carry out some landscape design at his estate, Trent Park at Southgate, Middlesex. The original landscape here was designed by Repton around a house that was described by Nikolaus Pevsner as 'a singular loggia in the Italian Style'. Some Victorian additions of 1894 were demolished by Sassoon when he took over the estate, and he commissioned the architect Philip Tilden to create a Georgian country home from the material salvaged from demolished buildings in 1926. From Sassoon's time is a wisteria walk and a pergola with Italian columns of pink marble, but it is not clear whether Connell carried out the work.

There was another garden design project for Connell at Lyme Park in Cheshire around this time. In addition, Connell did a few fit-outs for shops and restaurants, sometimes with his sister-in-law, AM Hargroves, who was also a talented architect. Most notably they did the Vitamin Café together on Oxford Street in 1930/31. During this time Connell had an office in Welbeck Street. Connell had married Maud Hargroves, Ward's sister, in 1930. Basil Ward joined Connell in practice at the tail end of 1930 as High and Over was nearing completion.

Among the projects designed by Connell and Ward before they were joined by Lucas were New Farm, the Sinah Lane houses on Hayling Island, Usherwood and what has always been called the Concrete House near Bristol, which (like the Flat Roof House in Little Frieth) straddled the partnership, indeed beginning shortly before it was formed.

The MARS Group
The revolutionary mood of the time demanded the creation of tight, if not always articulate or coherent groups or cabals, such as the artistic group Unit One that we have discussed. In architecture this happened nationally with groups such as the Miners' Welfare Office, set up in 1928.[47]

Internationally, CIAM was founded the same year through discussions among some of Europe's leading modern architects who argued that architecture should be returned to its true sphere – economic, sociological and 'altogether at the service of humanity'.[48]

Unsurprisingly, the new organisation took some time to make inroads into the closely guarded 'classical-modernist' circles of British architecture, and it was not until 1933 that an English branch of CIAM was established and Lucas, Connell and Ward, still in individual practice, were invited to become some of its first members.

Above:
The north facing elevation and glazed staircase of High and Over, 1928–31.

Opposite:
The MARS Group catalogue, cover design by Ashley Havinden.
Part of the MARS Group exhibition at the New Burlington Gallery, 1938.

In January 1929, a letter from the *bon viveur*, Eton and King's College-educated writer and critic P Morton Shand to the Swiss historian Sigfried Giedion, the Secretary of CIAM, suggested that the Director of Education at the AA School, Howard Robertson (Shand's cousin), should be approached to discuss the English presence at congress meetings. Robertson attended several CIAM congresses, ostensibly representing the 'English view'.

Following this, again at the instigation of Shand, Giedion wrote to Wells Coates in 1933: 'To our regret, no English group of the Congresses has been formed. Mr Robertson and some of his friends attended our Brussels Congress, but they soon afterwards informed us that no interest in our movement existed in England.... Please let us know if interest in the new architecture is still so lukewarm in England.'[49] It seems that Robertson's remarks to Giedion had been mischievous – he was soon overtaken by the young avant-garde and his assumption that there was no interest in forming an English group was probably a convenient way to retain his position as the CIAM representative. Shand may well have known that Wells Coates was, unlike Robertson, the sort of man to be provoked into action by Giedion's challenge; he would drum up interest and establish contact. This is exactly what he did.

In 1933 the formation of the Modern Architectural Research Group (MARS) was announced in a press release.[50] It was to be a new form of organisation that used publicity and exhibitions as tools to further its cause. Indeed, of the initial six 'modern architects and allied technicians' who formed the group half were architects – Wells Coates, D Pleydell-Bouverie and E Maxwell Fry – and half were writers and publicists – P Morton Shand (writer and critic), H de Cronin Hastings (editor of the *Architectural Review*) and John Gloag (historian). These were swiftly joined by Amyas Connell, Basil Ward, Colin Lucas, F Skinner, Godfrey Samuel, Berthold Lubetkin, John Betjeman, FRS Yorke (Treasurer and Secretary), Cyril Sweet and Geoffrey Boumphrey.[51] The selection of members of MARS was based on their commitment to the modern architec-tural idea. A list of people who would not make the grade, including Grey Wornum, Oliver Hill, Oswald Milne, Walmsley Lewis, Joseph Emberton and Howard Robertson, existed from the outset.[52]

The aim of the group's work was in line with that of the CIAM:

• To formulate contemporary architectural problems
• To represent the modern architectural idea
• To cause this idea to penetrate technical, economic and social circles
• To work towards the solution of the contemporary problems of architecture

Above:
The entrance exhibit of the MARS Group exhibition, 1938.

Torres, Weissmann, Giedion, Moser and Rudolf Steiger (a former Korn assistant).[54] The proceedings opened with a dinner on Saturday 19 May 1934 attended by Lubetkin and P Morton Shand. A Sunday meeting took place at the RIBA followed by a boat trip to Greenwich Hospital. On Monday the group were back at the RIBA for a day session and garden party, but in all this activity there was no mention of Connell, Ward or Lucas attending. Much later in 1939 Amyas Connell was delegated by the MARS Group to host Frank Lloyd Wright at the Arts Club when he came over from the United States to present the Sulgrave Manor Lectures at the RIBA.

Accused of deviating from the modern

Connell Ward and Lucas maintained that they never really felt an integral part of the MARS Group. This was exacerbated, no doubt, by their run-in with the MARS 'style police' in November 1935. In April of that year the MARS committee had found it necessary to draw up a list of the modern architectural 'characteristics and principles' of the group, listing them as: 'regularity ... the avoidance of brick or anything giving an ashlar wall surfacing.... No conscious striving for symbolism of function ... avoidance of axial symmetry ... avoidance of applied architectural ornament ... avoidance of stressing movement in the design not honestly derived from the nature of the structure.'[55] Connell Ward and Lucas were hauled up in front of a kind of MARS kangaroo court to explain why they had wandered off the straight and narrow of this modernist creed with a neo-classical competition entry for Newport Civic Buildings. The partners, realising that they were not going to win this much needed work with the design they wanted to submit, had come up with a scheme that might win them the opportunity to suggest a more 'modern' design solution subsequently. Ward recalled that 'MARS had become somewhat preoccupied with matters more political than architectural [and had] considered our action "revisionist"'. He continued, 'We thought this hardly cricket and turned up for the meeting dressed in tail-coats and top-hats for a discussion as silly as the thought behind the order to appear.'[56]

The MARS group was primarily preoccupied with the exchange of ideas; it did not collaborate on buildings. However, limited commissions were obtained through the work of the group and when MARS member Godfrey Samuel competed with Connell Ward and Lucas on a project in Chalk Farm in 1934, the latter were the victors. Kent House was their only built social housing scheme, and they were shortlisted for the competition through the MARS Group's involvement with the St Pancras House Improvement Society's Northern Group through 'New Homes for Old'.

Described in detail later in this book, the well-received Kent House scheme incorporated twenty flats in two linked modern blocks for families on low incomes. It

Wells Coates' new architectural currency looked first at human needs and secondly at the resources of technology. Drawing these two factors together and applying the formal vocabulary of modernism would, according to Coates, create 'the new aesthetic'. As JM Richards recalled in his Memoirs, another important purpose of the MARS group was to make international contacts: 'for without the reassurance of being part of an international movement they would have been discouragingly isolated'.[53]

MARS' first meeting with CIAM took place in June 1933 in Athens. All delegates had to prepare information on the nature of their nation's cities for the theme of the functional city. Nine maps were produced in London by the group as well as reports on geology, climate, historical and future trends of development. Coates, Boumphrey, Shand and Samuel represented the group in Athens. New members joined to help with the preparations including Ove Arup, Serge Chermayeff, Joseph Emberton and John Summerson. Connell Ward and Lucas' clients Sir Bernard Ashmole and Charles de Peyer were also invited at this stage; however, Ashmole declined.

Intrigued by the way in which England was changing, the CIAM visited the MARS Group in London in 1934. The meeting at the RIBA was reported in the *Architects' Journal*. Among those attending were Gropius, Korn, Le Corbusier, Merkelbach, Syrkus, Sert,

Above:
The garden section of the MARS Group Exhibition 1938.
The assembled founder members of CIAM in 1928 outside
the castle at La Sarraz.

illustrates the type of housing that, in the end, MARS encouraged; 'centralised, high density housing schemes' with carefully orientated flat blocks, individualised balconies and (where possible) personal gardens. This was exemplified in two competitions: the Cement Marketing Company competition in 1935 for reinforced concrete flats won by Lubetkin, Tecton and Ove Arup (Connell Ward and Lucas also did a scheme detailed later in the book), where internal staircases worked as access to each pair of flats and the cost was kept as low as £94.81 for each habitable room;[57] and a design for flats for the Birmingham Corporation in 1936, where MARS members specified a system of construction using prefabricated components.[58]

ATO

In 1935 Lubetkin and Skinner of Tecton split off from the MARS group and formed a separate society called the Architects' and Technicians' Organisation (ATO), which had a more political agenda and closer links with the Building Industry. At the centre of the group was the desire to work for better living conditions. It probed further into the reasons for the control of privilege and finance over the current architecture scene and with a commitment to fight fascism took on a more active political role than the MARS Group, questioning legislation among other things. For example, when the RIBA in 1935 recommended qualified architects to work in local authorities, thinking that private practitioners might raise the standard of public schemes, ATO rallied to defend the official architects, suggesting that the solution should be a greater opportunity for training.

MARS Group members on the other hand were confused; some were also on the RIBA board and it was difficult for them to have an opinion on this issue. Realising that it had been caught between a rock and a hard place, the MARS Group turned its attention to more concrete aims. They began planning a propagandist exhibition in a smart and fashionable gallery. It was a carefully, even ambitiously designed show that took up most of the available space in the New Burlington Galleries in the heart of Mayfair. But the preoccupation with the presentation, its spatial effects and displays – planned for 1937 but opened in January 1938 – led one reporter to write that 'the content of the exhibition was submerged in the form and the form seemed to explain nothing'.[59] The old 'fit for purpose' maxims were displayed, but how did they fit in with the emphasis on 'style' or 'aesthetics'? Where had all their research led them?

MARS Group individualism

Maxwell Fry, reflecting on the history of the group in a letter to Malcolm Reading in 1981, maintained that MARS did 'no collective research'. This word in the group's title suggested a scientific approach to modern architecture and some believed that it was just a word

that suited the letters of its catchy identity 'MARS' and had little to do with the role of the group. For Louise Campbell the opposite was true: she felt that there was a tendency among the members to rest on the research, to explore the definition of a problem rather than propose its solution.

To Maxwell Fry the MARS Group was 'a collection of individuals who having individually arrived at certain conclusions about contemporary architecture came together to defend and to extend the beliefs about which they felt strongly'.[60] Unlike Unit One, where the members could remain individuals under one banner, with MARS there was an amount of work that needed to be done as a group, and a particular bugbear of Lubetkin's was that there were problems with cohesion from the outset. The group struggled to present itself as a unified body.

Fry also remembers it fondly as a 'coming together of friends' and as an 'organisation sustained by goodwill and purpose ... an association of which the value lay in ideas'.[61] And despite the earnest nature of the group, the members were given nicknames – the Hungarian-born Ernö Goldfinger was known as 'fingers in the till', Connell Ward and Lucas as 'Columns, Walls and Lintels' and so on.

By 1937 there were 137 members of the MARS Group. The world-famous playwright and essayist George Bernard Shaw was roped in to write a short foreword for the 1938 exhibition catalogue, so elegantly designed by the noted graphic designer Ashley Havinden. Shaw described the group as representing 'a violent reaction against impressive architecture. It has no religion to impose ... it considers the health and convenience not only of the inmates [sic] but of their neighbours and of the whole town, as far as it is allowed to have its own way, though of course it is often baffled on this point just as Christopher Wren was'. He clearly had no idea what it was about.

The partnership

Mr. Colin Lucas, B. Arch., Cantab., has joined in partnership Messrs. Connell & Ward, of 25, Grosvenor Place, S.W.1, the firm to practice under the name Connell, Ward & Lucas, Architects. Telephone No. Sloane 4640.

22nd May, 1934.

*25, Grosvenor Place,
London, S.W.1.*

'Of all the agencies which made me realise as a student what architecture was all about, Connell Ward and Lucas are probably the most important.' Peter Smithson.[1]

Colin Lucas officially joined Connell and Ward on 22 May 1934. He remembered that it was Philip Scholberg from the *Architect and Building News* who had originally introduced them. They were all members of the MARS Group from its earliest days in 1933. Connell and Ward had also consulted Lucas, Lloyd and Co. for financial advice on concrete construction regarding the Ruislip scheme in June 1933. Between them, Connell Ward and Lucas designed upwards of twenty private houses as well as other projects in the five years they stayed together.

Over the period of their practice, Connell Ward and Lucas' work was covered by a multitude of journals, not least the *Architects' Journal* and the more internationally important *Architectural Review*. The *Architect and Building News* remained loyal from their publication of Connell's High and Over in January 1930 right through to the house at Frognal in 1938. However, Professor CH Reilly's slot every January in the *Architects' Journal*, 'The Year's Work at Home', more or less ignored them every year. In reviewing the work of 1936 some explanation was given: 'Though there are a number [of houses] by Messrs Connell, Ward and Lucas, none of them seem to come up to the fine standard they set themselves and other people in the original High and Over house at Amersham. I say "original", for in passing it the other day I saw it had brought forth a number of rather ungainly colt-like offspring in the field in front of it."[2] He was referring here to the Sun Houses leading up to High and Over by Ward.

Ward was the main spokesman of the firm, lecturing extensively on their work and ideas. The topics were challenging – it would be interesting to know what the Croydon chapter of the South-eastern Society of Architects made of his lecture 'Modern Architecture is ordered knowledge' in 1935, where he claimed that progress in architecture had been retarded by ignoring laws of physical and mechanical science, and criticised the status quo in which the study of history and tradition was an end in itself rather than a means to an end. Guests at the Exeter Rotary luncheon in April of the same year were treated to a talk on a MARS-related topic on new housing needs for the working class, planning for the future and regulating the outward growth of the city centre.

The practice's run-ins with the planners, particularly over the Ruislip houses and the house at Frognal, were covered in the architectural as well as the national press. 'Connell, Ward and Lucas are in trouble again', reported the *Architects' Journal* in 1936. The practice wrote a letter to protest that it was they that were being troubled, not that they were in trouble.[3] With such publicity and the majority of public opinion against modern architecture, the practice did struggle, and social and economic circumstances of the thirties made the private lives of all three partners even less comfortable.

Their eccentricities and character were joyfully remembered by a former assistant, Niall Montgomery, at the time of Lucas' death in 1984:

One would be saddened by the news of Colin Lucas' death were this not such a world as anyone were well out of. Gone too the noble Amyas Connell of the blue-black beard, dazzling in respect not only of miraculous pre-Marsmatic draughtsmanship.... Under the cloth cap Basil Ward, the reddish, late baroque moustache, the gold-buttoned waistcoat, the silver-knobbed walking stick, and occasionally over the horizon. Ward one Sunday reproached a student for taking an hour off from the St George's Hospital competition.... The student asked, 'What do you believe in, Mr Ward?' Glares through window at the backside of Buckingham Palace, broods... 'I believe in...', wheels around to face audience, 'Architecture!'[4]

Connell was a wonderful raconteur with a tendency, particularly as he matured, to forget which of his many anecdotal stories he had told, although nearly all of them benefited from repetition. A favourite is associated with the MARS Group's hospitality for Frank Lloyd Wright in 1939. Amyas' job was to take the Master out to lunch at the Arts Club in Dover Street. He later recalled in a conversation with Christopher Gotch in 1974 for the *Ham and High*:

I was pointing out the well-known architects in the coffee room, when Wright (perceptive as ever) said 'Who's that?' indicating a little old man curled up like a dormouse asleep in the corner. 'Voysey', I said. 'Not old Voysey,' he replied, 'He was responsible for me becoming an architect. He had done a house in Surrey called the Nest. This house so impressed me I became an architect. I must meet him.' I tapped Voysey on the shoulder, a rheumy eye opened, for by then he was very old and deaf. He said, 'there's an American architect who'd like to meet you.' 'What?' Voysey bellowed. He repeated it. 'There aren't any architects in America', Voysey exclaimed. Wright was standing behind his back like a naughty schoolboy. There was a long silence. Lloyd Wright said how much he had admired The Nest in Surrey. 'Never heard of it,' was the retort.

Connell left them together talking happily. In our version of the story he left them playing billiards in the games room.

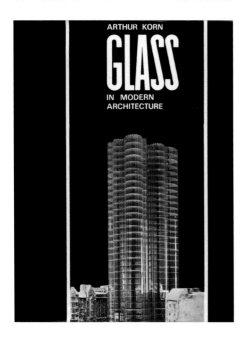

Above:
Paul Rotha's illustration, published in the *Architectural Review* of the flat roof-sunbathing trend that was gripping England, September 1932.
The practice's invitation to their client's official opening party at 66 Frognal, July 1938. The guest list included many of their previous and potential clients and other contacts in the artistic world; Henry Moore, Herbert Read, P. Morton Shand and Maxwell Fry.
The front cover of Arthur Korn's reprinted book *Glass in Modern Architecture*, 1967.

The practice's last joint competition was that for St George's Hospital, entered in February 1939, although Colin Lucas was job architect for 66 Frognal in Hampstead up until April 1939. This last house caused a local sensation and the invitation to its opening was duly inscribed with the recorded opinion of the bellicose Chairman of the LCC, Sir Robert Tasker MP. The house, Tasker declared, was 'one of the greatest pieces of vandalism ever perpetuated in London'. When Connell heard this, he thought, 'Fame at last!' How right he was. But by the end of June 1939 Connell and Ward were on their own again.

Little regard is now paid to the architectural views of Sir Reginald Blomfield, who lived adjacent to 66 Frognal, and few seem to visit his rather well designed villa. But whereas Blomfield brought traditional values and elegance to Hampstead, Connell Ward and Lucas brought revolutionary change, a new aesthetic and a sensibility to functional and practical design that, like any good work of art, has lasted and, for the avaricious, provided economic value.

The ethos of the practice

For Connell's early interest in modernist attitudes we have to go to Le Corbusier and to what Reyner Banham, in a perceptive essay entitled 'Louis Kahn: The battery-hatch aesthetic', referred to as the 'academic kit of tools that every French architect (including Le Corbusier) … inherited from the Beaux Arts Tradition … the idea of designs based on the assembly of so many "Elements of Composition"…. Each of these elements, ideally, a volume or room devoted to a single function…. These given volumes are juggled around until they make an elegant symmetrical pattern in plan.'[5]

Connell explained his own processes as follows:

> From inception to completion, each building for which I, as the architect, have been responsible has been the best that I could do. I have looked on each project as a projection of my past experience, and, on completion, it becomes the prime subject for exercising my critical faculty. I have travelled widely and have learned that the understanding of the timeless quality of a great work of art begins with the analytical study of social history related to the aesthetic expression of its creator, and grows with the realisation that those moments of delight and joy felt when one is in the presence of a great work of art are indelibly implanted in one's memory. Consciously or unconsciously they become part of one's aesthetic expression. So, a target is set for achievement, and the core of my critical faculty was established.[6]

There was 'much discussion of social custom and convention, discussion in which the prospective building owner … took an active part'.[7] As James Connell recalls: 'The zest was for living, and architecture was

part of that, not vice versa. Connell Ward and Lucas started with their clients, the lives they led, they got to know them intimately, even lived with them for a while, and around that knowledge they built the house.[8]

A reappraisal of the principles of architecture

The work of Connell Ward and Lucas was in essence the reappraisal of two of Vitruvius' three touchstones of architecture: 'Commoditas' or usefulness and 'Firmitas' or stability/firmness, the third being 'Venustas' or delight.

'Firmitas', described by Ward as 'the reappraisal of technique',[9] came first as a main interest was in technological advancement, particularly in concrete in the core structure of the buildings. Connell and Ward took as their departure point the Dom-ino houses of Le Corbusier, particularly point load foundations, floors designed as flat beams cantilevered beyond the line of columns, and self-supporting bent beam staircases. Through exploitation, they 'conceived the idea of a monolithic reinforced-concrete structure … and, thereafter, we caused floors, walls (where these were required), columns, beams, to be tied together to form a structural whole. In a sense, we designed floor slabs as horizontal flat beams and external walling as upright flat beams. Thus we eliminated any need for lintels over openings.'[10] Ward names Connell as the author of this structural advance, but we know that Colin Lucas came to this construction method simultaneously through his own early experimental work.

Next came the 'reappraisal of needs in architecture as a social function' or 'Commoditas'.[11] The reappraisal of technique facilitated the free planning of partitions, external walling, door and window openings in order 'to suit functional requirements of occupancy' and to embrace a new modern way of living: the creation of an architecture that 'enhances life'.

Arthur Korn, who was an enormously influential teacher in England at Oxford, the Architectural Association school and the Brixton College of Building in the post war period as well as the former secretary of the MARS Group planning committee, recognised these two key qualities in his important statement:

> Connell Ward and Lucas introduced a new language into British architecture at a time when there were hardly any British architects thinking in an uncompromisingly contemporary vernacular. Of their work two aspects now seem important: the great courage with which they exploited new materials – and the artistic vigour with which they conceived a new way of life in building form.[12]

As regards 'Venustas', Korn had identified a third aspect of their work worthy of note as 'classic purity', influenced perhaps by El Lissitzky or Van Doesburg,

which achieves an extraordinary richness of forms and voids.[13] Ward displays the same agitation at such an analysis of the aesthetic of their work as we can see in Colin Lucas' text for Unit One. Ward, in his essay in *Planning and Architecture*, dismisses Korn's allusion to the Russian's and the Dutchman's inspiration, saying 'we saw these men, who were in the main painters and sculptors, almost as romantics'. For Ward it was essential to differentiate between the non-functional forms of art and the functional ones of architecture. To ally their work with that of the artist was to misunderstand their *raison d'être*: 'Functional building structure was for us the basis for architectural form and we believed in what Nervi has since stressed, that a building is more likely to be beautiful if it is structurally right.'[14]

The placement of the envelope was derived from structural concerns; mindful of cracking, they 'avoided wherever possible large openings in or near centres of external wall slabs. As a rule, one side of each rectangular opening, whatever its dimensions, was taken to the line where two walls met, whether at a corner or at a re-entrant angle.'[15] There were also functional concerns; sometimes they used corner windows, but these elements 'were not consciously intended to be formalistic but to be functional. We saw the elements as being a logical outcome of the general monolithic structure concept … which allowed loads to be distributed in a certain way … less restrictive to architectural design than is the case with conventional brick or masonry wall building.'[16] But not aesthetic concerns? '50% of architecture is the statement of the problem….Art, we said would look after itself.'[17]

Individual signatures

If the architecture was purely derived from these same touchstones, perhaps it is surprising that the characteristic hand of each of the partners is apparent in the work of modern architects such as Connell Ward and Lucas. In his writing, Ward does not deny that there is something more in the creative act that is part of the individual, that there is 'romance to be sensed in all works of man. A line of division between thinking and feeling is impossible to draw.'[18] He says that 'the character and indeed, the force of a work of art depends upon the individual's will-to-form, therefore in any significant work, the act of creative will is bound to be expressed'.[19] The function can take a form so far, then aesthetic judgement comes into play. Ward is explicit about this when he says, 'in the aspect of aesthetics we found pleasure and satisfaction in attempts to solve problems of unifying or harmonising formal and spatial relationships'.[20]

In the composition of Lucas' building facades, lessons from the architect's Beaux Arts training at the Cambridge school are apparent, lessons reinforced by

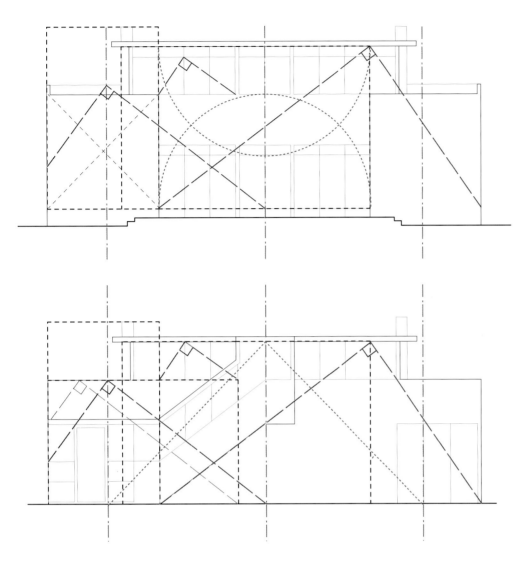

the pages of Le Corbusier's *Vers une Architecture* chapter on 'regulating lines'. Lucas uses the right angle and the golden section to generate the masses and proportion of his buildings, as Michelangelo did at the Capitol in Rome and Le Corbusier for his own villa in 1916. Le Corbusier states: 'The general mass of the façades, both front and rear, is based on the same angle (A) which determines a diagonal whose many parallels and their perpendiculars give the measure for correcting the secondary elements, doors, windows, panels etc. down to the smallest detail.'[21]

Lucas and Le Corbusier revealed their admiration for this mathematical harmony through measure, regulation and order, one that is evident in many of the great modernist compositions of the day. This visual harmony has been likened to underlying natural order where nature can be understood as 'something poised and reasonably made, ... something infinitely modulated, evolved, varied and unified'.[22] Colin Lucas was a spiritual man, his later writings and teachings on his own specific belief structure making him a respected teacher within his circle. This understanding of the world underpinned with natural order resonates within a unifying spiritual order.

Le Corbusier, like Connell, admired Michelangelo, singling him out as a sober 'creator' among other simply 'talented fellows' of the Renaissance. Writing in *Towards a New Architecture*, he said: 'The lesson of Rome is for wise men, for those who know and can appreciate, who can resist and can verify.'[23] Obviously considering himself as such, Le Corbusier admired the 'clear aim', the 'classification of parts', 'pure forms', a 'simple and direct' order, proportion, 'a sane morality', quantities, mass, rhythm, equations in specific examples of original Roman, Byzantine and Renaissance architecture. It is the discipline and the tools that transcend generations, movements and 'isms' that Corbusier admires – a universal truth akin to the pure perfection of the design of a machine that works. He aspires to this purity through his recognition of the problem of the house; this is, as William Curtis identifies in his book *Le Corbusier*, not a reduction of it to a machine for living in, rather an understanding that the practical concerns of the house are a 'sort of analogue of universal order'.[24]

Such clarity of form coupled with a pragmatic approach to living can be found at High and Over and probably prompted the positive responses to the house from unexpected quarters. For example, Augustus Daniel, then Director of the National Gallery and a distinguished art critic, wrote to Ashmole about Connell, saying: 'You have a real thoroughbred of a new kind.'[25]

Modern' meant to strip back what came before to get to the root, to set out the fundamentals, independent of style and aesthetic, from which to approach the

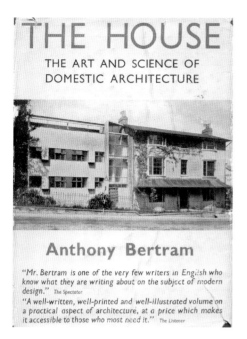

THE HOUSE
THE ART AND SCIENCE OF DOMESTIC ARCHITECTURE

Anthony Bertram

"Mr. Bertram is one of the very few writers in English who know what they are writing about on the subject of modern design." *The Spectator*

"A well-written, well-printed and well-illustrated volume on a practical aspect of architecture, at a price which makes it accessible to those who most need it." *The Listener*

The compliments of the season from

AMYAS D. CONNELL *R.S.*

BASIL R. WARD *A.R.I.B.A.*

COLIN LUCAS *B. ARCH.*

2 5   *Grosvenor   Place   London   S W* 1

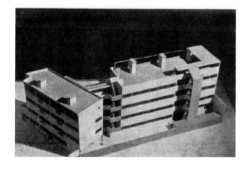

Above:
The dust jacket of Anthony Bertram's book *The House*, featuring Connell Ward and Lucas' project The Firs. Connell Ward and Lucas' Christmas cards featured images of their latest designs. This, c.1934, depicts a model of an early scheme for Kent House.

Opposite:
Overlays of Colin Lucas' elevations of the Flat Roof House at Little Frieth illustrate how the angle of the staircase, the proportion of the bays at either end of the building, even the proportion of the windows has been determined by regulating lines.
Michelangelo's Campidoglio in Rome, governed by the same proportional design principles that Le Corbusier adhered to when designing a facade.

solution to the problem. Adherence to principles ensures that a work of architecture transcends its time and is valued by other generations and other periods. Ward felt Connell Ward and Lucas' work had continuing credibility in 1968: 'Opportunities have expanded in technical scope as hitherto unimagined, also when new ways of life are a common cause in the community,'[26] and enjoyed the fact that critics in the late 1960s perceived 'freshness' in the work of the practice, 'freshness having a timeless quality'.[27] This was in contrast, he observed, to architectural work driven by the 'need to create a particularly individualistic and romantic manner' that is 'manifest in a kind of formalism, which has "life with very little truth in it"', such as 'nineteenth-century academic historicism' and 'twentieth-century eclecticism'.[28]

Anthony Bertram in his book *The House: A Machine for Living In* of 1935 was adamant that the underpinning philosophy of functionalism meant that 'architecture begins with use, but not that it ends there'.[29] Bertram's perception that the rules of the modern movement were not absolute but rather underpinned the creation of a more individual and personal architectural form was one shared by a great many architects of the period.

John Allan says this of Lubetkin, whom he describes as mastering the toolkit of modernism at an early stage in his career in preparation for his own journey of architectural discovery, which resulted in his own characteristic work. Connell Ward and Lucas would also have held this opinion. Basil Ward, looking back on the work of the practice, explained that they 'were in pursuit of the idea rather than the style ... we considered that architecture could only be approached on logical lines'.[30] 'Architecture embodies art (with its imaginative and emotive influences) and science (with its intellectual needs and its mental constructs). When art and science are in harmonious balance, significant architecture is the outcome.'[31] Connell Ward and Lucas were passionate that there should be truth to the technique and it is this that they stood up for. Here is Basil Ward again: 'A less uncompromising course might well have brought us more commissions.'[32]

Heroic deeds?
The young architects of the modern movement in England have been variously described as Turks, Pioneers, or Heroes. They referred to the battle in which they were engaged as an architectural crusade. Looking back on their work, it appears that both Connell and Ward were well prepared to roll up their sleeves and get involved with argument. This was a fact that became clear from Connell's radio broadcast with Sir Reginald Blomfield and Ward's romantic reminiscences of their youthful architectural antics. 'Youth is heroic, tending not to reckon cost, in personal and emotional terms....Youth scorns

convention ... and youth has some gift, perhaps of insight, which takes the place of experience.'[33] Less vociferous was Colin Lucas, who said, 'I find arguments on Aesthetics as meaningless as they are endless.'[34] This lack of interest in politics and debate did not, however, mean that his buildings are watered down; he can be seen to be the most tenacious of the three in terms of the modern material and aesthetic expression of his buildings throughout his career. There is little doubt that all three fought hard in the inter-war period to have the courage of their convictions and to create the buildings in the pages of this book.

We aimed at rationalism and, I suppose, functionalism, although the latter was an outcome of the rational to which we held. Functionalism was not a rigid rule to follow and we were suspicious of the 'machine aesthetic'. Nevertheless we got great pleasure from contemplation of the formal attitude of modern machines, for example aircraft designed to race for the Schneider Cup Trophy....The much misinterpreted phrase 'Form follows function', said to be a dictum of Louis Sullivan, was for us neither 'a jingle' nor a catch phrase.[35]

Charles Holden in *The Listener* in July 1933 on the subject of 'Is Modern Architecture on the right track' wrote: 'It depends what is meant by functionalism, the style or fashion of functionalism, or the principle of functionalism. If the style or fashion, I would say that it will have the life of a fashion and that it will be done to death by its own devotees,... the principle of functionalism ... is the vital force behind every great constructive period the world has known – the lintel, the arch, the dome and the vault.'[36]

Joseph Emberton, in the same issue, wrote: 'You ask is modern architecture on the right track, and you ask questions based on stylistic premises, framed with circumlocutions such as "ultra-modern", "functionalism", etc. which are barren, meaningless, trackless to the contemporary architect.'[37]

Ward, writing in *Architecture North West*, quoted Herbert Read as saying that the architect 'takes his tone, his tempo, his intensity from the society of which he is a member'.[38] The year 1939 represented the end of an era and for many, including Connell Ward and Lucas, a new way of life and, once the conflagration was over, new challenges and opportunities. As P Morton Shand opined, in the last of a series of important articles written over a decade for the *Architectural Review*: 'World War II checked the wider generalisations of what historians labelled the "New Architecture".'

The modern house

Above: Contemporary photograph of the
Weissenhofsiedlung exhibition, Stuttgart, 1928.

'In blood and in poverty the little man will start building a new order and a new house, a new machine for living in. It will have large windows to let in the light.'[1]

It has often been said that an Englishman's house is his castle, conjuring images of battlements and defences, a hard shell to protect a soft and private interior – a home. The house was the key 'object' of early discussions on modern architecture in England and questions of the why, how and where of housing were the subjects of numerous books, pamphlets, articles and broadcasts. It was over such questions that the more interesting – and sometimes most acrimonious and emotive – discussions took place either strongly supporting or attacking the tenets of the 'new architecture'.

The majority of projects completed by Connell Ward and Lucas before 1939, whether as sole practitioners or together, were houses, primarily private houses. At the core of their practice was the desire to solve satisfactorily the problem of a brief using modern materials and technologies. They cut through the nostalgia surrounding the notion of home and appraised modern domestic requirements, distilling them into a few primary factors to underpin their designs: hygiene and health, sunlight and air, convenience and economy. Few would accept such a scientific approach to nest-making.

The achievement of architects in England like Connell Ward and Lucas who attempted to re-examine the problem of the house from a modern standpoint appears minute in comparison with the total amount of housing that was built in the 1930s. Official figures indicate that some two million new homes were erected between 1929 and 1939. It was a boom time for the speculative builder and a time of expansion of local authority housing, but the scope for experimentation by modern architects and their (mainly middle-class professional) clients who believed in, or were persuaded by, the arguments for modern architecture was limited.

The proliferation of the English house
The garden city movement in the early years of the twentieth century underlined the general pattern of English housing development and set the seal on the ideal of an Englishman obtaining a rural house with a garden in a country situation. It proved to be a strong and irreversible trend. Although house prices were high, the ability of the general public to buy houses was increasing owing to the rapid growth of building societies. In contrast to pre-war Britain, more houses were for sale as opposed to rent and the aspiration to own your own home in suburbia came into its own.

Low-density development across the English countryside was encouraged by vast improvements in private and public transport. Many left the city to set up home more permanently in the country air, others with means bought or built second houses for escape at the weekends or in the summer months. Land was readily available from farmers subsidising their livelihood in an agricultural depression and people took advantage of

this on a variety of scales: individuals buying single plots to occupy with a new house, a disused bus or a railway carriage, and developers purchasing large tracts of land to be subdivided for bigger settlements.

From the mid-1920s, many took seriously the risk that England's green and pleasant land would be gobbled up by the sheer scale of this housing boom. The Council for the Preservation of Rural England was formed in 1926 to synchronise reactions to this problem. Their written message in Sir Patrick Abercrombie's *The Preservation of Rural England* and Clough Williams- Ellis' 1928 book *England and the Octopus* was cautionary:

> England has changed violently and enormously within the last few decades. Since the War, indeed, it has been changing with an acceleration that is catastrophic, thoroughly frightening the thoughtful amongst us, and making them sadly wonder whether anything recognisable of our lovely England will be left for our children's children.[2]

Protective building and planning legislation in the form of the Town Planning Act of 1925, with further acts 1932–35, allowed rural districts to prepare formal development plans in an attempt to preserve natural beauty in the face of the pressure to develop. Powers went to local authorities to regulate the size, height, design and external appearance of buildings and led to the rejection of buildings likely to seriously injure the amenity of the locality. Committees used their weight to protect their areas from over-development.

Hygiene and health, sunlight and air, convenience and economy
Le Corbusier's message that the house was a machine for living in was 'an inspiring call to action' for Connell Ward and Lucas. Basil Ward, looking back on the practice's work later said that this dictum 'was wholly acceptable … we believed in his statement on the house and we saw in it, and in his writings generally, a transcendent logic.'[3] Sir Bernard Ashmole's experience at High and Over was that Connell's views on Le Corbusier's now famous statement on mechanised domesticity were more measured than Basil Ward suggests, but Le Corbusier's 'The manual of the dwelling' in *Vers une Architecture* reads as a recipe for Connell Ward and Lucas' modern domestic design.[4]

The virtues of good ventilation and sunlight in relation to health had been long understood by the 1920s and during the inter-war period the merits of strength and vitality gained through outdoor activity were widely promoted. In 1937 the Physical Training Act was passed by Chamberlain's National Government, promoting exercise, a good diet and compulsory medical inspection. Being tanned from the sun's rays was becoming a sign of health rather than poverty. Connell Ward and Lucas' designs embraced this notion and

A NEW BOOK

THE MODERN HOUSE

BY

F. R. S. YORKE, A.R.I.B.A.

TO BE PUBLISHED DURING MAY   PRICE 21s. NET.

A HOUSE IN KENT, BY COLIN
LUCAS; the South and East elevations. The external staircase in
reinforced concrete is run across
the house as a continuous beam
supporting the first floor.

The modern architect designs houses that are intended primarily for living in. He does not
allow a preconceived idea of the appearance of the façade to interfere with the efficiency of
the plan. New materials are at his disposal and he employs new methods of construction.
This book outlines the requirements to be met in the new type of home, and discusses
at length its several parts—plan, wall, window and roof. It is illustrated by about 500
photographs, plans and constructional details of houses by architects in Europe and America.

An Illustrated prospectus will be sent post free on request to :

THE ARCHITECTURAL PRESS, 9 QUEEN ANNE'S GATE, WESTMINSTER

they improved the connection with and access to the outside through sunroofs and terraces, large opening windows and doors. Basil Ward, looking back at their work, felt that one of the most important aspects of what the practice achieved was a positive impact on interiors; he said, 'standards for larger lighter rooms really came out of this sort of building.'[5]

Internally, the clean modern lines of hard, smooth surfaces, simple profiles for skirtings and architraves and floor to ceiling fitted furniture were responsive to another health preoccupation amongst the middle classes – hygiene. The clutter of the typical Victorian interior had been gradually cleared of nick-nacks and heavy fabrics during the late nineteenth and early twentieth century as the link between dirt, germs and ill-health was more fully understood. That cleanliness could affect better health was a relatively recent discovery and owed much to the practices of Florence Nightingale learnt through tending the troops during the Crimean war. The message was spread to the public from the 1890s via schools and public health departments, through publications and exhibitions in a desperate attempt to improve conditions in the cities. By the thirties, health advice from the government was louder through advertising, broadcasts and household management publications. The message reached the middle-class housewife. Combining facts with emotive arguments, the state of cleanliness became equal to a state of grace, dirt to slovenliness; the good mother who took her responsibility seriously would take pleasure in keeping her house clean.

The impact of modern design was greatest on the interior of the homes of the middle classes as a direct result. Light, bright, convenient and easy-to-clean interiors were desirable, even if a modern exterior was still unpalatable to many, and Connell Ward and Lucas embraced the latest materials developed for this purpose. Plywood, formed from laminating thin slips of timber, was used extensively, especially for built-in furniture, often painted or even metal covered for tabletops, shelving and doors. Chromium, seventy-year-old technology newly introduced to building components such as taps, was increasingly used in decoration, as well as non-corrosive steels that had been discovered, by mistake, in 1913. Two new plastic materials, bakelite and beatle were popular and increasingly available, perhaps more in industrial design than construction; non-flammable, moisture and vermin proof they were excellent for easy maintenance.[6]

For floors, the practice generally used hygiene-friendly sheet materials such as cork, linoleum and rubber. However, the ultimate was a jointless floor and Connell Ward and Lucas experimented with the latest composite materials that could be laid in situ across whole rooms, and even up the walls. At Frieth, Lucas experimented with sawdust and screed, at Frognal he

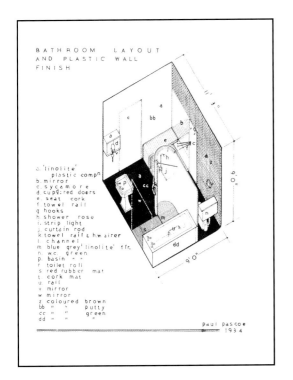

BATHROOM   LAYOUT
AND   PLASTIC WALL
FINISH

a. 'linolite'
     plastic compⁿ
b. mirror
c. sycamore
d. cupⁿ. red doors
e. seat cork
f. towel rail
g. hooks
h. shower rose
i. strip light
j. curtain rod
k. towel rail & hw airer
l. channel
m. blue grey 'linolite' flr.
n. w.c. green
p. basin " "
r. toilet roll
s. red rubber mat
t. cork mat
u. rail
v. mirror
w. mirror
z. coloured brown
bb "   "   putty
cc "   "   green
dd "   "   "

paul pascoe
1934

Opposite: An advertisement for FRS Yorke's book from the *Architectural Review*

Above:
A cartoon by Osbert Lancaster in his book *Homes Sweet Homes* illustrating the functional interior.
Connell Ward and Lucas' plastic bathroom design for the Contemporary Industrial Design in the Home exhibition at Dorland Hall, 1934, and, below, Connell Ward and Lucas' typically austere bathroom design at Temple Gardens, 1935.

was tempted by samples of a cork and rubber composition that had just come onto the market.[7]

As the emphasis on cleaning increased, the trend for domestic service decreased and had virtually died out by the early years of the Second World War. The fact that Connell Ward and Lucas' private houses often included living quarters for their servants is proof that their clientele were in the more affluent band of society. They could thus also afford state-of-the-art fitted kitchens with the latest gas and electric appliances and modern conveniences, another tick in the box of hygiene as dirty fuel was banished from the areas where food was prepared. The mass production of such modern conveniences that began inter-war was perfectly in tune with society's emphasis on hygiene. Advertisements promised they would save time and produce better results to improve the health of the family. They became more affordable to a larger audience and manufacturers began to reap the rewards of the public's obsession with the latest technology.

All these factors came together in the bathroom where scrubbing and cleaning also applied to the body. Plumbed-in bathrooms feature in all of the practice's projects, but bathrooms were quite a recent phenomenon, first appearing in middle-class houses from the late nineteenth century and in state subsidised houses from 1919. An enormous amount of fun was had in bathroom design in the 1930s. Suites of matching sanitaryware came into their own, often coloured and with concealed fittings – preferred as they gave order to the room. In a 1934 publication, bathroom designer Dorothy Braddell reported, 'nowadays no room is more popular than the bathroom and there is none on which people are willing to spend more time,

thought and money'.[8] The bathroom had become a palace to the body, a place of rest, contemplation and also of vigorous exercise.

Connell Ward and Lucas' design for the 'Plastic Bathroom' at the Contemporary Industrial Design in the Home exhibition at Dorland Hall in 1934, demonstrates the virtues of Linolite plastic composition on the floor and walls.[9] This is highly colourful: putty and brown on the walls, blue/grey on the floor, a green toilet, red bathroom cabinet and bath mat and doors in sycamore to add texture. A curved partition around the shower is illuminated with a curved strip light, concealing the pipes to the towel rail and shower. *The Architects' Journal* reporter, generally sceptical about the rest of the exhibition, awarded honours to Connell Ward and Lucas' design which he described as a 'neat and forthright piece of work'.[10]

The practice's interior designs were stark in comparison to the glamorous works of other contemporary designers. In 1938 the bathroom at Moor Park was featured in *The Studio Year Book* with its sunken bath alongside a design by D Pleydell-Bouverie. The latter with silvered glass wall tiles, a handbasin set in a slab of green glass and bath with radio set, two telephones and a teak floor is more infinitely more lavish and gorgeous. The closest that the practice got to such exuberance is in Connell's early shop designs and the interiors of High and Over. Elsewhere a more measured approach was taken, preoccupied with function and convenience. They focused on the neatest, most economic solution – often derived through experimentation – achieved in appropriate materials. The same preoccupations led to their almost unswerving use of reinforced concrete for the fabric of their buildings.

Private houses

Above: 66 Frognal, 2008, after the restoration by Avanti Architects.

Connell Ward and Lucas' private house commissions were often for clients with some wealth, generally professionals with a modern vision for their family life who were passionate enough to put up a fight alongside their architects for their modern masterpieces. The architects erected around twenty bespoke designs in total, each one a bookmark in the evolving story of their development of reinforced concrete construction. These are the projects for which the architects are best known and for which they received the most acknowledgement. Henry-Russell Hitchcock recognised their importance in the genre of modern architecture in England when he said:

> to the pool of memorable English production of this period, which led me to write in 1937 … that the English School then led the world in activity, Connell Ward and Lucas contributed a series of houses – the latest one built in Bessborough Road in 1938-39 – which are among the most characteristic examples of the time and the period.[1]

In the following pages we will chart the evolving designs and techniques of the practitioners through examination of these houses and give a snapshot of their history. Each house is attributed to its project architect, whose different signatures were recognised by Nikolaus Pevsner when he surmised, 'Connell's houses were original and flashy, Ward's sound and sometimes very good (The Firs, Redhill), and Lucas's often minor masterpieces (in Surrey, the house at Wentworth, also at 66 Frognal, Hampstead).'[2]

Over the course of the research for this book, several other houses by the architects have come to light but very little to flesh out the stories behind them: a project in Sowley mentioned in the Architects' Journal in June 1935; correspondence suggesting that a house was erected near Watford in 1934; drawings in the RIBA's collection for a house in the grounds of Melchet Court in Wiltshire for Hugh Quigley of Surrey and rather Miesian plans for a two-storey house designed by Basil Ward for Mrs RG Edwards, probably the client for the Preventorium project of October 1938.

High and Over

High and Over, Amersham, Buckinghamshire, 1928–31
Amyas Connell of Connell and Thomson

'The blow is falling; prepare to meet the shock! The modern-house-in-the-English-countryside has arrived – at least its portrait – overnight.'[3]

Perched on a bare hillside overlooking Amersham, High and Over has been recognised as the first major modern house in England. Its stark form, clearly influenced by early European modern architecture but ordered with classical proportion, is allied to a clear conception of contemporary domestic life. The project was a staggering opportunity and achievement for such an inexperienced architect. Howard Robertson, principal of the Architectural Association in London, admired the work of the young architect as 'adventurous, fearless in its openness'.[4] In 1964, Ian Nairn in his survey *Modern Buildings in London* reported of High and Over, 'This is where modern architecture – that is, as a conscious reflection of past styles – began in the London area.'[5]

The project was commissioned by Bernard Ashmole, the young director of the British School at Rome at the time that Connell took up his scholarship there, and his wife Dorothy Ashmole. When the couple returned to England from Rome in 1928 they wanted to live in the countryside but within easy commuting distance from Professor Ashmole's new job at University College, London. They soon secured twelve acres of land to the north east of the village of Amersham in Buckinghamshire. This was high ground that sloped gently down to the south with views over the Misbourne valley. Rail services in the village offered a convenient connection to central London.

Dorothy Ashmole gave the estate the name High and Over after Hindover Hill near Alfriston in Sussex's South Downs, and not just because of the similarities between the two landscapes. In 1924 three pranksters had climbed Hindover in the dead of night and carved a white horse into the chalk of the hillside to get into the news. High and Over was not created as a publicity stunt (although perceived as such by some traditionalists) but Dorothy obviously found the correlation between the locals' surprised discovery of the Litlington White Horse and the unveiling of her new house apt. It makes it all the more appropriate that the completed gleaming white house was described by Augustus Daniel, director of the National Gallery, as 'a real thoroughbred of a new kind.'[6]

Having given up on his third year in Rome in order to pursue this first commission, Connell completed initial design drawings for High and Over in November 1928. By mid-May of 1929, when the planning application was submitted to the district council, Connell had set up an

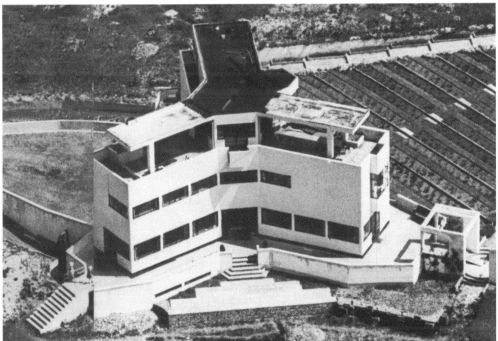

Above:
The completed house from the site of the swimming pool in the south, prior to the terraces being formed. This would have been the view from the road beneath the site. An aerial view showing the terraces.

Opposite:
Aerial view of High and Over with water tower.

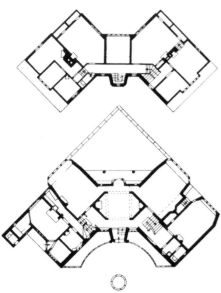

Above:
The entrance elevation of the The Barn, Exmouth, Devon by E S Prior, 1895–97.
Ground and first floor plans, The Barn.
Entrance elevation of the Freudenberg House, Berlin-Nikolassee by Hermann Muthesius, 1907–9 and ground floor plan.

office in Bloomsbury with a colleague, Stewart L Thomson. Thomson was an Australian who had completed his early training in Melbourne. He had travelled to England in 1924, like Connell and Ward, and had entered the competition for the same scholarships, medallions and prizes as his fellow colonials.7 Despite Thomson's name being on some of the early drawings, High and Over has always been attributed solely to Connell and by February 1930 the drawings bear Connell's name alone.

The design

The Ashmoles had a clear functional brief for their keen young architect and had given some thought to their general living space requirements and sizes. When discussions on design began, three primary factors emerged: 'the contour of the site, the maximum intrusion of sun into the house and also the view … being magnificent from the top of the hill', and as the project progressed the idea for a Y-shaped plan with wings 120 degrees from each other was established, as this, according to Connell, 'solved satisfactorily those three objectives'.8 This model gave the client the ability to enjoy 360 degrees of the hilltop view with the house set above a natural hollow to the south of the site where it would catch all of the scanty sunshine offered by the English climate.

Raymond McGrath in his book *Twentieth Century Houses* of 1934 recognised that this solution came from 'hard reasoning', and this was so, in a way that was worthy of a great modern masterpiece. Perhaps more surprisingly for a building like High and Over, its form was also derived from a plethora of historical precedents, drawn on by client and architect alike. Initially, the merits of an Elizabethan house plan were debated with a courtyard open to the south with two protecting wings, but the advantages of the Y-shaped plan became more obvious as they became clearer about the siting of the house. In relation to orientation, Ashmole remembered that they 'went on the principle, well known in antiquity, that a building facing south gains heat when the sun is low, in spring, autumn and winter, yet is particularly shaded inside when the sun is at its highest in summer'. The amount of glass used, Ashmole said, was 'no greater than for instance, in late Georgian houses, although differently disposed, and the gain of heat from the sun would exceed its loss through the glass'.9

Experimentation with 'progressive plans designed to catch the sun' was also a preoccupation of the Arts and Crafts architects and a topic Connell would have been aware of during his articles with Stanley Fearn in Wellington.10 The Y-shape can be seen as an extension of the butterfly plan of ES Prior's The Barn at Exmouth, 1895–7, an influence on MH Baillie Scott's planning for his well-known competition entry Dulce Domum, 1901, and also adopted by Muthesius in Berlin with the

Freudenberg House, 1907–8. In such designs, the hall and circulation was central to the plan with the accommodation arranged in two wings on either side.

At High and Over, Connell adopted a hexagonal central hall, a form that had been used in Arts and Crafts architecture and that Kornwolf and Pevsner, writing on the architecture of Baillie Scott and Edwin Lutyens respectively, recognised as historically rarely found outside Italian baroque architecture.11 Connell himself described High and Over as 'a centralised plan in which all the axes converge at one point … a well organised centralised and nuclear plan, similar to many buildings of the Renaissance', and said that it 'symbolised the unity thought to be evident in the Universe'.12

The form is a clear fusion of Italian and English traditions so pertinent to Connell's architectural education and Professor Ashmole's career. Connell's background had taught him to respect the lessons learnt from history and, most recently, his close studies in Italy had awakened in him respect for the architecture of ancient Rome and particularly the buildings of Michelangelo. He later said, 'I can't see how any person may project himself into the future without having the true line of descent of history behind him to give him direction'.13 However, both parties were clear from the outset that this house must be modern in order to be relevant to the day in which it was created. As Ashmole remembered, 'we both thought that a modern building should be in a modern style, as all the best buildings had always been'.14 For Ashmole, who was obviously familiar with Le Corbusier's writings, Connell's views on modern architecture were sensible: he too had studied the work of Le Corbusier and of modern German and Dutch architects, but dissented from the extreme view that a house was simply a machine for living in, unless beauty is considered as a part of living, and unless the house reflects in some degree the tastes and even the character of the client.15

Corbusier's mechanistic dictum that was clearly on the tip of the tongue when modern was under the spotlight – and its connotations of repetitive preformed solutions – is softened here. While the overriding expression of the form of the building – its whiteness, its windows, its unbroken surface and its volumes and hoods, even the construction method – would make a critic look straight back to the Continent, High and Over is bespoke. It is a machine for living in that is tuned to suit its client and its site and is responsive in its orientation. Ashmole reported Connell as saying, 'I want anyone to be able to see that this is the Ashmoles' house'.16

Arrangement

Connell arranged the accommodation in wings to separate its functions. On the ground floor the dining room and kitchen service quarters are housed in one

wing with the library in another and the drawing room in the third. Apart from the service wing, corridors are virtually eliminated and instead the generously proportioned spaces flow seamlessly and logically into one another. The central hexagon of the entrance hall and stairs is not only the unifying pivot of the plan horizontally but also vertically as a double-height space. The folding doors to each of the wings can be thrown open to unify the whole of the ground floor if required. At first floor two large bedrooms with dressing rooms are provided in two of the wings with the bathroom and maids' quarters in the third. The single bathroom shared by children, guests and parents was accessed from the central hall and one can imagine the theatre of inhabitants in dressing gowns timing their visits at bedtime and in the morning.

The second floor is dedicated to the nursery accommodation with the hexagonal day nursery at the centre and the night nursery and nurse's room stretching over the service wing. A second staircase is provided here for the nurse to access the maids' sleeping quarters on the first and the kitchen on the ground floor without entering the main circulation stair to the house. The Ashmole daughters remembered how they played on the two roof terraces at High and Over under the shade of the concrete canopies and imagined themselves on the deck of a boat. Standing in the balcony that protruded to the south and surveying the view beneath they felt themselves to be 'captain of the ship, sailing along'.[17] They were on a voyage into the landscape they could survey from their vantage point whilst also being able to retreat into the safety and comfort of the interior. Travelling large distances by boat was common in the early twentieth century and the experience seems to have inspired the architecture. Often it was the children who enjoyed this deck-top world. In later designs by Ward at Moor Park and Lucas at Frognal the rooftop is a playground where the younger generation could take advantage of the sun and air in their own private world, giving them independence whilst also removing them from the goings on of the grown-ups.

Disposition

The three main facades of the house, like the facing pages of an open book, are treated architecturally in very similar ways, yet each have different characteristics. The entrance facade, orientated to the drive in the north west, has more or less symmetrical but sparse fenestration and the blank wings concentrate the visitor's gaze on the central focus of the front door and triangular porch jutting out above it. At the centre of the north-east elevation three facets of the hexagonal form of the hall protrude, each with vertical strips of glazing to second floor level. Either side, the flat planes of the wings are penetrated with short strips of glazing arranged asymmetrically to suit the rooms; in the eastern wing a wall of library shelves prohibits windows at ground floor level.

Above:
Aerial view of High and Over.
The north-east elevation with protruding glazed staircase.

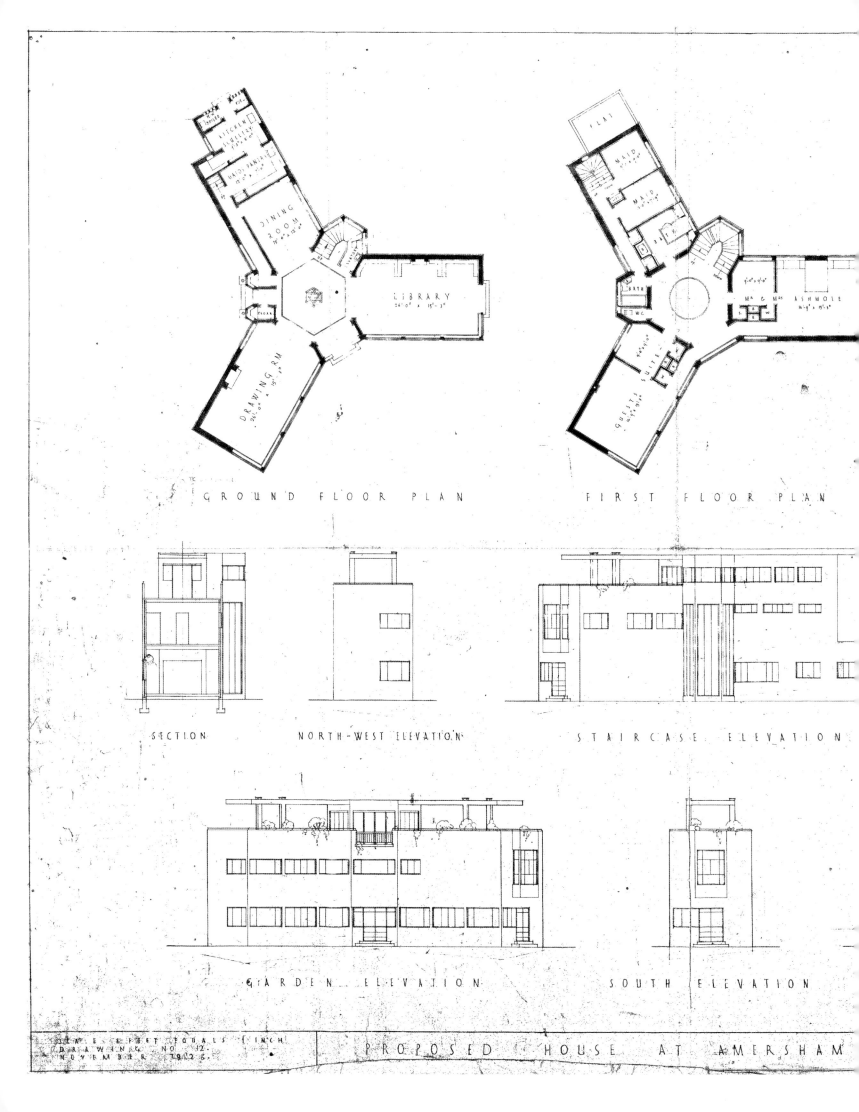

GROUND FLOOR PLAN

KITCHEN
SCULLERY
MAID PANTRY

DINING
ROOM

LIBRARY
26'0" x 15'-3"

DRAWING RM
26'0" x 15'-3"

FIRST FLOOR PLAN

FLAT

MAID

MAID

BATH

MR & MRS ASHMOLE
16'-9" x 15'-3"

GUESTS SUITE

BATH

W.C.

SECTION   NORTH-WEST ELEVATION

STAIRCASE ELEVATION

GARDEN ELEVATION   SOUTH ELEVATION

SCALE 8 FEET EQUALS 1 INCH
DRAWING No 12
NOVEMBER 1926

PROPOSED HOUSE AT AMERSHAM

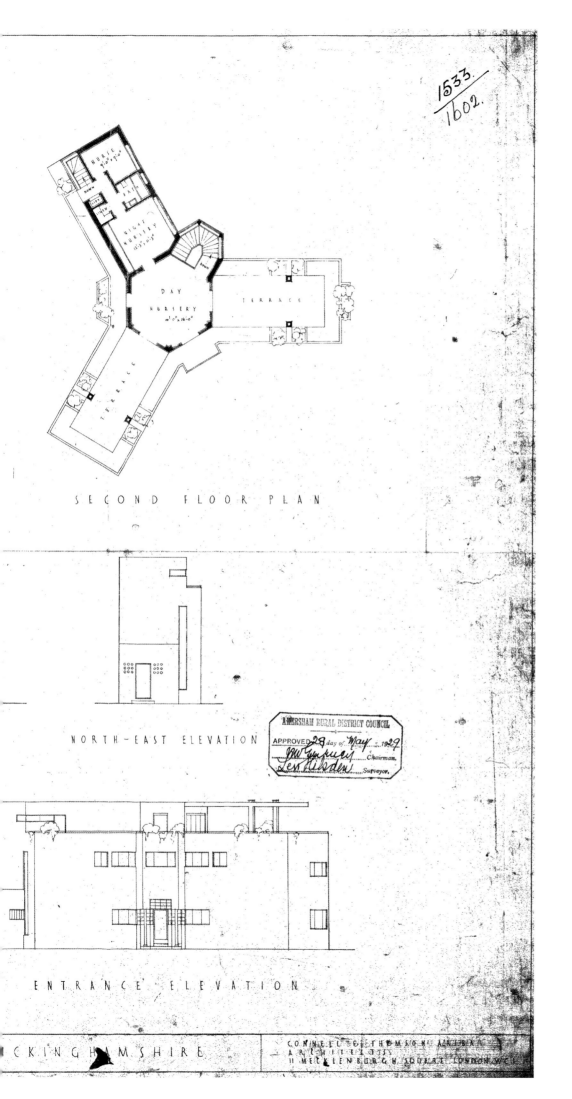

SECOND FLOOR PLAN

NORTH-EAST ELEVATION

ENTRANCE ELEVATION

CKINGHAMSHIRE

CONNELL & THOMSON AARIBA
ARCHITECTS
11 MECKLENBURGH SQUARE LONDON WC1

The plans and elevations of High and Over submitted to Amersham rural district council.

Below:
The original substation to the site was located at the base of the drive. The Sun Houses were later built on the stretch of rising land between it and the lodge at the left of this picture.
The lodge, built half way up the drive has since been significantly altered

Right:
Looking westwards along the balcony with the gardener's lodge in the distance beyond. The boat-deck quality of the children's play area is evident with the small projecting balcony like the captain's helm in the centre of the plan. This was a wonderful vantage point for 360 degrees of spectacular views beyond and good for spying on the adults on the 'decks' below.
The dining room, full of natural light. The light box in the recess is still in place today.
The north facing entrance elevation to the drive.

In contrast to the other two, the south elevation is glazed with almost continuous bands of fenestration at ground and first floor, allowing the best views from the library, drawing room and guest bedroom above over the landscape of the garden to the south west and across the undulating Chiltern hills beyond. Symmetry is avoided and the master bedroom fenestration is provided by a clean-lined modern interpretation of an oriel window that lines up on axis with the landscaping to the proposed swimming pool. The rising sun would have lit the Ashmoles' room through this window and filtered into the hall through the open treads of the staircase. The dining room and the servants' quarters would also have benefited from morning rays, and the nursery and the main garden facade would have been warmed throughout the day from the south, with the forecourt and main entrance bathed by the evening sun.

Construction

Connell planned to pour the house in reinforced concrete using recyclable metal shuttering in order to demonstrate that this was 'an economical method of construction and had a great future'.[18] The larger firms of contractors pioneering the use of this construction method were generally not interested in the relatively small scale of this domestic scheme. The client was forced to accept the tender of Messrs Watson of Ascot who had recently built Epsom grandstand but had limited experience in reinforced concrete construction. A less enterprising construction of concrete frame with brick and block infill was therefore adopted. John Winter, the architect who has had a large hand in refurbishing the house in recent years, has recognised similarities between this construction method and that used by André Lurçat at Villa Guggenbühl, completed in 1927, overlooking the Parc Montsouris in Paris. It was also the same method employed by Le Corbusier at the Villa Savoye at Poissy (1928–29). The rendering to the outside of the houses, like cake icing, gave a uniformity to the exterior finish, but it must have irked Connell that this seamless skin misrepresented the construction materials it shrouded.

Nevertheless even this hybrid construction method was a groundbreaking use of concrete in England, as, according to Architect and Building News in November 1931, High and Over was 'one of the first examples in England of reinforced concrete frame construction applied to domestic architecture'.[19] The frame, at roughly 8 foot centres and spanning approximately 16 feet gave the architect greater freedom than traditional load bearing construction in the size and regularity of the openings for windows and doors. The rhythm of this frame is most clearly expressed on the south elevation at ground level where it regularly interrupts the otherwise continuous ribbon of Corbusian fenêtres en longeuse, their metal frames painted black in a similar facade treatment to Le Corbusier's Paris houses – Maison La Roche et Jeanneret, 1923, and Maison Cook, 1926.

The oriel window on the south-east wing of High and Over can be read as a modern interpretation of the architecture of English country houses, but it is also formally extremely similar to the bay window at Lurçat's Villa Guggenbühl and the earlier Villa Besnus at Vaucresson by Le Corbusier of 1922–23.

The build, as any construction project, had its hiccups. With such an unconventional project, many new materials were used to varying degrees of success, causing stresses for the architect and his client. Ashmole later remembered that the original external render, Astroplax, which was slightly translucent and therefore had a fine ivory-like appearance, actually contained water soluble gypsum that washed away in the rain and had to be replaced with a waterproof alternative.

Interiors

The interiors at High and Over were precisely directed by the desires of the client. The decorative nature and richness of the material mix in some areas are characteristic of art deco. Ashmole remembered that the colour schemes 'had no particular relevance to function except that they were naturally appropriate to their positions, but were devised solely to give pleasure'. 'In short', he said, 'we considered that part of the 'function' of a house was to give aesthetic pleasure to

the owner by its form and colour'.[20] This approach was characterised by the hall at the very heart of the scheme where a fountain played from a glass bowl set into the floor and softly lit from beneath. The sound of the flowing water would have echoed off the polished limestone and inset glass floor and sparkling light would have reflected off the gleaming metal doors and frosted green glass lining the room, having the effect of dissolving planes and giving a magical illusion of depth. Sensual as well as aesthetic pleasure was delivered through the design. This ambience was captured in a short film made by British Pathé in August 1931 entitled 'The house of a dream'.

The *Architect and Building News* ran a series on the interior of the house that illustrated the opulent design. Connell used clean lines with strips and trimmings to give flashes of glamour. Ceilings are suspended throughout to hide the concrete down-stand beams and services run within them with light boxes fitted flush with the ceiling finish. Many of the walls are sprayed with easy to clean pale grey matt cellulose and the floors to library and drawing room are similarly finished with maple floors. The stainless steel lining to the fire and hearth enhances the glow and flicker of the flames. Connell's remit extended to the design of certain pieces of furniture and he worked with the hexagon motif as a 'harmonising element' in the stools in the nursery and in the door handles. There is a considerable amount of built-in furniture such as bookcases and cupboards with integrated electric light fittings arranged around fireplaces. The kitchen and pantry were tailored for the modern household, compact and space-efficient. Clever labour-saving contraptions are incorporated into the building, such as a metal trap door in the hearth designed to eject ash into a galvanised steel shute to the ash pit below in an ingenious, Heath Robinson fashion.

The landscape

The development of the estate also involved the design of outhouses, including an electrical transformer at the entrance of the site, a lodge to be occupied by the gardener and his wife and a water tower. Photographs of the estate taken in June 1931 show the house with all these pavilions in place and the landscaping in embryonic form. What is apparent is that Connell clearly developed a whole masterplan for the site where the landscaping was as important to the project as the construction within it. This is illustrated in the site plan that appeared in the *Architect and Building News* in January 1930.

The siting of High and Over follows the advice of Alberti (1404–72) in *De re aedificatoria* about planning the ideal Renaissance villa and gardens where he says that the best villa garden should have a sloping site with views over the countryside. He advised that the villa should sit high on the site and that the gardens should weave slowly to this pinnacle from which the view is finally revealed. At High

Below:
The drawing room with light boxes and fireplace trimmed in shiny chrome metal. The staircase is visible through the folding doors beyond.
Drawing of the house cut away to reveal the interiors.

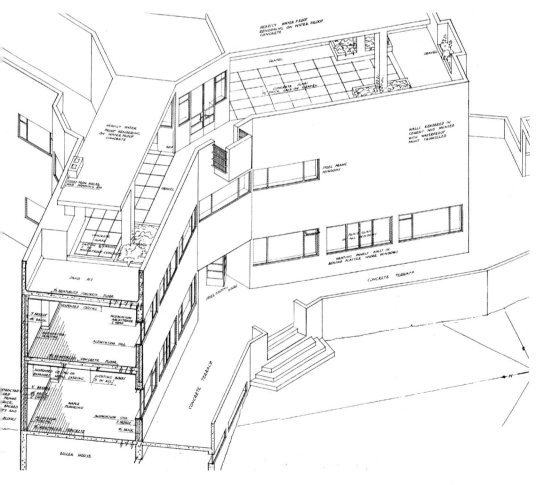

and Over just such a circuitous route is formed winding its way up from the bottom of the garden and following the contours of the site up the south-west bank. This path is punctuated by several nodes or stopping points at which a set of more formal, axial routes become apparent that relate back to the geometry of the house itself. Primarily these elements are ordered by a web of six routes that radiate from the centre of the hall, picking up the axes of the three wings of the house. In line with the south wing a cubic concrete pavilion begins a long pergola leading to the site of the future swimming pool. Another tree-lined avenue was planned on axis with the water tower. A separate triangle of paths holds the house at its centre, the three corners of which were the splayed tarmac drive at the entrance to the house and planting and terraces on the other sides.

In his studies of High and Over Michael Findlay has made a link between these landscaped features and the garden designs of Armenian-born modern architect Gabriel Guevrekian. In particular he cites Guevrekian's courtyard for the Robert Mallet-Stevens' villa built for Vicomte de Noailles on a hilltop at Hyères in around 1926.

The Ashmoles and their gardener put an enormous amount of time and effort into nurturing this extensive landscape into abundant life. A vast number of fruit trees were planted, a kitchen garden established and a triangu-

lar terraced rose garden planted to the north east of the house. Copious amounts of concrete bed edges were formed by the two men. The swimming pool, resited from Connell's original location, was also constructed by Professor Ashmole and his gardener in 1934 at the base of the steep slope to the south of the house.

Planning

The drawings for the house were submitted to the council on 16 May 1929. Surprisingly, they were approved just thirteen days later.[21] However the council made 'quite clear' that they did this under protest, 'with the greatest reluctance', not liking the plans but finding nothing to which they could legally object.[22] The water tower that formed a separate application was a different matter. Initially, the Ashmoles had approached the local authority about a new water supply to a swimming pool. When their request was turned down Connell and Thomson sent a drawing of a 50 foot concrete water tower design for an artesian well in April 1929, integrating an external fives court and games store. This was not seen as a 'necessary adjunct to the house' and the council rejected it. A ministry of health inquiry was held and the final decision went against the Ashmoles. A war of attrition began when the same plans were submitted by Connell showing the tower six inches lower with a promise that he had enough energy to ensure that this submission/appeal cycle would keep happening until the thing was passed. Howard Robertson wrote in support, 'let the design be original or different', he said, 'and the official devils are unloosed.'[23] The well was eventually sunk and the water tower constructed.

Ashmole remembers High and Over as 'a great success, we and our children loved it – its airiness, its lightness and spaciousness', although Ashmole reports in his autobiography that the family might have been too ambitious in size.[24] This suggestion that the house may have over-stretched the family may explain why, just a year or two after moving in, the Ashmoles sold off four plots on the estate for smaller Connell and Ward designed houses (described in later pages of this book) and may also be the reason for the Ashmoles' departure from the house not long after it was completed.

Over time the original steel windows to the main house have been largely replaced. The house was listed in 1971 with grade II* status. In recent years it has undergone careful refurbishment and, although now surrounded by a housing estate and with significantly less land, the integrity of the exterior of the house remains. Internally, the division of the building into two units has compromised the scheme primarily because the hall space no longer unites the three wings.

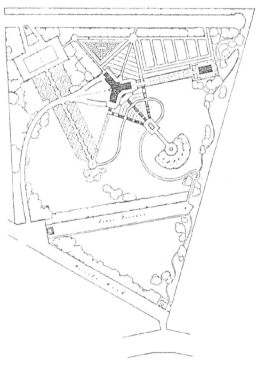

Above: Site plan showing the landscape design.

Opposite: Recent photograph of the house surrounded by mature trees.

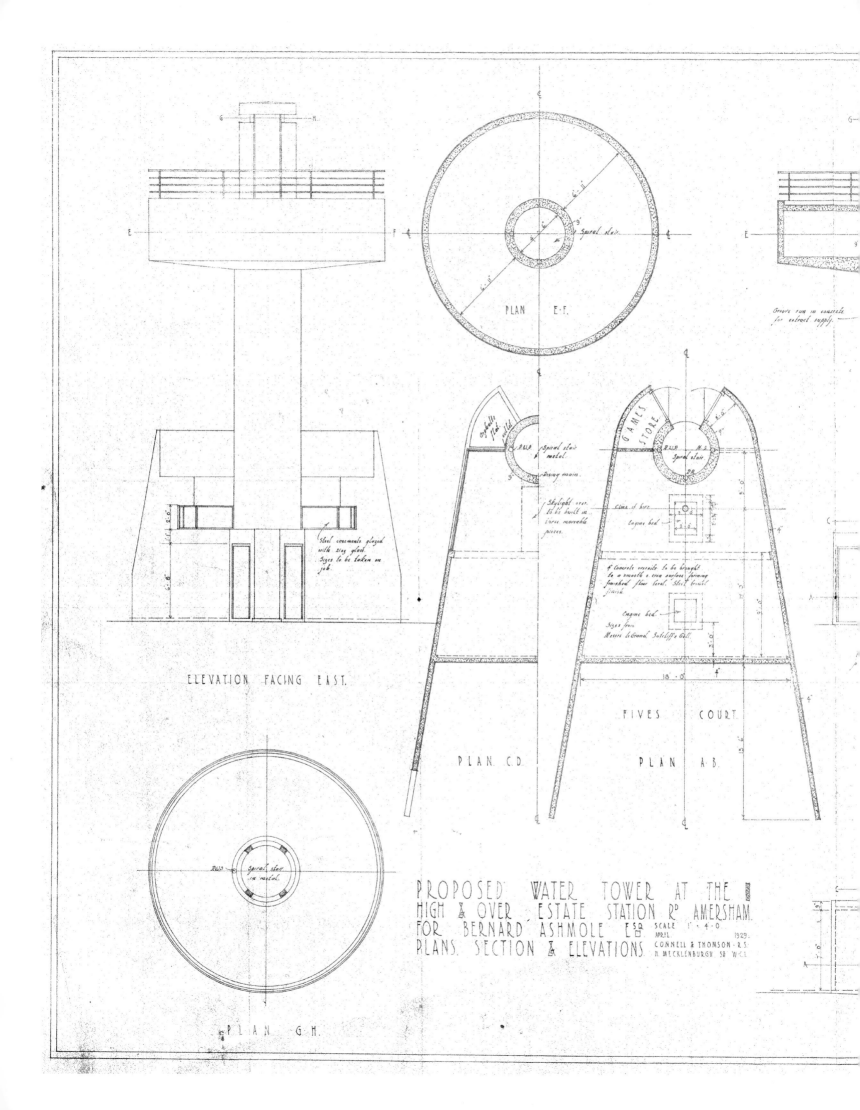

ELEVATION FACING EAST.

PLAN E.F.

PLAN C.D.

PLAN A.B.

PLAN G.H.

GAMES STORE.

FIVES COURT.

Groove run in concrete for extract supply.

Steel casements glazed with 21oz glass Sizes to be taken on job.

PROPOSED WATER TOWER AT THE
HIGH & OVER ESTATE STATION Rᴰ AMERSHAM.
FOR BERNARD ASHMOLE ESᵠ SCALE 1'·4·0.
APRIL 1929.
PLANS. SECTION & ELEVATIONS CONNELL & THOMSON· R.S.
11. MECKLENBURGH Sᵠ W·C·1

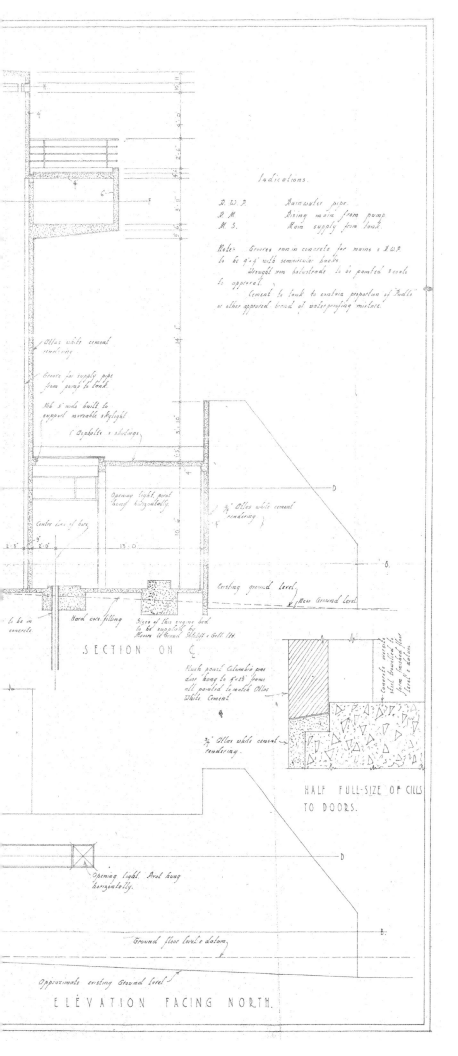

Indications.

D.W.P.   Rainwater pipe.
R.M   Rising main from pump.
M.S.   Main supply from tank.

Note: Grooves run in concrete for mains & R.W.P.
to be 4"×4" with semicircular backs.
Wrought iron balustrade to be painted 3 coats
to approval.
Cement to tank to contain proportion of "Pudlo"
or other approved brand of waterproofing mixture.

Atlas white cement
rendering

Groove for supply pipe
from pump to tank

10b s'work built to
support moveable skylight

1" asphalte & sheetings

Opening light, pivot
hung horizontally.

3/4" Atlas white cement
rendering

Centre line of bore

Existing ground level.

New Ground level.

To be in
concrete

Hard core filling   Size of this engine bed
to be supplied by
Messrs LeGrand Sutcliff & Gell Ltd.

S E C T I O N   O N   C.

Flush panel Columbia pine
door hung to 4"×2½" frame
all painted to match Atlas
White Cement

3/4" Atlas white cement
rendering

Concrete encased
steel bracketed to
form lintel to floor
level & datum

HALF FULL-SIZE OF CILLS
TO DOORS.

Opening light, Pivot hung
horizontally.

Ground floor level & datum.

Approximate existing Ground level

E L É V A T I O N   F A C I N G   N O R T H.

Above: The water tower.

Opposite: Working drawing by Connell and Thomson for
the water tower at High and Over.

Noah's House

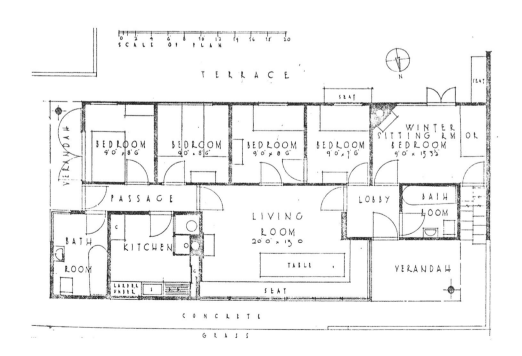

Noah's House, boathouse and outhouses, Bourne End, Buckinghamshire, 1929–34
Colin Lucas of Lucas, Lloyd and Co.

Noah's House was reported to be the first domestic building in England to be constructed entirely in reinforced concrete. This statement is significant, albeit difficult to verify. Noah's House was a less flamboyant and less marketable architectural debut than that of Amyas Connell, not least as a result of a more humble brief and budget. However, technically Lucas achieved in the construction of this project what Connell set out to do, but failed at Amersham. Here Lucas started the structural experiments in reinforced concrete construction that would preoccupy him throughout his career.

On leaving Cambridge in 1928 Colin Lucas went into the construction business with his father, joining his firm Lucas, Lloyd and Co. The Lucas family owned a riverside plot of land on the Thames between Marlow and Bourne End and enjoyed weekends and summer holidays staying in a houseboat named The Ark that was propped up on the shore. Noah's House, as it became known, was designed as a more permanent shelter on the site.[25]

Financial and practical constraints led to research into a cheap building solution that could be delivered to a site that was only accessible by boat. Ballast, transported on Thames barges, was adopted as an aggregate for all building elements: foundations, walls and roof in reinforced concrete. Reusable shuttering would keep costs down and all elements would be kept to a minimal thickness to reduce the cubic volume of concrete required. With water in plentiful supply, the additional materials required for delivery to complete the building envelope were few.

Lucas, Lloyd and Co. started an exploration of the structural properties of the material from first principles. Where conventionally the structure would be a distinct element of the design, like a frame or a set of load-bearing walls, here a solution was reached where the structure was working in three dimensions and formed the complete enclosure to the building, eliminating almost entirely the need for additional fixings or substructures. The disposition of these elements – walls, roof, floor – was dictated by the desire to create clean, simple living spaces with a strong connection between inside and outside.

Noah's House
Construction of the original house began in 1929. It was set well back from and parallel to the river on higher ground, leaving a generous lawn between building and water's edge and a practical buffer zone for when the river flooded. A reinforced raft foundation was used and from this, 4 inch walls were poured in one lift. Celotex insulation board was inserted in the shuttering and left in situ as the interior finish when

the shutters were struck. Free-standing columns were kept to a minimum and the strength of the concrete construction was used to its full capacity, with roof acting as lintel over window openings, only supported by steel mullions in the most open portions.

The aesthetic of the building can be seen to come directly from the structural solution. Primarily it is a composition of concrete planes balanced with voids and glazed elements. The south elevation is a uniform concrete wall with a rhythm of conventionally sized steel casement windows. The north elevation, facing the river, is more interesting. Here, a large glazed element to the main living room is set adjacent to a large wall plane that is punctured only with a single kitchen window. The metal-framed glazing in the living room is set right up to the underside of the roof without a conventional lintel over and the floating nature of the slim concrete roof element hovering above is expressed. This composition had in it the seeds of Lucas' future designs.

The original single-storey plans of Noah's House echo the spatial economy and simplicity of living on a boat. The formal shape is orthogonal with central circulation serving the open main living space, kitchen and bathroom on the riverside and bedrooms on the other. This main space with the focus of a prominent and large family table is strongly connected to the outside with the glazing we have described, from soffit down to the height of the built-in benching. A separate sitting room with a cosy fireplace is provided on the other side of the house for the winter months, alternatively it could be used to supplement the four bedrooms. A bathroom at either end of the house is provided. Adjacent to the main entrance, an external alternate tread staircase leads to the flat roof terrace above. Internally the insulation board was finished in a rich palette of Mediterranean colours – Provençal blues and greens. Externally, the walls were rendered with sand cement and the house was colour-washed terracotta brown.

The Boathouse
In around 1930 Lucas, Lloyd and Co. built another concrete structure at the river's edge to house boats and a workshop for Ralph Lucas and a study for Mary Lucas. This is a dry boathouse with a raked, stepped slab and large doors opening onto a slipway to allow Ralph Lucas to take his vessels out of the water to work on them. Excellent natural light is given to the workshop area at the curved end of the building through a continuous strip of glazing to the south and east elevations set under the roof. The slim slab of the roof overhangs like a curving hood, protecting the interior from the harshest summer sun.

Raised above the volume of the workshop and separately accessed from external stairs is the small music room. With a little fire and views back to the house and

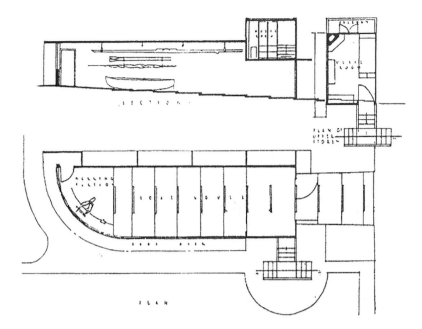

across fields to the west, it was designed so that Mary Lucas could compose here away from the hurly-burly of family life. The detailing, with unframed glass rebated directly into concrete apertures, is even simpler on these outbuildings than on the main house.

Later additions

Noah's House was a haven for the Lucas family until the 1950s. It was accessed over water for many years after its construction in 'an elegant electric canoe-shaped launch with a rear cabin'.[26] Colin Lucas' son Mark remembers that the river was a focus for their activities in and on the water, particularly in the summer, and a backdrop to afternoon tea that was always in motion with skiffs, punts, sailing dinghies and even paddle steamers passing by.

Over the years there were a few schemes by Colin Lucas to extend and adapt the house. In around 1933 a formal Parisian-style walled garden with an adjacent additional bedroom and bathroom was added to the west of the house. This little hard-landscaped and formal garden had similarities, like the garden at High and Over, to Guevrekian's garden for Villa Noailles at Hyères (1926). The bedroom could be fully opened to the external room in this private little backwater of the house. The vertical chimney for the main flues to the kitchen and living room appears to have been enlarged at this time, becoming a strong balancing element in the composition of the longer horizontal of the north elevation.

A later scheme was proposed that would have tripled Noah's House by extending and adding a first storey.[27] In fact, a less ambitious extension was carried out to the north west, adding another bedroom off the walled garden bedroom and a workshop adjacent to the garden wall. A corridor was also introduced in place of the original veranda to connect the new bedroom internally to the house.

After it was sold, the house was changed beyond recognition with a first floor added with a pitched, thatched roof. The boathouse with music room, now a listed structure, still stands at the time of writing, although it is in a disappointingly bad state of repair.

Above:
Plans and section of the boathouse and music room above. Formally arranged, the walled garden was a very private suntrap. Doors open into the bedroom beyond.

Right:
Furniture in the music room of the boathouse, much of which was built in, was contemporary.
The house in 1998. Noah's house has been completely shrouded by new construction.

Opposite:
The boathouse viewed across the lawn from the house. Lucas experimented with curved elements of concrete at stair balustrades and roofs at the entrance to the elevated music room in the boathouse.
The interior of the well-used boathouse in the 1930s.

The Sunlight House

The Sunlight House, Chelwood Gate, East Sussex, 1930–31
Colin Lucas of Lucas, Lloyd and Co.

In October 1930, under the mantle of Lucas, Lloyd and Co., plans were submitted to Uckfield rural district council for the construction of the Sun or Sunlight House at Chelwood Gate in East Sussex. This was another building for Colin Lucas' family, this time for his elderly grandfather, Francis Lucas, whose career had also been in engineering. He had been the managing director of the Telephone Construction and Maintenance Company and in 1897 was involved in laying the first telegraph cable between England and the USA.[28] With his wife Katharine he had bought some land at Chelwood Gate in 1914 for their retirement. Over time, they had developed several additional buildings on the site, Long Barn in 1915 which had a large open plan living area and bedrooms accessed externally above with a separate cottage, 'men's room' and gas plant, and later, in 1917, a bungalow named Streeter's Rough. Unusually, they lived between all these buildings in a home that was more like a set of pavilions than a conventional house.

The Lucas, Lloyd and Co., cottage project was undertaken eight years after the death of Katharine Lucas when Francis Lucas was in his eighties and it was designed primarily to create overflow accommodation for friends and relations. The compact layout, providing hall, kitchen, dining and living spaces downstairs and three bedrooms with a bathroom upstairs, was 'carefully arranged' to give 'the greatest possible amount of sunlight, fresh air and consequently good health that can be had in an economical design'.[29]

This is partly achieved through the careful positioning and orientation of the house on the half acre site; a closed entrance facade with circulation is backed up against trees in the north east allowing the south and west elevations to open onto a garden that slopes away to the south. The advancement of the concrete construction technique pioneered at Bourne End is, however, pivotal in achieving the Sun House's

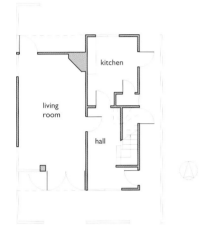

Above:
Ground and first floor plans. Circulation spaces are large in relation to the accommodation they serve.
West elevation.

Opposite:
At ground level the low concrete walls of the house continue into the landscape as garden walls 'embracing' enclosed paved areas adjacent to the house.

environmentally responsive design. Apertures are larger than conventional buildings and open right up to the underside of the soffit to allow maximum light penetration from the brightest part of the sky. Cantilevered balconies and overhanging roofs are engineered to keep out the sun during the hottest part of the day, the balcony to the south bedroom being larger (virtually doubling the size of the room when folding doors were opened) to give deeper shade to the living room and its veranda below, in turn allowing a greater area of glass. The plan stops just short of being entirely symmetrical because of this.

Fenestration is wrapped around the south and west corners on both floors of the house under the cantilevering structures without any secondary structure. From the inside, this heightens the visual connection with the outside, as do the lowered sills throughout the house. From the outside the corners of the house, conventionally where the supporting structure is, are eaten away. The elevational composition created with clean lines and a balance of planes, apertures and glazing is more sophisticated than that at Noah's House.

Initially the scheme was rejected by Uckfield rural district council for the reason that it was 'incongruous' and that the type of construction was 'generally unsuitable in a rural area' and a request was made for the owner to 'submit a design in conformity with the environment'.[30] The amusing ping-pong of correspondence between Lucas, Lloyd and Co. and the council during the remainder of the project reveals Lucas' determination to get his original design built.

In a reply to the council's request, Lucas voiced regret about their feelings that the amenities of the neighbourhood were compromised. He said, 'It has always been Mr Lucas' ardent wish to preserve the beauty of the neighbourhood' and that Mr Lucas was happy to sign an agreement that would allow the building to be pulled down if its appearance contravened the general amenities of the neighbourhood. However, at the council's recommendation, a zinc and tile mansard roof was added to the drawings before permission was granted

by the committee in November 1930. On the working drawings, the original scheme remained unchanged and a timber trussed structure was shown as a dummy roof to be bolted on later.

Lucas had little intention of heeding the authorities. He started constructing the original scheme prior to permission being granted, and on 21 October, following a site visit from the local authority, he begs to be excused for the unfortunate misdemeanour in starting preliminary work without their leave. On 26 October it was noted by the council that work was still in progress and later in March 1931 there are several letters from Uckfield pointing out that the agreed roof had not been constructed. In July 1931 there was a request from the local authority for the statutory notice of completion now that furniture was inside and someone was obviously living there.

Ralph Lucas replied this time stating that his father had built the cottage 'in this particularly sunny spot to give sun baths to London children who do not get sufficient light and air and he would very much like to reserve the flat roof for additional sunbathing space if required, he also wants it for his sunshine and ultra-violet ray recording instruments … he is very anxious, therefore, not to fit this roof … To this end he has tinted the whole house a good russet brown instead of putting on a russet brown roof … if the council would come and look at the completed form I feel sure that they would approve of it … Mr Lucas is not trying to evade their orders.'[31] At least one further visit from the district surveyor was made in early August and although the details are not known, the Sunlight House remained with its flat roof for many years after that time.

Whether or not he did have plans to provide such facilities for little Londoners at Chelwood Common, Francis Lucas sadly did not live much longer to carry them out as he died in 1932, soon after the house was completed. The estate was split up after his death and the Sunlight House changed hands quite quickly in November 1934. It still stands but it is unrecognisable as Lucas' design, having been extended and a pitched roof added in 1980.

The Hopfield

Above:
The staircase, an integral element of the structural scheme for the house is lands with a solidity that is clumsy in relation to the lightness with which the planes of concrete are articulated in other areas of the building.

Right:
The sitting room spills seamlessly out into the landscape beyond.

Opposite:
Ground and first floor plans.
View from the bedsitting room through to the open sleeping porch and the balcony and stair beyond

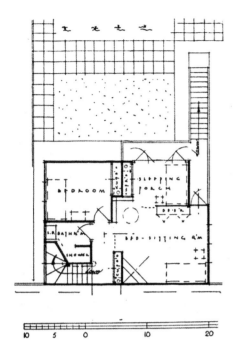

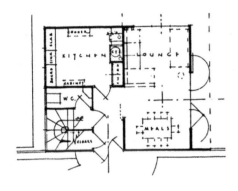

| | | | | |
|10|5|0|10|20|

The Hopfield, Wrotham, Kent, 1931–33
Colin Lucas of Lucas, Lloyd and Co.

Kent was an extremely convenient location for a bolt-hole from south east London, where Lucas, Lloyd and Co. was based, and a newly married Colin Lucas took a plot in a hopfield just outside Wrotham in order to build himself a weekend house. It was popular to have such a haven outside of the town and particularly amongst those who could afford cars. An *Architect and Building News* publication devoted to the typology in 1938 described it as a place in which a

> very special type of life may be enjoyed, consisting of complete change and relaxation, as free of as much bother and work as possible. The building should provide reasonable comfort and facilities for an open-air life, at low first and minimum upkeep costs, with a maximum amount of labour saving. It is mainly for summer use.[32]

An emphasis was placed on the health and vitality attained through communion with nature and, much like the Sunlight House, the Hopfield is designed to connect the user with the landscape and the elements.

For Lucas, the creation of a house for himself presented the opportunity to experiment further with his reinforced concrete construction method and at the Hopfield he develops a more rigorous architectural vocabulary. It is a neat cubist essay in concrete, refined in three dimensions. A compact, orthogonal plan generates a two-storey rectangular volume, broken only by a protruding linear external stair that connects the upstairs bed-sitting room and sleeping porch to the garden. Three of the five visible facets of the building are simple four-inch concrete planes with few apertures, the largest of which is a large glazed window to the internal staircase.

In direct contrast to this, Lucas uses large openings, overhangs and fenestration to disintegrate the south-facing elements of the volume. The reinforced concrete balustrade of the external staircase is a continuous beam across the house, providing one of the principal supports for the upper floor. The cantilever allows folding doors to be inserted to the sleeping porch; hence the entire wall can be opened up during hot weather. It also protects the living room below from the elements. A dramatic composition is achieved by setting aperture against concrete plane and defining the thin edges of the roof and walls. Hence, the concrete expanse of the entrance facade, punctured only by the front door appears to wrap up over the house to form the roof as one large cranked 4 inch concrete plane. The horizontal

banded expression of balconies and balustrades, much like the Sunlight House, is picked up in the enfolding garden walls that extend from the house to express the extent of the formal garden. Externally the render was finished in a subdued green colour intended to harmonise the house with the locality.

The staircase at the Hopfield appears to be a direct reference to those designed by Le Corbusier at the Maison Citrohan in 1922 and the Villa Stein at Garches in 1926–27. At the Hopfield the form is imbued with an instrumental structural role in the design. Overall, Lucas' early houses have a greater affinity with the forms of work by Dutch modern architects. Both the Hopfield and Sunlight House projects have distinct similarities with the external elevations of Gerrit Rietveld's Schroeder House in Utrecht of 1923–24 in the way that the fenestration wraps the corners, the roofs oversail and distinct planes of the building jut and float. There are also strong similarities, probably coincidental, with the spatial and material preoccupations of contemporary Belgian architect Louis Herman de Koninck.

Lucas felt it was a 'delightful house to live in – nice and warm, no draughts, no creaking floorboards or leaking tiled roofs'.[33] Downstairs there was an open plan lounge/dining area, a large separate kitchen and upstairs two bedrooms, the larger divided into a sitting area with openable sleeping porch. Flat ceilings, uninterrupted by intrusive downstand beams were covered with 'stout' lining paper and distempered. Lucas also designed the majority of the furniture and fittings for the house himself including beech laminate chairs and carpets.

The Hopfield was completed in summer 1933 for the sum of £1,200, which was equivalent to the cost of Noah's House. It was widely published in magazines and journals and, surprisingly, it was the only example of work by the Connell Ward and Lucas trio that appeared in FRS Yorke's seminal book *The Modern House in England* in 1937. It was the work that represented Colin Lucas in the Unit One exhibition and publication in 1934, appearing amongst works by leading contemporary artists such as Henry Moore, Barbara Hepworth and Ben Nicholson.

In around 1940 the house passed into the hands of bohemian artist and writer Denton Welch (1915–48), who mentions in his book *The Journals* that a bomb fell in the garden, unexploded, in August 1940. In 1944 there was a refurbishment and extension after a fire. Since then the house has been extended several times. The original building is still recognisable embedded in the additional accommodation.

New Farm or The White House

New Farm or The White House, Haslemere, Surrey, 1931–33
Amyas Connell of Connell and Ward

In 1931 Sir Arthur Lowes Dickinson (1859–1935) paid a visit to the office of Amyas Connell. High and Over had caught the 72-year-old's eye and, undaunted by the furore in the press it had provoked, he asked Connell to design his new home in Surrey. The client had an interest in new ideas and in supporting young people. Also, with a head for figures (having had a distinguished career in finance in America and England), he was intrigued by the cost implications of building using concrete construction.[34] Having heard Connell present his beliefs, remembered by the architect in 1977 as, 'an immature presentation ... expressed in Mars Group clichés', Lowes Dickinson remarked, 'Young man, I am an old man. I do not want a house to live in, but one in which I can spend my few remaining years and then die in.'[35]

For Connell, this was a welcome commission in a terrible economic climate. He had been making ends meet with small shop fit-outs and was delighted to get his teeth into a large domestic project of this nature. Basil Ward returned to London after three years of job-running in Burma during this period and joined Connell in practice. Athough he assisted with the New Farm project, it is Amyas Connell's name that is primarily associated with the design. Now known as The White House, the project had a variety of nicknames, Pollards, Aldings but more commonly New Farm.[36]

New Farm

The new family home was to be a phoenix rising from the ashes of Lowes Dickinson's own recent financial crisis. The outfall of the Wall Street crash had forced the Lowes Dickinsons to leave their rambling family home in Haslemere. Lowes Dickinson owned some farmland in nearby Grayswood and in January of 1931 he had received permission to convert some farm buildings there to create a cottage for his daughter. His subsequent application for Connell's designs on another part of the site caused a bit more of a stir at the council offices.

In 1976 Mr Field, an employee of the Hambledon rural district council from 1930, could still recall the arrival of the application for the house. It was, he said, 'a huge roll of plans, not the usual sheet or two'.[37] The proposed concrete wall construction at 4 inches did not meet regulation requirements and the architect was asked to provide calculations to prove structural stability. Figures were subsequently approved and the council grudgingly gave the go-ahead in July 1932. They registered their disapproval of the aesthetics by stating that 'erection of houses of this particular type throughout the district generally would be most undesirable' and insisting on a screen of lime trees to shield the unsuspecting passer-by from the shocking new building.[38]

CRITTALL WINDOWS

"NEW FARM," GRAYSWOOD, NEAR HASLEMERE, SURREY.
MESSRS. CONNELL & WARD, ARCHITECTS.

The windows are Crittall Standard "N" types, with a few of the same section made to special sizes. The 'daylight walls' to the staircase are made of Standard reinforced Sash Sections. The windows are painted dark maroon-red and the walls of the house are tinted pale pink.

Above:
Contemporary Crittall windows advertisement depicting New Farm.

Opposite:
Recent photograph of the refurbished house from the driveway.

Above: The main glazed staircase rises amidst the concrete volumes of the building, themselves punctured with slots of fenestration.
A detail of the canopy protecting the entrance.
The irregular and stepped plan can be fully appreciated on the roof terrace.

Opposite: The strong sweep of the driveway dominates the site plan and the house appears as a set of collected volumes positioned on its curve. External rooms are organised on axis with the front door.

ROOF
PLAN.

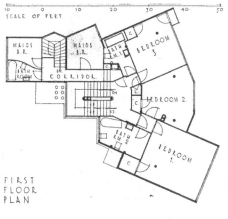

FIRST
FLOOR
PLAN

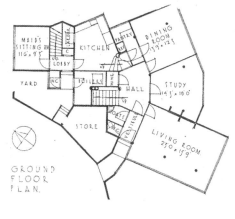

GROUND
FLOOR
PLAN.

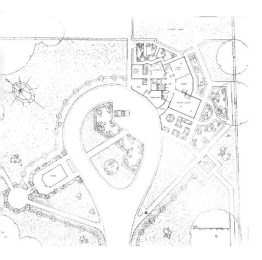

The house

With a build cost of £3,050 the scale of this project is closer to High and Over than the smaller early projects of Colin Lucas. The plan consists of three main reception rooms on the ground floor: study, dining and living rooms fanning out from the hall. These are supported by a kitchen and maid's sitting room on a slightly lowered level to the east of the staircase. On the first floor three bedrooms with associated bathrooms and storage are located over the living spaces and, again a few steps down, the servants' bedrooms are positioned over the service spaces. Surmounting the whole plan is an extensive roof terrace.

The great glazed staircase and main hall forms a pivot to the plan that fans out symmetrically from this north-west, south-east axis. Perpendicular to this, the servants' wing to the east is symmetrically ordered around its own, smaller staircase. While economical and giving good functional adjacencies, this distinctive plan of irregularly shaped rooms reflects Connell's departure from conventional orthogonal planning. Whereas Connell made the envelope of High and Over rigorously express its generating geometric principles, he is looser at New Farm. The plan bulges and extends making a more organic imprint with some surprising and playful twists.

At times, the visitor seems to be purposefully disorientated by the layout. The configuration of the entrance in particular contrasts strongly with the ordered, symmetrical arrival at High and Over. At New Farm the visitor is ushered through the side of the building. The front door is announced by a cantilevered concrete porch set into a curious single storey garden wall. This element, a physical interface of the garden and building, follows the curve of the drive and ignores the geometry of the house, leaving an awkwardly shaped infill store between. Visitors are brought into the centre of the house along a funnel-shaped curving passageway. They enter the central hall at a corner, perpendicular to the main axis of the building and then re-orientate themselves to enter the three main living spaces to the south. The arrival experience is thus more like an exploration than the clear logical progression of spaces.

At New Farm Connell developed a new aesthetic prefigured in the earlier Amersham house, synthesising historic references from his architectural background with technical innovation and reaching more deeply into the rich heritage of the English Arts and Crafts tradition. (It is worth comparing these plans with The Barn and Freudenberg House illustrated in the section on High and Over). New Farm was later described as, 'Among the most advanced houses of the decade'.[39] Although awkward in places, with this design Connell went some way to create an Anglicised modern language and while his subsequent work with Ward and Lucas

increased in clarity and formal confidence some have commented that Connell's work did not sing in such an exuberant way after High and Over and New Farm.

Light, air and elevation

As at High and Over, Connell primarily embraces the principles of 'sun, light and air' in his design of New Farm and these direct the orientation of the building and the treatment of its facades. The dining, study and living room face south for the optimum light throughout the day even though the principal views are away to the north (best enjoyed from the roof terrace and the staircase). The living spaces and bedrooms are lit through virtually uninterrupted ribbons of fenestration. These are kept narrow and long, as Corbusier extols, not taken up to the underside of the ceiling as is typical on Lucas' houses, and therefore they keep out the highest and strongest of the sun's rays. Externally they puncture and band the south, west and east facing two-storey envelope of the house in a similar but more seamless way than at High and Over.

At the entrance, this boxiness is entirely dissolved by the full glazing to the north and west faces of the staircase volume. This treatment reinforces the centrality of the staircase to the design. The thinness of the roof slab is revealed, likewise the raking stair within and thin folding planes of concrete to the entrance wall and porch in front add up to a rich and complex three-dimensional abstract composition. The staircase is a receptacle for the afternoon sun and ensures that from its very core the whole house is flooded with natural light. It washes all the main rooms and penetrates down into the house through small porthole skylights inset into the flat roofs.[40]

Connell employs the flat roof as a garden again at New Farm – an idea that has perhaps more currency for a dwelling in the city than here in the rolling Surrey countryside. The footprint of the building is evident here on this artificial landscape, unfettered by divisions. From the roof edges, the changing elevations below can be clearly understood: angular jutting planes of the successive roofs overlap beneath at the entrance and at the south sheer drops of the flatter facades are broken only by the projecting balcony to the bedroom.

From the roof terrace, the ordered layout of the verdant garden not far below is also made clear. The landscaping is dominated by the prominent sweep of the turning circle and parking area at the front of the house. This is bisected by a pedestrian route on axis with the front door and ends in the west with a rectangular pool and halts at the intersection of a network of other paths. There are formal areas where the beds are ordered and hard landscaping is formed from concrete but there are also less precious areas of the landscape where undulating lawns abut the stepping and faceted house.

Construction

This was Connell's first building constructed entirely in reinforced concrete. As the critic Baseden Butt recognises, the construction method is wholly integral to the form and aesthetics of the house. He said, 'The house at Grayswood would not have been achievable in shape or formality or even in terms of economy if it had not been realised using concrete.'[41] When the *Architect and Building News* covered the project in March 1933, they recognised the similarities of the construction method with one they had covered a year earlier at Bourne End. Later, Colin Lucas said of this coincidence, 'one of the strangest things I could never understand was that we had … independently hit on the same technique. As far as I know we were alone in this field.'[42] As with Lucas' houses, the structural elements were designed so as to standardise the shuttering as much as possible and four-inch concrete external walls were cast with an integral internal skin of insulation to mitigate heat loss.

There are some notable differences between the techniques. Connell does not use mass reinforced concrete so religiously for all the elements of his building. Slabs at New Farm are constructed in reinforced concrete beams with light hollow floor blocks and internal non-loadbearing partitions are formed of hollow blocks. Connell also relies more heavily on the use of columns in this design than Lucas. Later recalling that he was 'under the spell of Le Corbusier' at this time, the key architectural inspiration for him in this construction technique came from Le Corbusier's Dom-ino sketch from 1914–16, where the introduction of a frame with point load foundations released the architect from the restrictive load-bearing wall.

This schema is evident at New Farm where the reinforced concrete columns are the major structural elements around which the curtain walls can meander freely and can be more extensively glazed. The columns work to support the upper roofs and floors with the structural concrete stepping walls to the north and east. The concrete stair is cantilevered from the large central column in the hall allowing the staircase to be wrapped with glass on two sides from first floor level.

It is interesting to pause a moment to reflect on the earliest work of the two young architects in practice – Connell and Lucas. Lucas' architecture is rigorously expressed as a set of structural concrete planes working in three dimensions giving deep apertures, eroded corners and totally flat thin spanning slabs. Connell's facade treatment is more boxy and more referentially 'European Modern' with its flush horizontal ribbon windows and at the same time he plays formal games with historic references in elevation and in plan. His forms to this date are more complex than those of Lucas – they do respond to more sophisticated briefs – and they are also less beholden to structural, material integrity.

The White House?

Although the house at Grayswood has been painted white now for some time and has been rechristened the White House, something that is often overlooked (not least because the only contemporary photographic records of the building are in black and white) is the fact that colour was widely and boldly used from the very start in these architects' work, and indeed in modern architecture. The exterior of the White House was sprayed in waterproof cement that was finished in blush pink set against leaf green metal casement windows. It is unsurprising that the steel window company Crittall used the house for a contemporary advertisement for their windows.

Colour played an important part to accentuate shapes and emphasise planes internally as well as externally. The interior was decorated in rather garish colours and a plethora of finishes, including some antique tiles from Lowes Dickinson's collections used as wall decoration. A diagram in a contemporary article in the *Architect and Building News* of 10 March 1933 (see illustration) notes the colours and types of materials around the fireplace in the study. A pink terrazzo hearth, surround and curving shelves are wrapped around a column that is finished in black gloss enamel. The ivory walls contrast with a rather curious black sculptural form like a large paddle or rudder that boxes in the flue from the living room behind, traversing the chimney breast and diagonally bulging forward to receive a white opal recessed light fitting in its soffit.

Later history

New Farm has shown itself to be adaptable to the changing requirements of its succession of owners over the years, some of whom have made alterations and additions. Despite these (and probably due in part to its listed status) the original house remains clearly recognisable today.[43] The concrete fabric of the building has not succumbed to any major defects. The house was skilfully refurbished around 1993 by Avanti Architects.

Above:
The central column to the main stair (to the right edge of this photograph) also contained the boiler flue.
The sculptural fireplace in the study.
An impression of the original pink colour of the house.

Opposite:
The completed house before landscaping commenced.
A recent view of the garden elevation of the house.

42 and 44 Sinah Lane

Above: Saltings at the completion of a major refurbishment
by Barry Russell, 1976.

42 Sinah Lane (Saltings) and 44 Sinah Lane, Hayling Island, Hampshire, 1933–34
Amyas Connell of Connell and Ward

Locally nicknamed 'salmon' (42) and 'cucumber' (44) on account of their colour, these neighbouring weekend houses on Hayling Island in Hampshire were commissioned by two London doctors and their families. Number 44 was for Dr L Haydon and number 42, called Saltings, was for Dr RD Lawrence.[44] The two families became close friends when Dr Haydon became the General Practitioner for the Lawrence family in Battersea. Dr Lawrence headed the development of the diabetic department at King's Hospital at Denmark Hill in South London. Diagnosed with the condition himself in 1920, he was one of the first patients to be successfully treated with insulin and his experience led him to dedicate his career to developing this therapy. He founded the Diabetic Association with the writer HG Wells in 1934, the same year that his house on Hayling Island was completed by Connell and Ward.

With a strong friendship, children of the same age and mutual interests, the Haydon and Lawrence families looked for two plots together on the coast to build houses for weekends and holidays.[45] Their search ended at Hayling Island where they bought a quarter of a six-acre field at the south-west end of the island north of Sinah Lane. Each of the long sites reached down to the shore of Langstone Harbour and the protected waterways and surrounding open landscapes and beaches offered the perfect opportunity for fine summer days of childhood adventures. For rainy days, the cinemas and general seaside entertainments at West Town were conveniently close. A prestigious golf club at nearby Sinah Common was also a great draw for the two doctors. According to a 1930s advertisement for a school in South Hayling, this was the right place for a healthy year-round life with a high sunshine record and the 'mildest winter climate in England combined with uniquely invigorating air'.[46] The families could also enjoy a healthy diet of local fish, oysters and farm produce.

It is most likely that Robin and Anna Lawrence came to know Amyas Connell through mutual friends, the Boumphreys. Geoffrey Boumphrey was an inventor, engineer and author, and his wife, Esther, was an artist, writer and a great friend of Connell's wife Maud Hargroves.[47] Mrs Haydon was an actress, like Maud Hargroves, and Anna Lawrence a dancer and accomplished musician and all the couples moved in similar artistic circles in London associated with the Chelsea Arts Club.[48] With a generally forward-looking attitude to life – all three boys were educated at a progressive school in Wimbledon – in addition to their artistic interests, the Lawrences gave Connell and Ward the commission to design their weekend house. Both couples were particularly interested in how the designs could offer them an efficient house with flexible living arrangements that could also promote health. Basil Ward later said, 'You can imagine how exciting it was for two young architects full of Corbusier's ideas to get a commission like that.'[49]

The 1930s saw the growing popularity of Hayling Island brought about largely by an increasing ownership of motor cars that trundled over the timber toll bridge from Havant. The little country lanes were upgraded with more substantial surfaces.[50] Since the early nineteenth century Hayling Island had been a resort geared towards the upper end of society with a large terrace of impressive Regency crescent houses and a substantial hotel with excellent views to the sea erected at West Town in 1825. By the 1930s a permanent summer seaside fairground had replaced the more upmarket horse racing events of the previous century on the esplanade, complete with ghost train and boating lake with an island of marooned monkeys. Seasonal holiday camps and houses were also developed, particularly along the south coast and the far east of the island earned the nickname 'bungalow town'. The area around Sinah Lane was relatively rural and quiet.

It is likely that both Connell and Ward had a hand in the designs of this pair of houses. Although employing the same reinforced concrete construction methods for both, the two houses are notably different in form and size. Elements of the practice's contemporary speculative house designs at Saltdean, Amersham and Ruislip are, unsurprisingly, evident in the designs (see pages 132-51).

42 Sinah Lane

Number 42 (Saltings) is a substantial property with an L-shaped plan primarily running east/west across the shortest width of the site and projecting south towards the approach road. The main entrance is positioned at the internal corner of the L and opens immediately into the open plan hall/dining/living room area. To the north are the maid and kitchen quarters, to the west the boiler room, garage and external stores. A staircase adjacent to the entrance leads up to the sleeping quarters and on to the roof terrace.

The open plan dining and living space is reminiscent in scale to a wing of High and Over and is given a taller floor to ceiling height than the ancillary spaces to the west. The three main bedrooms and a dressing room are situated above this room and the children's accommodation, nursery, bedroom and balcony, are accessed from the half landing on the stairs.[51] Every room has built-in cupboards for storage. Two bathrooms are shared between the bedrooms and a wc is provided downstairs. With such an emphasis on outdoor living, the sleeping quarters are comparatively more generous than the living spaces beneath. The living room accounted for only half of the ground plan with the rest given over to storage, garage, kitchen and maid's quarters.

An innovative tri-leafed revolving door/shelf unit was introduced between scullery, maid's quarters and living room. A simpler version of this space-saving cupboard was incorporated into the practice's contemporary houses at Ruislip and Amersham. Practical cork floors, warm to the bare foot, were installed throughout. The house was furnished with imported Finmar furniture from Heals.[52]

The plan of Saltings is characteristically orientated in relation to the sun: living spaces have large areas of glazing to the south and west to maximise sunlight while glazing in the service spaces admits more constant north light for practical tasks. With a north/south orientated plot and the harbour away to the north the result is that the main living spaces give onto the drive rather than the long private garden with the harbour and views beyond as you would expect. The result is that the main body of the garden is separated from the living spaces, while the sunny front garden becomes a focus for the life of the house with large folding doors opening onto it from the living space. By positioning Saltings further north on the site than its neighbour the architects made this forecourt parallel with the rear terrace of number 44, allowing the spaces to be linked and reinforcing the connection between the two properties.

The upper floor and roof terrace get the full advantage of the views to the north. The master bedroom is projected forward from the rest of the north facade like a bay window to take the occupant one step closer to the harbour. Whereas, in the main, horizontal strips of fenestration are used, here in the master bedroom, as in the children's bedroom and in the living room, the architects take their glazing right up to the ceiling to bring more light in.

The treatment of the staircase is strikingly similar to Connell and Ward's Ruislip houses of the same date (see pages 134-38). A plane of concrete wraps up as a wall and over as a roof to the stair held apart from the volumes of the house with a band of two planes of glass. At the base of the stair, in a new composition of a now familiar characteristic of Connell's designs, the front door is protected by a thin concrete canopy. At High and Over this was a diamond shape, at New Farm a deep angular cantilevering hood. This one, triangular and curved, spans from the bathroom to form a 'lid' to the pronounced semicircular enclosure to the boiler. A tiny strip of windows beneath it makes this horizontal element appear to float. The transoms and mullions of the windows, painted black as at High and Over against dusky pink walls, appear to dissolve and the apertures rather than their divisions are accentuated.

44 Sinah Lane

The Haydons' house at number 44 was a more compact dwelling for a smaller family unit. Whereas the

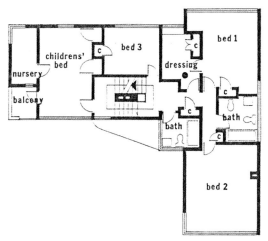

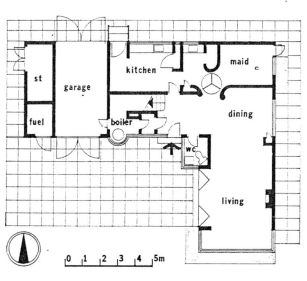

Above:
Saltings viewed from the south east.

Right:
Ground and First floor plans.

Above: 44 Sinah Lane front façade.

Below:
Mrs Lawrence at the 'front door'of 42, spring 1934.
Mrs Haydon and Mrs Lawrence sitting on the front door step of 44 Sinah Lane.

design of 42 had similarities to Connell and Ward's speculative houses at Ruislip, 44 is formally closer to their speculative houses at Saltdean – particularly its shapely external cantilevered staircase from first floor to roof terrace. It also has its entrance and circulation arranged at the centre of the plan, flanked by the living accommodation. On the east side is the dining area with a small kitchen to the rear and on the west an open plan living area with views down the long garden to the shore of the harbour. The tight staircase from ground to first floor was originally glazed to light the landing on the first floor. Around this, three small bedrooms and bathroom are arranged with a fourth bedroom over the garage to the north east. Built-in storage is incorporated wherever possible.

Planning and construction

Building regulation applications were considered simultaneously for both houses by Havant and Waterloo urban district council at their committee of 9 March 1934. On the same date an application was received for a larger modern house in the neighbouring plot of number 40 Sinah Lane for an Admiral Craufurd. Plots to the east of this were not built on until some time later. More details of the unusual four inch reinforced concrete construction were requested by the council from the architects and building commenced later in the spring. The contractors were a local firm who had never built in concrete before and there were considerable problems on site, not least because Connell and Ward, struggling in early practice, could not afford to get down to supervise during construction. There is even a family story that Saltings was built back to front but this seems unlikely. Practically, the roof leaked from the very outset, especially in the bathroom, however Dr Lawrence's son can remember no bad feeling towards the architect at the end of the project.[53]

During the construction period the families rented local accommodation on Hayling Island. The buildings were ready enough in six months for Saltings to be used in the autumn half term break in 1934. Thus started frequent and prolonged visits to the holiday homes. The Lawrence family with their three boys, a nanny and cook would go to the island for weekends perhaps once a month and would decamp to the house for the whole of the summer. They would even brave the weather at Christmas when the house was not so comfortable, relying on the coke boiler to take the edge off the cold and damp. The Haydons with their daughter Bridget were usually there at the same time and the families maintained a close friendship.

Fond memories of these times are held by the Lawrences' middle son Adam. The children were free to take off with a picnic in the morning and spend days exploring on and in the water in Langstone harbour, even venturing out into the choppier water of the Solent when they plucked up the courage. A number of

his parents' artistic friends came to stay, particularly from the ballet world, and one of his ingrained recollections is of Hugh Lane performing arabesques on the parapet of the roof terrace. At the age of six he heard the declaration of war in the living room of Saltings in September 1939. The family converted the boiler room under the stairs into an air raid shelter and continued to use the house until 1940 when he remembers seeing some of the first raids on Portsmouth from the roof terrace. Soon after this the inhabitants were evacuated from Hayling Island, furniture was stored, houses shut up and left. The island was used as a decoy to protect Portsea Island. Fires were lit to simulate the bomb damage of Portsmouth and to encourage enemy troops to bomb Hayling, thus protecting the more important military targets in the nearby city. The result was that Hayling Island was regularly bombed and when the families returned after the war the houses were still standing but in a sorry state of repair.

Later history

In August 1974, 42 and 44 Sinah Lane were both listed, an act that 'delighted' Basil Ward.[54] By this time Saltings had passed into the hands of Dr Lawrence's sister-in-law, and the house needed some attention to address problems of damp penetration in roofs and through walls. A substantial restoration of Saltings was carried out by architect Barry Russell from 1974 with funding from Hampshire County Council. The architect's findings form the first publication on this project in 1977 and give us useful insight into the original construction. Initial inspections suggested that deterioration of the concrete structure was to blame for the water ingress, however, the concrete, constructed using reinforcing mesh and bars in tandem was 'exceedingly dense' and 'suffered little from water penetration'.[55]

It became apparent that the windows were the major weak point. Originally steel painted windows had been fixed to unrebated concrete apertures with a sand cement fillet under sills but no damp proof course, drips or flashings – detailing Barry Russell describes as 'optimistic'.[56] Galvanised double-glazed steel windows were used to replace these in 1977 and lead sill flashings introduced. These windows have since been replaced with white plastic by a subsequent owner.

In 1942 the house at 44 Sinah Lane was bought by a local resident and was kept in the same family until 2006. In 1944 the north-facing glazing to the stair was removed and in 1949 the kitchen, hopelessly small, was extended. Consequently, it is difficult to understand the original design from the current rear facade. Number 44, having lost its green hue, has been known as the White House since 1974. At the time of writing a major refurbishment has just been completed by John Winter.

Usherwood

Above: Front entrance at Usherwood.

Right:
The Usherwoods inspecting the roof terrace and hood.
Sitting in the window of their incomplete house.

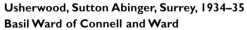

Usherwood, Sutton Abinger, Surrey, 1934–35
Basil Ward of Connell and Ward

In the depths of the Surrey countryside, this small bungalow for the Usherwood family was designed by Connell and Ward and completed after Lucas joined the practice in 1934. Like the Hayling Island houses this project was unpublished at the time and is little known. The client was a young couple whom we see in these photographs, exploring the house under construction. It is probable that he is the same T Usherwood who was the graphic designer working on *The Book of Parkwood Estate* that was being prepared to advertise the speculative housing scheme Connell and Ward were currently cooking up with contractors Walter Taylor Ltd in Ruislip (see page 138).

Of particular note is the glazed semicircular bay that accommodates half of the open plan living room area of the house. Such curvaceous expressive architectural gestures, seen also in the work of Mendelsohn, Chermayeff and Lurçat, were also used by Basil Ward in his design for Moor Park. Even with such a low house, a roof terrace is provided, with very close connections to the surrounding garden.

Above:
The curved bay of the south west facing living room.
North east elevation.

The Flat Roof House

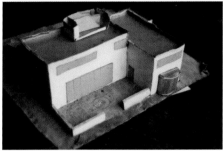

FIRST FLOOR PLAN

GROUND FLOOR PLAN

Above:
Margaret Sewell's design model of the Flat Roof House –
viewed from the entrance road and from the garden.
Ground and first floor plans.
Margaret Sewell and the gardener.

Opposite:
The house viewed from the garden.

The Flat Roof House, Little Frieth, Buckinghamshire, 1933–35
Colin Lucas

This commission was the last one that Colin Lucas started on site while still a sole practitioner and it was completed in February 1935, well after the trio formed their partnership. The house was Lucas' largest commission to date for a client from outside his family circle and it was the first one that he undertook without Lloyd, Lucas and Co. as contractors.[57] In the design of this surprisingly symmetrical building, Lucas' adherence to the ancient, ordering principles of architecture he learnt about at Cambridge, primarily the golden section, is more evident than in his other buildings thus far. Through a rigorous approach to the design, he tests how these design tools can be used to organise such a modern building technique.

The Flat Roof House, christened such by the postman, was commissioned by the miniaturist painter Margaret Sewell, a friend of Lucas' wife. Having been left a single mother in 1917 when her husband, also a talented artist and book illustrator, was killed in the First World War, she formed a strong bond with her daughter, Phillada Sewell. In the 1930s they made the decision to build a weekend house in the country in addition to their London home. After an extensive search around the Chilterns they bought a plot on high ground on the outskirts of the agricultural village of Frieth with glorious views across the Hambleden Valley. High Wycombe's nearby railway station had an efficient connection to their London home where Phillada Sewell, an actress, did her training and most of her work.

Margaret Sewell had very clear ideas that the new house should reflect the spirit of the age and prior to employing Colin Lucas as her architect she had modelled her own design in cardboard to show to the local authorities. This was largely inspired by her interest in the modern architects on the Continent, particularly Walter Gropius and Le Corbusier, whose work she had seen in publications such as *The Studio* magazine, but also first hand on her travels in Europe.[58] Sewell had read Frederick Etchells' 1927 English translation of Le Corbusier's text *Vers une architecture*, and many of the elements of her design – horizontal fenestration, roof garden and flat roofs – were motifs borrowed directly from the architecture described and illustrated in its pages.

The model depicts a building made up of three flat-roofed volumes. A pair at two-storeys are set at right angles to each other to make up the L-shaped body of the house and a third, a garage, is set apart from the house but tethered to it by a low wall running from a back door. This wall encloses a small kitchen garden. Central to Mrs Sewell's vision for the house is a main reception room, the dimensions of which reflect the

drawing room at Kew Palace. With the room set across the site and principally glazed to the south west, she orientates this to make the most of the garden and view. A curved bay window also protrudes from the garden elevation and the scheme is crowned with a small private sundeck on the roof.

The council was perturbed by her design. Besides disliking the 'factory aesthetics', they were incredulous at her unusual desire to have two bathrooms. She was not put off and in late 1933 or early 1934 she approached Colin Lucas to be her architect. She had admired the Hopfield in publications, possibly also visiting Noah's House at nearby Bourne End. Wycombe council received planning drawings from Lucas in May 1934, the month that Lucas joined Connell and Ward in practice.[59]

Lucas' solution

With a clear steer from his client, Lucas carefully considers her intentions and refers to her designs. Taking a close reading of the site at Frieth, its level changes and orientation, he refines the architectural language of the house, condensing the plan and economising the volumes. The deeds to the site stipulated that the new house should be set back from the road and Sewell's placement of the house across the short dimension of the plot, as close as possible to and parallel with the lane made sense to Lucas. The house divides a small arrival space for car and pedestrian at the front from the long sweep of the main garden, protecting the latter from the gaze of inquisitive passers-by and reserving the views into the valley for the householders.

Again, Lucas agrees with and adopts Margaret Sewell's orientation of the drawing room with the long side glazed to the garden. Understanding that this space is pivotal in her design, Lucas reinforces its presence by making it central to his plan. He uses the changing levels to the site to enhance the drama of arrival in this space. Access to the building is on the higher ground and, having passed through the hall, the guest is encouraged to pause at the threshold before descending several steps to the lower level of the room. The volume is made taller by the height change and the floor is detailed so that the internal finishes are flush with the external terrace. Hence, the room appears to flow seamlessly into the garden beyond (as at the Hopfield).

The rest of the ground floor accommodation, mainly service space, Lucas arranges in a horseshoe around the drawing room with the kitchen and garage/boiler/store flanking symmetrically either side and the staircase climbing behind. On the first floor the opposite is true as all the rooms are pushed into the centre of the plan above the drawing room, allowing the garden to occupy the periphery in two secluded balconies accessed from the bedrooms. These are enclosed by balustrades that are vertical extensions of

the external envelope of the building. Three bedrooms, a bathroom and wc are accessed from the central landing and an en suite bathroom is provided in the master bedroom, an element considered most luxurious at the time. The Flat Roof House is more rigorously and economically planned and internally more spatially advanced than any of Lucas' built works so far.

Regulating lines

Lucas uses regulating lines and the golden section to organise the facades following principles that have been in place since ancient times. The Flat Roof House appears to be more similar to his student design for a fisherman's weekend cottage than his more recent built work. The south-west elevation is entirely symmetrical. Three bays of windows with a rhythm of 3:2:3 panes are centred on the ground storey and held between two equally sized windowless box-like wings of concrete. On the first floor 4:2:4 panes are tucked up under the roof and overlap these wings, accentuating the detached over-sailing slab above.

On the entrance facade, a similar 4:2:4 pane rhythm is repeated at first floor level with smaller panes and higher window sills giving more privacy to the first floor accommodation. The symmetry of the elevation is significantly disrupted by a protruding cantilevered staircase. The two central panes of glazing are pulled forward with the stair element and the glazing line twists to follow its rake above the handrail down to the front door. Front door and garage door, one projecting and glazed, the other flat, solid and flush with the external wall, are balanced symmetrically at ground level. Although seeming to break all the rules of the organising symmetry, the angle of the staircase actually follows the line of a triangle drawn from the ground floor extremities of the elevation to the centre of the roof.

At the Flat Roof House Lucas employs his now characteristic four-inch thick concrete construction with in-situ wallboard insulation. The leanness of this construction is appreciable at window sills, balconies and at roof edges. Either side of the central bay of two window panes on north-east and south-west elevations are nib walls carrying beams that are expressed, unusually for Lucas, as down-stand beams in the first floor ceiling. These help to take the load of the roof and are cantilevered to pick up the projecting staircase structure in the north. The significant span of the drawing room ceiling is constructed as a two-way spanning reinforced concrete slab to achieve a flat uninterrupted surface.

While embracing such technologically advanced building methods it seems surprising that Lucas might look back to history and to his own traditional architectural education for inspiration to order these materials. The Greeks, the Egyptians and the advocates of the Renaissance among others used such regulating

lines to generate their architecture. However, it was a tool that transcended architectural style and a method of which Le Corbusier extolled the virtues in the pages of his book *Vers une architecture*. Regulating lines, he says, fix rhythm and geometry whilst safeguarding against whimsical design, they are 'a satisfaction of a spiritual order which leads to the pursuit of ingenious and harmonious relations'.[60] Lucas found such organising principles extremely useful in design throughout his career. He saw himself, like Le Corbusier, as part of a lineage seeking a universal truth or beauty in the rhythms and forms that transcend the issues of style or aesthetic. Such preoccupations are reflected in Lucas' writing for the Unit One book and were being stimulated by his contemporary involvement with the group. According to his son Mark Lucas, 'Colin used Golden Section intellectually and intuitively. The subject was of continuing interest and tied in with [his] long term enquiry into advanced maths, musical scales and the colour spectrum.'[61]

Inside
Interior decoration was predominately white, as the exterior. All fixtures and fittings echoed the simple, unornamented aesthetic of the house and a modern kitchen was fitted with a walk-in larder, a deep porcelain sink and purpose-built cupboards. A solid fuel boiler ran the central heating and was situated in the room behind the garage with the coal. Lucas ran pipes in the floor, where possible, to the radiators in each room.

The drawing room was decorated more lavishly with a maple floor and a fire surround of genuine travertine. This ample room was the heart of the house and was admired by many visitors over the years. Owing to the Sewell family's close connections with the contemporary arts scene, many of these were the great and the good of the music, theatre, film and latterly television worlds. The first Christmas at the house was celebrated with Margaret Sewell's sister, the pianist Rosamond Ley and her friend and fellow student of Busoni, pianist Egon Petri with his wife Mitta. Phillada Sewell remembered in her diary that the piano playing 'was a joy'.

The Sewells lived at the Flat Roof House until Phillada's death in 1998. Very little was altered in that time, apart from the replacement of the failing original steel windows. These had been set flush to the exterior walls and the omission of external sills led to water penetration and frost action over the years. The house was sold for the first time in 1999 and has since been extensively refurbished.

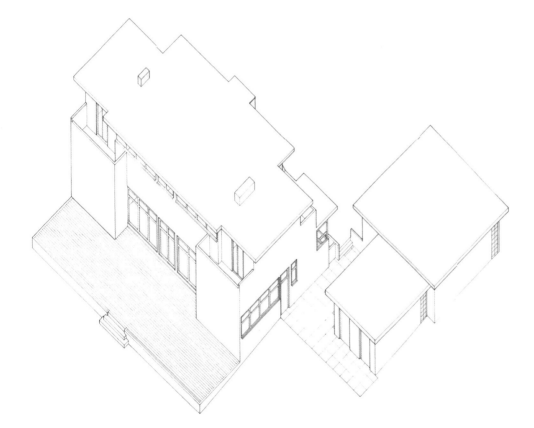

Top: South and north elevations in the late 1990s (left) and after refurbishment.

Above: Axonometric of whole house.

Opposite:
The two balconies accessed through end bedrooms were not heavily used and were perhaps always a Mediterranean conceit.

The Concrete House

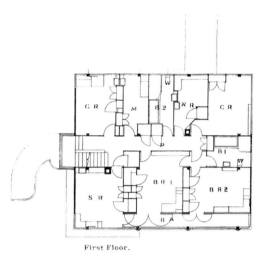

First Floor.

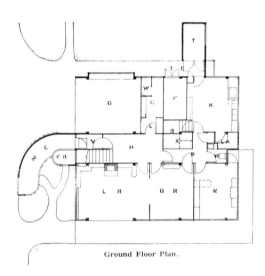

Ground Floor Plan.

Above:
Ground and first floor plans.

Opposite:
The approach to the Concrete House from the south.

The Concrete House, 4 The Ridgeway, Westbury-on-Trym, Bristol, 1934–35
Amyas Connell and Basil Ward of Connell and Ward

Like the Flat Roof House, this project in Bristol was executed over the period that Lucas joined the practice. Its designs originated from the Connell and Ward partnership but the specification, a copy of which still exists, drew on the experience of all three practitioners. This house was the furthest from London executed by the practice. It was for Mr Ronald Gunn, a director of Imperial Tobacco, his wife Jessie Gunn and their young son. Moving to Bristol from Somerset to be close to the docks, the Gunn family had acquired a site between Westbury-on-Trym and Brentry at the top of Brentry Hill with a fantastic aspect south across the downs towards the city. Westbury had evolved as a traditional Gloucestershire village until it was absorbed into the city of Bristol in 1904. Thirty years later Westbury and Brentry were in the process of being subsumed into the suburban sprawl of Bristol although the area was still a popular semi-rural afternoon tea stop on the trams from the city with good market gardens and nurseries. The site of this house was the last finger-like plot on a field next to Sheep Wood to be developed and was accessed by a new road.

Ronald Gunn's interest in building a modern house stemmed from his civil engineering training. Also a neighbour of the family, coincidentally from New Zealand, had built a V-shaped concrete house that had inspired him and it is likely that his acquaintance the architect Marshall Sisson gave him the name of the Connell and Ward partnership. Mr Gunn was taken to see High and Over and was impressed. He gave the architects a free hand with the design of his new home and both partners appear to have been involved in its design.[62]

Layout
The Concrete House is set well back from the road to align with its neighbours and the approach down a long straight driveway gives plenty of time for the visitor to admire the modernity of the design alongside its pitched roofed companions. The driveway delivers the visitor at the main entrance to the house at the centre of the plan on the west side.

The plan is largely orthogonal and is orientated on a north/south axis. It is divided structurally and functionally into three bays or zones. On the ground floor the service spaces occupy the north bay, living spaces are in the south (sitting room, dining room and nursery) and circulation in the centre. On the first floor the children's, maid's and guest bedrooms are tightly packed into the north bay, Mr and Mrs Gunn's en-suite bedrooms are located to the south with a sun room, and the circulation is again held between these spaces in

the central zone. This double-loaded corridor is daylit by the fully glazed staircase, reminiscent of that at New Farm, in the west. Eight-inch glass tiles are let into the roof to give spots of light in the darkest area of the first floor circulation space by the bathroom.

Given that the house incorporates facilities for a maid, it is surprising to note that Ronald Gunn had a strong interest in Socialism and was a member of the local Communist party, holding meetings at the Concrete House. He was also a Quaker. The family took lodgers and there is a curious little tale of their first lodger at the Concrete House, Klaus Fuchs. He was a German political refugee aged 21, a Communist from a Quaker family, who fled Germany in 1933 when the Nazis started to round up the Communists after the burning of the Reichstag. A previous lodger introduced Fuchs to the family and Ronald Gunn helped the talented scientist to become a researcher in physics for Neville Mott at the University of Bristol. As war broke out Fuchs' status was complicated by his ethnic origins and he was sent to Canada. Gaining considerable knowledge through his involvement in the development of atomic physics on both sides of the Atlantic, he began secretly to help the Communists and was later found guilty of stealing British and US nuclear secrets for the Russians in the Second World War.[63]

Construction

At Bristol, Connell and Ward explore the use of Le Corbusier's Dom-Ino principle more rigorously than in previous schemes. A grid of sixteen columns on raft foundations are the main load-bearing elements, their spacing determined by the standard width of insulation board. As at Colin Lucas' Flat Roof House, two main structural beams run parallel through the building and these define the circulation areas. The north and south elevations are treated in very different ways to suit the orientation of the building and its uses. The north zone of the house, with the service rooms, children's and guest bedrooms, bathroom, wc, kitchen and garage, is predominately solid with irregularly positioned strips of fenestration and the columns are incorporated into the external walls as nibs. In the glazed south elevation the structural elements are clearly articulated: at ground floor as piers between windows to the living room, dining room and nursery, at first floor three columns replace piers where the external walls step back to create a balcony as a secondary external circulation space to the master bedrooms.

The amount of glazing is remarkable at Bristol and the architecture is lean and light. Connell and Ward introduce two particular details to enhance this effect: they cantilever the concrete structure by several feet in the west and east and introduce glazing at each of the four corners of the house where one would traditionally expect to see load-bearing construction; also internally they reduce the partition width between rooms to just

two inches so that they can invisibly divide the internal spaces behind the glazing mullions and reduce the amount of solid wall required.

The symmetry of the south facade is disrupted at the west end. Floor-to-ceiling glazed doors with a deep metal frame replace the steel glazing in the living room (as at Saltings). At first floor the study or sun room is brought flush with the external envelope of the building to occupy the balcony space, and at the roof the balcony is lowered and replaced with a metal balustrade. Two fine concrete horizontal blades are introduced as shading above the fenestration. These interventions visually dissolve the three strong bands of concrete that would otherwise dominate this facade.

Several elements protrude from the otherwise rectangular plan. In the north a single-storey tool-shed is attached to the building to the north of the kitchen with the thinnest blade of a concrete roof that forms a porch to the back door. At the garage elevation on the north facade an L-shaped volume steps forward from the main body of the wall in a similar way to Lurçat's scheme for Hotel Nord-Sud in Corsica, 1929. The strip of glazing here gives good north light to Mr Gunn's workbench inside the garage, undoubtedly an important spot in the house that was serviced with heating coils and an electrical supply. Both elements, the two corner windows that seem to have escaped from the south elevation and the ventilation grilles, lift this facade from being otherwise flat.

The most notable excrescences are the staircase and porch at the main west entrance. The volume of the stair, just the width of the circulation zone at the centre of the plan, and glazed on three sides, continues up to the roof terrace with the thin blade of the roof extending eastwards to create a canopy. An expressive quarter-circular entrance canopy springs from the base of the glazed volume, the curve expressing the turning circle of the cars entering the garage. It scoops the visitor into the building past irregular swirling flower beds and a curved concrete planter.

The build

Correspondence between Connell and Ward and the city engineer at Bristol began in April 1934 and drawings were submitted at the end of June. The house was described as to be 'constructed in reinforced concrete in conformity with the new London County Council Reinforced Concrete Code and insulated throughout'.[64] More information was requested regarding the details of the walls and process of construction and once this information had been submitted, approval of the plans followed swiftly on 5 September 1934. Work commenced the same month and was undertaken by local Bristol contractors CA Hayes and Sons with a significant contract value of £2,800. This may have been

Above:
Detail (top) and view from the front door of the curved form of the canopy.

Opposite:
The stair and entrance canopy.

a reflection of a complicated mechanical and electrical brief.

Although the project drawings for Bristol were completed by Connell and Ward in May and June 1934, the specification dated June also bears the name of their new partner Colin Lucas. The specification reveals the depth of knowledge about concrete that the architects had accumulated to this point. The type of cement was stipulated for quality control purposes to be of British manufacture and supplied by the Cement Marketing Co. Ltd. There followed copious descriptions of the detail regarding the wetness of form work, time elapsing between mixing and pouring, height of tipping, ramming, type of mixing machinery permitted and joints between pours.

Wallboard insulation was specified to line internal faces of walls and columns, except the tool-shed and garage, to be 'fixed as shuttering' and left with 'true, cleanly butted joints without undulations'. Wallboard to the soffits and beams were to be well soaked with water before being laid so that the water of the concrete did not leach into them when it was poured. The surfaces of several of the floors were also to be covered with wallboard, for acoustic purposes, bedded on mastic and left to receive carpets.

To the exterior envelope a waterproofing compound was incorporated into walls, columns and chimney stacks to 12 inches above ground floor level to form a damp proof course and the surface of the concrete was also waterproofed. External walls and hoods were finished in two coats of spray Tungaline paint from Sissons of Hull in a 'biscuit colour' and a quarry tile coping was applied to the parapet.[65] The colour of the metal window frames is not clear, but they were dark against the buff of the walls.

Inside

Clearly inspired by the economy of an engineered solution, the house is tailor-made to suit the activities of the family and even their possessions. It embraces Le Corbusier's dictum of the house as a machine for living in, with each area designed for the utmost practicality. Mr Gunn fully embraced the latest technologies, incorporating gadgets and appliances into the house and the layout is designed to facilitate them.

Central heating is installed with the basement boiler room, like a ship's engine room, close to the centre of the house and accessible from the kitchen. Adjacent to it, a store area is provided with access so that dirty fuel could be delivered from the outside. The kitchen is equipped with an electric cooker and water softener. Wall cupboards are specifically designed for crockery, pots and pans and a special outdoor cupboard is incorporated so that tradesmen can leave things undercover when the occupants are out.

Each area is finished with a playful use of colour. The kitchen in white and blue enamel with battleship grey linoleum for the floor. The dining and living rooms with light green walls, a yellow ceiling, joinery in a sandy stone colour and an oak floor. A sliding partition in dark wine crimson meant that these rooms could be divided. The partition matched the undulating chimney flue in the living room. In the day nursery the walls and ceiling are in biscuit and the floor finished in blue linoleum. Cupboards are different colours to indicate use and the scale of the growing occupant is addressed in the adjustable height of the writing table.

In December 1935 the house won applause from *Decoration* magazine which cited it as 'house of the month', admiring the ease with which it could be run 'with housework reduced to the minimum'.[66] Mrs Gunn, however, would have preferred her kitchen to be cosier and more central to the family life, she found it too austere and also too hot. This was very much Mr Gunn's project, his wife would have preferred a 'more romantic home' and she remembered in a letter to researcher Jim Wood in 1976 that her friends generally shared her dislike of the scheme.[67]

Recent history

The Concrete House has been very well kept. Remarkably, most of the built-in furniture survives today, along with the original light fittings, electric clocks, built-in speakers, fireplaces and much of the door furniture.

Below:
The banded and symmetrical south elevation.

Opposite:
The garden (north) elevation set in a barren landscape soon after completion.
From the master bedroom the balcony and circular columns were visible beyond.

The Firs and Firkin

Above:
The vertical glazed element of the staircase separates the old from the new.

Opposite:
Floor plans and cross-section of the Firs. The section clearly shows the level change between road (on the right hand side) and the garden (on the left). The garage is tucked right under the living accommodation at the rear.

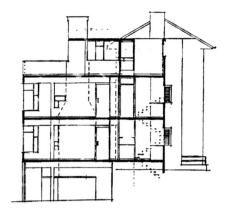

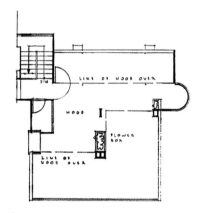

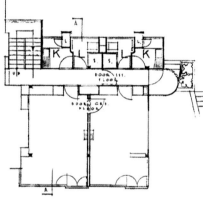

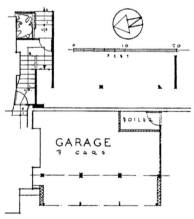

Right:
The main road elevation to the extension, with the Regency house beyond.
More generous windows on the west elevation give views onto the quieter garden.
View from the roof terrace looking east.

The Firs and Firkin, Redhill, Surrey, 1934–35
Basil Ward of Connell Ward and Lucas

The Firs was a curious extension to a Regency house with the same name on the main Brighton Road in Redhill. It was built for Miss Edith F Cooper as a new wing with four bedsits for four friends to live together but retain some autonomy. The planners were understandably concerned when they received drawings in August 1934 that this was a proposal for a new block of flats. The architects wrote to reassure them:

> Our client's purpose in building the new wing to the above is not for conversion into flats, she together with her sister and two lady friends have lived together for some time and the purpose they have in mind is to have bedrooms and living rooms looking onto the gardens on the west side and to be away from the noise of the traffic on the Brighton Road.[68]

The proposed bedsits each had a living room, bedroom, kitchen, wc and shower room and the shared living spaces and servants' quarters were kept in the old house.

Basil Ward was the architect in charge of the Firs scheme, project number 71 for the practice, and he took on a second project on the same site almost simultaneously. Mrs FM Unwin from Chiswick acquired a parcel of land in the grounds of the Firs from the owner, sold perhaps to fund the extension project, and approached the practice to build her a small weekend house amongst the trees. This house, approximately 20 foot by 20 foot had an open plan living space with large sliding folding windows to the garden beyond and a compact kitchen with one bedroom, a small bathroom and a sun terrace protected by a canvas curtain on the first floor. Aptly, this project later became known as the Firkin.

Planning permission was given for the Firs in September 1934 and in November for the Firkin. Construction began simultaneously on the projects and two of the architects' most frequently used contractors built side by side, West and Musgrave of Southfields on the Firs extension and Walter Taylor Builders Ltd from Harrow, on the Firkin. The architects appear to have jumped the gun on construction of the Firkin, commencing before the required details and calculations were submitted. A letter from Reigate's building inspector of 16 January 1935 reminds the architects of their obligations noting that 'the work is still proceeding'. Basil Ward's excuse was that his client 'would be inconvenienced and out of pocket' if they had not started the project. Overall, though, the architects' experience with the council on this project was an unusually positive one and as the Firkin neared completion in May 1935, the practice wrote to the

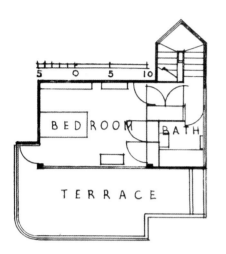

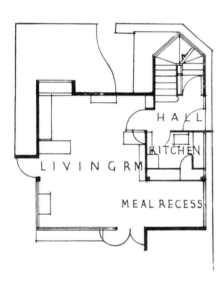

Above:
The ground floor and first floor plans of the Firkin. The north facade to Mill Street was more closed. The triangular staircase was glazed with obscured glass on one face. The exterior of the house was finished in grey.

Opposite:
The garden elevation, facing south, with the sun terrace above.

building inspector thanking him for his help and 'the considerate attitude … adopted towards this very new work'.[69]

Designing to fit with the existing

Anthony Bertram featured the Firs in 1935 in his book *The House*. Comparing a picture of the newly completed extension at Redhill with a picture of Stokesay Castle, he pronounced that all 'additions and adaptations, because they are to meet new social needs, must be in a new idiom'.[70] As the alterations and additions to the castle were added always in the style of the day, so, he argues, Connell Ward and Lucas' intervention is appropriate as a twentieth-century addition to an older house.

When publishing the scheme in June 1935 the reporter for the *Architect and Building News* admired in the design that 'the main lines of the old house find appropriate counterparts in the new: a compromise has been achieved without sacrifice of principle'.[71] This is most clearly illustrated on the east elevation to the road where the fine gutter line of the existing pitched roof is picked up and reinterpreted as a beam of concrete that hovers above the roof terrace supported on steels like rainwater pipes. Writing later in 1964, Ian Nairn remarked on the same point saying that the rhythms of the original house had been 'caught and counterpointed exactly … the pair of buildings reads as directly and eloquently as a piece of music'.[72]

The staircase is a key element in the design of the extension. The glazed structure architecturally separates the old from the new whilst also allowing access to and between the two parts of the property. The new building, as the original house, is constructed on a piece of land with a significant level change, such that the two storeys containing the four identical bedsits tie in with the ground and first floors of the original building at street level but an additional garage area can be incorporated beneath on the west garden side. Whereas the accommodation and the flat roof terrace above are constructed in reinforced concrete, this lower ground floor is built in brick, primarily to tie in with the existing adjacent brickwork. It is the first time that Connell Ward and Lucas used a brick/concrete hybrid construction, an idea that is explored further in the private house projects that follow.

The Firkin

Small but well planned, the Firkin was a little garden house built in reinforced concrete with integral masonite insulation. Like the Firs, partitions were constructed in breeze blocks, the roof finished in bitumen and internally a jointless Linolite flooring minimises upkeep. The half-glazed triangular enclosure to the staircase was a notable feature on the north elevation, and although asymmetrical on the elevation is reminiscent of the triangular bay on the entrance facade of

Peter Behrens' New Ways. Also on the north elevation there was an unusual sloping glazed bay window to the living room. Both elements are in opaque glass to increase privacy and the frames were light like the grey walls. The site was higher than the road and the small building would be more imposing were it not for the surrounding trees. These also protect the glazed south garden facade from prying eyes.

Later history

In 1951 Edith Cooper wrote to the council offering to sell the Firs to them as she had decided to move into the cottage in the grounds. She felt that with her offer 'the housing shortage might thus be relieved to some small extent'. It is not clear if the council took her up on this but by 1960 the new inhabitants had erected incongruous little pitched roofs over the larder vents on the road facade.[73] The building was listed but by 1985 it had fallen into disrepair and rather than attempt to renovate, developers applied to demolish it and replace it with reproduction Georgian houses. A public enquiry was held in the same year in which the Thirties Society successfully fought against the dismissive claims that this was a 'curiosity' and 'short lived style of architecture', claims that came from the developers and district councillors alike.[74]

It was Pevsner's view that the Firs was one of the only two buildings worth visiting in Redhill along with the parish church, and the building remains today with its pitched roofs removed and looking very close to the original from the outside. Sadly, however, the Firkin has been lost. In 1964 Ian Nairn reported, 'until a couple of years ago this was a very good small villa by the same firm, one of the best things they did. It has now metamorphosed into a house with a skin of yellow brick and weatherboarding in our present taste'.[75]

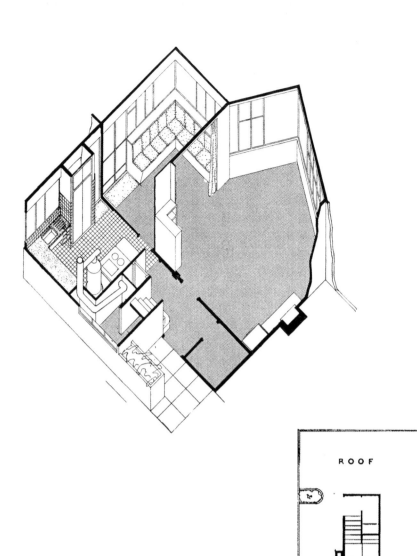

Literally down the Brighton Road from Redhill in the southern reaches of the village of Woodmancote, Connell Ward and Lucas constructed their next private house. This weekend home for Dr and Mrs Crow is situated on top of a ridge in a beautiful rural situation in West Sussex. Curiously this weekend house in the country was to be a respite not from the hurly-burly of the city but from the seaside town of Hove. In April 1936 the *Architect and Building News* reported of the completed building that its 'clean lines and arresting form, seems to strike a note more in accordance with present-day notions of fresh air, of sunshine and of simplified living and thus it can be said to reflect the outlook of the people of to-day'.[76]

Dragons was designed by Colin Lucas. He first put pen to paper to produce the earliest site plans in April 1935 and an application scheme was received two months later by Chanctonbury district council. Accompanying the proposal was a photograph of the site with the building roughly collaged onto it using white paint to give a crude impression of the house in its context. Despite its unconventional appearance, Dragons was recommended for approval just nine days later. In August 1935 the building surveyor received construction information.

Design
Set well away from the road the two-storey house occupies a ridgetop position at the south-west corner of the large site. It is designed to take full advantage of the views across the downs that fall away to the south. Perfectly square in plan on first and second floor, the house has three jutting extrusions at ground floor. The most notable is the glazed extension to the living room, angled at 30 degrees to the south elevation, that substantially extends the living room. A remarkably large square garage adjoins the house in the west and a small fuel store and tradesman's entrance are provided in the smallest east extension. A bite is taken out of the ground plan at the north-west corner creating a protected porch at the main entrance to the building.

A wall at the centre of the ground floor plan divides the south-facing accommodation – living room and adjacent open dining recess area – from the entrance hall, stair, wc and kitchen. Centrally located and contained fully within the square plan (rather than being expressed as a separate element on the exterior like the Concrete House and New Farm), the staircase delivers you to the centre of the first floor then continues fully enclosed up to the roof terrace. The sleeping accommodation on first floor is again, roughly speaking, divided by a central wall separating two larger bedrooms with gorgeous views to the south from the circulation, two small bedrooms and a bathroom.

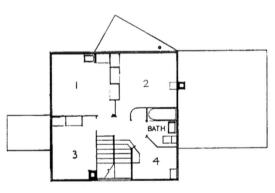

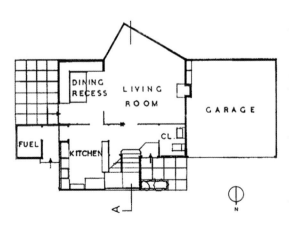

Opposite:
Continuous fenestration wraps around the south and east elevations. A thinner strip gives natural light to the garage. An angular bay projects from the living room space and the roof canopy appears to hover over the roof terrace.
The entrance (north-west) elevation can be simply understood as a C-shaped concrete block holding a rectangle of glazing between its top (roof) and base plinth. The glazing reveals the staircase zigzagging behind. A rectangular concrete block is propped against the glazing elevated above a single storey rectangular volume with a chimney.

Above and right:
Axonometrics from the *Architects' Journal* illustrating the construction and layout of the house.
Floor plans and a cross-section through the building.

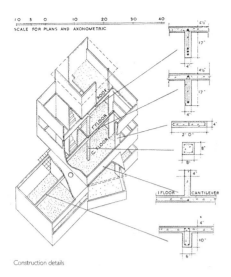

Construction details

SEASIDE HOUSES AND BUNGALOWS

BY ELLA CARTER

This book is uniform with "Houses for Moderate Means" which has run to two editions. It deals with inexpensive houses of the seaside type and with bungalows. Plans, constructional details and costs are given for each of the 50 houses.

Opposite:
The living room photographed on a sunny evening with the low sunlight penetrating deep into the plan. There is a strong sense of connection with the landscape beyond through the ample glazing. The floor is jointless magnesite flooring in light buff, walls are yellow and all internal windows and woodwork are finished in light green. The concrete nib visible towards the left of the picture is one of the main structural elements of the construction.
Low sills in the bedroom allow the views to be enjoyed even when lying in bed. Deep skirtings below the windows were incorporated to hide the pipework to the radiators. A built-in dressing table together with a stool (designed only a few years before the project was completed by Alvar Aalto in 1932–33).

Above:
Axonometric from the Architects' Journal illustrating the construction and layout of the house
A view of the roof terrace looking south. The curved planter wraps around the steel supporting column to the concrete hood.
Although a house near rather than on the coast, it was depicted on the dust jacket illustration of a book in the same year by Ella Carter entitled Seaside Houses. Design drawings of Dragons were also exhibited at the Royal Academy of Arts Exhibition of British Architecture 1937.

Construction

Having completed the Firkin and the Ruislip houses and by now adept in Connell Ward and Lucas' construction methods, Walter Taylor Builders Ltd took this project on site. Dragons was well publicised after completion and the Architects' Journal ran a comprehensive article analysing its construction. Lucas continues to keep stanchions to a minimum and make the walls and slabs do much of the structural work in this scheme, unlike the construction of the house in Bristol where a more plentiful grid of columns is taking the load. The amount of cantilevered structure at Dragons is particularly notable and how this allowed Lucas to introduce extensive corner glazing to the south-facing elevations and a deep porch area in the north.

Dragons is another compact house in the same vein as Hopfield and the Sun House. Here Lucas continues to explore the qualities of glass juxtaposed with hovering concrete volumes and wrapping planes. Viewed from the north west, the composition is strong and simple. The three-storey glazing to the staircase is held within a 'C' of concrete, its finer horizontal elements extending to create a planter at the entrance recess on ground floor and an overhanging roof at the upper floor terrace. The ground floor rectangular volume of the garage and main entrance appears to have been spun through ninety degrees from the rest of the accommodation and slips under the cantilevered volume of the bedrooms on the first floor. The expanse of solid concrete and its apparent weight set against the fragile glazing to the stair is particularly engaging, with the cranked concrete of the stair landings visible through the glass adding a playful ingredient to the composition.

At the south and east facades the planes of concrete are broken up with strips of glazing. Lucas uses the most characteristic element of this scheme, the prominent chimney-stack, as a balancing vertical element to these horizontal bands. This emerges from the single-storey garage volume and is separated from the house and expressed like a factory chimney. Circular in section and constructed out of 6 inch concrete, it is anchored back to the wall at high level by 1 inch diameter steel rods bolted through the full thickness of the wall.

As with the living room at the Flat Roof House, Lucas emphasises the living area with a freer treatment of its plan. He incorporates a glazed protrusion that has a rather uneasy relationship with the adjacent more solid volume of the garage as it neither continues it nor disengages from it. From the inside, however, the living room is dramatically enhanced by the effect of the bay, because it both increases the floor area of the living room and enhances the view.

Colour played an important part in the external composition at Dragons. Special 'lining oil' paint was painted directly onto the surface of the concrete in tints to harmonise with the surrounding landscape, light green on the front and back with buff on the side flanks, a combination described as 'refreshingly attractive' by the Architect and Building News.[77] The freestanding chimney was finished in light pink and doors and steel window frames in blue.

Later history

The house still stands and is still surrounded on three sides by fields although the saplings planted in the 1930s have matured and the site is less open than it was. Dragons has not been listed and since 1974 has been significantly altered through a series of extensions. There is an extension above the garage, the roof terrace has been filled in and at the ground floor the angled south bay has been subsumed in an extensive addition to the south and east. The outside has been covered in horizontal timber cladding and all the windows have been changed. The original form of the house is hardly discernible.

95 Salisbury Road

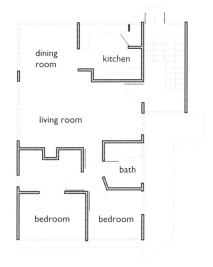

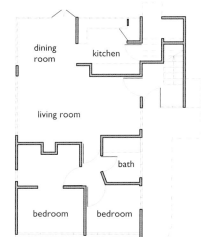

**95 Salisbury Road, Worcester Park, Surrey
1935–36
Amyas Connell of Connell Ward and Lucas**

This small dwelling in the growing suburbia of Worcester Park consisted of two floors containing identical flats. It was designed for Mr E E Minnion of Tooting Park, south London and was project number 90 in the Connell Ward and Lucas practice, contemporary with Dragons. The statutory applications were submitted to Epsom district council in July 1935, at a time when Salisbury Road was sparsely populated with buildings. The planning history gives no hint of the council being alarmed by the reinforced concrete construction.

Connell had the largest hand in this design. Much like the scheme for the house at Bristol, the main volumes of the house were orthogonal set against the more curvaceous forms of an entrance hood. Designed in an L shape, the main body of the house contains the accommodation and the short leg at the west end incorporates the stair and circulation with fuel store beneath. With the front door at the internal corner of the L, the long approach down the side of the building is protected by the canopy.

Ground and first floor have the same plan with identical fenestration. The bedrooms face east towards the road and the entrance drive and a small concrete protrusion cantilevers over the continuous fenestration here. These elements are more effectively employed on subsequent house designs above south-facing windows to protect internal spaces from the direct rays of the midday sun. At Worcester Park, they appear to be more of a formal invention integral with the canopy piece at ground level. A north-facing bathroom with high level windows for privacy is contained adjacent to the sleeping arrangements.

The rest of the plan is an open living/dining area with adjoining kitchen. The main living space is orientated to the south west, with fenestration wrapped around the corner on both elevations. With only one neighbour on the north side at the time of completion, the living spaces on the first floor flat had a lovely outlook onto surrounding fields and mature trees. An additional high, narrow strip of windows to the living area allows additional daylight into the room whilst being respectful of the privacy of the imminent construction in the next-door plot to the south.

Completed in early summer 1936, this project was not widely published. A planning application to demolish the building was refused in 1967 and sales particulars from the following year show the two flats by this time have been converted to one house. In 1987 the house was given grade II listed status. The main change externally has been that the fenestration and balustrading has turned white from its original dark tone.

Opposite:
From the road the porch to the main entrance protrudes forward to greet you.
The first floor to the staircase is fully glazed to west and east, making it transparent from the front and the back of the property and also distinct from the main body of the house.

Right and below:
Ground and first floor plans.
The dining room area of the ground floor flat viewed from the living room. The rooms were compact but with good site lines to the view beyond to the south west.

Temple Gardens

6 Temple Gardens, Moor Park, Rickmansworth, Hertfordshire, 1935–37
Basil Ward of Connell Ward and Lucas

The Moor Park project had a relatively long gestation period in the architects' office and working drawings date from April 1935 even though completion was not until 1937. No evidence has been uncovered that this delay was due to planning issues but the additional requirement to obtain permission from the Moor Park estate to build would have complicated matters. Temple Gardens was just one cluster of private houses to be developed within the grounds of the eighteenth-century house at Moor Park. The estate had been purchased by Lord Lever six years before his death in 1925 and was converted into an extensive country club. The eighteenth-century house became a luxurious club house and the mature grounds were reconfigured with a golf course and other sports facilities. The client for this five bedroom family house, Mr HS Tanburn, already resided on the estate. He worked as a diamond merchant in Hatton Garden, London's jewellery quarter, and no doubt enjoyed the benefits of residing in the countryside while being only a short distance from the Metropolitan line underground station at Moor Park that could convey him into the centre of London.

Temple Gardens, among the trees of the old pleasure grounds, was developed from the mid 1930s and the site for number 6 sloped up from the new access road. Ward, the project architect, arranged the living rooms of the house to face south east and elevated them to the first floor to make the most of the uninterrupted view of the golf course on the other side of the boundary fence and open countryside beyond. The house was finished in an olive green colour with buff sides. FRS Yorke acknowledged in his book *The Modern House in England* how the house harmonised sensitively with the mature woodland that surrounded it.

Structure
The architect R Randal Phillips, reporting on the house in *Country Life* in April 1938, described it as a 'house of the more advanced kind … sure to be regarded by some people as an affront'. Having anticipated that he would share this reaction, he is surprised to find that he is inspired and excited by the design. It is for him a 'sincere and functional accomplishment', its material and structural honesty being an important aspect in earning his respect.[78]

Randal Phillips praises the flexibility of design afforded by the concrete construction. Basil Ward, the project architect, remembered later in 1976 that the structure of the house was divined as 'a grid of columns (like the Dom-Ino concept of Le Corbusier) around which rooms and other spaces could be freely designed. The floor and roof slabs are cantilevered beyond the line of

supporting columns.'[79] However, this description, now familiar to this book, seems simplistic for the house at Moor Park. When the *RIBA Journal* appraise Moor Park with Connell Ward and Lucas' subsequent house at Wentworth in July 1937, they recognise a more advanced concrete construction method than that which Ward describes. Reinforced concrete, according to the *RIBA Journal*, 'lacks the background of almost instinctive use and expression possessed by older forms of construction' and in these projects a 'logical expression of reinforced concrete' is developed. They say:

> the fact appears to be emerging … that its most economical use is in the form of posts and structural panels, the former being capable of great irregularity in spacing and the latter of use horizontally, vertically or sloping, at the same time having extensive possibilities in cantilever construction.[80]

In this system the walls and slabs are designed as a structural unit where walls carry loads and combine their function with that of stanchions and beams. The structure is streamlined and the traditional requirement for heavy load-bearing masses at the perimeter is reduced. The result in architectural terms is an even greater freedom of design than the regular grid of the Dom-Ino house. The system allows larger spans with supporting structure (columns and beams) of smaller cross sections. These could be shaped to disappear as walls rather than march through the plan as regular and obtrusive columns. In short this is a description of the structure Colin Lucas employed in his early projects the Sunlight House and the Hopfield. At Moor Park and Wentworth, we see Lucas' post and panel approach wedded with Connell and Ward's Dom-Ino inspired structures.

Connell Ward and Lucas were not alone in employing this structural solution, Berthold Lubetkin working with structural engineer Ove Arup at Highpoint One, 1933–35, utilised a similar method, calling it 'panel and slab technique'. As John Allan describes, 'the real "art" of its structure is the way these [columns, piers and beams] are disciplined architecturally to occur only where they may be legitimately disguised or positively expressed'.[81] Each element of the construction worked hard structurally; external walls acted as beams and floors were hung from external walls with pillars. This building system made the construction leaner and lighter. Loads were concentrated at points so that there was a reduction in foundation trenches thereby reducing excavation work on site and saving time and money.

The architectural flexibility that this construction method afforded was explored by Ward. The volume of the house was nibbled out of the ground and first floors to give external terraces and routes under the

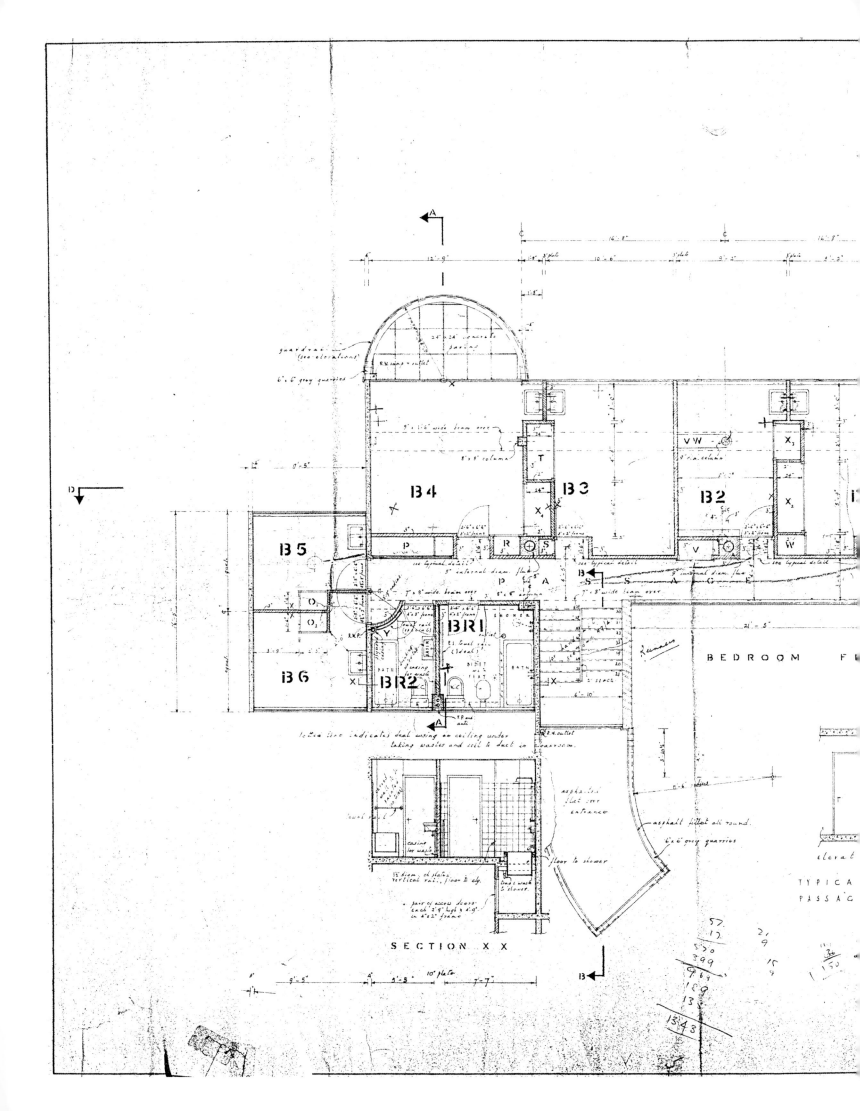

SECTION X X

TYPICAL
PASSAGE

BEDROOM FL

B 4
B 3
B 2
B 5
B 6
BR 1
BR 2

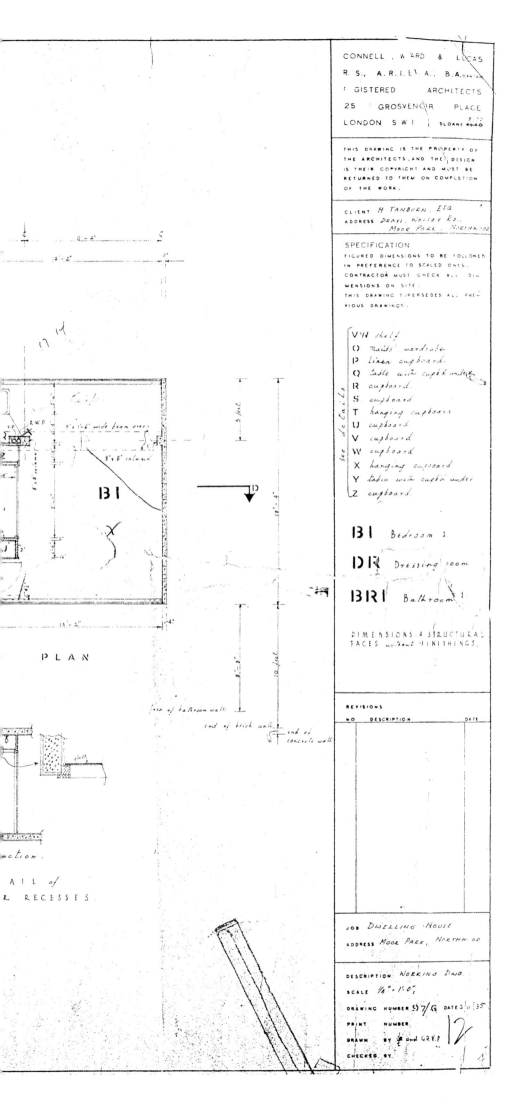

PLAN

B1

DR1

CLIENT H. TANBURN, ESQ
ADDRESS DRAYS, WOLLEY RD.,
         MOOR PARK, NORTHWOOD

SPECIFICATION
FIGURED DIMENSIONS TO BE FOLLOWED
IN PREFERENCE TO SCALED ONES.
CONTRACTOR MUST CHECK ALL DI-
MENSIONS ON SITE.
THIS DRAWING SUPERSEDES ALL PRE-
VIOUS DRAWINGS.

V W shelf
O maids' wardrobe
P linen cupboard.
Q table with cupb'd under
R cupboard.
S cupboard
T hanging cupboard
U cupboard
V cupboard
W cupboard
X hanging cupboard
Y table with cupb'd under
Z cupboard.

B1 Bedroom 1.

DR Dressing room

BR1 Bathroom 1.

DIMENSIONS & STRUCTURAL
FACES without FINISHINGS.

REVISIONS
NO	DESCRIPTION	DATE

JOB DWELLING HOUSE
ADDRESS MOOR PARK, NORTHWOOD

DESCRIPTION WORKING DWG.
SCALE 1/4" = 1'-0"
DRAWING NUMBER 57/G DATE 2/11/35
PRINT NUMBER
DRAWN BY and G.R.V.P
CHECKED BY

Working drawing of the second floor plan of Temple Gardens.

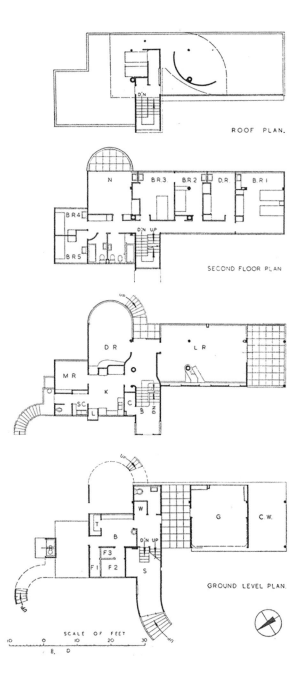

ROOF PLAN.

SECOND FLOOR PLAN

GROUND LEVEL PLAN.

SCALE OF FEET

Above:
Ground, first, second and roof plans.

Right
The near complete house viewed from the east.

Opposite:
During the winter months the fireplace would become the focus of the room.
The sitting room had substantial glazing giving a good, elevated view of the garden and golf links. In summer, the family would enjoy a seamless connection to the terrace beyond.
The architects' axonometric drawing of the living room. This was arranged with a bookstacks lining the north-facing elevation and a niche for the piano behind the fireplace and chimneystack.

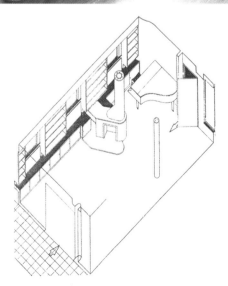

house. Visually, the resulting absence of walls, particularly at corners where structure would conventionally be found, gave the building a feeling of lightness and transparency that was accentuated on the south-east elevation with large tracts of continuous glazing. The poured monolithic concrete technique also allowed Basil Ward to develop the sweeping baroque shapes that characterise the house at Temple Gardens. Using specially adapted shuttering, Ward created the protruding cylinder of the dining room, the curved roof canopy and curling staircases. These elements added another layer of visual punctuation on the south facade.

Design

The house was well connected to the exterior with no less than four entrances in total from the surrounding garden. The approach to the main entrance is via a flight of stairs under the cover of the curvaceous projecting canopy. As at Bristol, this expressive form is locked into the glazed stair tower behind but unlike Bristol, where these organic shapes are an appendage to an orthogonal plan, at Moor Park the curves are more confidently integrated in the whole architectural composition.

The entrance hall leads up stairs and straight through the building to another entrance with an external stair that follows the curve of the dining room down to the garden. The mirrored S of this circulation both divides and connects the plan of the building – the living room to the south and the dining room with kitchen and maids' quarters to the north. The section can similarly be read as two elements staggered and linked centrally by the circulation. Arriving at a half level up from the ground, stairs ascend to the main living areas or down to the service areas at ground level with garage, boiler room and various stores.

At first floor the spacious living room with adjacent covered terrace is designed as a flexible space, loosely organised into several zones by the columns and fireplace. In the summer the south and east-facing fully folding, sliding windows can be opened so that the space flows out onto the raised patio and in the winter the arrangement can be re-orientated to the more solid west wall and fireplace in the north with book and music shelves punctured with three square windows. In the dining room, a distinctive glazed semicircular bay reminiscent of that at the Usherwood house (see page 76), cantilevers the diners over the lawn giving them delightful views and making the space a receptacle for south light.

On the second floor a corridor runs south to north through the plan, intersecting the main stair circulation. Single-loaded in the south, the corridor connects the south-east-facing master bedroom with adjoining dressing room and two interconnecting children's

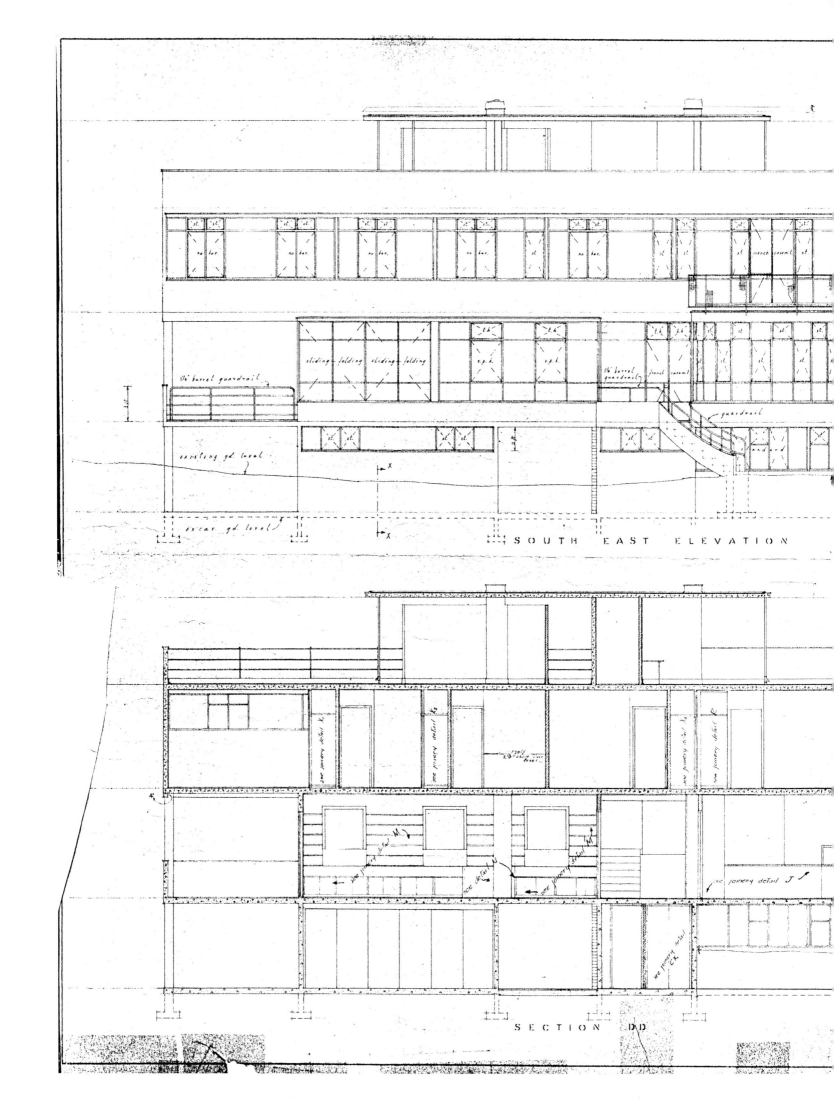

SOUTH EAST ELEVATION

SECTION DD

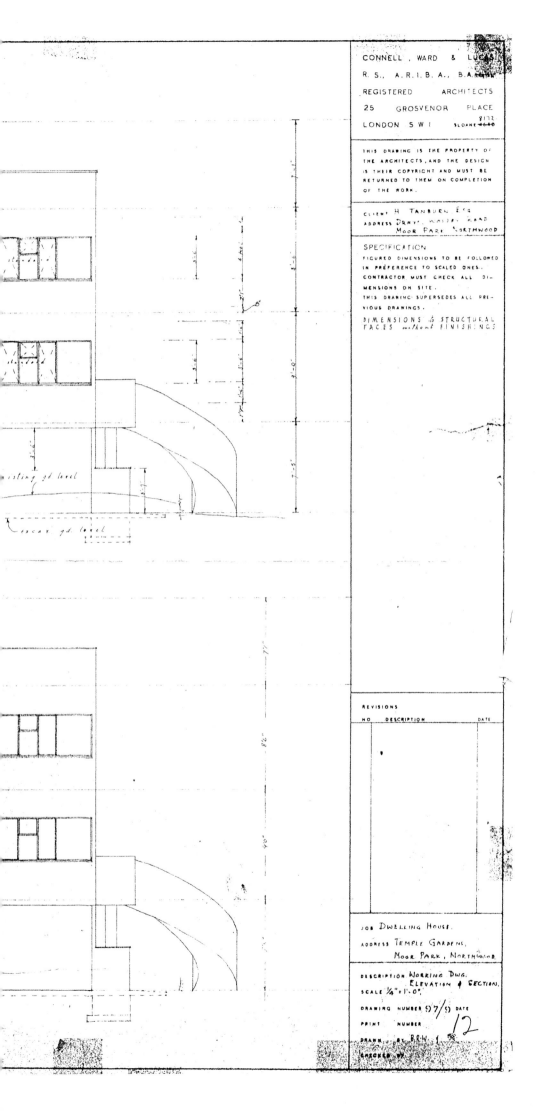

CONNELL , WARD & LUCAS

R. S., A. R. I. B. A., B.A.

REGISTERED ARCHITECTS

25 GROSVENOR PLACE

LONDON S W 1 SLOANE 8172

CLIENT H. TANBURN ESQ
ADDRESS DRAKES, WELLER ROAD
     MOOR PARK NORTHWOOD

SPECIFICATION
FIGURED DIMENSIONS TO BE FOLLOWED
IN PREFERENCE TO SCALED ONES.
CONTRACTOR MUST CHECK ALL DI-
MENSIONS ON SITE.
THIS DRAWING SUPERSEDES ALL PRE-
VIOUS DRAWINGS.
DIMENSIONS TO STRUCTURAL
FACES without FINISHINGS

REVISIONS

NO	DESCRIPTION	DATE

JOB DWELLING HOUSE.

ADDRESS TEMPLE GARDENS,
     MOOR PARK, NORTHWOOD.

DESCRIPTION WORKING DWG.
          ELEVATION & SECTION.
SCALE ⅛"=1'-0".

DRAWING NUMBER 97/9 DATE

PRINT NUMBER 12

DRAWN BY B.R.W.

CHECKED BY

Cross section through the house and south east elevation of Temple Gardens drawn by Basil Ward.

Left:
In amongst the trees, the house sits alongside its more traditional looking neighbours.

Below:
At the top of the stairs, the main roof terrace beckons beyond. Surrounded by mature trees, although stark in itself, the roof terrace appears verdant.
Under construction c.1936.

Opposite:
The roof was a playground for children and a sleeping deck for the adults. Rainwater pipes were embedded in the columns to the convex curved canopy on the roof. A concave concrete wall beneath orientated the views away from the drive towards the south and a swing is set up in the sunlight. A journalist in the *Studio Yearbook* marvelled at how the shiny blue soffit to the hood reflected the light that bounced off the pink pavers below.
The semicircular bay window of the dining space.
The roof terrace was used as a bedroom in the summer months.

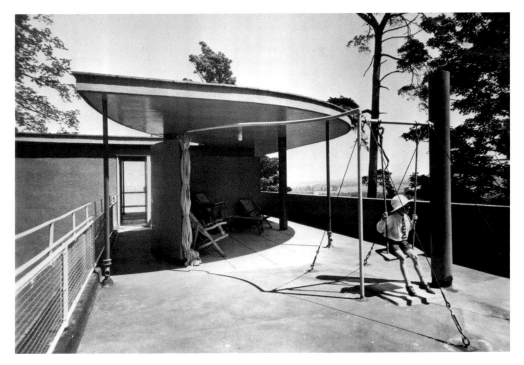

bedrooms. North of the staircase, the corridor becomes double loaded, serving the nursery, two bathrooms grouped above the kitchen (to economise on service runs) and the maids' rooms facing north and west. The plan ensures that the best views are reserved for the Tanburn family and that there is a degree of privacy from their servants.

The main stair extends a further flight to a roof terrace, to be used not only as a children's playground and for sunbathing but also for sleeping. The contemporary photographs of the house show two collapsible beds, bedding, bedside table and lamp all set up. These were stored in the cupboard at the top of the stairs and were used in the open air under the canopy overhang in the north to create a makeshift outdoor bedroom.

Service and utility areas are characteristically inventively detailed. A rubbish chute is introduced outside the scullery to discharge the waste into a lower bin area outside the house. The linen cupboard has two compartments for drying, one for airing. The main bathroom is spacious, not least because the bath was literally sunk into the upper part of the cloaks cupboard in the half landing of the hall beneath. The chimney stacks to the boiler and fire, expressed with shiny finishes on the first floor, are contained within the corridor walls on the second floor and appear again as they shoot through the roof to discharge above the canopy level.

Interior colours were vibrant, two or three colours were used to accentuate particular wall planes and built-in furniture. The living room walls were predominantly matt pink contrasted with one dark glossy blue surface behind the piano and light blue gloss pillars. All of this was set against an oak board floor. Linoleum was laid in the service quarters and a jointless magnesite composite floor on the staircase. A great deal of architect-designed laminate board and painted built-in furniture and fittings are integrated in the house together with the latest light fittings from Ultralux and Bestlite.

The house was covered extensively by the architectural press in England and in addition pictures were requested in February 1938 by P Morton Shand for their inclusion in the American monthly paper *Shelter*, for which he was a contributing editor, to illustrate work by the MARS group after their 1937 exhibition.[82]

In 1966 Basil Ward, then part of Murray, Ward and White, was invited back by the owners to create an enclosure to the roof terrace in aluminium and glass, an addition that was anticipated in a 1937 publication on the house: 'at an early date it is proposed to add a room on the north end of the roof'.[83] The house was grade II listed in 1985. Today Moor Park stands virtually in its original form with its walls having paled to white and a large number of window frames replaced.

Bracken (Greenside)

**Bracken (Greenside), Wentworth,
Virginia Water, Surrey, 1936–37
Colin Lucas of Connell Ward and Lucas**

Bracken was built on the private Wentworth estate for Harley Street doctor RA Williamson Noble, an opthalmologist and the queen's surgeon. The story goes that the doctor had bought the plot without telling his wife and began to build this country house as a surprise for her – an act that was not totally altruistic as he was a keen amateur golfer and the site had a grandstand view of the seventeenth hole of the famous Wentworth golf course. The plans were 'turned down flat by the estate people' and the appeal went to arbitration. Fortunately, said Lucas, they 'got the right arbitrator'.[84] But apparently, when built, Mrs Williamson Noble did not feel that her present had been worth fighting for. An advertisement in the *Homefinder* magazine published shortly after completion, shows that the house was to be let out. In contrast to these sentiments, the eminent American architectural critic Henry-Russell Hitchcock recognised Bracken as 'one of the best' of the houses by the Connell Ward and Lucas practice.[85]

The original owner's views have a strange and sad symmetry with those of the last owners of Bracken – or Greenside as it has been more recently known – and its subsequent demise. The last owner, also immune to the charms of the house and its incapacity to command a high market value, bulldozed Bracken in November 2003, despite not having obtained all the required consents. The 'Greenside Case' has been the subject of the sort of public furore to which Connell Ward and Lucas would have been accustomed in the 1930s. The reason for the recent furore was that the house was recognised as being of significant architectural merit and its destruction could have had far-reaching implications on the protection of listed buildings in Britain.

The original scheme

Given the similarity of programme and siting of Moor Park and Bracken amidst the trees, peering over the fairways of golf courses, it is quite easy to confuse the two projects, even Basil Ward did so in his 1968 article in *Architecture North-West*. Technically the same post and panel construction method was adopted. However, the planning and the architectonic quality of Bracken is quite distinct from Moor Park and illustrates beautifully the different design approaches of Basil Ward and Colin Lucas. The fact that Lucas and Ward's design signatures are recognisable in the different houses further undermines the argument that design of a modern house is purely an outcome of its function.

Although larger than Moor Park in terms of the number of rooms, Bracken was altogether more compact, more grounded and less curvaceous, in two and three dimensions. The main entrance to the house was

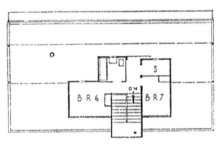

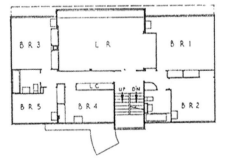

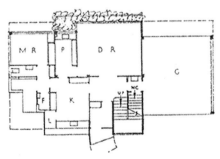

Above:
The entrance elevation. Standard Crittall metal windows with fixed lights between them were painted cream. Obscured glazing was introduced for privacy at the front of the house in the windows to the kitchen, larder and entrance hall.

Right:
Ground, first and roof plans.

Opposite:
Above the seventeenth hole at the Wentworth golf course and surrounded by tall trees, the house stood out in contrast to the dark foliage surrounding it. Here the nature of the concrete first floor hovering above the darker brick band of the ground floor building can be fully appreciated.

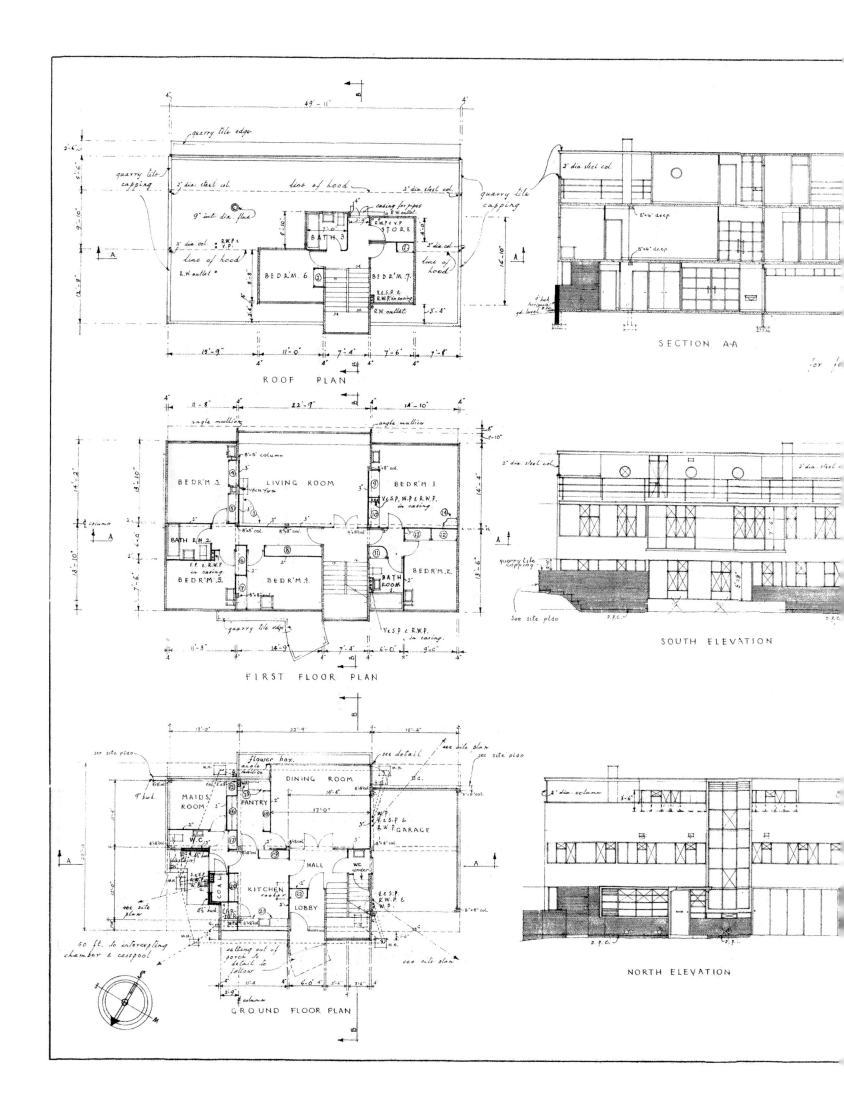

ROOF PLAN

BATH 3

STORE

BEDR'M 6

BEDR'M 7

SECTION A-A

FIRST FLOOR PLAN

BEDR'M 3

LIVING ROOM

BEDR'M 1

BATH R.M. 2

BEDR'M 5

BEDR'M 4

BATH ROOM

BEDR'M 2

SOUTH ELEVATION

GROUND FLOOR PLAN

MAIDS' ROOM

PANTRY

DINING ROOM

W.C.

COAL

CAR-DNER

KITCHEN

W.C.

GARAGE

HALL

W.C. under

LOBBY

NORTH ELEVATION

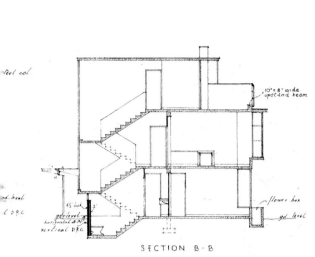

SECTION B-B

See also reinf. c. engin's drawings.

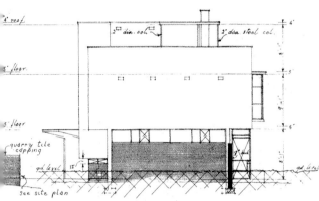

WEST ELEVATION

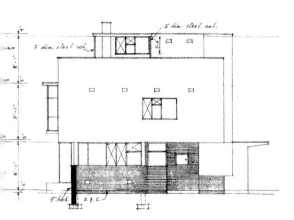

EAST ELEVATION

CONNELL , WARD & LUCAS

R.S., A.R.I.B.A., B.A. (CANTAB)

REGISTERED ARCHITECTS

25 GROSVENOR PLACE

LONDON S W 1   SLOANE 4640

CLIENT MR. WILLIAMSON NOBLE.
ADDRESS 27. HARLEY, ST. W. I.

SPECIFICATION
FIGURED DIMENSIONS TO BE FOLLOWED
IN PREFERENCE TO SCALED ONES.
CONTRACTOR MUST CHECK ALL DI-
MENSIONS ON SITE
THIS DRAWING SUPERSEDES ALL PRE-
VIOUS DRAWINGS.

· REINFORCED CONCRETE:
  BREEZE SLAB
· CRANHAM PARTITIONS:
· BRICKWORK:

· JOINERY FITTINGS: ③ etc
  (to future detail)
· METAL CILLS TO ALL WINDOWS
  EXCEPT THOSE ON BRICK WORK,
  THESE TO HAVE QUARRY TILE CILLS
  SIMILAR TO CAPPINGS

· DIMENSIONS ARE TO
  STRUCTURAL FACES
  WITHOUT FINISHINGS.

· SOIL DRAINS}
  (4" stoneware)}
  (minimum fall - 1 in 40)

· Rainwater & surface}
  Water DRAINS }
  (4" stoneware)
  (minimum fall - 1 in 40)

· Gullies: ⊓ G

· Vent pipe: V.P

· Soil pipe: S.P.

· Waste pipe: W.P.

· Rainwater pipe R.W.P.

· Manhole. M.H
· all drains below building
  to be surrounded by 6" concrete.

REVISIONS
NO	DESCRIPTION	DATE

This is one of the Drawings referred to in the Contract dated Sept 21. 1936 between Mr Williamson NV and Messrs J. J. Lovell.

Signed J. A. Williamson Noble

J. J. Lovell & Son

JOB DWELLING HOUSE.

ADDRESS WENTWORTH ESTATE.
VIRGINIA WATER.

DESCRIPTION WORKING DRAWINGS

SCALE ⅛" = 1'-0"

DRAWING NUMBER 93/9. DATE 23·7·36

PRINT NUMBER ⚹ ⚹ 18

DRAWN BY GRWP

CHECKED BY

The architects' contractural drawing of the plans, elevations and sections for Bracken.

112 Private houses

concrete that appear as a solid mass with strips cut out for fenestration. The house has a similar orientation to that at Moor Park and, likewise, the south elevation of Bracken is more glassy than the north. On the drawing board at the same time, it is very interesting to compare Lucas' designs for Wentworth and 66 Frognal and see how two different but related designs emerge from the same material concerns (we look at this in more detail in the section on 66 Frognal).

At Bracken Lucas uses brickwork alongside concrete. He wraps the ground floor accommodation in clay like Basil Ward's rear garage at the Firs (see page 000). Lucas describes this as 'a little brickwork ... only for non-structural walls at ground level, to emphasise the floating character of the superstructure'.[86] Looking at the north elevation, the light green volume of the first floor appears to hover over the clay as Lucas suggests. The multicoloured brickwork is not constrained by the floor plates of the house above and extends to form free-standing garden walls delineating external areas close to the house.

The superstructure over, horizontally banded like a sandwich with bread of rendered concrete and a glass filling, has a wedge driven into it in the form of a glazed staircase block. This appears as a hollow concrete rectangular box with its end sliced off and is picked out in light cream. The front door and kitchen window are similarly framed in concrete. The surround to the entrance porch swings away to the west, forming a curved wall of protection from the gaze of the maid at the kitchen sink. The dark brown tones of the render at the recessed second floor were intended to make it, too, dissolve.

at the ground floor. Glazed doors in the hall led into a dining room orientated and fully glazed to the garden in the south with an access door at the side onto a terrace. The kitchen and larder, pantry, fuel store and maid's room were adjacent to the dining room to the east and a large garage with folding doors for two cars was situated to the west. The living room, designed with Mrs Williamson Noble's grand piano in mind is elevated to the first floor level to take advantage of the views. Five bedrooms and a bathroom are packed in around this living room – children's and guests' bedrooms to the east and master bedrooms to the west. Two further bedrooms are provided on the second floor with an additional bathroom and store. The rest of the roof was terrace, orientated to south rather than the entrance drive.

Evident in Colin Lucas' composition is his continuing preoccupation with the relationship of volume and skin. Concrete planes wrap the internal spaces – their thinness revealed as they are used to outline the staircase and porch or to create a roof plane. This treatment contrasts with flat expanses of rendered

Cranham hollow terracotta blocks with good insulating qualities are used to create the non-load-bearing internal partitions. The interior of the reinforced concrete walls are finished in washable distemper on plaster finished Celotex (also soffits) each room is decorated using two to three colours on different wall surfaces. Floor finishes were oak blocks and boards in living rooms and bedrooms, whereas stairs and service quarters are finished in composition flooring and linoleum from the Linolite Flooring Company. The house was fitted with tubular heaters and electric fires with an open fireplace in the living room. Lighting, cooking and hot water are all electrically powered.

The roof terrace, a recreational space, is waterproofed using asphalt and finished with asbestos tiles. Round windows like portholes give light to the store room and bathroom at this level. The rectangular strip of a canopy rests on the volumes of a store and bathroom and oversails like aeroplane wings, pinned at either flank wall with fine steel columns. The chimney stack, within a fat round concrete column on the roof, penetrates the canopy and exhales above.

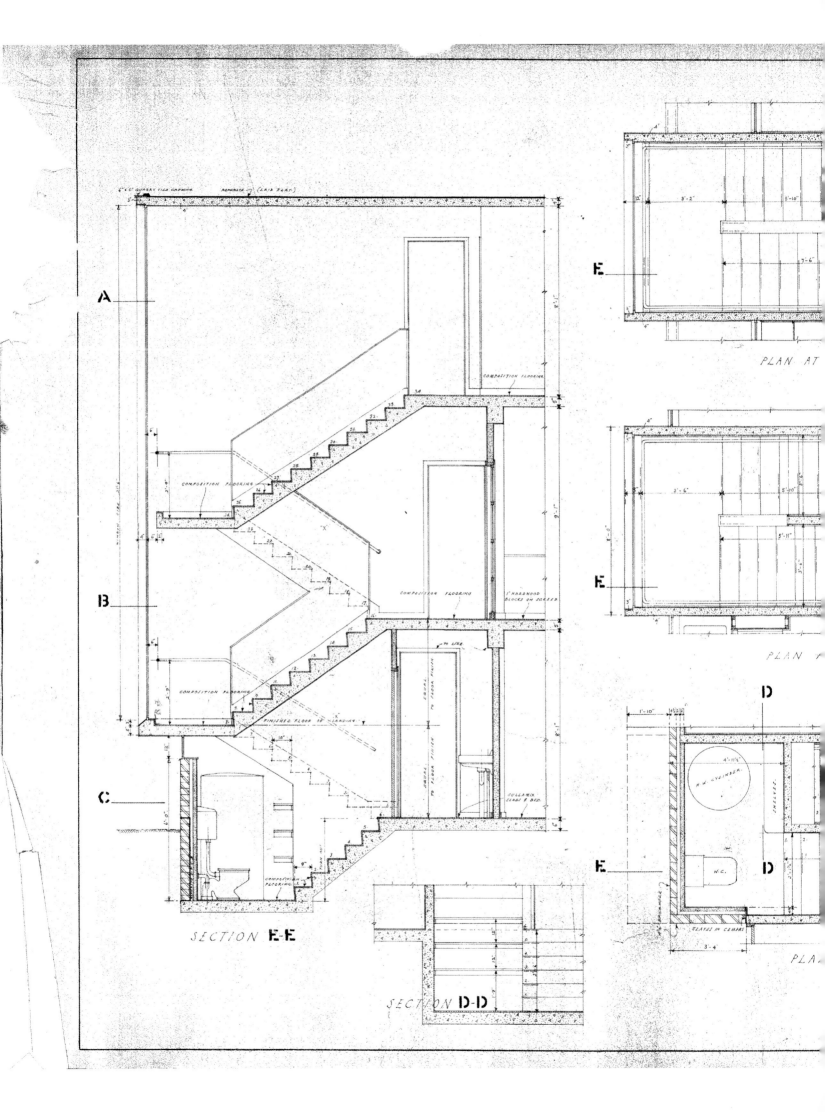

SECTION E-E

SECTION D-D

PLAN AT

PLAN

PLAN

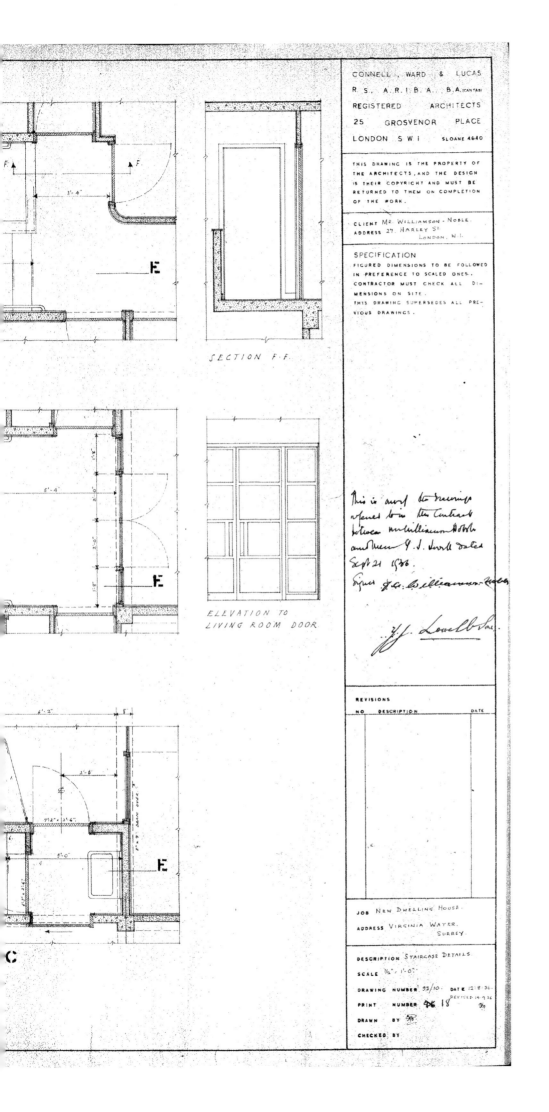

SECTION F.F.

ELEVATION TO
LIVING ROOM DOOR

CLIENT MR. WILLIAMSON - NOBLE.
ADDRESS 27. HARLEY ST.
LONDON, W.I.

SPECIFICATION
FIGURED DIMENSIONS TO BE FOLLOWED
IN PREFERENCE TO SCALED ONES.
CONTRACTOR MUST CHECK ALL DI-
MENSIONS ON SITE.
THIS DRAWING SUPERSEDES ALL PRE-
VIOUS DRAWINGS.

REVISIONS

NO	DESCRIPTION	DATE

JOB NEW DWELLING HOUSE.
ADDRESS VIRGINIA WATER,
SURREY.

DESCRIPTION STAIRCASE DETAILS.

SCALE ½": 1'-0".

DRAWING NUMBER 93/10. DATE 12.8.36.
REVISED 14.9.36
PRINT NUMBER 18

DRAWN BY

CHECKED BY

Contractural drawing of design details for Bracken.

Above:
Windows from the window bench to the soffit had fully glazed corners to make the most of grandstand views of the seventeenth hole. Glazed opening vents were incorporated in the middle section of the windows.

Right:
Two bedrooms on the second floor are surrounded by a roof terrace. The render was dark against a light canopy with a deep overhang to increase the effect of a horizontal plane floating above.

Opposite:
The solid balustrade at the centre of the main staircase contrasts with the lightness of the window mullions and transomes.

Publicity and later history

Bracken was erected between September 1936 and the early part of 1937 and photographs of the newly completed house appeared in the MARS 'New Architecture' Exhibition in 1937 and made their way into the first edition of FRS Yorke's famous survey of contemporary houses of note in 1937, *The Modern House in England*.[87]

English Heritage recognised the qualities of this house and listed Bracken grade II in 1988. Prior to that, in the 1960s planning consent was given for an additional garage with a staff flat over, a swimming pool enclosure was added in the year it was listed and the replacement of window frames was permitted a year later. At the time of its demolition the house itself was not much changed from the original scheme but it was in a bad state of repair. Finding it hard to sell for a similar market value to the neighbouring properties, the owners applied for the house to be de-listed for demolition in 2001. They, backed up by neighbours, blamed their misfortune on the fact that the house was an eyesore, 'extremely ugly' and 'unsuitable for modern needs'.[88] One went so far as to claim that international golfers were often put off their chips and putts when informed that the 'incongruous pile of rubble' was listed due to its architectural merits. In 2002 planning approval was granted to demolish Bracken and replace it with a house in a more popular style. This decision was successfully challenged by conservation societies in the High Court but a second application for demolition and replacement with an Edwardian style house was subsequently granted in November 2003, subject to the agreement of the Office of the Deputy Prime Minister. The planning committee came to this decision against advice, claiming that under the Human Rights Act the owner should have the right to maximise the value of the property. Just days later, not waiting to obtain listed building consent or to give the ODPM the statutory period to call in such decisions, the owner brought in the wreckers.

After the demolition, conservation groups led by the Twentieth Century Society tenaciously led a successful judicial review to challenge the decision of the committee, not least because this precedent of the case could have far-reaching consequences for all listed buildings. In November 2004 a public enquiry not only turned down the application for demolition of the house and dismissed the claims of infringement of Human Rights, but also, after reflection on Green Belt policies, turned down the planning permission for the building to replace Bracken. This ultimately meant that the land value would significantly diminish. In addition, in 2005 the owner was convicted of unlawfully demolishing the listed building and fined. Sadly, none of these actions can bring back the building that has been recognised as one of Lucas' finest houses.

117 Bracken (Greenside)

66 Frognal

Above:
Mature trees frame the views of the rear elevation.

Right:
The architects' axonometric drawing of the exterior of the house clearly shows the stepped nature of the terraces at the rear.

Opposite:
Geoffrey Walford with wife Ursula.
The entrance elevation viewed from the west soon after completion.

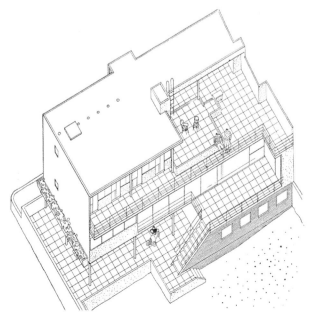

66 Frognal, Hampstead, London, NW3, 1936–38
Colin Lucas of Connell Ward and Lucas

66 Frognal is one of the best-known projects of Connell Ward and Lucas and widely considered as one of their finest and most assured buildings. It sits on a prominent site on Frognal in north London.[89] Ian Nairn recognised it as 'the best of [Connell Ward and Lucas'] pre-war houses, which is', he said, 'tantamount to saying the best pre-war house in England.'[90]

The Hampstead house was built for solicitor Geoffrey Walford of Piccadilly, his wife Ursula Walford and her four children from a first marriage. From the outset Walford had a desire for a modern house and a clear brief for his architects. His commitment to these principles was to be tested to the limit during a fierce debate surrounding the planning application that delayed construction by nearly a year. The designs for Frognal were described by opponents as 'one of the greatest acts of vandalism ever perpetrated in London'.[91]

When the dust had settled a little after Frognal's completion, Geoffrey Walford felt compelled to write about his house in the *RIBA Journal*. This precious account conveys the strength of conviction he had in the project. Despite the furore over planning approval, he described the process of building his own home as 'an experience of intense interest and delight'.[92] He wrote:

> It may seem surprising to some that this building is not symptomatic of exhibitionism, nor of iconoclasm, nor is it the result of any particular liking for

operating theatres or for the decks of ships ... it represents the logical conclusion to nothing more mysterious than the problem of how to live. ... I can only regret that this building should offend the susceptibilities of some people and be beyond the comprehension of others.[93]

Like Lucas, he felt that 'design was not a matter of erudition in style nor of aptitude for repeating the fine effects of other ages, but simply a matter of sensibility for structure, for the placing of masses and weights, and for materials.'[94]

Walford also believed that the life of his family would significantly benefit from their new home environment. During the planning period, he was quoted by the *Evening Standard* in 1937 explaining his reasons for a modern house:

> I did not want a house of several floors which would take four or five servants to run ... I wanted a covered entrance to the house and a garage, because I did not want to employ servants to fetch or drive a car, I wanted a covered open-air playground for children, whose sole recreation need no longer be confined to walking on pavements. I wanted windows that would give extra light and air, convenience in planning for rooms and a roof that could be used for sunbathing, and many other features. The house satisfies all my requirements ... in other words it represents, in my opinion, good architecture.[95]

Using his own professional expertise he fought for this architecture. Reflecting on his career in a lecture at the RIBA in 1976, Colin Lucas said of Walford's project, 'the house stands as a monument to his determination and as a symbol of the modern movement'.[96]

The design
Unusually, the plan of Frognal was largely conceived prior to the client securing a site. In fact, Geoffrey Walford had already started to design his home before he appointed an architect. He had made a presumption that a London site would typically have only a front and rear aspect. Walford stipulated that rooms should face either east or west to receive sunlight for a period every day and therefore the orientation of the future plot was an important factor in the purchase. When the corner site in Hampstead was secured for £2,600, the design was not adapted to take advantage of its third aspect, the flank elevation was left quite blank, with just two small square windows to let light and air into the bathrooms.

The floor plans at Frognal incorporate a greater range of spaces than Lucas' other projects, from the cellular bedrooms of the second floor to the vast open plan living areas of the first floor. The main entrance just to

the north of the staircase at ground floor is flanked by a large double garage and workshop for the owner-driver to the north and the children's playroom protected from the sun by the overhanging superstructure in the south. The living rooms on first and second floors are screened from the road noise by service rooms, corridors and a spine of storage cupboards. On the first floor the maid's accommodation and kitchen, with separate external stairs to a tradesman's entrance in the north west, serve the combined dining, living and library/music room areas to the east. A dressing room and bathroom in the south west complete the master bedroom suite with the east-facing bedroom.

The children's 'quarter' on the second floor is designed to be quite separate from the adults' accommodation, in a similar way to the designs of High and Over. Even the hardwood floors, made from New Zealand matai, were fitted on acoustic isolators to reduce noise transmittance through the house. Four small bedrooms face east with a bathroom and a sitting room in the west as well as a very large roof terrace for outdoor play. An additional playroom on the ground floor provides the young ones with a separate access to the garden. With this, Walford gives his four offspring a great gift of independence and probably gives himself and his wife a good deal of quiet, uninterrupted time. During term, with the children away at school, their bedrooms convert to guest bedrooms by rolling back retractable screens. In quieter periods, the second floor can be completely closed down to reduce running costs.

It was central to Walford's requirements that the house acted as a background conducive to conversation, reading, music and reflection. Lucas' design hit the mark. He said of his house:

> I find the simplicity and spaciousness of unbroken surfaces offer rest to the eye and to the mind. I find delight in the control of forms arising in the building itself and its appurtenances, rather than in superimposed effects. I find delight in the use of colour and in the play and variation of light. I find delight above all in the relation between house and garden.[97]

The external envelope
66 Frognal would have been on Colin Lucas' drawing board simultaneously with Bracken in early 1936 and the two can be read as a pair of architectural compositions. Lucas underpins the facade designs with the regulating lines of the golden section. He then manipulates the wall planes, pushing orthogonal volumes forward and back, sometimes literally and sometimes by introducing glazing and other surface treatments. Colour is also used to reinforce the compositions. Through a process of simplification and reduction he arrives at the eventual house designs.

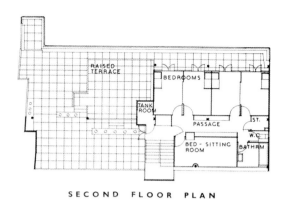

SECOND FLOOR PLAN

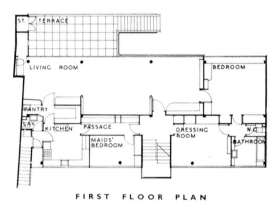

FIRST FLOOR PLAN

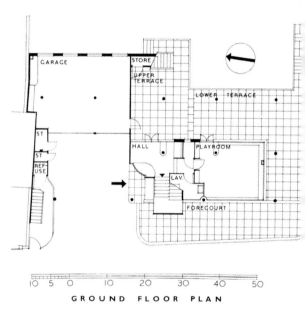

GROUND FLOOR PLAN

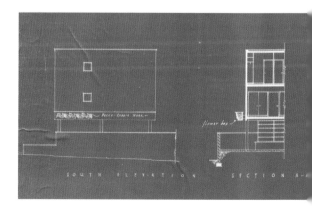

Above:
The living room from the music room. The alcove of the sitting room area is defined by the raised ceiling in the bay between two circular columns. A range of multi-coloured curtains ran on five curtain tracks, referred to by the family as 'Clapham Junction', in front of the magnificent 8ft high bronze sliding windows to the patio. These were provided with a curtain docking void. The family had a choice of two full length sets in dark blue velvet and pale grey, three-quarter sections in green, pink and yellow and further sections of 'flimsies' in white and in pale hues, pink, green, yellow and blue. Much of the loose furniture in the house was designed by Walford's friend Betty Joel, the famous furniture designer.
From the horizontal window, virtually free of mullions, in the master bedroom is a view of the mature trees of the gardens to the rear.
The relatively blank flank wall the house complete with planter at the base that was agreed on in the planning conditions.

Opposite:
Interior views.
Ground, first and second floor plans.
Drawing of the end elevation and planter.

The entrance to the house at Frognal, like Bracken, can be read in simple terms as a rectilinear box-like form containing the first floor, hovering above recessed ground floor accommodation and intersected by the strong vertical rectilinear form of a staircase. In the rural context, the staircase at Greenside is fully glazed and open to the surrounding woodland. In the urban context at Frognal, it has a solid wall to the road but is projected forward to receive light from strips of glazing either side. The non-load-bearing brick walls seen at Bracken at ground level slip under the projecting staircases and sills of the glazing at ground floor at Frognal too, and project out into the garden to form the perimeter wall. The load-bearing structure is brought to the ground as square columns at Bracken and as round pilotis at Frognal, a difference that is also picked up in the shape of the ventilators above the first floor windows. This structure is exposed as the volume of the houses are cut back around them to make garages and porches give almost fully glazed perimeters to ground floor rooms above the brickwork.

At second floor level in both projects, the volume of accommodation is reduced. At Bracken the two bedrooms become a little island in a sea of balcony, set back from the perimeter of the building and painted dark so that they recede like the ground floor. The blade of roof shading is held well back from the front and rear of the building and is made to hover above the roof terrace on thin metal columns. At Frognal the south-facing flank wall of the house, the full depth of the property, extends up and over the top to create a roof to the second floor accommodation in the south and, decreased in depth at the staircase, continues to the north flank wall to create a shading hood to the roof terrace at the north end. The strip of windows to the second floor accommodation are held back from the building perimeter so that either side of the staircase reads similarly.

At the rear of both designs, the overriding principle of raised living rooms transparent to the rear garden with generous windows is identical. At Bracken these living rooms hover above the ground, detatched from it, at Frognal, Lucas makes full and inventive use of the relatively tight site by introducing stepped terraces to maximise the garden and create a surprising variety of external spaces that interlock with the principal bedrooms and living spaces. A balcony is pushed forward at the second floor level to shade the first floor windows and the deeper balcony at first floor connects the living spaces to the garden via an external stair.

The planning battle
Hampstead borough council were initially confused by the plans of the house when they were submitted. The town planning and building regulation committee felt that the volume and disposition of the proposal were acceptable but that its design and proposed construction methods were not. They claimed that it would injure the appearance of the district, a view put forward by various opposing bodies, adjoining owners and architects. Loudest was the protest from local residents, amongst them distinguished architect Reginald Blomfield who had locked horns with Connell in the broadcast debate 'For and against modern architecture' in 1934 and who owned one of the neo-Georgian villas adjacent to the site. Other local architects added their signatures to an objection letter sent to the council. Letters were also received in support of the application.

The scheme was referred to the London County Council for a decision. With so many conflicting arguments, the Hampstead committee could not advise the council to withold consent. It did, however, ask the LCC to impose conditions on the external appearance. During the meeting, a number of people came forward to speak out in favour of and against the proposals. Local politicians also got stuck in, Sir Robert Tasker (Conservative member), supported by the traditionalist architects neighbouring the site, opposing the scheme, and J Dugdale, Labour councillor for South Islington, opposing him. Tasker saw the house as an 'act of vandalism'. Dugdale launched a personal attack, 'there are many famous architects', he said, 'who consider Sir Reginald Blomfield is by no means a gentleman who should be considered as an arbiter of good taste'.[98]

The London County Council passed the scheme with conditions in July 1937 by 70 to 33 votes. The conditions stipulated that colour and texture were to harmonise with the adjoining house on the road and asked that the exposed flank wall should be 'satisfactorily architecturally treated'. It was reported in the newspapers of the time that the chair of the committee, Mr H Berry, sympathised with Walford and his architects, understanding that the role of the innovator is always hard. Although he did not personally like the building, he felt that the council should not stand in the way of progress.[99] However, agreement to the conditions was withheld and the matter went to arbitration. On hearing that this was decided in favour of the residents, Walford took his own case to the High Court and won. The judge here set aside essential parts of the arbitrator's award on a 'technical legal point' and Walford won the case. Approval of the detail of the flank wall was not given until October 1937.

Construction
One of the main reasons that Walford had chosen Connell Ward and Lucas as the architects for his project was that they were one of the few architectural practices of the time embracing reinforced concrete construction as a building method

that was separate and distinct from masonry construction. He said, 'their work appealed to me as having that structural quality which, personally, I find missing in nearly all other contemporary work with the exception of some engineers'.[100]

At Frognal, Connell Ward and Lucas took a departure from their previous structural solutions and the house was designed as a grid of free-standing reinforced concrete columns. On account of poor subsoil and made-up ground on the site, these columns had to be built off continuous strip foundations rather than more economic pad foundations. The columns supported flat reinforced concrete beams that stood down from the ceilings in the interior of the house. Floor slabs were constructed using a method similar to the lost-tile construction Le Corbusier had learnt from the work of the French engineer François Hennebique: hollow tiles were laid onto movable shuttering on temporary steel beams and reinforced using steel rods, then concrete was poured on to encase the tiles and steel.[101]

The external walls of the house were cast as steel reinforced concrete. Lucas increased the thickness of the insulation at Frognal to an inch and a half of cork as opposed to the thinner wallboard previously employed. He also introduced a bituminous coating on the warm side of the insulation to prevent condensation. Internal walls were constructed using non-structural terracotta blocks.

The tender process for construction took place before the planning permission was obtained and the favoured contractors, YJ Lovell (the contractors who had just completed Bracken) waited for ten months until summer 1937 to start on site. An eight-month building contract for a massive sum of £7,206 overran to roughly a year and the Walford family lodged with the Connells for part of the delayed construction period. Lucas remained the project architect until around April 1939 when correspondence states that Connell was dealing with the last issues relating to the project. This probably coincides with Lucas leaving the practice.

Colours
The colours of the house were a subject of discussion from 1936 when Walford suggested ochre/buff or grey for the walls and roof of the entrance with a covered play area in pale yellow or warm pink. Lucas advised that it would be easier to settle on the colour when the shape of the house could be seen and the subsequent planning conditions also swayed their decision. Mrs Walford later remembered the colours of the completed house in conversation with Tim Benton in a recording for the Open University. The front elevation was pinky-beige on the staircase with upper floors in pinky mushroom. There was a dark mauve tradesman's entrance, a dark brown wall at the entrance to the garage, raspberry pilotis and a bright

yellow curved front door (to match their Rolls Royce), and metallic blue ventilators. A reporter in the News Chronicle as the house neared completion in July 1938 described it as 'a refreshing spectacle in brown cement with a row of bright, circular metal baffle plates across the front which have baffled and hurt everybody'.[102]

Later history
The house was completed just months before the outbreak of the Second World War and soon afterwards the Walfords were forced to evacuate amid fears that the amount of glazing would be particularly dangerous if the area was bombed. The Walfords sent their three boys to Canada with Dione Lucas and her first son, Mark. Their little girl, Angela, stayed in England with her mother and stepfather and they rented a house in Virginia Water.

In September 1939 the London County Council took possession of the ground and first floors to use the house as a fire alarm station, providing a mess for seven men. There was some trouble with a leak in the asphalt roof so that in 1941 the house was sealed off. In 1942 the Ministry of Works and Buildings salvaged the railings for use in the war effort.

During the war, in December 1942, an advertisement for the sale of 66 Frognal appeared in Country Life and The Times. The house was sold to Sir Richard Acland MP in June 1943 for £6,750, nearly £2,000 less than the original asking price. Geoffrey Walford, devastated by leaving the house that he had put so much of himself into, had also lost a significant amount of money through the project. He remained in close contact with Colin Lucas and his second wife Pamela right up to his death.

The house was grade II listed in 1973 and upgraded to grade II* in 1999, particularly in relation to its exterior. Prior to this, the architect Trevor Dannatt designed an infill to the sun deck to the north of the building to give new bedrooms with a design that was reportedly approved by Connell Ward and Lucas.[103] Later, an indoor swimming pool was added on the ground floor and the rear wall of the hall was pushed out towards the rear garden to extend the ground floor accommodation.

In 2000, new owners decided to breathe new life into the house. Rather than working to reinstate the detail of the original building, Avanti architects have concentrated on restoring the integrity of Colin Lucas' design while adapting it for the use of a twenty-first century client. This has involved the creation of a more meaningful extension to the roof, the reinstatement of internal partitions on the first floor and also the reintroduction of the original colours to the exterior of the building.

Potcroft

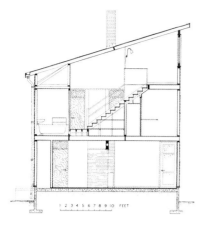

N ▲

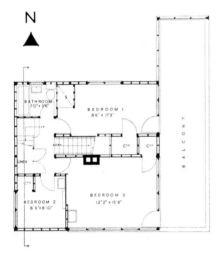

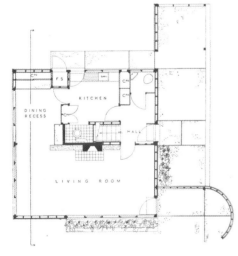

Above:
Plan and section of the original scheme.

Opposite:
The south elevation of the house, 2008.

Potcroft, Sutton, Pulborough, West Sussex, 1937–38
Colin Lucas of Connell Ward and Lucas

It may be surprising to see this timber house in the pages of a book that is dominated by sand and cement. In fact, the original intention was to build in concrete, but complications led to the house changing site as well as material and form before it was finally executed on the proviso that it would be surrounded by a screen of trees. At this point in the late 1930s, timber was being used by many British modern architects who were exploring modern design with softer and more textural, earthy materials. Probably the best-known of these is Serge Chermayeff's house Bentley Wood at Halland, East Sussex.[104] The emergence of this architecture has long been understood as an influence from Scandinavia and particularly the work of Alvar Aalto in Finland who was experimenting with the technical capacities of traditional building materials such as wood and brick as well as reinterpreting historic forms of vernacular architecture in a modern architecture.

These influences had some effect on Connell Ward and Lucas' work. Judging by the authorship of the drawings, Potcroft was designed by Lucas. At Bracken and Frognal he had started to introduce more textural brick elements into design but his main preoccupation really remained with concrete – as his later career reinforces. The decision to design this house entirely in wood was a concession for the practice, rather than a deliberate intention, as timber was likely to deliver the aesthetic that would halt objections to the proposals. Nevertheless, in 1938 when AC Beardsmore covered the house extensively in an article in *Focus* magazine, he recognised it as an 'outstanding example of the new use of timber'.[105]

The client for Potcroft, Dr Llewellyn Thomas, a bachelor and doctor from Worthing had an interest in a plot of land near the end of a lane on the outskirts of the beautiful small village of Sutton in West Sussex, owned by a body of people who were 'administrators of large estates in England'.[106] The architects designed a reinforced concrete house for their client. However, restrictive covenants forced the doctor and his architects to respond to the criticism from the vendor's surveyor that 'this type of house is not suitable for erection in this very rural district so adjacent to a rectory and a church'.[107] Dr Thomas did not want to alter the design, nor to enter into a costly legal dispute, so employed the architects to start again on the less conspicuous adjacent site and to design something that could be let or sold in the future if he was able to secure a site for the original scheme.

Ironically, objections were then received to the planning application for the timber house and the local authority refused the scheme on the grounds that 'it is considered that this locality is only suitable for buildings of timber with brick fillings or plaster panels, or brick and stone, or brick entirely, with roofs of clay sand faced tiles and similar in all respects to characteristic Sussex buildings'.[108] The architects lodged an appeal against the decision with the Ministry of Health and at the same time continued to discuss the scheme with the planners, complaining that their decision had been unreasonable. The planners made it clear that they would accept the plans if a screen of trees was planted around the building, the eaves increased, the roof altered to a lower angle and the house moved further down the hill. Rather than going to arbitration, Dr Thomas instructed his architects to amend the scheme and the project went ahead.

Arrangement
Potcroft nestles into the side of a relatively steep site that slopes down from the east to the west. Most notably unusual in this design, apart from the mono-pitch roof over the house, is that the staircase is not expressed in Connell Ward and Lucas' usual fashion on the exterior of the building. It is instead buried in the square building plan, located just off centre and running straight to first floor. At the landing a second flight runs at right angles to the first to the 'sun parlour' that is squeezed under the highest part of the roof pitch. The layout of first and second floor is identical to the Saltdean houses of 1934, with the second stair flight made internal rather than expressed on the outside.

The cedar-lined stair is dead ahead of the front door to the house with a horseshoe of accommodation arranged around it. To the south is the large living room that occupies half of the plan. This flows, partitionless, into the dining room recess behind the stairs and leads to the kitchen that has a second doorway leading back to the entrance hall via a small vestibule with a wc. There is a back door into the kitchen for deliveries from the outside, but the owner, without servants, can access the kitchen from the front door without having to pass through the living spaces. At first floor, two good-sized bedrooms are provided either side of the stairwell and a bathroom and third smaller bedroom are accessed from the hall at the west end. The efficient plan minimises circulation space by eradicating corridors. Storage is neatly tucked into any spare space: above the entrance hall, under the second flight of stairs and under the pitched roof adjacent to the sun parlour. The ceiling follows the pitched roof line above the first floor landing and the circulation space is open to the sun parlour above.

At Potcroft, the flow of space through the building – around the circuit of the ground floor living areas, up and past the bedrooms to the sun parlour on the second floor – is more of a journey than in many of the preceding houses. Within a simple square plan, the

architects achieve a spatial sophistication in this project more akin to the much-celebrated experience of Le Corbusier's Villa Savoie, which is likened to a promenade, than was evident in their earlier houses.

Designing in timber

Drawings of the timber house are mainly executed by Colin Lucas and date from August 1937. As their only non-concrete house this project is revealing about the integrity of their approach to architecture. Their concrete buildings to this point are expressed as concrete and the architects push the structural capabilities of concrete to shape the architecture. When approaching building with a new material, they naturally do the same thing, feeling that the 'aesthetic value of the timber should be made use of in full' and that it should be put through its paces structurally.[109] The firm settled on just one type of timber for the entire construction, cedar, which was chosen as its properties would allow it to be used for all elements: the structure, weatherboarding and internal linings. This has achieved a purer expression of construction than their concrete buildings. The same timber is expressed both internally and externally in its raw state, whereas with concrete they had to apply coats of render and insulation to finish it.

External walls are made up with three skins of Canadian cedar shrouding a timber frame and utilising the natural insulating property of the wood. Horizontal cedar weatherboarding is fixed back through building paper to a diagonal rough boarding that is in turn fixed to minimum 4 inch by 2 inch studwork. The structural frame is doubled at the corners and at the centre of the plan where a double beam, supported by the brick fireplace at its centre, traverses the building and supports the joists to the floor above. Roof joists are 6 inch by 2 inch and are finished in boards and felt. There are vents between the joists at the eaves to help any moisture trapped in the construction to evaporate. By framing and bracing the sides and front of the house, 'similar to a lattice girder construction', they are able to create a large overhanging balcony over the entrance of the building approximately 8 foot by 40 foot with the minimum of additional support.

Internal wall linings are tongue-and-groove horizontal boarding. The architects found the material flexible and quick to construct and also liked the fact that the timber was in a 'great variety of shades'.[110] The brick of the chimneybreast and flue is exposed – the architects enjoyed the 'conformity' of the textural qualities of the materials. The ground floor finish is robust and forgiving timber block, all wall linings are timber with ceilings and fitted furniture finished in unpainted birch plywood.

Timber windows by a Swiss manufacturer were installed, the panes opening inwards and fully back onto the fixed portions so as to form unobstructed openings. This reduces the sight lines of the timber frames, which was of great importance to a group of architects used to working with the ultra-fine frames of steel Crittall windows. It also avoids the nuisance of windows banging in the breeze. As with their concrete houses, the fenestration is in strips and is sometimes wrapped around the corner of the house, but with the timber structure at the four corners of the house the glazing cannot be continuous. In the living room the glazing is brought down to the floor along the south facade, forming a greater visual connection between inside and outside.

Although comparison between the external architectural language of Potcroft and that of the practice's other houses reveals some significant differences, its banded facade compositions and glazed corners (as far as they could be achieved with timber frame) are not dissimilar from its concrete cousins. If the aesthetic of Connell Ward and Lucas' architecture, as they asserted, was a direct expression of the structural integrity of the material they built in, then why should a timber building resemble a concrete one? It is clear – and it is inevitable – that although the structural integrity of the material is extremely important to their design, a subjective aesthetic judgement does come into play.

Later history

At the time of writing, Potcroft has only had two owners since Dr Thomas. Although it has not been listed, some of the original Best and Lloyd light fittings and the built-in furniture remain, with the windows, structure and internal linings still well preserved, although some of the linings have been painted. An extra skin of cedar shingles have been added to the south elevation. The house was significantly damaged in the storm of 1987 that devastated large areas of the south of England but it has been repaired with care and attention to detail. The efficient plan has not, like many of the other houses, required much modernising.

Above:
The house photographed shortly after completion.

Above right:
Interior of the open space plan living space, 2008.

Opposite:
The stair from ground to first floor lined in cedar with the stair to the sun parlour visible at the top of the flight.

26 Bessborough Road

Above and opposite: The oversailing roof, the cantilevered balcony and the planter beneath all project south west and step out into the garden.

26 Bessborough Road, Roehampton, London SW15, 1938–39
Colin Lucas of Connell Ward and Lucas

Lucas was the architect for this project, the last completed by the Connell Ward and Lucas practice before they disbanded. His client was the Proudman family. Philip Proudman was a civil engineer who worked on railways and had recently retired from a teaching post in Harrogate, his wife was a painter who had trained at the Royal College of Art and their young son, Anthony, was only six when the house was completed.

With inherited money, Mr Proudman bought the plot of land on Bessborough Road in south west London to build his own house. The site, purchased in around 1937, sloped gently and the land beyond fell away quite steeply to the west revealing beautiful views across towards Richmond Park. The couple were forward-looking with a keen interest in modern design and technology. Anthony remembers how they had a television on approval as early as 1939 out of curiosity. They also had strong left-wing convictions, although an interest in social housing was not their motivation to build a modern house. The reasons for their choice of the Connell Ward and Lucas practice is not clear; they were probably familiar with their work from publications. They got on very well with Colin Lucas and remained in touch with him well after the war.

The design
Two early options were drawn up by Lucas from January 1938. The larger of the two schemes, including a second floor with a north-east-facing studio for Mrs Proudman, was approved by the building engineer at Wandsworth in May 1934, so if the council had any concerns over design or construction, they were quickly resolved. Tender documentation was put together in June and post-tender, a cost-cutting exercise prompted the reduction in size. By September construction had begun on the two-storey house. Photographs show that building was completed for the summer of 1939.

The plan of Bessborough Road is set up as a very simple square grid of nine reinforced concrete columns that support concrete slabs above. At the two north facades these columns are tied into the external wall planes, at the two south facades, they are free-standing. The staircase, as at Potcroft, is at the centre of the plan, rather than manifest on the facade and it is made to curve around the central column as it rises to first floor. The ground and the first floor slabs are rectangular, projecting to the south west and the garden. The ground floor accommodates living spaces and the first a cantilevered bedroom balcony. The roof slab follows the line of the external walls to the north facades, but to the south facades extends beyond the envelope, shading the interior.

North-west and north-east elevations are largely blank, with slots of windows punched into them. These light the garage, boiler room and storage areas at ground floor and the maid's room, bathroom and part of the master bedroom above. The south-west garden elevation and the south-east-facing entrance elevation are largely glazed. At first floor this glazing is continuous under the roof, giving daylight to all four bedrooms, at ground floor the kitchen has high-level glazing and the dining room and living spaces have almost full-height glass. The perimeter of the ground floor is indented in the east at ground floor, so that the entrance door is brought close to the centre of the house, opening directly into the core circulation space. A deep undercroft acts as a porch and protection to the forecourt to the garage.

Much like his earlier scheme for the Hopfield, Lucas seems to start with a cubic form that he then manipulates, erodes and projects in ways to accommodate the brief and to create the form that works best with the orientation of the site. Walls that project from the plan are dynamic elements in the three-dimensional composition, one rendered and shaped like an umbrella handle – the curve containing the bin store and tradesman's entrance, its straight end leading the visitor to

the front door. The second wall, in brick, is embedded in the building and divides the kitchen from the garden, then extends to separate the entrance court from the garden. Viewed from the south, the rendered parapet wall that cantilevers with the balcony appears to hover over this wall, perpendicular to it and separated with a band of glazing. The roof above is a third strong horizontal plane in this composition.

In contrast to this corner, with its stepping facade, is the blanker west wall. At the Hopfield such an element is finished in concrete, here, Lucas uses non-load-bearing blue engineering brick – the largest element of brick in his designs so far. The wall wraps the concrete construction and the balcony, finished in yellow-grey Colourcrete, appears to slide out from behind it. At ground level, a planter, similar to that at the base of the flank wall at Frognal, wraps over the brickwork and round the fully glazed corner of the house, hovering over the turf of the garden lawn.

Internal spaces
The design of the open plan living and dining areas at Bessborough Road was particularly well judged. Lucas sunk the living space lower than the dining room depressing it down to the lower level of the landscape beyond. Using the same timber fenestration at Bessborough Road that he had at Potcroft, Lucas designed the main windows to the drawing roomto open fully back on themselves to let air and sunshine fill the room.

All the spaces were finished in colours chosen by Mrs Proudman and the architect. In the living area, the low wall between dining and living room and the soffit to the staircase were finished in mid-blue linoleum; the full-height wall was painted a yellow lime green. The hardwood floor was detailed as little 'bricks' of hardwood parquet, laid in a staggered bond. As always, there was plenty of built-in furniture and storage cupboards to all the rooms.

Completion and later history
The outbreak of war in September 1939 was announced a very few months after the completion of the house and Mr Proudman volunteered for the army. His family left Roehampton to accompany him in his nomadic existence over the war years in the south of England where he used his engineering expertise to aid the war effort. Young evacuees from East London came to live at Bessborough Road and the family only returned to their house in 1945, when their second son, Julian, was born. Mr Proudman died quite soon after this in 1951, but his wife carried on living in the family house until 1964, when she sold and moved out of London. The family was extremely proud of the house, their only criticism being that the children, in their teenage years, found that the open plan element made it more difficult for them to assert their independence.

Ben Nicholson's son bought the house from MrsProudman and stayed there for five years until a compulsory purchase order was served on the house by the Greater London Council to extend the adjoining housing estates in the creation of Alton West. Lucas, then involved with the Alton East scheme, ensured that the house remained standing, although it lost some of its extensive garden. A period followed when the home was carved up to house a doctor's surgery, the reception in the kitchen, and the living room divided from the dining area to become a sunken waiting room to the consulting room above. The upstairs was at that time converted into a caretaker's flat. The house was listed grade II in 1986 and sold by Wandsworth council to private owners in 1993 and has since been lovingly restored.

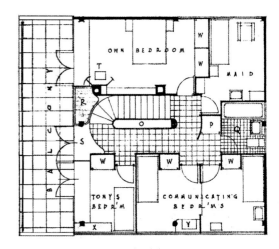

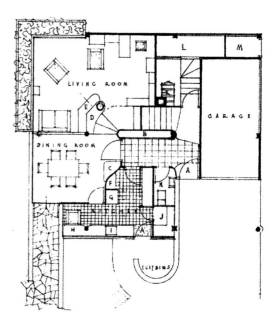

Above:
Young Anthony Proudman, photographed from his bedroom standing at the top of the stairs, peering into the mosaic tiled fishpond.
The base of the staircase projects into the living space, behind the chimney flue, curving like a twisted ribbon up to the ceiling. The free-standing fireplace and flue is similar to that at Temple Gardens.

Right:
Ground and first floor plans.

Opposite:
The empty site in August 1938.
13 September 1938: the slabs are being cast. Anthony Proudman stands in the foreground with wheelbarrows.
Early October 1938: the formwork is going up.
20 October 1938: the ground floor columns are struck and the shuttering is going up for the first floor.
28 October 1938: the shuttering is prepared for the roof slab.
11 November 1938: the concrete is struck and the bones of the house are in place. It is remarkable how little concrete structure there is: the columns, some slabs and a rear concrete wall.
3 December 1938: blockwork internal partitions are being constructed and window frames fitted.
April 1939: the house is fully glazed, weathertight and almost ready for occupation.

Speculative housing

Above: One of the speculative houses at Saltdean by Connell and Ward, 1934-5.

The strongest validation of the practice's preferred construction method was its potential economy of scale. From the earliest days of practice, the architects sought to bring their lessons in concrete to bear on larger projects and although some opportunities did present themselves, they hardly ever came to fruition. Playing on the strength of their experience in the housing sector, Connell and Ward identified that their best chance for greater volume was through the ballooning speculative housing industry and channelled their energy in the early years of the 1930s towards tapping into this. Where they could not find the opportunity, they instigated it.

Aesthetically their architecture was wildly at variance with the speculative housing market, wildly, too, at variance with the average householder's desires for their house. Disdain from all corners of the architectural profession was expressed about the quality of architecture delivered by the speculative builder. Connell Ward and Lucas' answer was a modern approach and the practice were involved in at least four schemes with which they hoped they could 'beat the speculative builder at his own game by providing more convenience for the man in the street purchaser of semi-detacheds'.[1] Ambitious projects for large estates

resulted in disappointingly small clusters of houses at Amersham, Ruislip and Saltdean and an even less fruitful involvement in the Frinton Park development scheme with Oliver Hill. The speculative housing market peaked in 1934 with the completion of 72,750 houses, and with it the practice's foray into speculative development.

Architects to the rescue

The trio were answering the call made at the Ideal Home Exhibition in 1934 for the architect to 'come to the rescue of the speculative house'.[2] Developers generally operated without the aid of an architect and to maximise their profits. At a time when material costs were relatively more expensive than labour, they squeezed specifications and floor areas. Architects, it was thought, would bring a quality control to construction. The RIBA held a competition for housing at Gidea Park through which they hoped to bring architect and speculative builder together for mutual benefit to create dwellings at modest prices that celebrated simple living. Certain of the houses were erected on selected sites and opened to the public in summer 1934 with projects by LW Thornton White, Euston Slamin, Schultz and Concannon, Scott, Chesterton and Shepherd, but for the likes of Connell Ward and Lucas Gidea Park was not rigorous enough and for them it was the policing of the integrity of design that was as important as the liberation of the housing market from poor construction.

It was usual for developers to construct dwellings using modern building techniques and then wrap them in a skin of jumbled stylistic architectural motifs, more often than not with historic reference. Such an approach provoked disapproving reactions from architects and commentators on architecture; traditionalists and modern thinkers alike. Professor Albert Richardson, head of architecture at the Bartlett who had taught Connell and Ward about Georgian architecture and had 'little sympathy' with their modern views said, 'to my way of thinking the chief trouble before the learned societies and educational bodies is ... the emancipation of democracy from the enormities of shoddy building.' He went on, 'Better by far the universal adoption of concrete for terrace groups in the suburbs than the serrations of 'mock' Tudor which perpetuate Victorian snobbery.'[3] Anthony Bertram from a very different position, writing in support of Le Corbusier's ideas on domestic design in his book *The House: A Machine for Living In*, vehemently stated:

> Tudoresque villas are the most tremendous symbols of the architectural rottenness which have infested most people in this Middle-Ages-ridden country ... the man who builds a bogus Tudoresque villa or castellates his suburban home is committing a crime against truth and tradition; he is denying the history of progress, denying his own age and insulting the very thing he pretends to imitate by misusing it.[4]

Above: Connell Ward and Lucas' designs for the unbuilt Wellington Flats, c.1935.

There is an ethical dimension to these convictions that are reiterated in Lucas' statement for Unit One written in 1934, a year earlier than Bertram and Richardson's pieces. Here he criticises the premise of architectural discourse in England:

> buildings are regarded from the two viewpoints of structure-economy-efficiency on the one side, and appearance-style-art on the other. And needless to say, when dissected so ruthlessly from the unit, appearance becomes a sham, and economy expires … If only those in authority could clear their minds of this duality … there might be a chance of finding a sane viewpoint, and sooner or later an ordered layout of 'clean-looking' structures would replace this chaos in our architecture, which eats into our minds and hampers our every action.[5]

In all three excerpts, the authors express the view that the use of old styles for new technologies in the postwar climate is not just grating, it is dishonest and that this nostalgic, faux-historic approach is a symptom of a slovenly, undisciplined way of thinking that the English would do well to shake off. This sentiment, a sort of 'truth to age', has similar ethical overtones to William Morris' call for truth to materials of decades earlier.

For Lucas the appropriate architectural solution in 1930s England is one that inextricably links structure and form, and the modern approach, not style, was what such architects wanted to bring to the housing market. They believed that socially as well as physically, their architecture would make England a better place, but it was not easy to affect change. Connell Ward and Lucas completed only small clusters of modern houses and the take up was poor. Some said that it was the aesthetic of modern houses that limited their appeal. Others, such as the editor of the *Architectural Review*, put it down to the fact that demand always follows supply, 'as every caterer knows', he said, 'the public is inarticulate, doesn't demand for anything'.[6]

As the decade wore on, Basil Ward did observe that 'Continental influences were having an increased effect upon architecture in Britain'.[7] In speculative building terms, rather unsatisfactorily for Ward, this tended to manifest itself in a smattering of 'art deco' and 'moderne' buildings that jostled side by side with the 'Tudorbethan'. It was difficult to persuade the developer that modern design was anything more than a style; the cherry on top of the speculative fruit salad. Basil Ward said that the modern house was:

> being expressed more in the form than in the content. Modern buildings were appearing which were a reflection of this failing and of compromise and this midcourse way was seen by us as a social-cultural feature in British life. Architecturally the phenomenon was one of eclecticism and of romance, in which

structure played a conventional part and function was made subservient to form. … We were inclined openly to remark on such considerations about which we felt very strongly. As to our own designs, these received critical and scathing notices in the Press and in some of the technical journals.[8]

The sort of modern domestic architecture that Connell Ward and Lucas were creating would remain scarce as long as building societies, local authorities and owners remained sceptical about modern construction techniques and contractors inexperienced in their application.[9] In England this remained the case throughout the twentieth century.

The (high) rise of the pied-à-terre

In the context of the urban fabric of the city private housing development largely took the denser form of blocks of flats. The demand for efficient and low maintenance pieds-à-terre was increasing in the 1930s, to such an extent that by January 1939, in his yearly review of the 'Year's work at home' for 1938 in the architectural press, CH Reilly commented that the block of flats was the most frequently illustrated building type for the year. Unlike suburban developments, architects were often involved in these projects and Connell Ward and Lucas had at least two commissions, one of which we will cover in more detail in this section.

Perhaps because flats were an emerging building typology of a scale that demanded modern construction methods, a contemporary approach to their design was more accepted. Clean lines and curved bands of brick cladding a concrete frame, and decorative fenestration commonly associated with art deco architecture, characterise many of the blocks of this period, and perhaps owe a little to the Amsterdam school. More modern designs were also executed by Lubetkin at Highpoint I and II in Highgate and by Wells Coates at Lawn Road in Hampstead (1933/4), Palace Gate in Kensington (1936/9) and Embassy Court in Brighton. There was also Pullman Court at Streatham Hill by Frederick Gibberd and Jan Pillichowski (1936) with 218 units designed specifically for the young professional.

Of Connell Ward and Lucas' two designs, Wellington Court and Lord's Court, only the latter started on site although it was never completed. The scheme for Lord's Court is curiously organic and decorative for Connell Ward and Lucas' work. That of Wellington Court, illustrated here in an artist's impression, is more rigorously modern.

DESIGNED for your every convenience

CONSTRUCTED for maximum light and air

INSULATED against heat and cold

BUILT AT

PARK WOOD ESTATE

EACH HOUSE HAS
Sunbathing roof garden
Fitted kitchen Tiled bathroom
Built in wardrobes in all
bedrooms Ample cupboard
space and boxroom Covered way
to garrage good garden space
COMPLETE DETAILS FROM
WALTER TAYLOR (Bilds) LTD.

Parkwood Estate

Parkwood Estate, Ruislip, Middlesex, 1933–35
Basil Ward of Connell and Ward (and Lucas)

Connell and Ward teamed up with the contractors Walter Taylor (Builders) Ltd, the builders for the Usherwood house, Firkin and Dragons, for their first foray into speculative building. The contractors put up the capital for the venture and Connell and Ward provided the designs. Mr Taylor enjoyed living in a house 'of modern design' and it was his view that it would not be long before the speculative builder forsook 'Jerrybethan' and built more desirable and pleasant modern houses.[10] The team hit a stumbling block at the planning stage and the much-publicised 'Ruislip case' probably served to put more developers off modern architecture than were encouraged to fire up their concrete mixers.

Park Wood
The site identified for this experiment was west of London in Ruislip, on land Henry VIII originally bequeathed to King's College, Cambridge. The site was already earmarked for residential development within an existing masterplan and the plots were chosen in spring 1933 from those still available on the college estate 'with regard to the general healthiness of the district, immediate open spaces and wooded areas'. Indeed the plots on Park Avenue backed onto Park Wood and fronted a designated open area south of the road.

In May 1933 Connell and Ward met with the bursar of King's College, the well-known economist John Maynard Keynes, to discuss their proposals. He was enthusiastic and the college offered to accept deferred payment for an initial parcel of land big enough for six houses. By June, the Abbey Road building society had injected the necessary finance for the contractors to obtain the freehold of the land, against which they borrowed the money for building. They set the prices for the initial units at £995 and had plans to construct higher priced units near the shops and railway station at a later date.

At the beginning of June 1933, Basil Ward sent a letter to Colin Lucas describing the project and asking him to come to their offices with his father to discuss it. We

cannot be sure if an alliance was formed with Lloyd, Lucas and Co. at this time but it is likely that the discussions focused around common construction techniques and also that they went well as Lucas joined Connell and Ward in practice less than a year later.

The design
Each unit was designed to accommodate two compact family homes and Basil Ward, the project architect, described it as follows:

It was the Adam Brothers type plan ... with a room at the front which was the kind of parlour, a room at the back which was really where the family did all its living, with a kitchen on one side, a staircase going up to three bedrooms, ... and a bathroom. This plan is repeated all over the country. My plan showed the same kind of arrangement, but I opened up the front living room and had only a divider, which is a quite common expression these days in contemporary design, with the kitchen on one side serving into this dining portion ... I took the staircase outside the building. The dimensions of these rooms were, on the whole, larger than those you would find in the speculative built house of the same kind, and type, and cost. Furthermore we built in quite spacious cupboards to each bedroom so that this was in itself an innovation. It was amply supplied with plugs for the owner to use his own electrical form of heating.[11]

The external form of the housing is crisply Teutonic with Bauhaus-like balconies that project out of the main bedrooms to break up the otherwise flat facade. The middle segment of the rectangular volume of the building appears to explode upwards and outwards, pushing a strip of concrete wall and roof higher and wider. This creates a shade on the roof terraces and turns through 90 degrees at either end to become the enclosing wall of the otherwise glazed staircases. The garage 'wing' on a single level protrudes forward of these staircases to form the bookends of each double block. It is a simple and strong composition, sliced through with horizontal bands of fenestration. Here, standard metal casement windows with fine sight lines were painted in a dark tone of blue against the bright white of the walls.

Construction
Concrete beams, floor and roof slab tie into the monolithic structure, with walls acting as beams above and below long strips of windows. The main structural members are 4 inches thick, founded on pad foundations with the party wall between two dwellings increased to 6 inches to comply with local authority regulations. External walls are insulated with wallboard and internal partitions are constructed in patent block. A progress report from Walter Taylor to Connell Ward

Above: The glazed staircase of one of the semi-detached Ruislip houses, viewed from the rear.

Opposite: Draft of a contemporary poster advertising the Parkwood Estate houses.

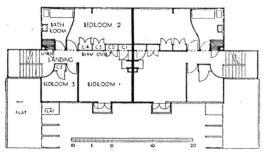

FIRST FLOOR

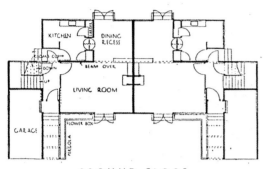

GROUND FLOOR

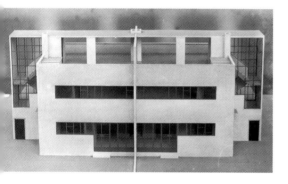

Above:
Ground and first floor plans of the Parkwood Estate houses.
Contemporary model showing the garden elevation at the rear.

Opposite left:
The original elevation design, 1933.
Annotated redesign proffered by the planning authority, June 1934.
Contemporary photograph of the staircase as it was built, fully glazed.

Opposite right:
The approved elevation design with opaque panels to the staircase glazing.
The *Architects' Journal* report of the latest news on the Ruislip case, June 1934.

and Lucas in October 1934 illustrates how the contractors experimented with the external wall finishes as they progressed:

> We have completed the foundations and have erected most of the walls up to Ground Floor level, and have included Sika in this part of the work for waterproofing.... We have carried out the shuttering with planed boards and find that this leaves a very good concrete surface, but for other portions of the work we propose to use prestwood boarding and compare the results.[12]

This flow of information between contractor and architect was invaluable to the progressive development of the construction techniques.

The Ruislip case

Well publicised in the *New Statesman* and other newspapers in addition to the architectural press, the planning process was difficult and drawn out. Ruislip-Northwood urban district council received the original plans for the houses at the end of September 1933. They refused the application on the grounds that it did not comply with the provisions of several statutes, bye-laws and regulations. Translated this meant that they had concerns that the aesthetic and materials were not suitable for domestic construction.

The council used new powers under the recent Town and Country Planning Act of 1932 to refer the case to the local advisory panel of the RIBA for their comment. Panel member Edwin Gunn wrote in the report that the plan was 'not an ignorant, but a consciously modern design, which in external form, is deliberately odd'.[13] In the light of such comments, the council refused to vary their initial decision, saying that concrete was 'cold, noisy and no cheaper or quicker than brick so that there appears to be nothing to justify its use in domestic work'.[14] Basil Ward, scathing of these criticisms found comfort in the thought that heroic architects from the past had encountered such antipathy, 'Deliberately odd, not new but of Continental origin', he said, 'a dark thought and spirits of Wren and Inigo Jones and others hovered.'[15]

Walter Taylor appealed the decision and in late April 1934 the case was taken to arbitration. Ernest Allen, appointed by the RIBA, sat as arbitrator, WA Fearnley Whittingstall represented the builders and Mr Gordon Taylor the council. The architects gave evidence in support of their design and others supported their cause; P Morton Shand generally recommended the designs; Professor Dixon gave calculations showing that the acoustic and structural characteristics of concrete were appropriate to domestic construction; an agent of King's College voiced support for the scheme saying that the type of house was 'by no means detrimental to the proper development of the district'.[16]

Mr Gunn, the vocal dissenter on the original RIBA panel, stated that he disagreed with 'every particular' of the expert evidence put forward. However, under cross-examination he revealed that he was most opposed to the prominent long windows at the stairs because the owner might be seen going up and down in his pyjamas. Such exhibitionism might be all right for continentals, he said, but certainly not for Ruislipians.[17] Mr Allen's report concluded that the design was 'injurious to the amenities of the neighbourhood' but that the council were not in a position to discount the scheme out of hand. Ruislip-Northwood were directed to inform Walter Taylor of reasonable alterations required for the scheme to be approved and were charged the larger portion of the arbitrator's fees.

The council duly outlined their amendments in a letter to the architects of 12 June, enclosing a drawing of what they had in mind.[18] This illustrates a complete redesign of the building, reducing the area and disposition of the fenestration and embellishing it with decorative transoms and mullions. Connell Ward and Lucas wrote a long letter to their client at the beginning of July accompanied by diagrams that highlighted the areas of change in the council's proposed scheme. The architects discussed the merits of each of the council's alterations in the light of their brief, giving practical, structural and economic critiques.[19] A diagram of a preferred resolution was also included showing a scheme very similar to their original one but with reduced glazing to the street elevation.

Revised architect's drawings were placed before the committee on 20 August 1934 and approval was finally given to a scheme that showed the central panes of the staircase windows as solid. The jubilant architects arranged a pre-contract meeting and construction finally began. In translation from drawing to reality, the full glazing to the staircases returned but with some of the panes in opaque rather than clear glass.

Three main principles of the Ruislip case preoccupied the architectural press and brought it wide coverage. The first was that the rejection of the initial scheme was dressed up as a regulatory issue when it was quite blatantly based on subjective aesthetic judgement. The second, a related argument, was that the council had spoken untruthfully about the qualities of concrete to support their rejection and even though these statements were withdrawn at arbitration they were prejudicial to the case. The Architects' Journal also argued a third, that it was damaging to the architectural profession that the RIBA member of the architects' panel was seen to uphold the decision of the council and undermine the authority of the architect. The scheme's eventual approval dismissed what could have been a dangerous precedent for planning law and also encouraged the RIBA to examine the role of their representatives.

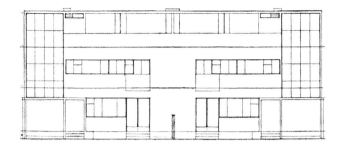

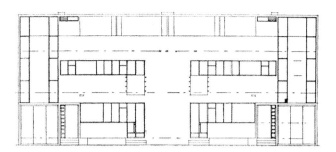

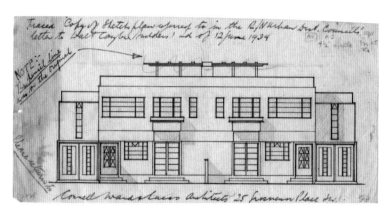

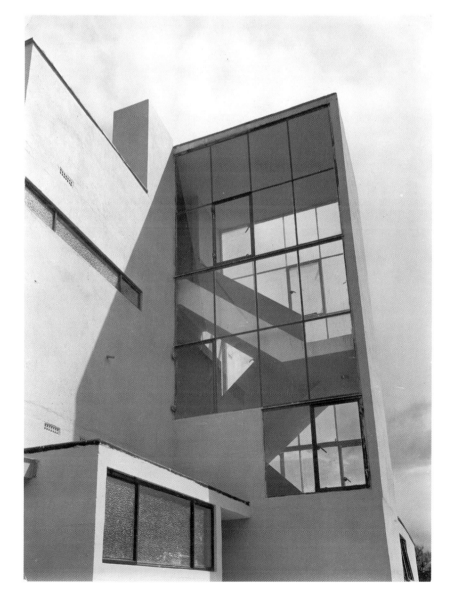

THE RUISLIP CASE — LATEST

The Ruislip-Northwood Urban Council have now issued an announcement of the modifications they require to be made in the house at Ruislip illustrated above, designed by Connell and Ward. The original design, it will be remembered, was rejected by the Council, who were advised to persist in their rejection by the local Advisory Panel, their decision being upheld by an arbitrator appointed by the R.I.B.A. Under the present law they have to announce the modifications they require within 28 days. Following is the text of the Council's announcement, as issued to the clients :—

PLAN No. 4179.

Dear Sirs,—My Council yesterday considered Clause 7 of the Arbitrator's Award (in respect of which you were good enough slightly to extend the period of 28 days) and passed the following Resolution :—

That the Council require that Plan No. 4179 be modified as follows :—

(1) By the re-designing of the staircase wings so as
    (a) materially to reduce the area of glass therein, and
    (b) to reduce the height and the width thereof.

(2) By the re-designing of the bedroom windows so as to provide breaks in the continuity of the glass. In this connection I have to state that, quite unofficially, a sketch plan has been prepared, which gives some indication of what the Council have in mind. If you think that it would assist you, we shall be very pleased for you or Messrs. Connell and Ward to inspect it here.

Yours faithfully,
(Signed) GORDON H. TAYLOR
Clerk to the Council.

[The story of the Ruislip case, together with an account of the arbitration proceedings, appeared in our issue for May 24. See also Astragal's note in this issue.]

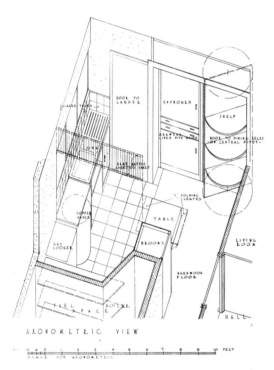

AXONOMETRIC VIEW

SCALE FOR AXONOMETRIC

Above:
Contemporary model of the detached houses.
Axonometric drawing of the kitchen design showing an ingenious rotating shelving unit used for serving and clearing to and from the adjacent dining area. A similar feature was repeated in the Sun Houses at Amersham and also at 42 Sinah Lane.

Right:
The Parkwood Estate book.

Opposite:
The only completed pair, photographed from the front gardens and showing the garage, porch and balconies, 1935.

For the architects, however, winning the planning case was 'a Pyrrhic victory'. Ward later said that 'the development, held up in time and ridiculed, did not go beyond two pairs of houses'.[20] King's College had patiently held up any development on the land earmarked for the Walter Taylor scheme, but having spent thousands of pounds installing infrastructure they were becoming painfully aware that they could not recover costs while the plots remained empty. In October 1934, concerned that they might miss the peak of the building boom if they waited any longer, they wrote to the practice saying that the question had arisen 'as to how far the college can endeavour to meet your views and give you every chance of going ahead with your scheme, or at any rate a very large part of it and without prejudicing their general interests'.[21] Not content to cut their losses, Walter Taylor wrote offering to purchase 200 feet of land on the west side of their building site and 93 feet on the east side.

Their optimistic attitude did not, however, result in many more houses. The first pair of houses was completed in 1935 and each were sold for £1,090. The council passed plans for a second pair without objection by 27 September 1934, but this was only half complete when development ceased. The scale of the project was disappointingly small and had little of the impact for which the team had hoped. Plans to embark on a similar venture in Mill Hill had to be shelved.

The Book of Parkwood Estate

It was imperative to the success of this venture to engage the public in an advertising campaign selling the idea of the Ruislip houses as the first few were constructed. Walter Taylor commissioned graphic designers to create posters and a pamphlet entitled *The Book of Parkwood Estate* to promote the scheme. As well as making the most of the local sports facilities and efficient public transport routes in Ruislip they used many of the arguments they had rehearsed during the planning process to convince the punters that the aesthetic was right, the construction materials superior and that the quality of life infinitely better in a house on the Parkwood Estate.

These are, it pronounced, 'The first houses that are a fit setting for living today.' 'Look at the houses about you', it said, 'they are imitative, conventional, bad copies of bygone styles; they possess neither grace of design, beauty of proportion nor true individuality, at Parkwood your home will still be pleasing to you when the houses on a thousand other estates are looking dowdy and out of place.' Such grace and beauty, it went on, is achieved through the use of modern materials. Concrete construction gives you 'warm quiet damp-free rooms' that are cheaper to heat as the walls and roof 'give greater insulation than a brick wall of more than double the thickness'. As well as lasting longer, the booklet points out that the houses could be rated

more cheaply for fire insurance than a traditional house, that concrete walls take less space and that 'foundations are safer'.

The booklet describes how the units are specifically planned 'for modern needs', demonstrating that alongside the creation of delightful light and airy rooms with flexible arrangements, the pragmatics, such as a lobby between hall and kitchen to reduce cooking smells in the rest of the house had been thought through. Robust wall finishes – to be decorated according to an initial colour scheme by the architect – and hardwood floors would equate to less time spent cleaning and thus promised a superior quality of life.

Later history
Number 101, the single house, originally number 85, was bought by Mr Hill who was a builder.[22] His son later remembered that his family moved into the house in 1938 and stayed for about twenty years. Originally the houses were locally nicknamed 'Blue Peter' (due to the blue window frames), the 'Ruislip Glass house' and even 'Casa Blanca'.

During the war the houses were superficially damaged when bombs fell nearby. All three were grade II listed in 1989 and remain gleaming white amongst the brick and tile of the surrounding development. A rear extension was added to number 101 around 1950 and the balcony was largely filled in a few years later. Number 97 is less changed, with a smaller rear extension and original windows. It has been restored in recent years by passionate owners.

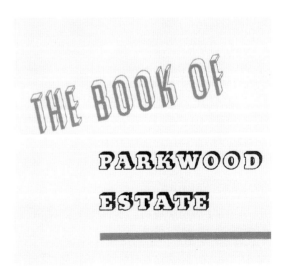

THE BOOK OF

PARKWOOD

ESTATE

The Sun Houses

Above:
Contemporary image of a completed Sun House in 1934.

Right:
Recent photograph of the houses viewed from Station Road. The mature trees hide the original High and Over house behind.
View from the rear garden of a particuarly well preserved example of the houses.

Opposite:
The site plan of High and Over with the Sun Houses.

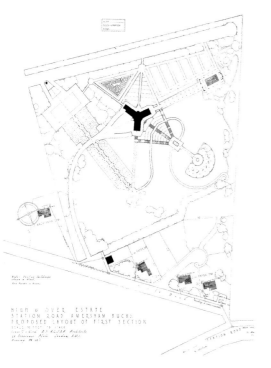

The Sun Houses, 4, 5, 6 and 8 High and Over Estate, Station Road, Amersham, Buckinghamshire, 1933–35
Connell of Connell and Ward

While Connell and Ward were fighting the planners at Ruislip, a second housing development was on the drawing board. The Ashmoles had been working on an idea to develop as many as thirty houses in the estate that surrounded their house, High and Over at Amersham. Connell was again invited to execute the designs for four plots they had sold at the base of the drive. These Sun Houses were drawn up from late 1933 and designs submitted to the planners in March 1934. In contrast to Ruislip, they received immediate approval. Three were to be constructed to the right hand side of the drive below the lodge, for a relative of Mrs Ashmole, Mr Charles de Peyer, for whom the practice had undertaken a flat refurbishment in north London. The fourth dwelling for Mr James MacGibbon of Bloomsbury was situated on the left of the rising driveway and was the first completed.

Design
Connell designed two types of Sun House; three type A and one type B were executed. Type A offers a very similar layout to the Ruislip houses with three bedrooms and a bathroom upstairs and a living room open to dining area and separate kitchen downstairs. As the site slopes up from drive to rear garden, the living area is split level with the dining area higher to be level with the rear garden. The main entrance positioned between garage and living room, opens directly into the hall and the staircase climbs from here to the roof where there is an internal sunroom with glazing facing south as well as a terrace. The garage is slipped back to be in line with the main body of the house. For a different shaped plot, the type B house is separated from its garage.

Not dissimilar to Ruislip, the staircase is fully glazed to the front with a concrete flank wall wrapping over the top of the building and finishing in a distinctive cantilevered shading hood to the roof terrace. To the south and east elevations, strips of glazing of differing heights are punched into the solid concrete walls and the north elevation has no windows at all, to protect the house from the gaze of the neighbouring south elevation. The composition of the west facade, where the full-height glazing to the stair with a jaunty roof balances with the more solid two-storey element, is the most successful. Otherwise the houses are quite boxy, lightened a little by the windows that are wrapped around the south-east corners and the jutting concrete *brise soleil* that protect the lower windows in the south and east elevations from too much sunshine.

The concrete houses were completed in spring 1935 by the contractors, West and Musgrave, who had constructed High and Over several years before and were co-currently working on the Flat Roof House at Little Frieth for Colin Lucas. Characteristically, there was a large amount of built-in joinery internally including benches around the dining area and the same inventive space-saving revolving shelf-doors between kitchen and dining room as at Ruislip. Each came to a total cost of £1,000 with central heating.

Later history
On completion, Mr MacGibbon had some issues with Amersham council who were concerned that no completion inspection had been carried out, no water certificate issued and that the plot had decreased in size since the original application had been received. When these issues had been addressed in 1936, he sold his Sun House at a loss. The purchasers stayed in the house for about forty years and a few years after their departure in 1979, all the houses were grade II listed. The other houses have been well preserved and extended generally in keeping with the original design. This group of four houses gives the best indication we have of what a larger estate designed by the architects would have been like.

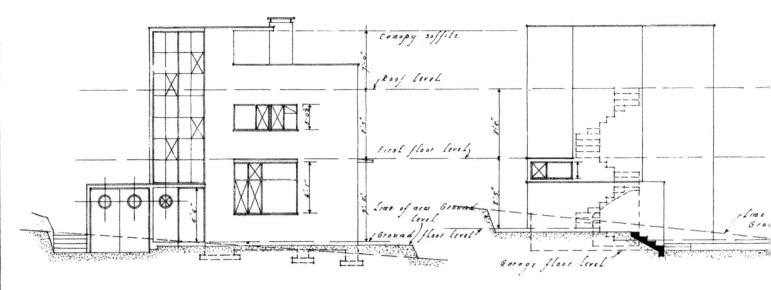

WEST   ELEVATION

NORTH   ELEVATION

Note. Building is a reinforced concrete
frame structure with 4" thick insulated
reinforced concrete walls and 6" concrete
oversite; weights concentrated on R.C. foundations
First floor, roof & canopy in R.C. slab construction
All in accordance with L.C.C. reinforced concrete code.

Note- All habitable rooms to have
requisite permanent ventilation. Lavato
& Bath ditto arranged with airbricks h
in walls.

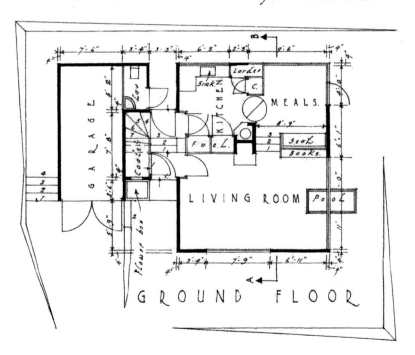

GROUND   FLOOR

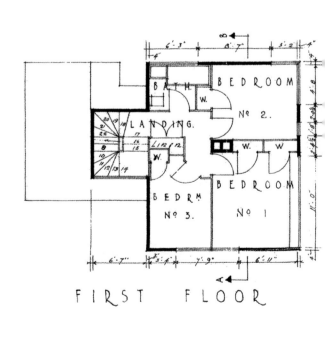

FIRST   FLOOR

DRAWING Nº 63/1
SCALE ⅛" = 1'·0"
FEBRUARY 1934
DRAWN BY

COPY
Nº
2

HIGH & OVER ESTATE
PROPOSED HOUSE FOR J.
THE WORKING DRAWING

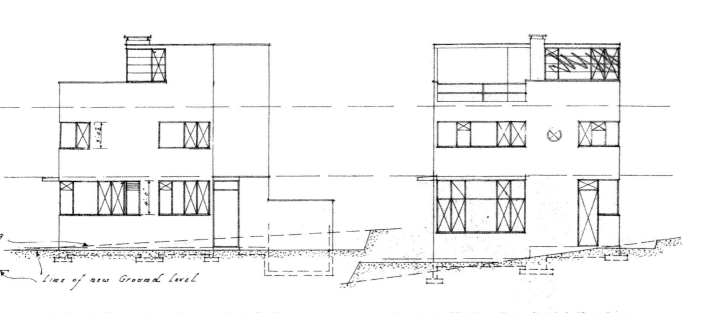

ting
el]

Line of new Ground Level

E A S T   E L E V A T I O N   S O U T H   E L E V A T I O N.

AMERSHAM RURAL DISTRICT COUNCIL.

APPROVED under Byelaws and Town Planning Acts
This 20ᵗʰ day of March 1934

~~~~~~~~~~~~~~~~ Chairman.

~~~~~~~~~~~~~~~~ Surveyor.

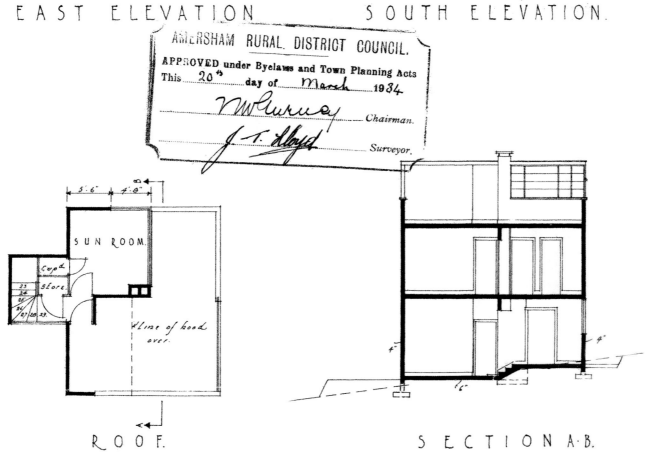

SUN ROOM.

Cupᵈ
Store.

line of hood over.

R O O F.   S E C T I O N A·B.

ATION ROAD   AMERSHAM
C GIBBON   Esᴏ̲

CONNELL & WARD
R·S· A·R·I·B·A ARCHITECTS
25. GROSVENOR PLACE
LONDON   SWI

Saltdean

Above:
Foursquare viewed from the south west
The first house under construction photographed in 1934.
The view from the property towards the coast was at this
stage uninterrupted by development.

Opposite:
The characteristic projecting staircases in this scheme are
interesting to compare with Le Corbusier's Pessac houses.
Typical ground and first floor plans. Although the footprint
was the same, the houses are each slightly different.
These plans are for 'One Other' - the northernmost
house. Garages adjoined each of he buildings.
Neville's magnificent Saltdean Lido designed by RWH Jones.

56, 62 and One Other, Wicklands Avenue, Saltdean, East Sussex, 1934–35
Connell and Ward

Published a month later than the first completed buildings at the High and Over estate, this was the first of two housing development projects undertaken by the architects at the coast. Of their three houses built on Wicklands Avenue, ironically the one originally named Unique, number 56, is the only one to survive relatively intact. The client, Mr Snow, required that the houses should have a 'seaside atmosphere' and that they should be an aesthetic improvement on the south coast developments typical at that time.[23] The *Architects' Journal* article reporting their completion disclosed that more were to be completed in the same year but these do not seem to have been built.

Saltdean, described by Nairn and Pevsner in 1965 as 'seaside gaiety and a cosy housing chaos' was the second and smaller of two major developments along this stretch of the Sussex coast dreamt up by the entrepreneur real estate businessman Charles William Neville.[24] Neville had spied his development opportunity while holidaying in Eastbourne just before the First World War and from 1915 he poured his energy into creating Peacehaven on a one and a half mile stretch of sparsely populated farmland over the brow of the hill from Newhaven. Wider use of the motor car, more regular and efficient train and motor bus services had encouraged people to set up outside the city and there was a marked move to populate the British coastline more permanently. In 1911 England and Wales had approximately 100 substantial seaside resorts of 2,000 or more, by 1931 five per cent of the population were living in seaside towns.[25] Peacehaven, one of the most prominent developments of the time, was a large grid town divided into plots and supported by good transport facilities including an aerial landing ground.[26] When the subsequent opportunity arose to expand his empire at Rottingdean and Saltdean, Neville seized it with both hands.

Neville's companies purchased land from 1916, securing the last major areas in 1925. Miles of looping avenues and roads were established from 1923 and the estate office was set up on the coast road to tempt in the passers-by.[27] Plots were advertised on the backs of London tram tickets and promoted as competition prizes. New houses began to appear in around 1924 but business was slow in the early years, marred by the severe recession in Britain. By 1929 just two houses existed on Wicklands Avenue. Contemporary photographs taken in 1934 show Connell and Ward's three houses sitting regally in vast swathes of grassland with only one other bungalow in close proximity.

Increasing from 103 houses in December 1931 to 802 in February 1938, development peaked at Saltdean in

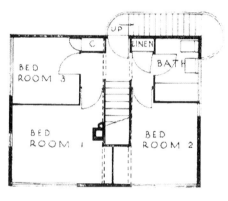

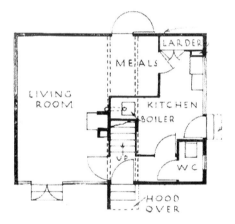

the years immediately preceding the Second World War.[28] By 1938, when nearly all the plots in Wicklands Avenue were occupied, Neville had turned his attention to the seafront. The sandy beaches were popular and the success of other developments at British seaside towns in the 1930s encouraged him to be bold with his interventions. In late 1937 he unveiled a majestic reinforced concrete lido designed by architect RWH Jones (1900–65) that was lauded by *Building* magazine as 'one of the really first-class designs of its type in the country' holding 300,000 gallons of water and accommodating up to 500 bathers.[29] A car park was planned for 1,000 cars with regular buses and shops close by. At the same time, the vast Ocean Hotel, another of Jones' designs, was being completed on a four and a half acre site at the corner of Wicklands Avenue and Long Ridge Avenue. For £300,000 Neville built a hotel for 600 guests with an American style bar, ballroom, exercise room and swimming pool that dominated the town.

Design

Connell and Ward's compact little houses offered the same accommodation as the Ruislip and Amersham houses but differently configured. The main stair, immediately ahead of the front door runs up through the centre of the plan, dividing the kitchen, hall and wc on one side from the living area on the other. A dining niche is situated beneath the rising stair, adjacent to the kitchen and open to the living space, joining the ground floor accommodation in a horseshoe shape around the stair. Upstairs the semicircle of accommodation is reversed, a small landing serves two main bedrooms either side of the stair and the third opposite the shared bathroom at the south of the plan. Another door gives access to an external staircase that runs to the roof terrace above.

The unifying vertical glazed elements that typically accompany the staircases on Connell and Ward's buildings to date are absent on the houses in Wicklands Avenue but still the articulation of these elements is the most remarkable aspect of the designs. Prominent on the simple cubic form of the dwellings, the stairs from first floor cantilever and curve, arriving at the roof under a rectangular protective canopy that is tied into the chimney stack. Their design is clearly borrowed from Le Corbusier's scheme for workers' housing commissioned by the industrialist Henry Frugès at Pessac in Bordeaux, a scheme that was completed in 1926 and which the architects had visited. Connell and Ward had also incorporated the same stair into their contemporary design for Doctor Haydon's house at 44 Sinah Lane (see page 75).

The roof canopy, stair and garage elements are integral parts of the balanced composition of the three-dimensional form of each house. In this respect, the scheme is reminiscent of Lucas' the Hopfield. When the two are compared the design signatures are quite distinct. At Saltdean the cubic volume of the building is less eroded, the fenestration punched into the walls rather than set into recesses between horizontal bands of concrete and the paper-thin quality of the concrete somehow more pronounced, as if the four walls could fall in on each other like balanced cards. Lucas' concrete is no thicker, but the horizontal and vertical planes seem to be knitted together to create a more robust form.

Construction

The most compact and economic of Connell and Ward's housing types, this trio were completed with garages for a total of £1,650 in late 1934 or early 1935. They are constructed in concrete using twisted square sections of steel for reinforcement. The first floor is carried by a pair of concrete beams flanking the internal staircase of the house in a similar structural scheme to that of their house at Bristol. The beams cantilever from the external walls to pick up the bottom of the external staircase. Internally, portions of the 4 inch walls are built in concrete to support the beams and slab floors, other partitions are constructed in breeze block. Masonite insulation lining the walls and roof is skimmed internally then finished in distemper. Low-maintenance composition, rubber and parquet floor finishes were originally installed and three radiators, fuelled by coke, provided minimal central heating.

Later history

Nairn and Pevsner reported in 1965 that Connell and Ward's houses stood 'forlorn among their conformist brothers and sisters … perhaps a little dispirited'.[30] When an application for listing was turned down in 1982, number 56, named Unique, was still close to its original form, number 62 or Foursquare was much altered and One Other to the north of Wicklands Avenue had been demolished following a fire. Planning history shows that in 1949 Foursquare was being used as the Saltdean Nursing Home when an application to extend the lobby was granted and that it had reverted to a house by 1952 when plans for a new study to fill the northern portion of the roof terrace were submitted and approved. In 1994 permission was granted for the house to be demolished and replaced with a new bungalow.[31]

Frinton Park

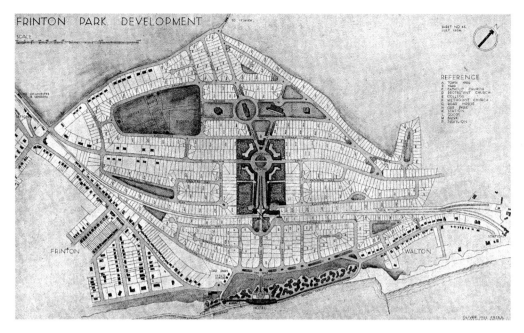

FRINTON PARK DEVELOPMENT

Above:
Frinton Park development, general layout by Oliver Hill.

Below:
Elevations of the Connell Ward and Lucas scheme, road elevation at the top.

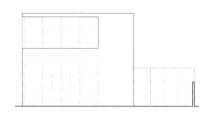

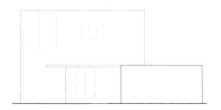

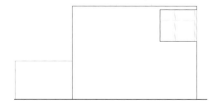

House design for Frinton Park development scheme, Frinton-on-Sea, Essex, 1934–35
Connell Ward and Lucas

After Colin Lucas had joined the practice in 1934, the trio were invited to join a team of architects designing houses for the modern quarter of an ambitious development at Frinton-on-Sea in Essex. Although Connell and Ward had limited success with the public and the planners, their speculative ventures up to this point had been with financers who believed in and builders who had experience in constructing modern houses. At Frinton the developers were interested in a style of flat roofed white house but had little patience for arguments about the integrity of modern architectural design and Connell Ward and Lucas found it impossible to compromise their art and step into line with the finance and programme-driven directives of the project. Their design for just one house was therefore never realised.

Frinton Park development scheme

Frinton itself was, and still is in the early twenty-first century, a discerning and selective seaside town. The first fish and chip shop arrived on the high street in the 1990s; the high street shops are still privately owned and run and the houses are pricey. A protected greensward sweeping along the whole seafront and separating the residences from the sea does not form the usual platform for the British seaside paraphernalia; not a kiosk in site, not a clink of a penny arcade.

In the mid 1920s a virgin site of 200 acres of woodland between Frinton and Walton on the Naze was earmarked for a substantial development but the difficult economic climate ensured the same slow start as at

Saltdean. Early in 1934, with only a little of the infrastructure in place, the South Coast Property Investment Company Limited bought the site and Frinton Park Estate Limited was set up with Francis Arnatt as managing director.

Oliver Hill was appointed consulting architect to oversee the masterplan and design quality of the development. Recognising the importance of establishing the overall character of Frinton Park development from the outset and 'anxious to avoid perpetuating another Peacehaven', Oliver Hill submitted a masterplan to the district council in July 1934.[32] They envisaged a 'gleaming white' town of 1,100 dwellings. The focus of the plan was an axial route lined with shops from a new town hall in the north west to a glittering hotel on the sea front in the south east. Around this the housing was arranged in four quarters, two north of the railway and two south. Hill's audacious scheme for the hotel, a linear building hugging the coastline at sea level required the major reconstruction of the shore with a new man-made sea wall to replace the sandy beach. A menu of different styles of homes were to be available in the different zones, reflective of Oliver Hill's chameleon-like adoption of various architectural styles over his successful career. The council, no doubt pleased to be offered an alternative to the usual haphazard bungalow growth, approved the design.

Primarily, Hill was keen that the Frinton Park development would be an exemplar of the most talented modern British designers, similar to his Dorland Hall exhibition of 'British Industrial Art in relation to the Home' a year earlier through which he had brought the cream of modern design to the public.[33] The first area to be developed was the 'modern zone' south of the railway line and Hill's list of suitable designers, including Connell Ward and Lucas, reads as a summary of the great and the good of the architects working in the modern vein. Architects such as Clough Williams-Ellis, Goodhart-Rendel and G Grey Wornum were employed to design the 'more picturesque houses' north of the railway line.[34]

The team of designers

From the outset the development company were keen to keep the architects on a tight rein in order to deliver the buildings on time and on budget and Hill, their architect, was to have the final say on the designs. The modern team met several times without Hill to discuss the strict terms and conditions of their employment at Wells Coates' and at Connell Ward and Lucas' offices. They signed a petition requesting a larger design fee and voicing concern about having to use Hill's quantity surveyors, builders and particularly his specifications.

The latter proved to be a major sticking point. The developer intended to adopt a hollow block construction method and was not prepared to allow

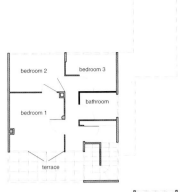

Above :
Ground and first floor (top) plans.

Below:
One of the first structures to be built at Frinton was the round estate office, designed by Oliver Hill. Now a family home, a floor mosaic was created illustrating the plan of the estate for the agent to orientate the prospective purchaser.
Today, completed houses sit amongst those of other styles.

monolithic reinforced concrete construction. The reasons for this were three fold. Firstly, Arnatt believed that they could popularise modernism by using flat roofed designs but that the sceptical public would not have enough confidence in the poured concrete construction method to buy the houses. Secondly, none of the builders on the project demonstrated the ability to build in reinforced concrete and thirdly the local authority, backed by legislation in the 1932 Town Planning Act, were apparently not happy to accept even 6 inch concrete walls and asked for prohibitively expensive 8 inch construction. For many of the architects including Connell Ward and Lucas, where construction method was integral to design, this restriction could not be tolerated.

Despite continued arguments on this point, many of the architects completed their designs. Connell Ward and Lucas deposited plans with the district council at the end of November 1934 for a house constructed from their typical recipe of 4 inch reinforced concrete with integral insulation on plot no. 260 on Grace's Walk. Reinforcement designs by Twisteel Reinforcement Ltd were also submitted at the same time. In their accompanying letter the architects had defensively outlined their experience in executing houses 'of this type' in England and pointed out that it was a method of construction approved of by the Ministry of Health and the London County Council. Surprisingly, the scheme was approved in January 1935.[35]

Arnatt began to get colder feet as prospective purchasers started breaking off negotiations when they understood that the new houses were to have flat roofs. The development company did not abandon the idea of the modern quarter, but the squabbles with the principled 'concrete' architects over what appeared to be irrelevant details began to frustrate them. Arnatt said that although he found the architects 'individually charming', together they were 'simply childish' in their refusal to build in the requested way.[36] The issue was eclipsed by the fact that the development was being strangled through lack of finance and the build programme was increasingly pressured. The directors and a local builder had to step in to fund the first dozen houses and a building society injected some capital on the proviso that none of the new buildings were to be of concrete construction.[37] The need to build twenty houses by the end of March 1935 was swiftly superseded by the need for thirty-six in February, then fifty by Easter 1935. Under pressure, Arnatt started to encourage Hill to reduce his specifications, to use cheaper foreign materials and to economise on foundation size.

There were neither the means nor the expertise to construct the designs of the uncompromising designers, Connell Ward and Lucas among them, so they simply dropped out of the project. Hill completed a dozen modern houses and designs by Frederick

Etchells, RA Duncan, Howard Robertson and Marshall Sisson were also completed.[38] The resident architect for the estate, JT Shelton, who was used to building more traditional styles of speculative houses, designed about twenty houses under the direction of Hill's specification with asphalt flat roofs, metal windows and cement render finished in white with pale blue, pink or green.

Continuing arguments between Arnatt and Hill, primarily over the inexperience and slowness of the builders, compounded by the time and money pressures of the project, eventually meant that even the developer and architect fell out. The company became insolvent by September 1936 and the whole venture was taken over by a local estate agent but never finished. The partially realised Frinton Park development is nevertheless one of the largest collections of flat roofed white rendered houses in the country. To the north of the railway, the one-eighth completed shopping circus, incongruous on the edge of a dense wood and with render falling from its brickwork construction, is a rather sad monument to a dream to elevate modern design and catch the imagination of the British public.

The Connell Ward and Lucas house

The layout of the Frinton Park house is most similar to the Worcester Park flats. Two storeys are laid out on a 24 feet 4 inch square footprint. The easternmost three-foot slither is a single storey volume with entrance door, hall and storage with garage adjacent, kept well back from the road. The living spaces are contained in the remaining rectangular volume. Orientated to the south east with full-height glazing, the living room faces the road and is semi-open plan with the dining recess (also fully glazed). The kitchen is accommodated in the far north corner of the plan, accessed from both the hall and the dining area. Large amounts of glazing to the front and rear elevations (south and north) contrasts with the minimum on the west and east elevations that face the adjacent plots. At first floor, three sides to the staircase become external walls as bedroom accommodation is cut back to give a generous roof terrace to the master suite, and two sides to the stairwell are side-lit with glazing. The three bedrooms and bathroom are accessed from a double loaded corridor at the centre of the plan.

Although the project architect is unknown, several aspects of the design hint at the influence of Colin Lucas. This is noticeable particularly at the south elevation where a bedroom terrace, in itself characteristic of Lucas' house design, is incorporated. Full-height glazing is taken to the underside of the ceilings rather than arranged in long bands and the general form of the external concrete walls – the two-storey blank facade that gives privacy to the stairwell reducing to a band of concrete as a perimeter balustrade to the roof terrace – are reminiscent of the Sunlight House and the Hopfield.

Lord's Court

Flats and Shops, Lord's Court, 32-36 St John's Wood Road, London, NW1, 1935–38
Connell Ward and Lucas

Amongst the archive documents of Connell Ward and Lucas held in the RIBA drawings collection are over a hundred drawings relating to their largest commission to go on site. The project for the seventy-seven flats in St John's Wood began in 1935 and was halted while under construction in 1938. Very little is known about how the project came about, the client or the brief. Fortunately it is possible to piece together a little of its history from the drawings and construction photographs.

Accommodating the middle class
St John's Wood, at the fringes of the leafy expanse of Regent's Park, had become a prime area for luxury flat developments from the mid-1930s. Local newspapers reported the influx of flat dwellers, noting the particular enthusiasm for the 'small service flat' among 'the recently married'.[39] This marked a sea-change in the development of the English city which had always differed from that on the continent where apartment and flat living is usual. Private developers, often large companies, seized development opportunities where they could and secured low-rise residential sites.

As well as instigating a dramatic shift in the scale of the urban fabric, sustained by government-led upgrades of the existing infrastructure, this construction boom fundamentally altered the socio-economy of the area. Developers served notice on the local working-class population to empty large tracts of their houses for the influx of the upper middle classes. In the period of 1933–36, 300 families were ousted from the area. Schemes such as Viceroy Court by Marshall and Tweedy of 1936, Stockleigh Hall by Robert Atkinson and AFB Anderson of 1937 and the 125 flat scheme Oslo Court, also by Robert Atkinson in 1938, were criticised for their lack of social conscience, the latter alone prompting the removal of thirty houses and not necessarily offering affordable alternative accommodation.

Mr FS Bennett, the client for Lord's Court, purchased three large houses with significant gardens that were certainly not working class at 32–36 St John's Wood Road to reshape into his new nine-storey scheme. A major attraction of the site, as its name suggests, was its adjacency to Lord's cricket ground. Elevated flats would give many of the new tenants grandstand views of the matches. The earliest proposals with a cruciform plan, date from July 1935. By February 1936 Mr Bennett had secured another property on the road, increasing the site area, and the architects extended the north-east arm of the cross to create a crescent shaped extension. Subsequent sketches show that the ambitious client had desires to incorporate the sites of another two properties on the road.

Highpoint I by Tecton and Lubetkin is likely to have been an inspiration to the practice. Completed in 1935 just as Connell Ward and Lucas were putting pen to paper, this was a project for sixty units on North Hill in Highgate. It was commissioned by the largest employers in north London, the Gestetner family. Cosmopolitan, wealthy and progressive in outlook, they wanted to create flats for the firm's employees, but when the DIA exhibition in 1934 displayed a typical flat, pre-lets were secured and the block was inhabited by private purchasers. Similar in scale to Lord's Court, this seven-storey block was laid out as a double cruciform plan incorporating two types of flat – one three bed flat in each of the arms with four units accessed from one set of stairs and lifts and with kitchen lifts and services shared by two flats.

Using this pattern on a larger scale at Lord's Court, four limbs of the cruciform plan typically contain two flats back to back. Per floor there are eight two and three bedroom flats, all accessed from the central circulation zone. Kitchens and main service ducts are clustered around the access area and bedrooms pushed beyond living areas with bathrooms at the extremity. Servants would have arrived invisibly up one of four hidden staircases arranged around the hall at the centre of the plan, accessible from the kitchens.[40]

On the first floor extensive roof gardens over the ground floor accommodation are provided in lieu of balconies. The deep plan, daylit using rooflights, is designed to cater for a mixture of uses, mainly retail. Rootes' garage and the India Tyre Company, both neighbouring the site, extend their premises into the new building. The grand central entrance hall has porter's desk, public telephones, lifts and stairs with smart new car showrooms to one side and an estate agent's office and a modest shop for the inhabitants on the other. An underground car park, ramping down from St John's Wood Road, is conveniently accessed via this main circulation spine. A second entrance hall and circulation spine is introduced when the plan is extended in 1936, giving access to the three additional flats on each floor in a variety of one, two and three bedroom configurations. At ground level there are fourteen maid's rooms with bathrooms and a common room.

The large surface area that the long extruded 'limbs' give to the plan maximises the opportunity for windows and balconies. The curved balconies to the bedrooms and living areas, like webs at the internal corners are its most distinctive feature. Such 'sunbathing verandahs' had been recognised as major selling points for the earlier flat developments such as Viceroy Court, where they could be used 'for sleeping out during the summer months or incorporated in the living room to increase the latter's size'.[41] For the four flats that did not enjoy views of the cricket pitch from their outside space, there was the bonus of direct sunlight from the south.

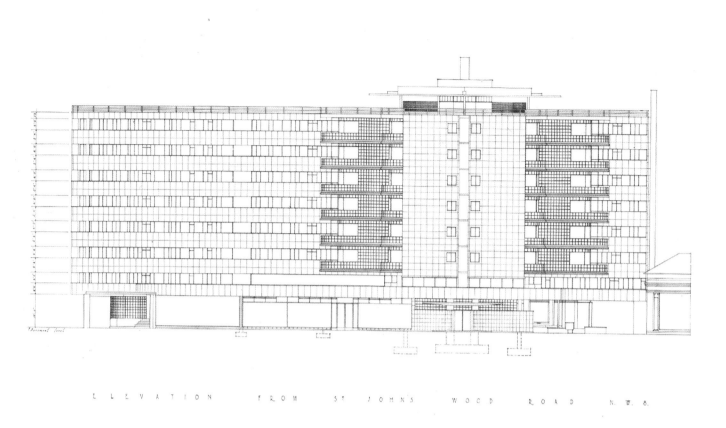

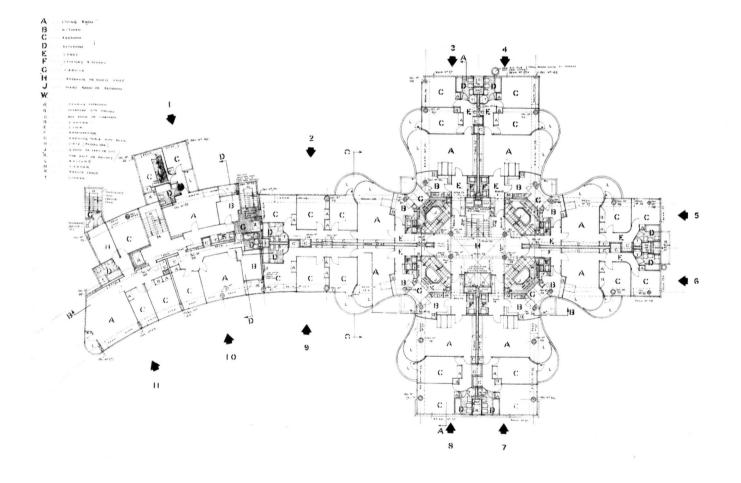

152 Speculative housing

Opposite:
Front elevation drawing from February 1936.
First floor plan showing the internal arrangement of flats.

Above:
View of the building under construction c.1937. The main entrance canopy, the raw interior at the central core and view from the first floor roof terrace – the grandstand at Lord's is visible through the trees beyond.

Structure

By the time this project came into the office, the partners had been working with reinforced concrete construction for over six years. Together with their contemporary project for film studios at Shepperton, this was their greatest opportunity to test the favourable cost implications of the large-scale use of concrete. Analysis of their working-class flats competition submission and the completed Kent House was favourable and, being a larger beast altogether, the practice were poised through the construction of the Lord's Court flats to prove even greater efficiency through the standardisation of components and reuse of shuttering.

Although usually carrying out their own structural calculations, when faced with these larger schemes the architects employed a leading engineer, Felix Samuely, to help them with the design. Early sketches in November 1935 show a hollow box ring girder on columns at the centre of the building. As the scheme progressed, this steel was replaced with reinforced concrete. A grid of columns radiating from the centre of the plan supported the concrete floor slabs. Walls were woven around the grid and at the outer reaches of the crosses, the columns are close to the slab edges, sitting just behind the windows and restricting views.

The structural solution at Highpoint, devised by Lubetkin with engineer Ove Arup, was the panel and slab reinforced concrete construction that Connell, Ward and particularly Lucas had been working with in their individual house designs. This allowed columns and piers to be hidden in walls to create clean lines. Given Connell Ward and Lucas' knowledge of concrete construction, it is disappointing that Lord's Court is not more innovative structurally and more progressive architecturally.

Having always committed to the expression of the construction material on the exterior of their buildings, the artist's impressions and elevations of Lord's Court come as a surprise. The whole building is clad with 'special, precast glass aggregate slabs in colours' applied in a grid of square panels and cast curved to follow the streamlines of bulbous, curved balconies. Unlike the planar modern blocks constructed by their contemporaries, the practice curiously seem to have steered a path between modern and art deco. Connell's earliest elevation sketches show caryatids holding the entrance canopy, a motif similar again to Lubetkin's Highpoint. By November 1935 these had disappeared but a vertical 'sculpture panel', reminiscent of Auguste Perret's Rue Franklin flats in Paris at the turn of the century, rises up the centre of the front facade. At this point the scheme is thoroughly symmetrical. Almost continuous strips of windows stretch down each of the long sides of the flats contrasting with limited glazing to the service areas at the internal corners and at the elevations to the end of each 'finger'. When the extension north east was added it was treated similarly with strips of glazing and cladding panels applied to the strips of structure between.

In the final design an oval entrance canopy announces the entrance to the building. The slab-like quality of this hovering element is accentuated by open corners and full-height glazing beneath to the showrooms. Internal finishes were to be fairly luxurious with travertine paving at the entrance and in the showroom and Austrian oak block floors to the shop and the internal areas. Each flat, of course, had a large amount of built-in furniture, with a spine wall of cupboards.

Construction

Between February and the end of June 1936 seventy drawings were executed for the project and preliminary approval of the scheme was given by the Ministry of Health in October 1936. Numerous details of the ground floor areas of Rootes' showrooms and garage were produced in December 1936, suggesting that construction started late in 1936 or early 1937. The last revisions are dated 1937 and leafless trees in photographs of the cast entrance area show that the construction continued at least into the winter of 1937. Later planning history confirms that the ground and first floors were built to the original design. Construction on the site ceased until the early 1960s.

It is unlikely that the onset of war was the reason that progress on the flats was halted. The construction industry was affected by local shortages of labour and increased wage costs for skilled labourers from 1936 due to an increase in war-related construction work, however, the pace of construction remained fairly healthy until 1939. The government encouraged private house building and continued its social housing programme in an attempt to fulfil its promises and between August 1939 and the end of March 1940 about 28,000 houses were still built. It was not until as late as October 1940, over a year after war was declared, that the licensing of civil building was agreed upon and became enforceable under defence regulations. This called to a halt 'luxury' building in order to relieve what had become severe labour shortages and regulate the use of materials. It is probable that building work stopped because the developers of Lord's Court became bankrupt.[42]

In June 1959 permission was refused for the completion of Lord's Court by erection of a six-storey extension. In May 1961, however, outline planning permission was granted for the 'completion' of the first floor for use as offices and erection of three storeys over to contain sixteen maisonettes. A scheme was carried out by Trehearne & Norman, Preston & Partners. Thirty years or so later in December 1997 an application was granted for demolition and redevelopment of the site and a block of flats was under construction on the site in October 2000.

Social housing

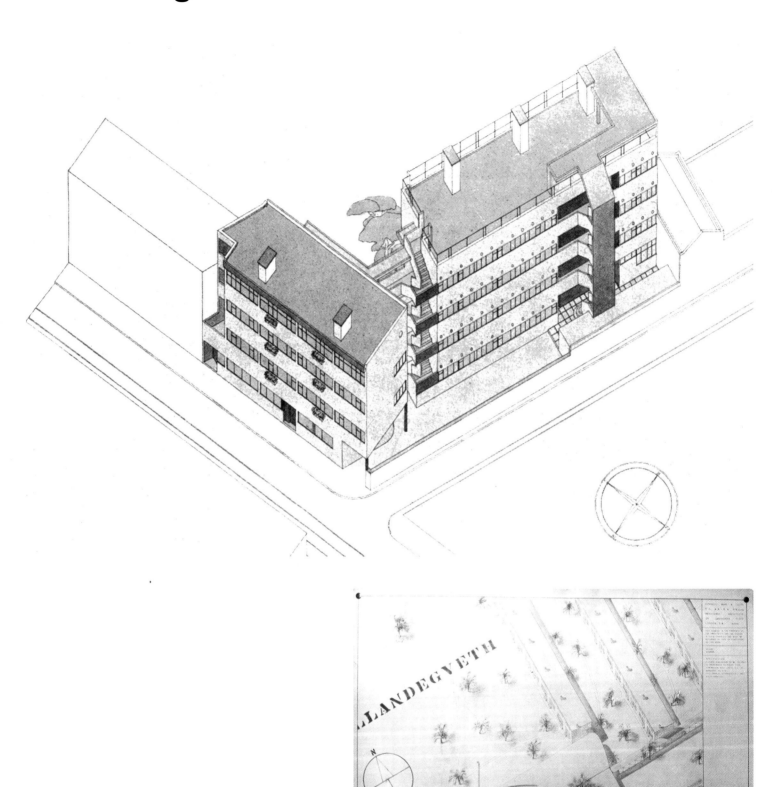

'If the urgent problem is the transformation of a million slum dwellings into cities of order, light, health and convenience, the men who will be engaged on the practical problem of such a transformation will find questions of ornament and decoration singularly futile and academic – a waste of time and money. Their problem is not academic, but human and rational. They have to design houses which embody an ideal of decent living on a communal scale; to do this they will need imagination and science.'[1]

The social agenda of modern architecture on the continent demanded solutions to facilitate the mass building programmes of national governments immediately after the First World War. Across Europe, countries developed strategies for the creation of affordable housing. Swifter, cheaper production of dwellings for large social housing projects was being made possible with the advancement of new building materials and technologies and the tenets of modern architecture emerged as an expression of these developments.

In 1919 Lloyd George was faced with a housing crisis; a general shortage of homes exacerbated by a large amount of substandard existing housing stock and the simple fact that England had not built for four years. His government subsidised local authorities to build unlimited numbers of new houses with controlled rents under the Housing and Town Planning or Addison Act of 1919. This was not just an attempt to clear slums, it was also intended to restructure the building industry as part of a larger plan to kick-start British industry, to lift morale generally at a time when a quarter of a million workers were on strike and to create a Britain worthy of the heroic demobilised troops returning from France and beyond. The Addison Act proved expensive and its effects fizzled out by the early twenties.

In the thirties, despite reformists' pressure on the National Government led by MacDonald, Baldwin and later Chamberlain, no over-arching interventionist plan emerged to tackle these social issues. Two Acts of Parliament were passed to regulate the clearance of slum dwellings and housing subsidies were distributed on a local level, mainly into the private market to provide the lion's share of dwellings. The first came in 1930 in the face of a collapsing economy. Ramsay MacDonald's housing act of his dying Labour government charged local authorities with the duty of identifying and replacing slum clearance areas, instigating a renewed programme of work. This was put on hold as the country limped through the early years of the thirties. As soon as a healthier glow was perceived in the economy, money went into rearmament and not until the Housing Act of 1938 was there another wave of incentives to progress slum clearance. This commitment to social reform came, surprisingly, on Conservative Chamberlain's watch. The radical approach of a national plan for Britain bubbled under

the political crust but would not gather enough momentum to break through until the end of the Second World War.

There was little opportunity for architects like Connell Ward and Lucas to get involved with social housing projects on the scale of those erected in Amsterdam, Vienna, Berlin, Frankfurt and Hamburg. Perhaps the closest England got to this was very late in the 1930s with the exceptionally large Quarry Hill Flats in Leeds designed by architects employed by the city council, particularly RAH Livett. This was inspired by French housing projects and construction techniques. Utilising a system of factory assembled steel frames and precast concrete units the need for a skilled labour force was eliminated. The first of over 900 units were occupied in March 1938.

Housing associations instigated many English urban projects. Marylebone Housing Association, for example, was executing schemes such as Wilcove Place by Louis de Soissons for 137 flats close to Lisson Grove. Here a relatively large site of densely packed housing was cleared and replaced with six blocks of five and six storeys at a total cost of £75,000. Each flat contained well-planned kitchens with ovens, built-in furniture and tiled walls, but the construction is unremarkable and typical; concrete floor slabs, steel filler joists and solid load-bearing brick walls.

Working for a forward-looking housing society, Connell Ward and Lucas were able to prove the advantages of their construction methods in a more modest scheme for just twenty flats in Chalk Farm. The Cement Marketing Company, looking to promote their product and giving the work of architects like Connell Ward and Lucas a good airing at the same time, held a competition in 1935 for a much more ambitious scheme, albeit on paper, for 200 flats. We know very little about a rural scheme for a centre for the unemployed in Llandegveth in Monmouthshire that was drawn up by Basil Ward in 1938. The drawing suggests that this was some kind of meeting place with rows of smaller repetitive units, perhaps some sort of co-operative noted as 'subsistence production'.

Alongside this trio of social housing projects, Connell Ward and Lucas were involved with many designs for health and welfare projects with a strong social conscience that we will examine later in the book. One might assume that the practice was motivated by the progressive socialist beliefs that certainly inspired modern architects like Berthold Lubetkin to action. Although they naturally gravitated to the forward-looking brief-makers of sometimes pioneering social projects, there is little evidence to suggest that Connell Ward and Lucas themselves had radical political leanings.

Above: A royal visit from the Duke of Kent to give Christmas presents to the inhabitants at Connell Ward and Lucas' newly completed Kent House, 1935.

Opposite:
A drawing of the original, competition winning scheme for Kent house, 1934.
Isometric of a centre for the unemployed at Llandegveth in Monmouthshire, designed by Connell Ward and Lucas c.1935 but unbuilt.

Kent House

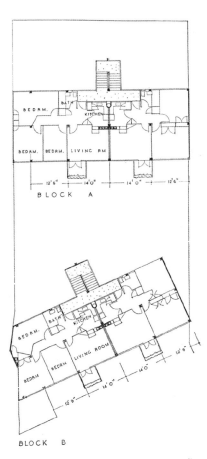

BLOCK A

BLOCK B

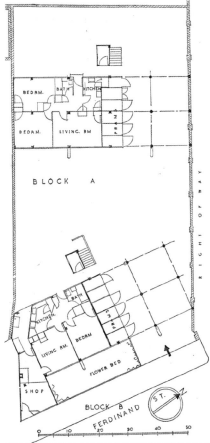

BLOCK A

BLOCK B

FERDINAND ST.

Above: Plans as built – typical ground plans below and upper plans above.

Opposite: Front elevation to Ferdinand Street.

Kent House, 13–17 Ferdinand Street, Camden, London NW1, 1934–35.
Connell Ward and Lucas

The commission for this block of working-class flats came from the St Pancras House Improvement Society Ltd, a public utility society based in Euston that was established in the 1920s to provide affordable housing alternatives for deprived city dwellers. The founder of this society was an extraordinary man of the cloth, Reverend (John) Basil Lee Jellicoe (1899–1935), who dedicated his short but impressive life's work to clearing the slums in and around Camden, north London.

A film called *Paradox City*, directed by Leonard Day and Gerald Belmont and made for the society in 1934 to appeal for funds for Kent House, documented the grim reality of slum dwellings and described the society's dream for the future in the recently completed flats, Athlone House in Somers Town, London. It compares the homes of a 'favoured few' in Park Lane apartment blocks, 'the substantial homes of the well-to-do' in Georgian terraces and 'the healthy homes of many' in suburban semi-detatcheds with the 'appalling shelter of thousands of decent citizens' in the slums. With views of cramped and dirty conditions and painful poverty, the camera sweeps up to rest on serried ranks of smoking chimneys perched on the crumbling Victorian housing stock. 'Every chimney', the narrator says, 'represents a family of from five to eight people cooking, living and sleeping in one or two rooms.'

The fundraising was successful and the south-west sector of the St Pancras group, formed in May 1934 to deliver Kent House, honed their brief and sought an architect. MARS had been involved with the St Pancras House Improvement Society's northern group 'New Homes for Old' exhibition and Connell Ward and Lucas beat other architects including Godfrey Samuel to the post through a design competition.

The design
The brief was for two blocks of rent-subsidised flats containing twenty units for families on low incomes. The original scheme provided more flats on the site in one block than the authorities would allow, so the design was modified from a pair of linked blocks joined at an upper level by a walkway to two separate blocks shown here. One block faces Ferdinand Street and continues the street edge, the other is placed to the rear of the narrow, rectangular site. Planning around two courts allowed for the maximum light and air to reach all the flats. On Ferdinand Street a small fish and chip shop is incorporated into the scheme; no doubt very convenient for all the tenants.

In each four-storey building there are two compactly planned flats per floor, there is no need for access decks, since each tenant steps directly off the centrally positioned stairwell on to their own entrance balcony, cantilevered directly off the floor slab and large enough to accommodate a table and chair. Each of the twenty flats have two or three bedrooms with all rooms opening off the entrance hall. Kitchens and bathrooms are clustered at the centre of the blocks to keep service runs simple and each living room has a projecting balcony a good six foot square. Electricity is supplied to all the flats with an immersion heater to provide hot water; they each also have a fireplace. Kitchens have electric ovens and other labour-saving devices such as a rubbish chute that disgorges into a shared bin store at ground floor. Rounded skirtings and an average of six built-in cupboards per flat also helped reduce housework and increase storage. In addition to the amenity space provided around and under part of each block at ground level with copious pram stores, the roofs were accessible and surrounded with metal grille balustrades. The new tenants received all of this for a weekly rent and service charge of just 13s 6d.

Construction
The flats are constructed from reinforced concrete. The structure for each block is arranged as a regular grid of three rows of five columns, the sixteenth integrated into and supporting the staircase. Beams run between these, incorporated into the 4-inch walls above the windows. Strips of fenestration, identical on each floor stop and start around the columns therefore pronouncing their positions on the external envelope. Balconies are cantilevered from floor slabs, thinning to their outer edge with small vertical upstands. The staircases, originally open to the elements, are beautiful, the pleasing abstract shapes of their zigzagging raked concrete forms work dynamically against an architectural composition that is otherwise quite stiff and banded. At the ground floor the walls are partially stripped away to exposed the forest of columns.

It is notable that the architects decided to use a beam and column construction method where the columns and beams protrude internally. With the technology at their disposal to entirely subsume the structure into the walls as Lucas had done at Hopfield, Sunlight House and at Dragons, they still chose this method. Perhaps it was thought that this grid system with internal partitions entirely divorced from the structure would allow a greater spatial flexibility in the long run.

Cost was a major focus for the society and for the architects. The build cost of £7,525 was analysed by Cyril Sweett, the quantity surveyor, who reported in the Architects' Journal that this was a cheaper form of construction than more traditionally constructed contemporary schemes such as Tabard Estate in Southwark and China Walk in Lambeth.[2] By using Walter Taylor (Builders) Ltd, by now masters of Connell Ward and Lucas' concrete construction, they ensured that the greatest cost advantages could be

Right:
On the rear elevation of Kent House the strong abstract shapes of the circulation stair contrast with the flat façades.
The staircase as well as the access to each flat was designed to be open to the elements.

Below: Kent House under construction.

Opposite:
Roof terraces to both buildings were to be used by all the residents in addition to the courtyard at ground floor.
The front elevation nearing completion.
The model of the competition winning entry with link bridges connecting the two blocks. There is a significant amount of additional accommodation and less external amenity space in this scheme.

attained. They also guaranteed a quick completion. This project was constructed at a frightening speed, the contract was signed in June 1935 and the building opened just six months later, at the beginning of December 1935.

The flats were opened by Sir Wyndham Deedes, a deeply religious man who had worked as chief secretary in the new administration in Palestine in the early twenties but had dedicated his latter career to social work in deprived areas of London. He proclaimed, 'each flat is an Englishman's home … your society is not only opening flats, you are opening avenues, windows, doors to new lives for men, women and most important of all, the rising generation'.[3] The parliamentary secretary to the Ministry of Health, Geoffrey Shakespeare, was also at the opening and applauded the cheerful colours. Colourful it was; the rendered walls were mainly brownish pink with turquoise windows and the box-like projection at the roof was in vivid blue; upstands to the projecting balconies, supporting columns to the ground floor, the door in the fish and chip shop and ventilation discs above the windows were in strong vermillion. All the ironwork was glossy black and the walls to the shop canopy yellow.

The Duke of Kent visited the project in the fog a few weeks later on 23 December, laden with Christmas presents for the children. One small child asked if he would like to come and have a bath in her new bathroom. Leonard Day took photographs of this visit to be included the new film he was directing called *Castles in Chalk Farm* which documented the construction of the flats.

Recent history
Kent House has been grade II listed. It underwent a half a million pound upgrade in June 2006, when steel double glazing replaced the original single-glazed windows, kitchens and bathrooms were upgraded and the exteriors were repainted to the original colours. Now reduced to fifteen homes, the block is still run by St Pancras Housing Association.

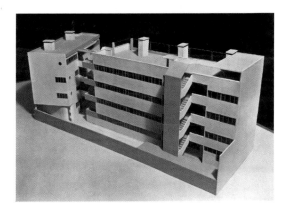

Working-class Flats Competition

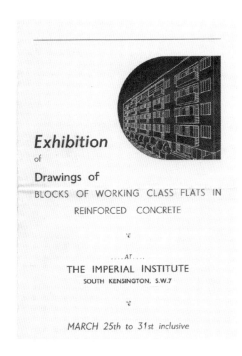

Exhibition
of
Drawings of
BLOCKS OF WORKING CLASS FLATS IN
REINFORCED CONCRETE

....AT....

THE IMPERIAL INSTITUTE
SOUTH KENSINGTON. S.W.7

MARCH 25th to 31st inclusive

Above:
The pamphlet from the exhibition of the entrants

Below:
Plan of two identical three room flats.

Opposite:
Model of the scheme by McCutcheon.

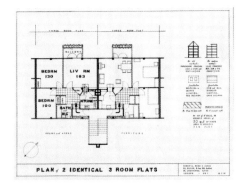

PLAN. 2 IDENTICAL 3 ROOM FLATS

Competition for working-class flats in reinforced concrete, 1935. Connell Ward and Lucas

In February 1935, while Kent House was on the drawing board, Connell Ward and Lucas along with 122 others, entered a competition for working-class flats in reinforced concrete set up by the Cement Marketing Company Ltd. The company hoped to secure designs for five-storey blocks of flats for working men, demonstrating from the estimated costs that the construction method compared favourably with any other type of construction. Emphasis was on collaboration between architect and engineer and Connell Ward and Lucas also listed quantity surveyor Cyril Sweett in their team, who was also working with them on Kent House. However, they failed to win over the judges, who included the architect of the Royal Corinthian Yacht /club at Burnham-on-Crouch, Joseph Emberton. They awarded first prize to Lubetkin and Tecton, second and third prize to lesser known practices and Connell Ward and Lucas only made the highly commended list. However, their scheme was published in the Architect and Building News in March 1935.

The teams were given a site and a clear brief. Flats of specific ratios of varying accommodation should be limited to 50 flats per net acre and no more than 50 in one five-storey block; five storeys because this was the height that was most acceptable to local authorities. Minimum floor areas and floor to ceiling heights were stipulated for each type of room and electric lighting, clothes washing and drying, cooking, refuse disposal, pram and cycle storage, cupboards and larders all had to be included for in the design. As well as drawings, each team had to submit a construction report and a cost estimate per habitable room.

Connell Ward and Lucas' scheme accommodated 200 flats at an average cost per habitable room of £119. In their report they outline some of the most important features of their design:

> all flats opening onto common hall space as in medical opinion it affords ample means of ventilation; separate kitchens with good ventilation from the hall space; back to back stoves and fires providing cooking facilities in the kitchen and open fire in the living room at a low running cost from one grate; balconies provided to every living room of sufficient size to enable meals to be taken out of doors in the summer and small children to be wheeled out for sleep during the day; a private entrance with flower box and wicket gate for each flat, giving an open air play pen for small children under the eye of their mother from the kitchen; Cupboards in every room – linen cupboards, larders etc.[4]

In addition to living accommodation, welfare centres for adults and children were provided in the blocks.

The orientation of the blocks was an important factor for the judges. The winning approach was to position blocks so that either morning or evening sun would bathe each flat in light. Many of the other applicants, Connell Ward and Lucas included, straddled the blocks with each flat, prioritising the primary living spaces on the sunnier side over the service, circulation and additional bedroom spaces on the other. Their living spaces on the front facade faced south east, so that the service areas would receive some evening light. Blocks were therefore arranged diagonally across the rectangular site, a fact noted by the Architect and Building News as being particularly unusual. 'It is curious', they said, 'to imagine the effect of a large area rebuilt in this way, with the avenues between the houses cutting across the street plan.'[5] The layout meant that the site became more like a park with buildings set into it, each block having its own vehicular access route and with the shared open spaces between wide enough to ensure that none of the buildings overshadowed their neighbours. These early approaches to planning blocks of flats are particularly interesting to note in relation to Colin Lucas' work with the LCC after the Second World War.

This exercise seems to be typical of the way marketing supported social housing construction in the thirties. In addition to this, modern architecture could enhance their self-promotion. A good example is the Kensal House flats scheme for the Gas Light and Coke Company completed in 1937. The company instigated an innovative working-class social housing experiment at Ladbroke Grove where they conformed strictly with the Housing Act and therefore qualified for generous subsidies to provide the 68 flats for rehoused slum-dwellers. Designed for large families, the development incorporated a clubroom, circular nursery school and playground, all built on the site of a disused gas holder. Maxwell Fry's design was inspired by German social housing projects and the project happily acts as a showcase for both the latest domestic fuel applications and modern architectural design.

Other projects

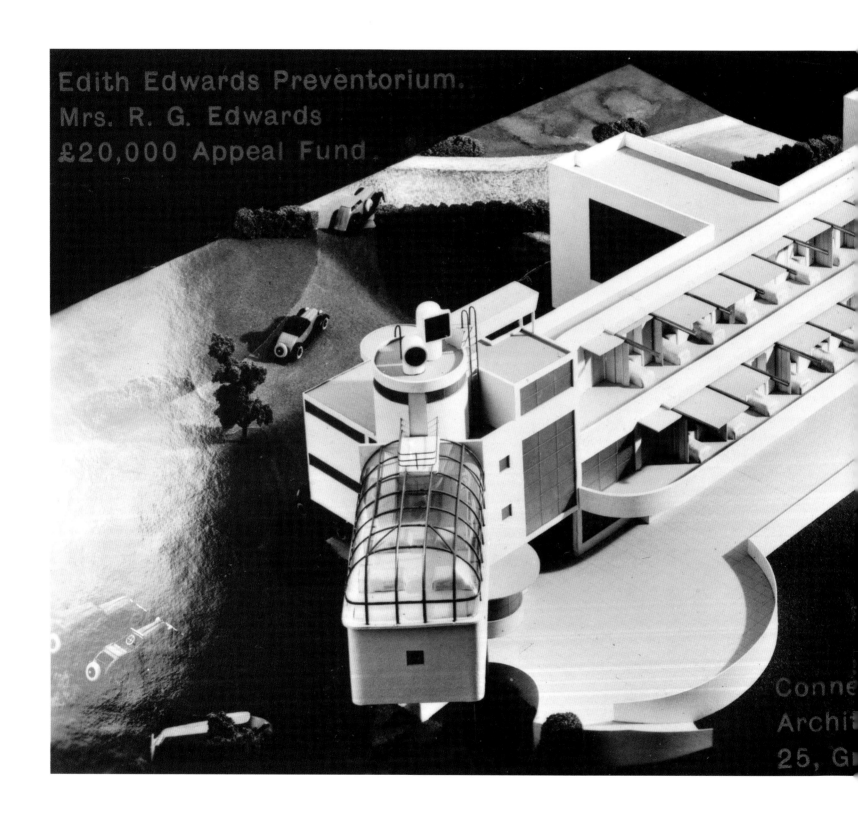

Edith Edwards Preventorium.
Mrs. R. G. Edwards
£20,000 Appeal Fund.

Conne
Archit
25, Gr

Clients with progressive briefs also sought the three architects for innovative design solutions on a number of non-domestic projects. In the early years of practice this was on the humble scale of interior designs for retail outlets and restaurants. The inherently transient nature of such projects means that none survive but documented designs include Lucas' wife's first cafe and cookery school in Sloane Street and a health food shop and cafe by Connell. Many young modern designers found that the modest scale of these interior projects gave them the opportunity to be expressive and playful with modern materials, they were also a vehicle for much-needed publicity.[1]

A scientific approach to building reached its full potential when used to solve the problems of technologically advanced briefs. In the mid-thirties ground-breaking designs for a tuberculosis preventorium, the first of its kind in England, and a vast health centre were drawn up by the practice. Different technical demands predicated a commission by the head of Shepperton Studios to design new sound studios for his site. With funds for film-making more ready than healthcare, Shepperton was the only one of these three designs to be completed.

Other documentation exists illustrating projects about which we know very little; a welfare centre and nursing home probably for Burnham-on-Crouch in Essex, a model of which was exhibited at the RIBA Health, Sport and Fitness Exhibition of 1938; three sketch designs by Lucas in 1937 for a St John Ambulance meeting hall for a Miss Audrey Stables from Haslemere in Surrey; a £300,000 block of offices with showrooms on the Headrow for S Newman (possibly thwarted by Sir Reginald Blomfield who carried out a significant redevelopment of this main shopping street in Leeds in the 1930s); designs for Sherwood School for Mrs Barclay of Epsom (who could have been the same Mrs Barclay on the committee of management of the St Pancras House Improvement Society, client to the Kent House project) and illustrations of a scheme for a boathouse on a quiet stretch of river.

Opposite:
Designs for a tuberculosis preventorium at Papworth were executed by the practice from 1935. The image of the model became an important fundraising tool.

Above:
A drawing from the practice files of a boathouse, also unrealised.

Ecole du Petit Cordon Bleu

Above:
Lucas' shop window design is a simple composition of rectangular flat planes fixed horizontally to become shelves and turned flat-on to become signs. This is not dissimilar to his treatment of form at a larger scale in his house designs.

Opposite:
The pay desk at the entrance to the restaurant.
The teaching space was kitted out with a futuristic looking horseshoe shaped demonstration desk, with a curving condiment shelf under, supported on five sturdy metal legs. The restaurant led through to the teaching room/kitchen. Circular motifs are repeated in the porthole windows, displays and light fittings.

Ecole du Petit Cordon Bleu, 29 Sloane St, London SW1, 1931. Colin Lucas

Dione Lucas, wife of Colin, set up the Ecole du Petit Cordon Bleu as a cooking school and restaurant in Chelsea a year or so after they were married in 1930. A creative and talented lady, Dione Lucas had training in a variety of fields: firstly jewellery design, for which her father was famous; then music when she learnt the cello at the Conservatoire in Paris, and finally cooking when she went on to join the Cordon Bleu school in Paris. Here she excelled, earning the coveted Grand Diplome Le Cordon Bleu, and her culinary career took off. 'The preparation of good food', she said, 'is merely another expression of art, one of the joys of civilized living.'[2] With fellow chef Rosemary Hume she took additional examinations to allow them to set up the official Cordon Bleu school in London. The first of their students were taught from a one-room school in Chelsea and within a year they moved to larger premises on Sloane Street where they incorporated a small restaurant alongside a demonstration room and named it 'Ecole du Petit Cordon Bleu'. Rosemary Hume ran the restaurant where 'special dishes were made to order' and Dione Lucas did the teaching 'in simple cookery of France and the Continent'.

Colin Lucas executed the designs for his wife's venture. He stripped back the interiors of the property, creating a space with an orderly, uncluttered feel. An elegant display in the glassy shop front on Sloane Street framed by shiny, sparkling curtains enticed the passer-by into a comfortable waiting area. A curved, sleek and glossy pay booth signalled the entrance through more lustrous drapes to an unostentatious roof-lit dining space. This had fixed bench seating, chrome and lacquered wood chairs to match tables and a smooth concrete or composite floor with rafia matting. Circular motifs on the display shelving, the pay desk and lighting were repeated in the porthole window in the door to the teaching room beyond the restaurant.

Through her restaurant, Dione Lucas seized the opportunity to educate a race traditionally associated with bad cooking in the pleasures of gastronomy. In her book Au Petit Cordon Bleu published in 1936, she said, 'not so long ago this country displayed little interest in questions of cookery ... things have changed and people are doing their utmost to make up for lost time'.[3] Interest in food and cooking was increasing as domestic help decreased and people were engaging in more 'Do-it-yourself' dinner parties. This was just the place to brush up on your soufflé technique and proved very popular. Within three years Hume and Lucas moved on to another restaurant and through her work Dione Lucas supported the minimal income of her husband's architectural practice, as well as her employment of Beatrix Connell as a helper. Towards the end of the decade, between 1937 and 1938, Lucas designed another restaurant for her, Au Petit Potager at 142 Wigmore Street.

The Vitamin Café

Connell and his sister-in-law designed this progressive eatery in Oxford Street to house a 'food reform restaurant' that, through the provision of wholesome meals, aimed to educate about health through diet. For its size, the project was quite extensively published in 1931, 1932 and again in 1934. The primary focus of these articles was the use of innovative materials for decoration. The architects boxed in areas of the soffit and clad with metallic surfaces similar to those used at the hall of High and Over and then set these against opal glass light boxes and curved fittings. The play of light on the shiny surfaces made them appear to fade away and the rooms feel larger.

To achieve this end, Connell and Hargroves used a new product which was a polished metal-faced plywood called Plymax that particularly interested the architectural press. Plywood, a relatively new material in its own right, was literally sprayed with molten metal projected from a spraying pistol on a blast of compressed air at a speed of about 760 miles per hour. This apparently cooled so quickly that the hand could be held in the spraying flame, four inches from the mouth of the pistol.

The small entrance vestibule acted as both the threshold to the cafe and the library or dietary information centre. It also housed the cashier's desk behind a little grille. Open shelves and counters were ordered under sections denoted by distinctive typography and displayed a range of wholewheat and healthy foods. Two sets of shiny double doors led to the cafe beyond.

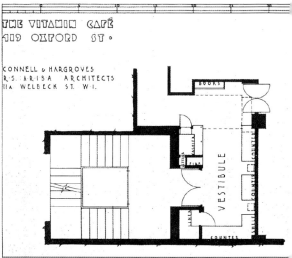

Health Shop

Above:
The display cases on the shop floor of the Health Shop, a design by Amyas Connell and Basil Ward in association with AM Hargroves.

Opposite:
The futuristic feel of the entrance vestibule is created with boards finished in polished aluminium. The planes of reflective material make the true volume of the space elusive, dissolving the walls and increasing the volume of the space.
The plan of the Vitamin Café.

Health Shop, 70-71 Welbeck Street, London W1, 1932. Connell, Ward and Hargroves

Recently joined by Basil Ward who had returned from Rangoon, Connell and Hargroves completed this shop fit out in 1932. In close proximity to Harley Street and Wimpole Street, an area of London densely populated by medical consultants then as now, this shop fit out was done for Edgar J Saxon Ltd. They had set up a forward-looking retail outlet to sell health food products and disseminate literature on the benefits of healthy diets to both prevent and cure disease. The shop is testament to the growing contemporary interest in this field.

An 'unconventional layout' is created here to house the 'unorthodox' stock of soya cream biscuits and the like in this pharmacy of foodstuffs.4 Counters are lowered to promote interaction between the assistants and customers who went to the shop to consult as well as buy. Six showcase counters to the outer perimeter of the shop give a large central milling space, these cases are framed in stainless steel and their contents well illuminated by strip lights. Stock drawers below are concealed by sandblasted glass screens with travertine plinths. The low window display helps to make the shop visually more accessible to the customer and a glazed screen allowed a good overview of the shop from the administrative area at the back.

The cashier's and enquiries desks are taller, dividing the information library and the goods display. Perhaps for confidence, the customer is encouraged to address an assistant through slatted metal strips, akin to a confessional. Adjacent is a writing desk for making notes and a notice board by the entrance to display announcements. The library holds books such as The healthy life and pamphlets – The healthy diet, The causes of cancer – all displayed in fittings of 'hygienic value'. The black and white photographs do not do justice to the flamboyant use of colour throughout the shop design. Mandarin red furniture was set against primrose shop walls and woodwork finished in chinese blue.

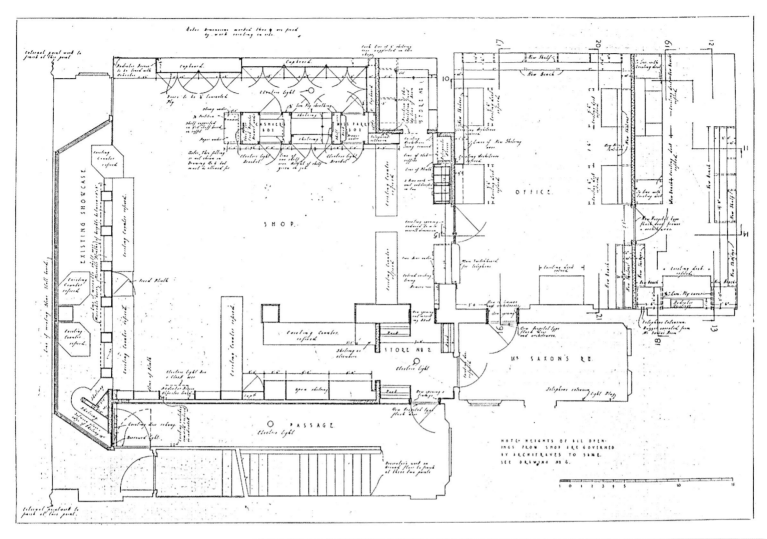

Above: The Health Shop layout with the shop office behind, published in the *Architects' Journal*, August 1932.

Right: The cash desk is a very small booth that effectively hides the cashier.

Opposite:
Built-in furniture divides the shop floor from the information library.
View through the displays to the well-lit shop front.
The library is an important feature of the shop that had an ambition to act as an information exchange as well as a retail unit.
Glass counters and ordered shelves.

The Edith Edwards Preventorium

MRS R·G EDWARDS £20,000
MARGARET STREET HOSPITAL PREVENT

Above: A drawing of the preventorium scheme showing the
retracting sunroofs and walls around the bedrooms.

APPEAL

RIUM FUND

The Edith Edwards Preventorium, Papworth, Cambridgeshire, 1935–39
Connell Ward and Lucas

Diptheria, whooping cough, pneumonia, bronchial disease, malnutrition and childbirth all played their part in high mortality rates in the twenties and thirties, particularly in dense urban areas. The most prevalent disease, however, was tuberculosis, a condition that severely affected the working class and killed between 30,000 and 40,000 people each year, often when shockingly young. There were a number of sanatoria for tubercular sufferers but a full recovery was a slow process and places were often limited by financial constraints.

Thoughts turned to the relative impact that preventative methods might have on tackling the disease and in the early 1930s, Connell Ward and Lucas were approached by a team of pioneering clients to design the prototype for a new kind of building – a tuberculosis preventorium. Although new to England, the advantages of such an interceptive approach had already been realised in France, Germany, America, Italy and Russia where preventoria had already been constructed. The building would house women and children suspected of tubercular symptoms, supporting therapeutic and community facilities and allowing doctors to observe patients and develop a greater understanding of ways by which the disease could be short-circuited.

The design
The project was for the Margaret Street Hospital for Consumption in Marylebone, London and was led by Mrs RG Edwards in memory of Edith Edwards. The site for the first preventorium was to be near to the Papworth Village Settlement in Cambridgeshire. Founded by Dr Pendrill Varrier-Jones, Papworth had been developing a long-term approach to the treatment of tuberculosis since 1916. Their staged rehabilitation programme offered patients employment in sheltered accommodation, allowing them to sidestep the stress associated with the return to work that often triggered a relapse. The preventorium would be a welcome addition to their village.

Rural Cambridgeshire was purposefully a far cry from the dense urban fabric whose inhabitants the preventorium would be built to benefit. Sunlight and air were recognised as major factors in the treatment of tuberculosis and hence one of the key aspects of the brief was to 'provide an open air sleeping accommodation together with special wards'.[5] The practice embrace this wholeheartedly in their design, producing a highly technical scheme with controlled air temperature, pressure and lighting conditions. Three of the four walls around individual rooms as well as the hoods over them are fully adjustable, allowing for a range of conditions from fully enclosed, air-sealed rooms to open air sleeping.

The building is arranged around an entrance core from which two main wings extend. The longest of these accommodates the dissolving bedrooms that are lined up in wards of ten on first and second floor tiers, all facing the same way, presumably south, to catch the sun. Beyond the main circulation corridor to these areas are blocks of supplementary accommodation, probably dining and therapy rooms protruding to the north. At the core a gentle ramp is provided in lieu of a main stair for taking exercise and for wheeling patients from area to area. It is not clear what is housed in the shorter wing of accommodation jutting from this circulation. It is raised above the ground on long columns or pilotis allowing the huge paved terrace to slide underneath forming a vast flat hard landscape in front of the building from which the patients and visitors can descend into the surrounding wooded landscape.

Built of insulated reinforced concrete, the familiar solid bands with areas of glazing characteristic of the practice's designs are supplemented by curved elements; balconies, a circular drum at the core of the building and the bulging glazing of a conservatory. The building is modern and dynamic, physically animated by the changing enclosures of the ward rooms. It clearly doffs its hat to the design of Alvar Aalto's tuberculosis sanatorium at Piamio in 1932 and Jan Duiker's tuberculosis aftercare centre, Zonnestraal (Sunray), at Hilversum in The Netherlands, completed in 1931.

Owen Williams' Peckham health centre of 1935 is worth noting as an example of a contemporary modern building embodying the progressive medical ambition. Described by JM Richards as a 'field experiment in applied biology', client doctors G Scott Williamson and IH Pearse provided facilities for all ages of the community with swimming pool, restaurant, dance hall and meeting rooms under one roof, where they could work among the community and offer practical advice and support to encourage a healthier social and physical family life.[6] The building helped to make this project a success, popular amongst the community and effective through its message.

Connell Ward and Lucas admired the work of the architect-engineer Owen Williams and aimed for a similar architectural spirit in their own designs for the preventorium. Judging by publicity in relation to the Peckham experiment, this would have been a seminal building for their practice. Although the design was widely published during the intense fund-raising period – particularly by the New Zealand press who enjoyed reporting the adventures of their boys in England – achieving the goal of £20,000 proved difficult and the war displaced the project. Connell kept in contact with Papworth. In 1943 when he was based in Hampshire and practising alone, he did a set of housing designs for the village settlement.

L. WARD & LUCAS

ECTS,

SVENOR PLACE S.W.

Individual Health Centre

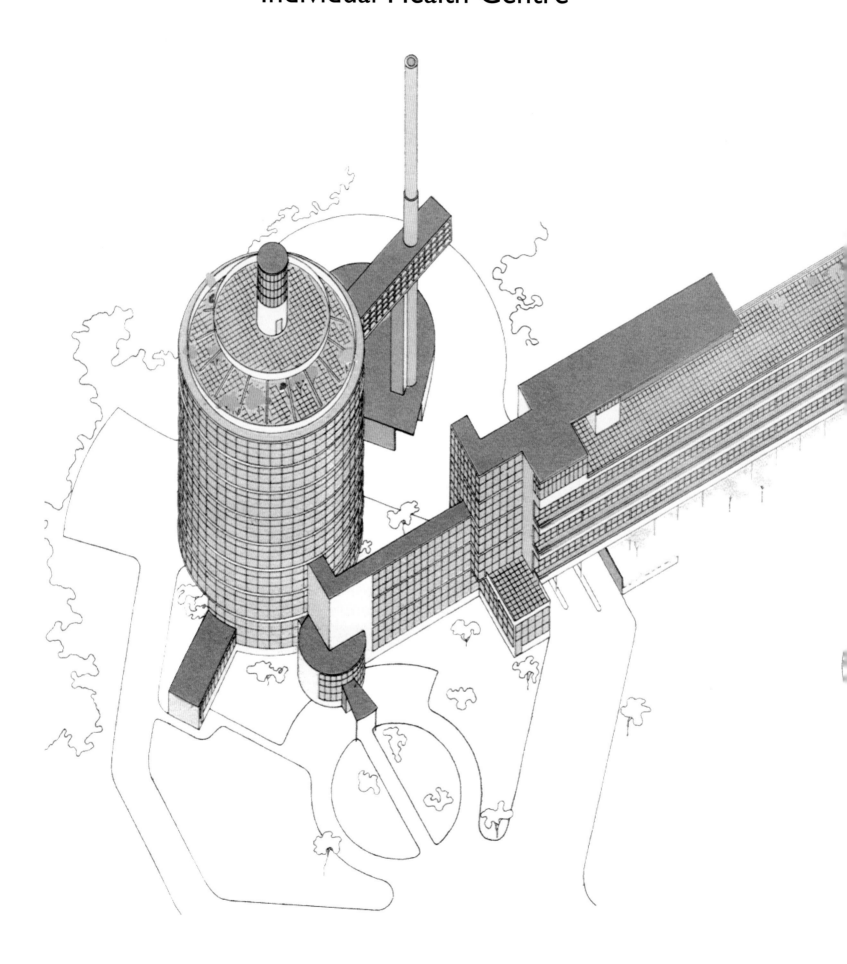

Individual Health Centre, 1935–36
Amyas Connell of Connell Ward and Lucas

The Individual Health Centre, the size of a small hospital, was to be a significant building for a group of doctors and would probably have been sited on the south coast.[7] It is disappointing not to be able to write more about this scheme, but sadly it remained a paper exercise that was very sparsely published. Amyas Connell who was responsible for the design later said, 'It could be suggested that the history of the modern movement in England may have been considerably affected had this project proceeded and been built.'[8] The scale and design would have made it comparable with seminal modern healthcare projects on the continent.

The design

The fact that this was called the 'individual' healthcare centre may have been significant to the brief. The scheme delivered research facilities in an eight-storey glazed circular volume, which suggests that the building was for observation and experimentation in addition to treatment, perhaps along the lines of the tuberculosis preventorium. The drum has a core type plan with floor slabs cantilevering from a central structure. The box-beam spanning to the chimneystack is the animal house, raised high above the ground. Three and five storey rectangular blocks dominate a collection of single-storey elements and are dedicated to in and out patient facilities and supporting administration.[9] Paved roof terraces surmount the main volumes of the buildings, presumably one for the research staff and one for the patients.

Above: J.A. Brinkman and L.C. van der Vlugt, Van Nelle Factory, Rotterdam 1925-31.

Opposite: A colour drawing of the Individual Health Centre. This would have been their most ambitious scheme if it had come to fruition.

The architectural language of the design – its glazed link bridges and light, glassy facades – are reminiscent of the Van Nelle factories of Jan Brinkman and Leendert van der Vlugt of 1925–31 in Rotterdam. The treatment of fenestration is remarkably close to Walter Gropius' seminal Bauhaus building at Dessau of 1925. Connell Ward and Lucas' scheme unsurprisingly was to be constructed in rendered concrete. The axonometric drawing of the scheme is one of a kind, indicating the architects' favoured disposition of colour: yellow to the south-facing planes, red to the west, to the prominent vertical chimney and to the series of pilotis that raise the patients' accommodation from the surrounding landscape. The caption to the published drawing states that even 'the natural green colour of the large grass expanse has been fully considered in the preparation of the colour scheme'.[10]

Sound City, Shepperton

**Sound City film producing and recording
studios, Shepperton, Surrey, 1934–36
Connell Ward and Lucas**

Connell Ward and Lucas had connections with the realist film industry in the 1930s through their friendship with Paul Rotha (1907–84), a headstrong and talented documentary film-maker and theoretician. This acquaintance almost certainly led to Basil Ward becoming the chairman of a committee supervising the creation of a series of architectural films by Gaumont British Films and it is quite likely to be the reason for the practice's commission to masterplan the expansion of Shepperton Studios for Sound City Ltd in 1934.

Sound City was the brainchild of Norman Loudon, a Scottish businessman who had made his money in creating 'flicker' booklets – series of photographs that when flicked together animated the scenes they depicted. Aged only 26, Loudon acquired Littleton Park at Shepperton in 1928 and with additional land purchased in 1931 he founded Sound City Ltd the following year. Just outside the picturesque village of Littleton the site was conveniently near to London whilst offering a wealth of beautiful rural locations for shooting. The large house, built under the direction of Sir Christopher Wren, with orangery and glass houses, was surrounded by a working estate with 60 acres of garden, wood and parkland with lakes and a river running through it.

The film industry in Britain had a strong start in the late nineteenth century but was flagging by the mid-twenties behind America's technical advancements and the formidable output of Hollywood. Buoyed by the 1927 Cinematograph Films Act that had stipulated that a certain percentage of films shown in British cinemas were to be made in Britain, the market for film making in the early 1930s was good. A number of film studios, Shepperton included, sprang up to meet the demand. In his first year Loudon turned out two feature films and three lower quality 'quickies' to feed the quota in a modest studio at Littleton Park. Two years later, with business continuing to go well, he drew up a programme of works to modernise and expand his facilities, a venture backed by four well-known producers who scheduled twenty-six feature films to be made at Shepperton by the end of 1936.

The design
Loudon's aim was to create a centre equipped with the latest technology to rival Elstree and Ealing studios in the setting of an exclusive country club. The architects were to prepare a masterplan to locate suitable accommodation, relaxation and refuelling facilities for personnel and artists as well as six new sound studios. These highly specialist buildings had to be technically capable of supporting a clear set of processes along with good delivery access and logical adjacencies.

Above:
A contemporary image of the studio entrances.
A view from the same angle taken in 2003.

Right: Axonometric drawing of the two studios showing a bridge between the two at high level. This was originally proposed to allow supers to move easily from one unit to the other, it was omitted in construction.

Opposite: The raw concrete finish is apparent on the end elevations of the studio building. The protruding curved staircase gives access to the first floor of the dressing room block beyond.

Loudon wanted 'film stages with dressing rooms etc. at a price sufficiently low to show large profits and yet to give acoustic and filming amenities which would make the stage more attractive than any yet produced.'[11] Connell Ward and Lucas relished such a functional brief. They researched examples of studios by Otto Kohtz in Berlin while developing the optimum layout for the stages and their associated facilities.

The masterplan shows new technical facilities next to the old, just north of the main house with a new access road (now defunct) arriving at the site between two new large and impressive buildings housing four sound studios (two must have been dropped).
These give a total floor area of 67,000 square feet of studio space, with two new stages per unit which can be used separately or opened up together to create the largest throw in the United Kingdom at the time at 265 feet. Tanks are incorporated under the floor for the filming of specialist scenes such as sea battles.

The two-storey dressing room blocks adjacent to each studio are independent structures. They house garages for mobile sound units, camera repair shops, loading rooms, still studios, property stores, paint shops, electricians, stores and art studios on the ground floor and on the first floor 265 feet of stars' dressing rooms, crowd dressing rooms and wardrobe rooms with bathrooms for the vast casts of the swashbuckling movies of the 1930s.

Construction and other technical requirements

The design of such vast shed-like studio spaces demanded a different engineering approach to that with which Connell Ward and Lucas were familiar. No doubt aware of their experience in welded steel construction at Mendelsohn and Chermayeff's De La Warr pavilion, the practice invited structural engineering firm Helsby, Hamann and Samuely to design the steel structure to achieve a 120 foot span. The practice's chief assistant, Colin Penn, introduced Samuely into the project.[12] Fifteen secondary trusses were spaced between four primary ones, the latter spaced at centres of thirty feet, and all connected by angle purlins. The largest member was dictated by transport constraints and a mixture of welded and riveted joints employed. Forty-foot gangways and a grid of steel members were provided for fixing lights and other equipment. The trusses are supported on rolled steel sections that are embedded in most locations in a 4 inch concrete external structural wall.

Fundamental to film production was the control of sound. Since 1929 all new films had sound and the studios had to be acoustically isolated from the outside, from each other and from any mechanical equipment to facilitate recording. To this end, Connell Ward and Lucas designed a completely independent internal acoustic partition to sit inside the external walls,

separated from it with a wide cavity. This was made up of timber with two inches of asbestos sprayed onto a wire mesh with a muslin covering. Where this internal structure is supported it is isolated using cork pads. Acoustic separation of the two stages within one unit is achieved with two skins of soundproof doors with a roofed brick-built fifteen foot passageway between. Mechanical plant is housed in these gaps and special measures adopted to line and deaden the machinery and ducts. All doors to and from the studios are also soundproofed.

Construction was rapid. The tender of contractors Walter Taylor Ltd, who were extremely well versed in Connell Ward and Lucas' specifications by this time and a safe pair of hands, was accepted in October 1935 and by July 1936 the new facilities were complete and immediately put to use. The vast walls of the studio sheds were finished in a concrete more raw than the domestic houses.

Later history

The completion of the stages at Shepperton increased productivity and the studios produced twenty films a year for 1936 and 1937, riding above a nationwide slump in the industry that resulted from a failed attempt to expand into the American market. However, from 1937 business slowed down considerably. During the Second World War the nearby Vickers–Armstrong aircraft factory was hit by German bombers and the studios were requisitioned. The technicians from Shepperton were employed in making decoy airfields, towns and military bases to confuse the German bombers across Britain. In 1945 the studios resumed film making and a year later Loudon retired from the industry and Alexander Korda took up the reins at Shepperton. The Connell Ward and Lucas studios are still in use today.

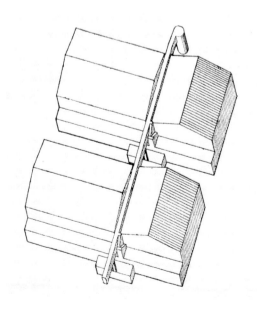

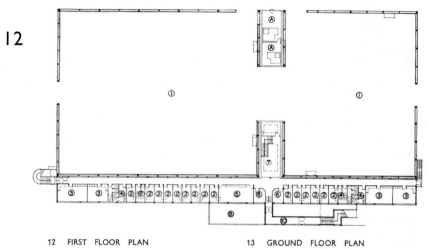

12 FIRST FLOOR PLAN

1 : Studios.
2 : Dressing Rooms.
3 : Ground Rooms.
4 : Lavatories.
5 : Wardrobe.
6 : Pay Office.
7 : Stairs to Studio.
8 : Fan Rooms.
A : Fans.
B : Flat Roof.

13 GROUND FLOOR PLAN

1 : Studios.
2 : Offices.
3 : Tanks.
4 : Lavatories.
5 : Art Room.
6 : Workshops.
7 : Camera.
8 : Sound Van Garage.
9 : Property Store.
11 : Scaffold Store.
12 : Tea Room.
A : Sliding Doors.
B : Ventilation Ducts.
C : Calorifier.

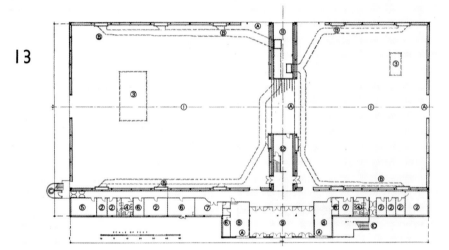

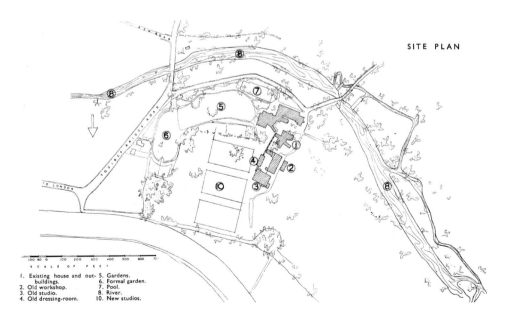

SITE PLAN

1. Existing house and outbuildings.
2. Old workshop.
3. Old studio.
4. Old dressing-room.
5. Gardens.
6. Formal garden.
7. Pool.
8. River.
10. New studios.

176 Other projects

Right:
The south-facing and well glazed two-storey dressing room block.
The shed-like interior of the studio space under construction.

Opposite:
Floor plans.
Site plan showing the outline of three, rather than two studios.

Opposite top right:
A site photograph superimposed with the new studios and the proposed new access road.
The interior of the new studio near completion, c.1936.

Architectural competitions

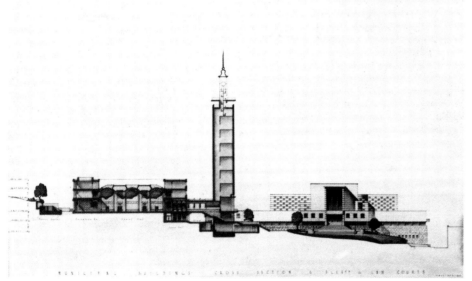

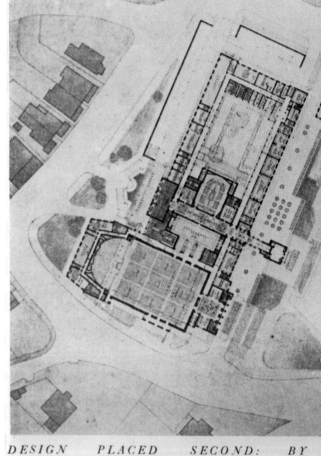

DESIGN PLACED SECOND: BY

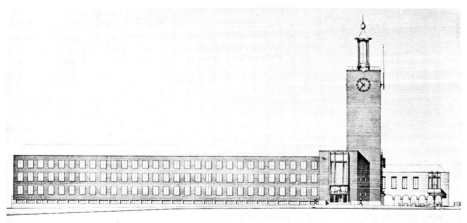

Architectural competitions were not just time fillers for a firm like Connell Ward and Lucas but an absolute necessity to ensure the continuity of the practice between jobs. Their interest in competitions was a serious attempt to get the firm's name before a wider circle of potential clients. The small modern house was all very well but was not financially viable for a practice with three partners. Looking for commissions on a larger scale, they entered competitions for civic buildings and hospitals, drawing out their schemes with energy and precision. In the event nothing came of their efforts.

Wholly committed to the Corbusian cause, though classically trained, they recognised that their design preoccupations would not sway the judges. So what could they do in these rather desperate circumstances? Go the way of Le Corbusier and lose out or pursue the way many an Englishman would go and resort to compromise? They chose compromise. They felt, according to Ward, that they could 'present designs likely to suit the taste of assessors of the day, taste largely of a romantic historicist flavour'. He recalled: 'We determined to enter the field of architectural competitions in order to obtain work. In the event of our winning we would have larger professional scope than hitherto, also we would ease our financial difficulties.'[13] Large areas of brickwork took them downstream to the more modest modernism of the Dutch Dudok school rather than the familiar waters of the Corbusian aesthetic. Georgian window proportions were simply not an option for their contemporary colleagues, although Connell Ward and Lucas attempted to get away with them in a 'modernised' way.

They shared third place in the Hertfordshire County Hall competition in 1935 with Grey Wornum, the architect of the RIBA building. It was a well-considered design that was highly praised in the Architects' Journal. It reported, 'the interest of Connell Ward and Lucas' scheme lay in examining how a firm usually so resolutely progressive would react to tiles and brick and stone facings. They do it superbly.'[14]

For the Newport Civic Buildings competition of 1936 they were awarded second place (for which they received the sum of £500). It provided a hard-earned premium and national notoriety at the same moment. Their scheme was cleverly planned and detailed, a distinct reflection on the state of their struggling practice with time to spare. Executed in a 4H pencil as sharp as a needle and subtly shaded in grey washes with the skill of an experienced watercolourist, Connell produced an immaculate set of drawings, enervated perhaps by their near miss in the Hertford competition. Their carefully considered functional plan put due emphasis on public accessibility and bureaucratic exclusivity.

The design caused a rancorous response from some MARS Group members who demanded Connell Ward

and Lucas explain their inconsistency in submitting what the group described as a 'middle of the road scheme', rather than a modern one. The competition, was won by a T Cecil Howitt, well known as a designer of cinemas from Nottingham. His design had clearly pampered even more to the grandiose desires of the assessors with its relentless compacted Roman symmetry, thrusting phallic monumentalism and doleful, uninspired U-shaped plan. In contrast Connell Ward and Lucas' scheme looked modern. It was brick faced in a Scandinavian way, sober and restrained in its open functional, asymmetrical layout. It was flat roofed with a simple layout of just two major blocks set at right angles on the generous site. However, and this may well have been the rub for the men from MARS, it was dominated by a thin clock shaft of a tower articulating the entrance to the public spaces, an element that caused the dissent expressed by the group.[15] Indeed, it was a submission based on compromise and controversy as Basil Ward later recalled.[16]

For the Newport competition they had submitted a superbly finished product but had naively, perhaps, not reckoned on how deeply offended their colleagues in the group would be to such a submission. The offended members of the group – led principally by Berthold Lubetkin and Maxwell Fry – saw the submission as a deliberate departure from the MARS party line and therefore indefensible. With a distinct touch of antipodean irony (good on ya!) and a distinct lack of British subservience the trio were delightfully defiant. Afterwards, an irritated Morton Shand from the MARS panel was reported to have said, 'They refused to take it seriously. Connell was jocular'.[17]

The final competition entry by the practice, in the year that the war began, was for St George's Hospital with Gabriel Guevrekian. Fifty designs were submitted for a hospital design on a site just a stone's throw from the offices of Connell Ward and Lucas on Grosvenor Place. WH Watkins and partners submitted the winning design. There were no daring solutions to the problem posed by locating a hospital on this prominent piece of land at Hyde Park Corner, and the winner was a traditional, classical scheme satisfying the pragmatic requirements of ward layouts and other education facilities. Connell Ward and Lucas' scheme, no. 35, was unplaced and a diagram of it in the Architects' Journal shows a long main facade on Knightsbridge with an axial route north/south and symmetrical wings either side. A surprisingly classical approach was also taken by Erich Mendelsohn and Hannes Schreiner (if it is properly attributed). It suggests that this approach was a prerequisite for the scheme. In a climate of uncertainty, one can assume that both practices were extremely keen to get the work.

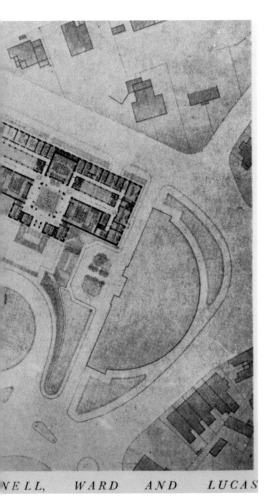

NELL, WARD AND LUCAS

Above:
Site plan of the Newport Civic Buildings.

Opposite:
Elevation of the competition scheme for Newport Civic Buildings.
A section through the proposed Newport Civic Buildings.
Entrance elevation of the Hertfordshire County Hall competition design.

Later years of Connell, Ward and Lucas

Connell Ward and Lucas ceased trading, like many other architectural firms, at the outbreak of war in 1939. They never reconvened. The partners went their separate ways carving out very different and distinctive careers for themselves and eventually losing touch for many years. Each pursued an individual career.

It was in March 1976 that they were briefly reunited at the RIBA in London when they came together in a forum on their work. The forum brought together, nearly forty years after the closure of the practice, Amyas Connell from East Africa, where he had set up Triad Architects in Nairobi, Basil Ward from private practice in the Lake District and visiting lecturer at the Manchester Polytechnic and Research Fellow at the Visual Arts Centre at Lancaster University, and the reclusive Colin Lucas from retirement in Highgate where he painted.

The RIBA forum was an odd occasion. The three guns were firing in different directions. It was obvious too that, apart from Basil Ward, the historian manqué of the trio, they had largely forgotten the detail of what they had done and accomplished in the 1930s. They were also somewhat taken aback that anyone should be interested in it and that it had any relevance for new generations.

Their post-war careers indicate what had become their new preoccupations. Of the three it had been Basil Ward who had kept the lamp burning on the CWL work of the thirties. Basil, ever the mandarin, acted as a modernist apologist, an amanuensis and cultural ambassador for the late firm. He went to New Zealand as a kind of visiting guru, introducing their work to new generations of architecture students and celebrating his own notoriety. Connell was to continue his career away from England, as he claimed that 'the bureaucratic yoke' had become too strong. Lucas joined the housing division of the LCC's housing department, working quietly to develop the use of concrete on housing estates while cultivating his private spiritual interests.

Opposite: Detail of the perforated sun screen wall of the Crown Law Building.

Amyas Connell

For a short period at the outbreak of the war Connell continued to practise as an independent architect working on a competition entry for the new Anglican cathedral at Auckland, New Zealand with Thornley Dyer. Their design was placed second. There were also designs for houses at West Winterslow and Papworth. However, for most of the wartime years Connell served firstly in the British Army as a garrison engineer in the Royal Engineers and then, when he refused to shave off his beard and was told to leave the service, he worked from 1943–45 as an assistant architect to the Ministry of Works as a war damage assessor.

With war over Connell set up a small practice and entered the competitions for the Crystal Palace (receiving a special commendation with colleagues George Simonek and Linden C Cooper) and the Liverpool metropolitan cathedral, before being tempted to move to East Africa in 1947.[1]

This fortuitous move to Africa was precipitated by a chance meeting at the London Arts Club with Mr Ernie Hitchcock (later Sir Eldread Hitchcock), chairman of the Tanganyika Sisal Growers Association, who was at that time seeking an architect to plan a new sisal estate in Tanga, Tanganyika (now Tanzania).[2] Tanga was a neat port town to the north of the country and a few miles south of Mombasa. Sisal hemp production was introduced to the area in what was German East Africa in 1893 by Dr Richard Hindorf, an agronomist who had been searching for a suitable crop for the dry and hot conditions on the coastal plains of East Africa.[3]

For Ernie Hitchcock Connell designed and built a sisal farm and a small village community a few miles outside Tanga at Kanga, and a fine cinema, the Novelty Talkies, in the old town – a structure that has adapted well to a more recent conversion into a computer training college. Additionally a number of houses were designed for executives connected to the sisal company, for Barclays Bank officials and other clients. Most have been altered.

Quite by coincidence Connell had begun his work in East Africa a decade or so after the arrival there of one of Germany's pioneer modern movement architects – the former Frankfurt City Architect and CIAM vice president Dr Ernst May.[4] After a number of years in the USSR, May had decided not to return to Hitler's Germany but to settle in Tanganyika, initially as a farmer in 1934. He soon reverted to architecture and his first African project was the Murray House in Arusha in 1936. He then opened an office in Nairobi, Kenya in 1937 but was interned locally during the early war years by the British.

After falling out with Hitchcock in the early 1950s, Connell moved on to Nairobi at the invitation of his former colleague and friend Thornley Dyer. Dyer was then the British government's architect and the invitation to Connell was initially for him to assist in the design of the new legislative assembly buildings that were to become the new Kenyan parliament buildings after the country's independence in 1963. Connell designed the buildings in two stages.

Through his reputation as a significant architect in Britain in the 1930s and through his ongoing work in East Africa, Connell exerted a considerable influence on the younger generation of local architects working there. Many of them had come from the United Kingdom keen to perpetuate the modernist principles that they had learned in the British architecture schools, such as the Architectural Association and the Regent Street Polytechnic (now the University of Westminster). Connell was elected president of the East African Architects Association in 1954–55. He was a long-term East African Architects Association council member and his work for Triad was widely published in their journal.

The most architecturally interesting building designed by Connell in Nairobi was undoubtedly the hospital he built for the local Ismaili community: the HH Aga Khan Platinum Jubilee Hospital (later called the Aga Khan Jubilee Memorial Hospital), 1956–62. It received an

Opposite: Amyas Connell out fishing!

Right:
Connell's new buildings - hospital, shops and administrative offices - for Kanga village in Tanganyika (now Tanzania) for Bird & Co., 1947.
Kanga village mosque, also designed by Connell for Bird & Co. in 1947.
Manager's House, Raskajone, Tanga for African Mercantile Co. Ltd., 1950.

RIBA bronze medal and was featured in the cover of the *RIBA Journal*. This was an unusual but highly appropriate choice of a building so far from London. It was probably the most Corbusier-influenced building Connell ever designed and used the route promenade idea in an open link between the wards and the operating theatres. The routes traverse the site as they weave through the clearly defined functional elements. This interesting building has great character and also adopts a version of Le Corbusier's brise soleil (or in this case 'light shelves') for its sun-facing facades. It resolved the numerous circulation routes within the hospital complex with a series of ramps, walkways, stairs and lifts articulated in a manner that resembles Le Corbusier's Armée du Salut building in Paris.

The success of the whole complex of buildings for the Aga Khan hospital (including the later nurses' home extension) rests largely on the clarity that emerges from this combination of closed and open routes, the plant-filled courtyards and the open airy, sunny character.

Originally the hospital was situated on an open site (no longer so, alas) adjacent to the fine, tall nurses' home with its prominent spiralling concrete external staircase (echoing Le Corbusier at Pessac) and some of the smaller-scale external stairs incorporated in houses that Connell Ward and Lucas had designed in their earlier years. The plan and the layout echoed that of Kent House, although the nurses' home far exceeds in scope and scale anything the practice did in the 1930s. It has more recently suffered from unsympathetic alterations.

A further scheme, the Law Courts for the new Kenya government, signalled a departure from the Corbusian aesthetic, moving much more towards the kind of architecture advocated for tropical climates by Maxwell Fry and Jane Drew. Connell recognised the value of the elevational treatment pursued in traditional cultures, notably the decorative screen walls from Persia and India. These seemed to Connell more suitable examples related to the local climatic conditions of East Africa than Le Corbusier's brises soleils.

For Connell the parliament building was a difficult design problem with the administrators demanding a miniaturised version of the gothic Palace of Westminster to be set in the centre of the city of Nairobi. His attempts to retain a modern idiom were somewhat undermined by a pastiche of the Big Ben tower. There is a close relationship between his final scheme and the design he had submitted for the Newport Civic Centre competition in the mid-thirties (see pags 178-79).

Connell was able to reconcile his own Corbusian influence and rational thinking with a gradual acceptance of local conditions. He saw a transfer of his innovative ideas to a new kind of tropical modern architecture.

One or two of Commell's projects achieve a high standard innovative design, as those at Amersham, Grayswood and Rickmansworth had done. Indeed, the East African buildings were far more complex than anything he or his partners had carried out in Britain in the 1930s. They heralded the beginnings of a new East African modern architecture.

Later additions to the parliament buildings, including the new assembly chamber, again reverted to Connell's interest in the architecture of Le Corbusier. A few years later, after the completion of the first stage of the parliament buildings and when designing the new Crown Law Offices (1960), Connell began to question his commitment to Le Corbusier. As he became better acquainted with the local climatic conditions and building traditions, he carefully examined previous examples of colonial architecture. For his 'light shelves' he drew not so much on the international modern architectural clichés but decorative screens based on Timurid and Moghul examples, particularly from the Taj Mahal and the screens of the Itmad-ud-Daula tomb in Agra.

In this way he also attempted through his architecture to express the mixed ethnic and cultural nature of East African life. In a sense he pursued the idea of a more regional modern architecture, seeking an authentic African architecture without recourse to mindless vernacularism or tribal pastiche or for that matter a reiterative functionalism.

With these buildings Connell changed his commitment to modern architecture. In a sense he became a 'post-modernist', taking motifs from historical and vernacular examples which appeared to be relevant to the tropical region in which he was working. He also attempted to express the mixed cultural nature of East African life. Having lived through the terrible Mau-Mau years, he understood and recognised – probably as well as any other local architect – the challenge that had emerged among Africans to seek an independent identity and to develop a new and relevant architecture appropriate to the burgeoning political situation under President Kenyatta. It would have been fairly easy for an architect to pick up ideas in planning and architectural form-making from the various vernacular tribal buildings in rural areas. But Connell eschewed this also. It seemed to him an inappropriate source for a fast-expanding urban area like Nairobi. It probably appeared architecturally inadequate as well. It was also alien to the traditions in which he believed. It was unknown in its application. Like other colonials he looked to those other traditions that had matured in tropical or semi-tropical climates: to Moorish Spain and Moghul India in particular. His own house and studio, Mile Seven in Limuru, was designed in a kind of Spanish gothic or Spanish Islamic style, which he used to cloak the functional interiors and his innovatory bedroom which incorporated a famous sliding wall – it

Opposite: The Nurses Home at the Aga Khan Hospital, with its Corbusian inspired fire escape stairs.

Right: The circulation spaces of the Aga Khan hospital.

Opposite:
View of the 'Big Ben' tower of the Parliament Buildings, Nairobi, Connell designed with H Thornley Dyer.

Right:
View of Parliament Buildings, first stage.
View of Parliament Buildings, second stage.
External circulation at the Parliament Buildings.

came down to separate the two parts of the marital bed – and the splendidly spatial mono-pitched living room. This latter device – probably borrowed from Marcel Breuer, if not directly from Le Corbusier – was also used by both Connell and May for their farmers' houses built in the 1950s.[5]

Ernst May, however, had not stayed long enough to mature his own ideas in this area. He left Nairobi at the end of 1952 – having lasted in East Africa for two decades – the year that the social and political unrest created by the Mau-Mau began. A few of his later buildings were completed after he left for Germany, all of them in a 'Modern Style'. His firm, Dr Ernst May and Partners, still operates from its Mombasa offices, but now in the charge of the British architect Tom McKenzie.

But Connell stayed and reflected more on the role of decoration and ornament in contemporary African architecture. He renewed his interest in using the decorative tradition of India for inspiration for the next stage of his career and developed patterned screen

Connell's magnificent pen drawing of the completed Parliament Building in Nairobi.

walls for the Dutch ambassador's house in Muthaiga (circa 1970). To understand his position in relation to the developing ideas for a decorated architecture we must return to the letter he wrote to his young assistant in December 1969. In it, as mentioned earlier, he eulogised Le Corbusier but went on to deplore 'the new Brutalist stuff … in which all sense of architecture has been lost', in which 'the emotional content has been drained away by an eclectic intellectualism'.[6] He clearly saw this lack of emotion as being a direct result of architecture having lost sight of individual human need, a fault which he laid at Le Corbusier's feet. Quite understandably, Connell felt that his helpful remarks to his younger assistant showed that Le Corbusier had attempted to understand this aspect of architecture but had failed: 'Although he postulated the human need as one of his prime movers, his grasp has proved ephemeral.'[7] But more pertinently, perhaps, Connell too took the argument in a different direction, out of the area of a priori human needs and to the whole new question of how to deal with ornament in relation to modern architecture. According to Connell, Le Corbusier 'lacked an understanding of the meaning of ornament. In his middle age the need for the adornment of structure led him to trifle with painting in a confused Léger mannerism'. Connell was to surmise: 'Had he realised that all traditional ornament was the atavistic expression of man's philosophic and theologic belief in his early period, his work might have been great.'

In the mid-seventies Connell returned to Britain for medical reasons and was eventually to die in London in 1980. He took up a designer's desk to work in the Triad office in Westminster with his sons James and Graham and among the last buildings he designed was a large villa for Sayed Hamr Bin Hamood in Oman, 1976-7, and an 'eco' house in Hemel Hempstead for a relative of his first client Sir Bernard Ashmole. This project was turned down by the local planners until Amyas, in one of his characteristically charming telephone calls, persuaded them they really were vetting a design by the architect for High and Over on Amersham Hill. He was told the decision was not final and would be reversed.

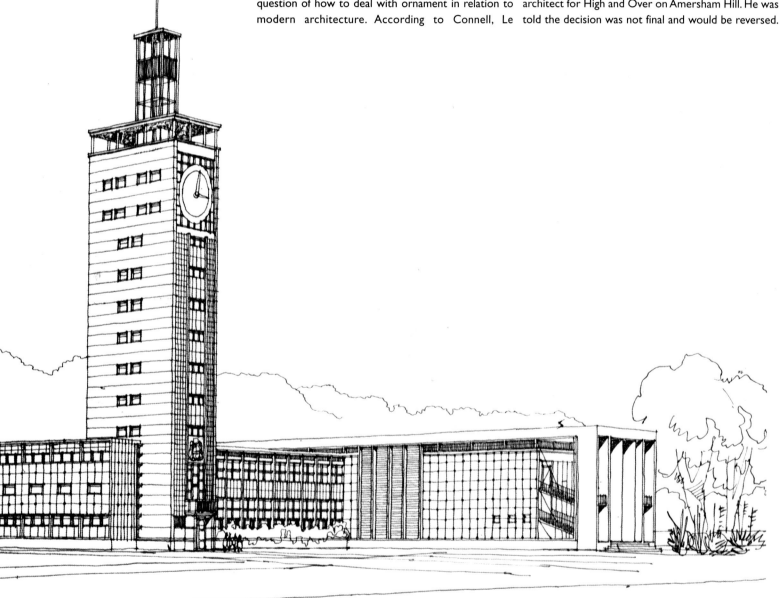

Above and opposite:
The main entrance of the Cyclotron building,
Hammersmith Hospital by Basil Ward when with Ramsey,
Murray and White.

Below:
Proposed development of Hammersmith Hospital.

Basil Ward

Basil Ward moved in very different circles in the post-war period to the colonial world of Amyas Connell. He enjoyed the political arena, teaching and telling. He loved England, but for a short and memorable moment in 1973 he was lauded as a pioneer of modern movement architecture in his home country of New Zealand.

After service in the Royal Navy, he worked on a number of projects before becoming a partner in Ramsey, Murray, White and Ward (made up largely of New Zealanders), which was succeeded by Murray Ward and partners with offices in Heddon Street. Little is known in detail of his own architectural work with the London practice, with the exception of the major projects for Hammersmith Hospital which included the metabolic research unit and the linear accelerator and cyclotron building, which he described at length in *Ark*, the student journal of the Royal College of Art in 1952. He was also the partner in charge of the new metallurgy laboratories for the University of Oxford and the test facilities building for Rolls Royce in Derby.

Two more personal projects included a pavilion for England's oldest cricket club at East Molesey in Surrey of 1955, where he took up a vernacular idiom (just as Connell had done in East Africa around the same time) with an elegant but essentially traditional timber framed building with sidings and a traditional veranda front. In the early sixties Ward was, not surprisingly, asked to make some alterations to Temple Gardens, the house he had designed at Moor Park in 1936. What is surprising was the ruthlessness he displayed in removing the original open roof terrace with its hovering canopy and replacing it by an extra bedroom. Plastic double-glazing units were also inserted into existing openings, but it is unclear whether Ward had any involvement or whether the new owners had been seduced by double-glazing sales people. Anyway it was not an improvement for the listed building.

Above:
Laboratory interiors at Hammersmith Hospital.

Right
Sketch of new entrance to Hammersmith Hospital.

As the philosopher-architect and the artist of the original CWL trio, Ward considerably enhanced his own reputation in Britain through his election as the first Lethaby Professor of Architecture at the Royal College of Art, beginning his stint of three years in 1953. During his tenure he gave a series of inspiring talks on WR Lethaby and his educational ideas and organised a series of lectures for the college, drawing on an impressive list of friends and colleagues in the profession. He also introduced a new (1957) edition of Lethaby's book *Form in Civilisation*, originally published in 1922.

Ward had a great regard for Edwin Lutyens and particularly for his work in India, which he spoke of in lectures that often also referred to the admiration he had for Dr Joan Evans' work on gothic art and aesthetic theory.

While working on the Provincial Insurance building in Kendal, Ward became attracted to life in the English Lake District and eventually settled there with his wife Beatrix in a house on a prominent estuary site near Ambleside. From there he began a second career in education and was welcomed as a much valued and revered teacher in the north west, firstly at Manchester Polytechnic (now the Manchester Metropolitan University), where for a while he took over as head of school. In 1967 he became a part-time arts lecturer at the University of Lancaster which had been designed by Shepheard Epstein and Hunter. There he helped establish the short-lived visual arts centre which was run by his friend and colleague the architectural historian Dr Geoffrey Beard. He was a Research Fellow at the centre from 1974.

During this time Basil Ward was determined to keep alive the importance and memory of the CWL interwar work through lectures and articles, often remaking in slide form original pictures from his collection of contemporary photographs, copies of some of which were given to Lancaster University.

Basil Ward's last major public appearance and talk was appropriately given at the RIBA, where he had taken on the chairmanship of the RIBA Drawings Collection for the council. The night was auspicious. The audience was enthusiastic. It was the night of the aforementioned RIBA forum in 1976 when Connell, Ward and Lucas all took part. Clearly moving towards the twilight of their individual careers and slightly forgetful of what they had achieved together, they were seen as come-back kids. Their pioneering works of the thirties was given a new impetus, but they did not appear as innovative and imaginative designers responsible for the best houses in the great decade of English modernism but as a trio of dedicated architects who unselfconsciously created their own piece of architectural history. Basil Ward, whose speech reflected his scholarly and professional knowledge of the trio's work, did more than the other two to establish Connell Ward and Lucas' postwar reputation.

Above:
The Provincial Insurance Company building proposal at Kendal.
The Rolls Royce test facilities building, Derby.

Above: Roehampton Estate Alton West Estate headed up
by Colin Lucas in the Housing Division of the LCC.

Right: Dione Lucas outside her restaurant on 117 East 60th
Street, New York, c.1943.

Colin Lucas

Lucas is in many ways the most enigmatic of the trio. He made a significant impression on the architectural scene in Britain during his later career and was instrumental in a number of major modern housing projects at the London County Council (LCC), and yet his voice is absent from the architectural press. Lucas had little interest in public debate, self-publicity and approval from his peers. He advocated earning a living with your left hand and dedicated time to his spiritual development and to his other interests: sailing, skiing, travelling, music, science, painting and writing poetry.

When pressed by his colleagues at the LCC, he would remember Basil Ward and Amyas Connell with respect, admiring their input into modern architecture between the wars more than his own. Roy Stout, his colleague at the LCC, described him as 'an unusual architectural talent, reticent and retiring', and that although he was 'a shy man', he was a man 'with ideas and a great underlying determination'.[8] Lucas is intriguing because of the seeming contradiction between the sensitive, retiring, spiritual teacher and his strong monolithic architectural output which was generated by an unerring commitment to concrete and the modern engineered solution. It is tempting to examine the separated spiritual and architectural strands of his life for any confluence, but just as art and mathematics are so often seen to be mutually exclusive, their age-old marriage is undeniable.

Lucas' contribution to the war effort was to bring his expertise in reinforced concrete construction to bear on the development of protective and defensive structures at the British Research Station at Princes Risborough. He based himself with his parents at Noah's House and commuted the short distance daily by motorbike. His wife Dione, pregnant with their second son Peter, left England for Canada at the outset of the war with seven-year-old Mark and the three sons of Ursula Walford (the client of 66 Frognal). She stayed initially in Ottawa with Colin Lucas' aunt and uncle, Sir Gerald and Margaret Campbell.[9]

When peace returned, Lucas travelled to reunite with his family, now in Manhattan where his wife was establishing herself as a chef and teacher. He undertook some architectural advisory work with the British Council while she ran the Egg Basket restaurant at Bloomingdale's and set up her own restaurant and cooking school on Upper East Side. In 1947 she published the *Cordon Bleu Cook Book* and in 1948 she became the first female featured on a television cookery programme, 'To the Queen's Taste', an experience that was to launch her successful career in broadcasting. Colin Lucas was less inspired by the architectural opportunities in America and the couple decided to separate at the end of the 1940s when he moved back to settle in England.

Lucas returned to a tough climate in England, but one with prolific architectural opportunities afforded by the destruction of both building fabric and pre-war attitudes. Government had advanced an interventionist strategy, unrecognisable from the thirties, supporting nationwide building programmes to reconstruct the built and social fabric of Britain. Two and a half thousand schools were to be built in a decade and the New Towns Act of 1946 called for ten towns on the model of Letchworth Garden City with substantial populations ranging from 20,000 to 70,000. Materials were scarce and architectural solutions had to be innovative.

Leslie Martin helped Lucas to join the development section of the LCC and he became one of the first members of the newly formed housing division of the architects' department. The work gave Lucas the perfect opportunity to bring to fruition the ideals of his pre-war practice and to test concrete as the construction technique to deliver social housing on a large scale. In Henry-Russell Hitchcock's view in 1958, the best of the mid-century urbanism projects, 'greater than the new towns', were the LCC housing estates at Loughborough Road, Ackroydon and Roehampton, for which the benchmark had been Westminster Council's Churchill Gardens housing scheme by Powell and Moya.[10] Colin Lucas was involved with two of the three LCC schemes that Hitchcock praised so highly.

Lucas' first project was to develop housing on sites at Princes Way and Wimbledon Park Side for the Ackroydon Estate under Robert Matthew, Leslie Martin and Michael Powell. The site in Wimbledon incorporated the grounds of four Victorian and Edwardian properties, including some landscaping thought to have been laid out by Paxton. There was an intention from the outset to preserve the open nature of the site and the scheme was developed as a series of housing blocks of differing sizes scattered amongst the five hundred or so mature trees that peppered the site.

The tallest of these were four T-shaped blocks designed for the highest ground. Standing at around one hundred feet they contained eleven storeys of up to three flats per floor accessed from stairs in the centre. The central spaces were naturally lit and ventilated and the T shape, an economic compromise from earlier star-shaped proposals, still allowed good views and daylighting to each of the flats. These were constructed using reinforced concrete frames with in-situ concrete roofs and floors. Externally, flank walls were finished in brick and spandrel walls in reinforced concrete. More traditional load-bearing masonry construction was reserved for the lower housing blocks, offsetting the higher cost of the tall blocks. These were a mixture of two, three, four and five-storey buildings containing maisonettes, some with staircase and some with balcony access

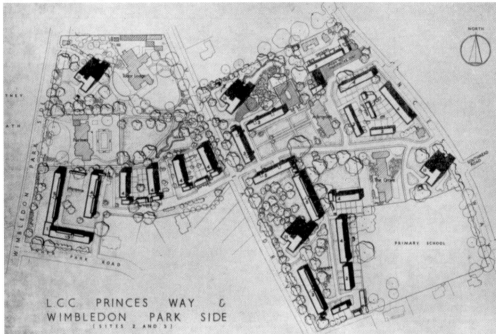

L.C.C. PRINCES WAY &
WIMBLEDON PARK SIDE
(SITES 2 AND 3)

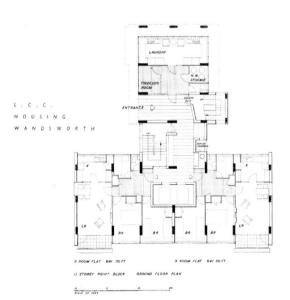

L.C.C.
HOUSING
WANDSWORTH

Planning approval for the Ackroydon scheme was given by the end of 1950 and the following year Lucas was invited to head up one of the teams designing the Roehampton Estate. For Lucas this was a seminal job: 'I was in charge of that from the very beginning to the very end', he said, '... I think I learnt more about architecture and how to run jobs with that than in the rest of my career.'[11] His team included John Partridge, Bill Howell (who worked mainly on the slab blocks), John Killick and Stanley Amis (who worked mainly on the point blocks). The four set up in practice together as Howell Killick Partridge and Amis at the end of the job in 1959.

One hundred acres of undulating mature landscape adjoining Richmond Park to the south-west of the village of Roehampton was earmarked for the housing estate and the project was split into two areas – Alton East and Alton West. Each contained a number of different high and low-rise blocks in clusters of accommodation. Alton West was completed in 1959, a little after Alton East. The project was not without its headaches, with cladding condemned by the district surveyor and large claims from the contractors.

The appropriateness of modern architecture and, by association, concrete for housing projects was the subject of much discussion in the early 1950s and a heated debate in the LCC reached a crescendo in the housing division over the Roehampton project. Put simply, the use of a 'New Humanism', named as such by the editorial of the Architectural Review and typified by the shallow pitches and brick construction of Sweden's welfare state, was advocated as a friendlier, softer architecture than the more brutal offerings of those following the modernist canon.[12] John Partridge, Lucas' colleague at the LCC, remembered that the housing division 'became locked in a heated debate between the followers of Le Corbusier and Mies and the followers of the Scandinavian school of humanist housing architects'.[13] The former in the Alton West camp, the latter in the Alton East team. He remembers that Lucas kept quiet on the subject, 'aloof in the total certainty that there was no debate for there was no architecture in Scandinavia of the relevance and stature of that of Le Corbusier and in consequence he felt there was no need for argument.'[14]

Another interpretation of this silence is that Lucas still believed what he had set down in his statement for Unit One in 1934 and was reluctant to get drawn into arguments on style or aesthetic. This is backed up by a statement from Lucas in this post-war period, quoted by his son:

My work as an architect was originally – and is still – inspired by a feeling for the material one is using, and particularly its structural possibilities. This, combined with the three-dimensional disposition

of space dictated by the client's requirements, combines to give the opportunity for the expression of certain proportions in the structure as a whole. Thus materials, space and proportion are the three main design elements. Whether the building is doomed to be reminiscent of this or that period or style is irrelevant. Ideally it should have no style other than its own.[15]

Lucas is still maintaining that architectural language is the outcome of a simple, unimpassioned, functional equation.

The architectural merits of the Roehampton Estate have been widely acknowledged and it was awarded a RIBA bronze medal in 1959. Lucas' personal achievement was rewarded with an OBE in 1972. It was received without celebration. As his son Mark Lucas recalls, his family used to joke with him that his awards were kept in the back of his drawer at work with his peppermint creams. This came, Mark Lucas says, from his background in 'a family disinterest in institutionalised dogma, fuss and formality'.[16]

Socially, such high-rise projects have had a less favourable legacy. When asked to comment on this subject by James Dunnett shortly before his death, Lucas said:

> I think it was definitely one of the solutions. I feel very disappointed by what has happened afterwards, going back to little almost neo-Georgian houses – a complete throwback … high rise housing was not a mistake. It all goes back to Gropius' idea of developing high buildings in a park landscape … but you need the other too, not just high-rise.[17]

Lucas' career at the LCC and latterly the GLC (from 1965) continued until he retired in 1978. He did not accept promotion after Roehampton, preferring to stay more closely involved with guiding teams 'at the 6B pencil stage' and having opportunities to spend time on site. John Partridge recalled that 'he had around him changing groups of younger architects all of whom he infused with great respect and confidence'.[18] His later projects included the Ferrier Estate, Kidbrooke, south east London, a scheme for 2,000 homes built on the site of an obsolete military store using prefabricating techniques. This estate has not attracted favourable appraisals architecturally or socially and at the time of writing is being completely redeveloped.

Lucas remarried in May 1952 to his cousin Pamela Campbell (1912–94). She was a textile designer and screen printer and had worked with him in the 1930s designing furnishings for Dione's restaurant. They lived in a studio in St John's Wood which was the former home of painter Dame Laura Knight. Visitors remember a gentle, studious atmosphere in a home furnished with unostentatious pieces of modern furniture.[19]

From the philosophical teachings of Ouspensky, studied by his mother, and to a lesser degree those of Gurdjieff, in whom Dione Lucas, his brother Tony and also Amyas Connell were interested, Lucas developed a very particular understanding of consciousness, space, time and cosmology which he shared with his second wife and taught to others.[20] In the 1960s he had a breakthrough in his spiritual development when he learnt the meditation methods taught by Maharishi Hahesh Yogi. These helped him to tap into an inner creative energy he had always believed to be there but that he had only been able to access sporadically.[21] He wrote of this elusive core:

> Everything one wants is there, deep inside one. All the energy one so badly needs, all the happiness and sense of fulfilment one hopes to get, all the beauty and the loveliness one finds in Nature. It is all there now, just exactly where one is at this moment – there is no need to go anywhere. But one has to dive very deep to find it.[22]

More prolific in his writing on this subject than on architecture, Lucas left a number of papers written for the informal meditation and discussion groups which he ran from the time he was at the LCC. Notes from talks he gave in 1982 go into detail about a specific and complex classification of the world, where all things, tangible and intangible form part of a spectrum of 'physical, subtle and causal parts', each assigned a material value. A much closer study of this belief system is necessary to begin to explain it, but a basic link between Lucas' spiritual and architectural concerns is evident even to those of us without this insight. His structured understanding of the universe is allied with the natural, ancient and mathematically derived order of the golden section that he used intuitively from his architectural schooling in his design. The golden section has been understood over the centuries to generate the most aesthetically pleasing relationships based in the Fibonacci sequence. Mark Lucas explains that this 'tied in with Colin's long-term enquiry into advanced maths, musical scales and the colour spectrum. Growing sunflowers for their left and right hand spiral count, which tends to 1.618, was a family pastime'.[23]

And it is to his family that we return time and again with Lucas; they were a major source of his inspiration and his strength. The innovations of his father and the creativity of his mother, coupled with a strong spiritual interest, sowed all the seeds which he spent his life nurturing. It is with affection and respect that his colleagues and family remember him.

Above: Colin Lucas photographed in front of the Roehampton Estate in the 1950s by Peter Lucas.

Opposite:
Site model of the Ackroydon estate, Wimbledon.
Site plan showing the disposition of housing blocks.
Typical plan of a point block.
Perspective drawing of the proposed point blocks.

References

Early years of Connell, Ward and Lucas, pages 8-17

1. Ward, Basil, 'Connell Ward and Lucas' in *Planning and Architecture: Essays presented to Arthur Korn by the Architectural Association*, London, 1967, pp.73-89.

2. Shaw, Peter, *Louis Hay Architect*, New Zealand, 1998.

3. ibid., p.74.

4. Fearn, Stanley, *The Aesthetic Use of Building Materials*, NZIA Journal, November 1926, p.114.

5. ibid.

6. ibid., and reported in *N.Z. Building Progress*, September 1921.

7. Modernist, Genius in Architecture Two talented New Zealanders, *New Zealand Freelance*, 18 September 1935.

8. ibid., p.74.

9. Ward, Basil, *AAJ*, 1956-7, p.209.

10. ibid., p.78.

11. Ward, Basil, speech at the RIBA, 2 March 1976.

12. Ward, Basil, interview with Dennis Sharp for Open University, 3 January 1973.

13. Ward, Basil, 'Connell, Ward and Lucas', op.cit., p.78.

14. Ward, Basil, interview with Dennis Sharp for Open University, 3 January 1973.

15. Ward, Basil, 'Connell, Ward and Lucas', op.cit., p.78.

16. ibid.

17. The Henry Jarvis scholarship was first won by Louis de Soissons in 1913.

18. At the end of the course, the scholars were exempted from the RIBA examinations.

19. Students had to pay their own way as well as an examination fee.

20. Le Corbusier, *Towards a New Architecture*, translated by Frederick Etchells, published by Rodker, London 1927 (1923)

21. Barbara Hepworth had won a one year travelling scholarship in 1923 to Italy where she met and married John Skeaping in 1925. They stayed in Italy and spent some time studying the technique of marble carving under an Italian master-carver. They returned to England late in 1926, six months earlier than planned due to Skeaping's ill health.

22. Campbell, Louise, 'The Rome Prize and early Twentieth Century British Architecture', *Journal of the Society of Architectural Historians of Great Britain*, Vol. 32, 1989.

23. Ward, Basil, speech at the RIBA, 2 March 1976.

24. *Express and News*, 'How outcast Connell became a legend', 11 January 1974.

25. Ashmole, Bernard, *Bernard Ashmole 1894–1988 An Autobiography*, Kurtz, Donna (ed.), Oxbow Books, 1994, p.51.

26. Lucas, Colin, letter to John Allan, 1 December 1971.

27. Dunnett, James, 'A Modern Briton', interview with Colin Lucas, *AJ*, 9 May 1984, p.28.

28. Casson, Hugh, 'Kit Nicholson' in *The Nicholsons: A story of four people and their designs*, York City Art Gallery, 1988, p.52.

29. Morrissey, Martin, 'Colin Lucas – Architect: A British modernist in the Nineteen Thirties', University of London, *Science in Architecture*, September 1995, p.2.

30. Worthington-Williams, Michael, 'Unorthodox Evolution', *The Automobile*, March 1997, Vol.15, no.1, pp.76-80. Apparently the first public appearance of a valveless car was in 1907 at Olympia.

31. de Syllas, Justin, in conversation with Martin Morrissey; see, Morrissey, Martin, 'Colin Lucas – Architect: A British modernist in the Nineteen Thirties', University of London, *Science in Architecture*, September 1995, p.2.

32. Dunnett, James, 'A Modern Briton', interview with Colin Lucas, *AJ*, 9 May 1984, p.28.

33. Casson, Hugh, 'Kit Nicholson' in *The Nicholsons: A story of four people and their designs*, York City Art Gallery, 1988, p.52.

34. Anthony Jackson in *The Politics of Architecture* (London, 1970) recognises leaps of progress between the first and the second, the Thurso house, and laments that his teaching post at the Polytechnic of Central London prevented him going further in the profession.

35. Lucas would have been aware of Raymond McGrath's extensive 'modern' rebuilding and refurbishment job for Mansfield Forbes at his Victorian house, Finella (1927). McGrath was an Australian who had graduated from Sydney in 1926

and came on a travelling scholarship to Cambridge where he became the first research student in architecture.

36. McGrath, Wells Coates and Serge Chermayeff met Valentine Goldsmith, who, as one of the directors of the BBC, later sought them to design a number of interiors at the new BBC premises. Helene Lipstadt has observed that class and school ties facilitated the construction of modern buildings to a large extent, as did the university degree course which had become the normal form of architectural training by the 1930s. By the end of the 1930s such relationships underpinned the patronage of modern architecture in Britain, the prerogative of a special breed of radicals and outsiders, even liberal professionals and upper classes and eventually the aristocracy.

Architecture of the Devil's Decade, pages 18-31

1. Cassou, Jean, Emile Langui, Nikolaus Pevsner, *Sources of Modern Art*, Thames and Hudson, London, 1962. i.e., The reappraisal of technique using reinforced concrete and the reappraisal of the social function of architecture.

2. Smithson, Peter, *AA Journal*, December 1956.

3. Korn, Arthur, 'Connell Ward & Lucas', *AA Journal*, November 1956, p.94.

4. Hitchcock, H-R, 'The acclimatisation of modern architecture in different countries', AA Journal, June/July 1946, p.4.

5. *Modern Architecture International Exhibition*, reprint of the catalogue to accompany the exhibition 10 Feb to 23 March 1932, New York, 1969, p.24.

6. *Modern Architecture in England*, reprint of the catalogue to coincide with the exhibition of the same name at MOMA, New York, in 1937, Greenwood Press, Connecticut, 1970, p.9.

7. Here, High and Over was substituted for Noah's House and the Hopfield, two projects completed by Colin Lucas in practice before joining Connell and Ward.

8. *Modern Architecture in England*, op. cit., p.25.

9. Priestley, JB, *English Journey*, London, 1934.

10. *Modern Architecture in England*, New York, op. cit., p.27.

11. Pevsner, Nikolaus, *Northamptonshire*, Buildings of England Series revised by Bridget Cherry, London, 2nd edn 1973 (2002), p.346.

12. ibid., p.71. New Ways is the earliest work in the twentieth-century style in the whole of England and as such deserves a Grade 1 designation in the official list of protected buildings (Listed Grade II, 1967).

13. Waugh, Evelyn. *Decline and Fall*, London, 1928.

14. Cheney, Sheldon, *The New World Architecture*, New York, 1929. See reference to Thomas S Tait, whose work he links with 'Le Corbusier and the German functionalists and not with any tradition in England', p.242.

15. Ward, Basil, 'Connell, Ward & Lucas' in Sharp, D (ed.), *Planning and Architecture*, London, 1967, p.80.

16. Hitchcock, Henry-Russell, 'English Architecture in the Early 20th Century: 1900–1939', Zodiac, Vol. 18, pp.6–9, p.7.

17. ibid., p.7.

18. Gropius was met by Jack Pritchard and Maxwell Fry at Victoria Station on 18 October 1934, where he arrived from Rome. The two had been encouraged by P Morton Shand to make arrangements to bring Gropius to England, where he stayed for less than three years. He made his home in Pritchard's apartments at Lawn Road designed by Wells Coates, also a haven for László Moholy-Nagy, Marcel Breuer and Arthur Korn and refugees from the Spanish Civil War. John Gloag and Agatha Christie also lived there.

19. Hitchcock, Henry-Russell, 'English Architecture in the Early 20th Century: 1900–1939', Zodiac, Vol. 18, p.9.

20. Ward, Basil, *AAJ*, 1956–7, p.208.

21. ibid.

22. Summerson, John, 'The MARS Group and the Thirties' from 'English Architecture Public and Private', John Bold and Edward Chaney, *Essays for Kerry Downes*, London, 1993, pp.303-9.

23. Ward, Basil, 'Things Remembered – Heroic Relics', *Architecture North West*, June/July 1968, p.12.

24. Blomfield, Reginald, *Modernismus*, London, 1934, pp.71-2.

25. Baillie Scott, MH, 'Is modern architecture on the right track?' *The Listener*, 26 July 1933.

26. *Wasmuths Monatshefte für Baukunst u. Städtebau*, Berlin, 1931, WMM, XV 9, pp.466-70.

27. Blomfield, Reginald, *Richard Norman Shaw*, London, 1940, p.32.

28. ibid., p.37. Blomfield held a particular grudge against concrete which he considered a material of doubtful value.

29. Esher, Lionel, *A Broken Wave: The Rebuilding of England 1940–1980*, London, 1981, p.19. The book cynically described the typical young architect of the 1930s trained under articled pupillage as 'a mildly artistic boy from one of the "minor" public schools.... With his gift for drawing he would have been steered by his parents, themselves probably professional people, into this gentleman's profession in which mediocrity would matter less than art.'

30. See *Focus* No. 4, London, 1939.

31. Dunnett, James, 'A Modern Briton', *AJ*, 9 May 1984, p.28.

32. ibid.

33. ibid.

34. Wells Coates (1895–1958), Canadian but born in Tokyo.

35. Paul Nash's letter to the editor of *The Times*, 2 June 1933, published 12 June.

36. In a similar way to Mansfield Forbes' group in Cambridge, it opened a forum for discussion about what is the art of today and what is meant by contemporary spirit.

37. Coates: letter to Nash, 3 March 1933.

38. Frances Hodgkins, a New Zealander, later resigned and the artist Tristram Hillier (1905–83) took her place. Hillier was born in China but of Huguenot stock, studied under Meninsky in Paris and was influenced by surrealism – see autobiographical sketch 'Leda and the Goose'.

39. Many of the artists of the group were chosen from exhibitors in the 'Recent Developments in British Painting' exhibition in 1931.

40. Herbert Read was a friend of Henry Moore and Paul Nash and prolific art critic of the time. Read had in 1933 been appointed editor of the *Burlington Magazine* and began a long association with Moore, Nash and later with Naum Gabo. The publication was a precursor to *Circle* – the first major tract on modern art and architecture to come out of London, edited by Gabo with Ben Nicholson and JL Martin and published by Faber. He wrote the introduction to and compiled the book for the group.

41. Read, Herbert (ed.), *Unit 1: The Modern Movement in English Architecture, Painting and Sculpture*.

42. *New Zealand Daily Telegraph*, 25 September 1935.

43. Ward, Basil, interview with Dennis Sharp for Open University, 3 January 1973.

44. Burmese press cutting, from the *Burma Times*, unknown date.

45. Ashmole, *Bernard, Bernard Ashmole 1894–1988, An Autobiography*, Kurtz, Donna (ed.), Oxbow Books, 1994, p.51.

46. Amyas Connell's letter to Simon Johnson, 5 December 1969.

47. In the same year that Connell's High and Over went up in Buckinghamshire another group of architects made their presence felt on the London scene. A typical group of enthusiastic young architects, the Miners' Welfare Office, who were drawn by the published manifestos of continental modernism, eventually produced a remarkable series of pithead bath buildings in a unique interpretation of modern architecture. The deputy architect of the group, Cecil Kemp, was heavily committed to the modern brickwork designs of the Dutch architect WM Dudok and this influence lies at the root of an extensive body of work. See Henegan, Tom, *An analysis of the beginnings of British modernism through the study of the group of the miners' welfare committee architects 1929–1939*, AA Student dissertation (unpublished), 1976.

48. See also Mumford, Eric, *The CIAM Discourse on Urbanism 1928–30*, Cambridge, 2000, pp.91–92.

49. Correspondence in the *AJ*, 10 May 1933, p.623.

50. Although to become strictly linked with the CIAM, it was in a sense a follow-on from the ill-fated and short-lived 'Twentieth Century Group' that had stemmed from the enthusiasm of the Cambridge don Mansfield Forbes and had included Coates, McGrath, Etchells and Howard Robertson.

51. Maxwell Fry (b.1899) was educated at Liverpool and wrote for the *AJ* from 1929–1930, on the relationship between the philosophy of modernism on the continent and its relation with the problem of low-cost housing in Britain. He and John Gloag were also involved in the Design and Industries Association that had been formed in 1915 to promote closer relations between designers, retailers and industry. In the 1930s the DIA identified itself with the Modern European Design Exhibition at Dorland

Hall in London. It was too crafty an exhibition for the alignment of the MARS Group with the DIA at this time, but the MARS Group did benefit from the social network of clients, designers, architects and a new breed of professional consultants on tap through the DIA and Unit One (and Paul Nash's connection with the Society of Industrial Artists).

52. Reading, Malcolm in his thesis 'The History of the MARS Group 1933–4, University of Bristol, 5 September 1986. Part of the reason why Robertson was barred from the group was no doubt because of the lack of integrity of his word.

53. Richards, JM, Memoirs of an unjust fella, Weidenfeld and Nicolson, London, 1980, p129.

54. Arthur Korn, who had been the secretary of the Berlin group of architects Der Ring, had arrived in London first for a CIAM meeting at the RIBA in 1934. Later he came on a more permanent basis in 1937 from Yugoslavia, where he had supervised the construction of a hospital won in competition. Korn soon become involved with the MARS Group, producing with the members of its Town Planning Committee the famous MARS Plan for London. This was eventually published by the Architectural Review in 1942 soon after Korn was released by the British government from detention in the Isle of Man. The article was termed a master plan for London, a brilliant plan promoted as a recipe for reconstruction after the devastation caused by the Luftwaffe. It was considered 'a clever piece of ruthless reconstruction' by advocates of the Garden City movement such as CB Purdom.

55. MARS file note held in AA Library (April 1935: unnumbered)

56. Ward, Basil in Sharp, D (ed.), Planning and Architecture, London, 1967, p.86.

57. Connell Ward and Lucas' scheme inserted welfare centres between blocks.

58. They were disappointed when G Grey Wornum and Anthony Tripe won with a scheme for an even distribution of flats built around courtyards, constructed in a system of clothed concrete. The subsequently expensive-to-maintain material with which they 'clothed' the concrete later forced their demolition in 1981.

59. AAJ, February 1938, p.388.

60. Reading, Malcolm in his thesis 'The History of the MARS Group 1933–45, University of Bristol, 5 September 1986.

61. Fry, Maxwell, Art in a Machine Age, London, 1969, p.112.

The partnership, pages 32-37

1. Smithson, Peter, AAJ, December 1956.

2. Reilly, CH, AJ, 14 January 1937, pp.91–102.

3. See AJ, 11 June 1936.

4. In AJ, 26 September 1984, p.39. 'Colin Lucas wore one of those special flat felt hats (of Cambridge provenance?), escaping from under which thin brown drapes of hair almost hid the distinguished mouth, locus of the pipe, whence now and then thin streams of meiosis lazily floated. He had a smashing telephone manner: "Lucas … Colin Lucas… No, Colin … No, no, no, Colin, C for cretin, O for omadhaun, L for lunatic, I for imbecile, N for nitwit".'

5. AR, March 1962, pp.203–6, p.203.

6. Amyas Connell quoted by John Winter, in Contemporary Architects, London, 1980, p.165.

7. Ward, Basil, 'Houses of the Thirties', Concrete Quarterly 85, April–June 1970.

8. A note from James Connell.

9. Ward, Basil, 'Connell, Ward & Lucas' in Sharp, D (ed.), Planning and Architecture, London, 1967, p.73.

10. ibid., p.80.

11. ibid., p.73.

12. ibid., p.78.

13. Korn, Arthur, 'Connell Ward & Lucas', AJ, November 1956, p.94.

14. Ward, Basil, 'Connell, Ward & Lucas' in Sharp, D (ed.), Planning and Architecture, London, 1967, p.94.

15. ibid., pp.80-82.

16. ibid., p.82.

17. Ward, Basil, interview with Dennis Sharp for Open University, 3 January 1973.

18. Ward, Basil, 'Things remembered: Heroic relics', Architecture North West, Vol. 29, June/July 1968, p.13.

19. ibid., p.12.

20. ibid., p.86.

21. Le Corbusier, Towards a New Architecture, Oxford (1927), 1989, p.80.

22. ibid., p.74

23. ibid., p.175.

24. Curtis, William JR, Le Corbusier, Phaidon, London, 1986, p.53.

25. Daniel, Augustus, in a letter to Bernard Ashmole.

26. Ward, Basil, 'Things remembered', op.cit., p.12.

27. ibid., p.15.

28. ibid., p.12. Ward later said that colonial friends who greatly helped him included Ian Reynolds, Maxwell Gregory and Peter Stiles, George Buzuk and Alan Cordingly.

29. Bertram, Anthony. The House: A Machine for Living In, London, 1935, p.1.

30. Ward, Basil, Speech to the RIBA, 2 March 1976.

31. ibid.

32. Ward, Basil, 'Connell Ward and Lucas: Origins, Influences and Sources' in Planning and Architecture, Essays presented to Arthur Korn by the AA, ed. D. Sharp, London, 1967.

33. ibid.

34. Read, Herbert, Unit One. London, 1934.

35. Ward, Basil, 'Connell, Ward and Lucas' op.cit., p.83.

36. Holden, Charles, 'Is Modern Architecture on the right track?' The Listener, 26 July 1933, p.125.

37. Emberton, Joseph, Is Modern Architecture on the right track?' The Listener, 26 July 1933, p.125.

38. Read, Herbert, 'The Meaning of Art", quoted by Basil Ward in 'Things remembered: Heroic relics', Architecture North West, vol. 29, June/July 1968, p.12.

The modern house, pages 38-41

1. Bertram, Anthony, The House: A Machine for Living in, A&C Black, London, 1935, p.115.

2. Williams-Ellis, Clough, England and the Octopus, Geoffrey Bles, London, 1928, p.15. Clough Williams-Ellis was the architect of Portmeirion and one of the founders of the CPRE.

3. Ward, Basil, 'Connell Ward and Lucas', Sharp, Dennis (ed.), Planning and Architecture, essays presented to Arthur Korn by the Architectural Association, AA London, 1967, p.79.

4. ibid.

5. Ward, Basil, reported in the Daily Mail by Stuart, Malcolm, 6 May 1976, p.30.

6. Neoprene was invented in 1931 and polythene in 1933.

7. Lucas, Colin, in a letter to GH Walford, the client of 66 Frognal, of February 1936.

8. Braddell, Dorothy, Decoration, April–June 1934, vol.4, no.2, p.70.

9. This was published in the Architects' Journal in May and November 1934.

10. Frost, AE, Architects' Journal, 29 November 1934, p.645.

Private houses, pages 42-131

1. Hitchcock, Henry-Russell, 'England and the outside world', AA Journal, November 1956, p.94.

2. Pevsner, Nikolaus, source unrecorded.

3. Robertson, Howard, 'An experiment with time: A house at Amersham by AD Connell', Architect and Building News, 3 January 1930, p.12.

4. ibid.

5. Nairn, Ian, Modern Buildings in London, LT, 1964, p.100.

6. Daniel, Augustus, quotred by Ashmole, Bernard, Bernard Ashmole 1894–1988 An Autobiography, Kurtz, Donna (ed.), Oxbow Books, Oxford, 1994, p.57.

7. Thomson (1902–90) subsequently pursued a career in architecture. His modern house St Raphael on Nelmes Way in Hornchurch, Essex, was published in the Architectural Review, December 1933, and was included in Myles Wright's Small Houses and R Randall Phillips' Houses for Moderate Means. After the war he went into partnership with Hector Corfiato.

8. Connell, Amyas, interviewed by Baker, Geoffrey, 'English Houses of the Thirties', short film for the Open University course, A305, 1975.

9. Ashmole, Bernard, Bernard Ashmole 1894–1988 An Autobiography, Kurtz, Donna (ed.), Oxbow books, Oxford, 1994, pp.53-54.

10. Girouard, Mark, Life in the English Country House, Yale University Press, 1978, p.303.

11. Lutyens' Papillon Hall of 1903 utilised a central plan with more than three wings and an expanded hexagonal 'core' of rooms.

12. Connell, Amyas, interviewed by Baker,

Geoffrey, 'English Houses of the Thirties', short film for the Open University course, A305, 1975.

13. ibid.

14. Ashmole, Bernard, letter to Allan, John, 21 June 1972.

15. Ashmole, Bernard, *Bernard Ashmole 1894–1988 An Autobiography*, Kurtz, Donna (ed.), Oxbow Books, Oxford, 1994, p.51.

16. ibid.

17. The Ashmole children, quoted from the television programme 'Marvels of the modern world', 2006.

18. Ashmole, Bernard, *Bernard Ashmole 1894–1988 An Autobiography*, Kurtz, Donna (ed.), Oxbow Books, Oxford, 1994, p.55.

19. 'High and Over Amersham Bucks – V: A concrete frame house', *Architect and Building News*, Supplement no.151, 20 November 1931

20. Ashmole, Bernard, letter to Allan, John, 21 June 1972.

21. At this time, May 1929, the Ashmoles lived at Eastbourne, near Dorothy Ashmole's parents.

22. Ashmole, Bernard, *Bernard Ashmole 1894–1988 An Autobiography*, Kurtz, Donna (ed.), Oxbow Books, Oxford, 1994, p.54.

23. Robertson, Howard, 'An experiment with time: A house at Amersham by AD Connell', *Architect and Building News*, 3 January 1930, p.12.

24. Ashmole, Bernard, *Bernard Ashmole 1894–1988 An Autobiography*, Kurtz, Donna (ed.), Oxbow Books, Oxford, 1994, p.57.

25. Letter from De Syllas, Justin, to the authors, June 2000.

26. Lucas, Mark, unpublished paper 'Colin Lucas – a view of a creative life', 2005, p.10.

27. This may have been when Lucas' parents planned to retire to Bourne End.

28. Rawlings, Derek, 'Streeters Rough and Beaconsfield Road on Chelwood Common', *Danehill Parish Historical Society Magazine*, vol.5, no.10, May 1997, p.7.

29. Lucas, Colin, letter to chairman of works and town planning committee, Crowborough, 21 October 1930.

30. *Surveyors Report on Plans*, rural district council of Uckfield, signed HRW, 14 October 1930.

31. Lucas, Ralph, letter to Mr Burdett, the surveyor, 5 August 1931.

32. 'Planning for the Week-End' in Planning – An Annual notebook, E and OE, *Architect and Building News*, London, 1938, p.31.

33. Lucas, Colin, from the transcript to his speech to the RIBA, 2 March 1976.

34. Arthur Lowes Dickinson's father, Cato Lowes Dickinson was a prolific portrait painter, painting Queen Victoria, the Prince of Wales and Gladstone. His pre-Raphaelite connections echo those of Connell's father, an artist in New Zealand.

35. *Architectural Review*, December 1977, RSVP, p.326. In fact, according to Alan Powers, this was not Lowes Dickinson's first commission. Architect Ernest Cole had designed and built him a flat-roofed house at Worsted Burrows in 1926.

36. The house was called Pollards after the avenue of lime trees proposed on the site. Aldings was a word derived from Arthur Lowes Dickinson's initials augmented with his penchant for adding 'ings' to the end of nouns.

37. From the RIBA file information on Connell Ward and Lucas held at the RIBA Library.

38. Quoted by Mace, PMH, 'New Farm, Grayswood, nr Haslemere', Open University thesis, 1978.

39. Turnor, Reginald, *The Smaller English House 1500–1939*, Batsford, London, 1952, p.202.

40. These portholes also serve to illuminate the external terraces after dark, emanating the artificial light from inside the building.

41. Butt, Baseden, 'Advantages and costs of concrete experimentation in domestic architecture', *Design for To-day*, October 1933, pp.220-23.

42. Lucas, Colin, from the transcript to his speech to the RIBA, 2 March 1976.

43. The house was listed grade II in January 1971 and upgraded to grade II* in May 1992.

44. A salting is an area of coastal land regularly covered by the tide as the shore at the end of the garden at nos. 42 and 44 Sinah Lane.

45. The Haydons' daughter, Bridget was the same age as the Lawrences' eldest son.

46. Excerpts from a 1930s guidebook of the island *The book of Hayling Island and Langstone*, Rogers, Peter, Halsgrove, Tiverton, 2000, p.59.

47. Geoffrey Boumphrey was the editor of the *The Shell Guide to Britain*.

48. Anna Lawrence was later a pianist for the Ballet Rambert.

49. Ward, Basil, reported in the *Daily Mail* by Stuart Malcolm, 6 May 1976, p.30.

50. Alternative transport from Havant came in the form of Terrier tank train engines, locally known as the 'Hayling Billy' and a ferry crossed passengers from Portsmouth in the west.

51. Dr Lawrence used the third bedroom as a study.

52. Finmar was founded in 1934 by Geoffrey Boumphrey and P Morton Shand to promote and distribute Aalto-designed furniture in England.

53. Francis, Marianne, from a letter describing her stay at Saltings in 1933.

54. Ward, Basil reported in the *Daily Mail* by Stuart Malcolm, 6 May 1976, p.30.

55. Russell, Barry, 'Mending the Modern Movement', *Architects' Journal*, 30 March 1977, p.582.

56. ibid., p.583.

57. The planning drawings bear the name of Colin Lucas solo, without Lloyd, Lucas and Co.

58. In April 1928, for example, there was an article on 'Concrete Architecture and House-Building' by Dresdner, Albert, pp.231-38. This covered work by Behrens, Hans Poelzig, Le Corbusier and Oud's housing estate in Rotterdam.

59. Through Phillada Sewell's first cousin, John Moody, there was a connection to Unit One. Moody, himself a painter, theatre designer, actor and producer was married to Nella Burra, the first cousin of artist Edward Burra, who was one of the eleven members of Unit One with Colin Lucas.

60. Le Corbusier, *Towards a new architecture*, Butterworth-Heinemann Ltd, 1992 reprint, Great Britain, p.75.

61. Lucas, Mark, from his unpublished paper 'Colin Lucas – a view of a creative life', 2005, p.35.

62. Mrs Gunn, letter to Wood, Jim, September 1976.

63. Simpkins, Becky, 'Klaus Fuchs, a man with many motives' also Sir Neville Mott, 'Bristol Physics in the 1930s', both sourced from the internet.

64. Letter from Connell and Ward to the city engineer at Bristol, 21 June 1934.

65. Notice to accompany new plans from Connell Ward and Lucas, 29 June 1934.

66. *Decoration*, December 1935, pp.18-19.

67. Mrs Gunn, letter to Wood, Jim, September 1976.

68. Letter from Connell Ward and Lucas to the borough of Reigate, 24 August 1934.

69. Letter from Connell Ward and Lucas to the building inspector, borough of Reigate, 10 May 1935.

70. Bertram, Anthony, *The House: a machine for living In*, A&C Black, 1935, p.ii.

71. Anon., 'An addition to a house at Redhill', *Architect and Building News*, 7 June 1935, p.280.

72. Nairn, Ian, *Modern buildings in London*, LT, 1964, p.110.

73. Anon. 'Cuckoo', *Architects' Journal*, 1960, p.594.

74. Astragal, *Architects' Journal*, 9 October, p.33.

75. Nairn, Ian, *Modern buildings in London*, LT, 1964, p.110.

76. Anon., 'A house at Woodmancote, Sussex', *Architect and Building News*, 17 April 1936, p.73.

77. *Architects' Journal*, 30 April 1936, p.661.

78. Randal Phillips, R, 'A modern house in Moor Park', *Country Life*, 2 April 1938, pp.358-59.

79. Ward, Basil, transcript to his speech at the RIBA, 2 March 1976.

80. Anon., 'Reinforced concrete Houses', *RIBA Journal*, 17 July 1937, p.901.

81. Allan, John, *Berthold Lubetkin Architecture and the tradition of progress*, RIBA Publications, 1992, p.270.

82. Shelter was then edited by Maxwell Levinson assisted by Richard J Neutra. Other contributing editors included Maxwell Fry, Walter Gropius and Frank Lloyd Wright.

83. Lander, Susan, 'A reinforced concrete house at Moor Park', *All England Homefinder*, October, 1937.

84. Lucas, Colin, transcript to his speech at the RIBA, 2 March 1976.

85. Hitchcock, Henry-Russell, source unrecorded.

86. Lucas, Colin, transcript to his speech at the RIBA, 2 March 1976.

87. Yorke, FRS, *The Modern House in England*, The Architectural Press, London, 1937, pp.101-03.

88. Glancey, Jonathan, 'Pain in the grass', *Guardian* architecture section, 4 November 2002, p.12.

89. This is not the only modern house to be built in this area at the time, Maxwell Fry's Sun House of 1935 is also just around the corner in Frognal Way.

90. Nairn, Ian, *Modern buildings in London*, LT, 1964, p.44.

91. Tasker, Robert, LCC council meeting, 1936, quoted on the invitation to the opening of Frognal.

92. Walford, Geoffrey, 'A client on his house', *RIBA Journal*, 19 December 1938, p.185.

93. ibid., p.181.

94. ibid., p.185.

95. Walford, Geoffrey, quoted by the *Evening Standard*, 1937.

96. Lucas, Colin transcript to his speech at the RIBA, 2 March 1976.

97. Walford, Geoffrey, 'A client on his house', *RIBA Journal*, 19 December 1938, p.181.

98. Dugdale, J, reported at the LCC council meeting, 1936.

99. Berry, H, reported in a press cutting from *The Times*, 1936.

100. Walford, Geoffrey, 'A client on his house', *RIBA Journal*, 19 December 1938, p.185.

101. François Hennebique (1842–1921) was a civil engineer who devised techniques of reinforced concrete construction for the building industry. His systems were widely used and his influence on the modern architects using concrete was great.

102. Article in the *News Chronicle*, 14 July 1938.

103. Cherry, B, and Pevsner, N, *Buildings of England London 4: North*, Penguin, p.229.

104. Other timber houses of the period include: E Maxwell Fry's Little Winch, Chipperfield, Hertfordshire, 1934; Gropius and Fry's The Wood House at Shipbourne, Kent, 1937; Raymond McGrath's Land's End, Galby, Leicestershire, 1937–9; Samuel and Harding's Overshot, Oxford, 1937; Anthony Chitty's Avalon, Churt, Surrey, 1935.

105. Beardsmore, AC, *Focus*, no. 2, winter 1938, Percy Lund Humphries, p.33.

106. ibid., p.31.

107. ibid.

108. Draft of Beardsmore, AC, article in *Focus*, no. 2, 1938, p.4, from Connell Ward and Lucas papers.

109. ibid., p.1.

110. Beardsmore, AC, *Focus*, no. 2, winter 1938, Percy Lund Humphries, p.29.

Speculative housing, pages 132-53

1. Ward, Basil, from the transcript to his speech to the RIBA, 2 March 1976

2. 'The architect and the speculative house', *Decoration*, special edition on the Ideal Home Exhibition, April-June 1934, vol.4 no. 2, p.54

3. Richardson, AE, *The Listener*, 26 July 1935, p.126

4. Bertram, Anthony, *The House: A Machine for Living In*, A&C Black, London, 1935, p.21

5. Lucas, Colin, in Herbert Read (ed); *Unit One: The Modern Movement in English Architecture*, Painting and Sculpture, London, 1934

6. The editor, *Architectural Review*, 'give the public what it wants', April, 1930

7. Ward, Basil, 'Connell Ward and Lucas', Sharp, Dennis (ed.), *Planning and Architecture*, essays presented to Arthur Korn by the Architectural Association, AA London, 1967, p.82

8. ibid.

9. Other estates of modern houses built in England include the Bata Estate 1932-7, Unity Estate Braintree Modern Homes Exhibition, Angmering & Goring in East Sussex

10. Anon., *The Observer and Gazette*, 'Sun Trap Houses', 27 April 1934

11. Ward, Basil, interview with Dennis Sharp for the Open University, 3 January 1973.

12 Correspondence from Taylor, Walter, to Connell Ward and Lucas dated October 1934.

13. Reported in the *Architects' Journal*, 24 May 1934, p.812.

14. ibid.

15. Ward, Basil, from the transcript to his speech to the RIBA, 2 March 1976.

16. Letter from Keynes, JM, to Connell and Ward, 5 March 1934.

17. Gunn, Edwin, later did a review of FRS Yorke's *The Modern House in England* and mentions Bracken as a house of particular interest – was this remorse? *Architects' Journal*, November 1937.

18. Letter from Ruislip-Northwood urban council to Walter Taylor (Builders) Ltd., dated 12 June 1934, published in *Architects' Journal*, 27 September 1934, p.455.

19. Letter from Connell, Ward and Lucas to Walter Taylor (Builders) Ltd., dated 3 July 1934, published in *Architects' Journal*, 27 September 1934, pp.455-57.

20. Ward, Basil, from the transcript to his speech to the RIBA, 2 March 1976.

21. Letter from King's College to Connell Ward and Lucas, October 1934.

22. The houses were renumbered when the rest of the houses in the road were built.

23. *Architects' Journal*, 7 February 1935, p.226.

24. Nairn, Ian and Pevsner, Nikolaus, *The Buildings of England: Sussex*, Penguin, Harmondsworth, first printed 1965, 1985 edition, p.601.

25. Walton, John, *The British seaside – holidays and resorts in the twentieth century*, Manchester.

26. Lowerson, John, 'Resorts, Ports & Sleepy Hollows – Sussex Towns 1840–1940', in Alan Sutton, *Sussex Environment, Landscape & Society*, 1983, p.221.

27. D'Enno, Douglas, 'Saltdean Past the beginning of Saltdean', published on the internet, an extract from his book *The Saltdean Story*.

28. ibid.

29. Nairn, Ian and Pevsner, Nikolaus, *The

Buildings of England: Sussex, Penguin, Harmondsworth, first printed 1965, 1985 edition, p.601.

30. ibid.

31. Strutt, Jack, Lewes District Council in a letter to the author dated 31 January 2000.

32. Lever, Jill, 'Deauville in Essex', *RIBA Journal*, November 1979, p.496.

33. See Connell Ward and Lucas' bathroom design submission to this exhibition illustrated in the houses introduction section above.

34. Lever, Jill, 'Deauville in Essex', *RIBA Journal*, November 1979, p.497.

35. Yorke, FRS, like Connell Ward and Lucas pursued a 4 inch thick wall construction and a Mendelsohn and Chermayeff scheme in 5 inch concrete appeared in Ella Carter's book *Seaside Houses and Bungalows*, Country Life Ltd, London, 1937.

36. Lever, Jill, 'Deauville in Essex', *RIBA Journal*, November 1979, p.498.

37. ibid., p.497.

38. ibid., p.498.

39 *The Marylebone Record and West London News*, February 1936.

40. Later alternative designs dated December 1936 show four flats per floor off the main access three 4 bedroom flats and one 8 bedroom flat from the main lobby. The rest of the layout is blocked in, suggesting that it did not alter.

41. *The Marylebone Record and West London News*, 4 April 1936.

42. Whittaker, Chris, letter to Sharp, Dennis, 17 September 2007.

Social housing, pages154-61

1. Read, Herbert, *Art and Industry*, Faber and Faber, London, 1934.

2. *Architects' Journal*, 19 December 1935.

3. Scott, Nigel, (ed.), 'The North and South-West Groups', *Housing Happenings*, no.21, summer 1936, p.39.

4. From Connell Ward and Lucas' competition submission report, 20 February 1935.

5. *Architect and Building News*, 'Competition for working-class flats in reinforced concrete – a review of unpremiated designs', 29 March 1935, p.406.

Other projects, pages162-79

1. Other such projects by modern contemporaries include Wells Coates' shops for Cresta circa 1929 and Erno Goldfinger's designs for 'Helena Rubinstein', London, 1926.

2. Lucas, Dione, as quoted on Wikipedia internet site, unknown publication.

3. Lucas, Dione, and Hume, Rosemary, *Au Petit Cordon Bleu*, London, 1936.

4. 'A Health Shop in Welbeck Street', *Architects' Journal*, 17 August 1932, pp.193-96.

5. Connell Ward and Lucas' notes regarding the project.

6. Richards, JM, 'The Idea Behind the Idea', *Architectural Review*, 1935, p.203.

7 Correspondence from Connell Ward and Lucas to Quick, Stanley, 31 January 1935.

8. Ward, Basil, filenote in CWL archive, date unknown.

9. Ward, Basil, 'Things remembered: heroic relics', *Architecture North West*, no. 29, June/July 1968, p.15.

10. unknown publication.

11. Descriptive text from Connell Ward and Lucas' papers.

12. Penn, Colin, interviewed by Saint, Andrew, *The Thirties Journal*, no.4. 1984, p.33.

13. Ward, Basil, 'Connell Ward and Lucas', Sharp, Dennis (ed.), *Planning and Architecture*, essays presented to Arthur Korn by the Architectural Association, AA London, 1967, p.86.

14. 'The Hertford Competition: diverse Outlooks', *Architects' Journal*, lxxx11, 1935 p.627.

15. For the winner's report and illustration of the premiated designs see *Architects' Journal*, 17 December 1936, pp.835-39.

16. Ward, Basil, 'Connell Ward and Lucas', Sharp, Dennis, (ed.), *Planning and Architecture*, essays presented to Arthur Korn by the Architectural Association, AA London, 1967, p.86.

17. Penn, Colin, interviewed by Saint, Andrew, *The Thirties Journal*, no.4, 1984, p.33.

Later years of Connell, Ward and Lucas, pages 180-97

1 *A&BN*, 10 May 1946, p.90.

2. Hitchcock died in 1954.

3. Doctor Hindorf had read about sisal hemp production in the Yucatan, Mexico in a copy of the *Kew Journal* (no. 62, February 1892), soon after which in 1893 he ordered his first assignment of bulbs from Mexico via Florida forwarded to the port of Hamburg, Germany and then, with the few bulbs that had survived, to Tanga. The first crop grew at Kikogares, south of the River Pangani. Dr Hindorf died at the age of 90 in 1954. See GW Locke, *25 years' Sisal research*, London, Longmans, 1962.

4. Sharp, Dennis, 'The Modern Movement in East Africa', *Habitat International*, Vol. 7, no. 5/6: Otto Koenigsberger Festschrift, 1983, pp.311-26. Also Herrel, Eckhard, *Ernst May: Architekt u. Stadtplaner in Afrika 1934–1953*, Frankfurt am Main: DAM, 2001. He opened an office in Mombasa, which still operates today under the name Dr Ernst May and Partner but stayed in Nairobi in a self designed house. In 1952 he produced designs for the 'luxury' Oceanic Hotel, a distinguished curved concrete structure of six storeys overlooking the ocean (demolished). By the time of completion in1956 May had returned to Germany. In Nairobi he designed the splendid modernist 'Delamere' flats and a local vernacular-style Boy Scouts centre. Another innovative May project was the Aga Khan Trust school in Kisumu, 1951-2, with its elevated classrooms and concrete *brise-soleil*.

5. ibid.

6. Letter to Simon Johnson, 5 December 1969.

7. ibid.

8. Partridge, John, 'Lucas in London', Connell, Ward & Lucas, *Modern Movement Architects in England 1929–1939*, Dennis Sharp (ed), Book Art, London, 1994, p.61.

9. Sir Gerald Campbell was the British High Commissioner in Ottawa at this time.

10. Hitchcock, Henry-Russell, *Architecture: nineteenth and twentieth centuries*, first pub. London,1958, 1989 edition, p.566.

11. Dunnett, James, *AJ*, 9 May 1984, p.28.

12. Frampton, Kenneth, *Modern Architecture; a Critical History*, first pub. London, 1980, 1990 edition, pp.262-63.

13. Partridge, John, 'Lucas in London', Connell, Ward & Lucas, *Modern Movement Architects in England 1929–1939*, Dennis Sharp (ed), Book Art, London, 1994, p.61.

14. ibid.

15. Lucas, Colin, quoted by Lucas, Mark, unpublished paper 'Colin Lucas – a view of a creative life', 2005.

16. Lucas, Mark, unpublished paper 'Colin Lucas – a view of a creative life', 2005.

17. Lucas, Colin, quoted by Dunnett, James, 'A Modern Briton', *AJ*, 9 May 1984, p.28.

18. Partridge, John, 'Lucas in London', Connell, Ward & Lucas, *Modern Movement Architects in England 1929–1939*, Dennis Sharp (ed), Book Art, London, 1994, p.61.

19. Dunnett, James, obituary of Colin Lucas, *AJ*, September 1984, p.52.

20. Ouspensky lectured in London in the 1930s and 40s but we do not know if Lucas attended these lectures.

21. Lucas, Colin, quoted by Lucas, Mark, unpublished paper 'Colin Lucas – a view of a creative life', 2005.

22. Lucas, Colin, in a letter to Caroline Lucas of 1972.

23. Lucas, Mark, unpublished paper 'Colin Lucas – a view of a creative life', 2005.

Appendices

**Geoffrey Walford: A Client on His House: No. 66
Frognal, Hampstead**
Journal of the Royal Institute of British Architects,
19 December 1938, pp.181-85

I have some doubt on the value of an attempt on the part of the 'building owner' to account for the building which represents the result of his efforts. Our powers of analysing our motives and reactions are unfortunately in the realm of sheer speculation. So complex are the threads that constitute the sum total of experience of each individual, so varied are the contacts of individuals connected with any new building, that no case can be more than a law unto itself.

However, the comments of many who have seen this house, the overheard remarks of many who stop in the street to stare in bewildered amazement and the violent opinions that have been expressed seem to indicate that some attempt at explanation may be of interest. It may seem surprising to some that this building is not symptomatic of exhibitionism, nor of iconoclasm, nor is it the result of any particular liking for operating theatres or for the decks of ships – that is, so far as I am aware. It may seem more surprising that to me it represents the logical conclusion to nothing more mysterious than the problem of how to live.

It may be that most, or possibly all, creative work springs from some frustration or restriction. The problem of determining the organisation and mode of living necessarily involves the acceptance of some restrictions and the escape from others. The individual can determine the problem, so far as it is affected by the building forming his environment, by accepting or adapting what others provide for him, or by creating a building in accordance with his own solution of the problem. Moreover, the problem is one that goes further than the determination of mere accommodation and the use of space. It includes the determination of a background and environment of emotional significance.

In this particular case the desire to solve the problem with a new building sprang from impatience with the compromise of adaption, both from the aspect of efficiency and background. The houses of a past age and the contemporary imitations called for an imitation of the more formal life of a past age, and involved a strain on personal effort and resources no longer necessary or of any apparent value. On the one hand a more precise use of space and a greater reduction of labour seemed possible. On the other hand, the use without pretence or shame of materials and methods now available seemed to offer the basis of a background sympathetic to existence in his age. In the distracting and stimulating conditions of work and pleasure outside the seclusion at home, my need is for relaxation, and for a background conducive to conversation, reading, music and reflection. I find the simplicity and spaciousness of unbroken surfaces offer rest to the eye and to the mind. I find delight in the control of forms arising in the building itself and its appurtenances, rather than in superimposed effects. I find delight in the use of colour and in the play and variation of light. I find delight above all in the relation between house and garden, whereby the terraces and garden may be an extension of the interior of the house and whereby the interior is screened rather than enclosed from the open air, trees and sky.

The plan of this house was governed by the requirement of accommodation for two people and four children in the school holidays, and for two people only in school terms. Isolation of the children's accommodation was desirable not only for the obvious benefit to them and to other occupants in the holidays, but for convenience of upkeep in their absence. Isolation by separate floors rather than by separate wings seemed to be the only solution for a house required to be in London. One floor, therefore, must constitute a complete living unit for two people and possibly one servant. The next consideration was garage and workshop accessible under cover for an owner driver, together with an entrance to house and garage under cover. The benefit of arrival and departure by car under cover seems so obvious as to be a necessity for town life unless chauffeurs or other servants are employed. This requirement, together with the complete living unit, appeared to cover too much site area; consequently the living unit was placed on the first floor, which had other advantages for a town house. The detachment of the first floor from the garden could be overcome by a terrace over part of the garage with a flight of steps down to the garden. This first floor living unit had to consist of a living room, including space for dining, for piano and for bookshelves, a bedroom, dressing room and bathroom, a kitchen and pantry and a maid's bed-sitting room. The living room alone should be planned generously, the remaining rooms taking the minimum reasonable space. This layout on one floor gave the advantages of using the bedroom and dressing room as private sitting rooms, and of living without servants in the absence of the children. The space required by this floor governed the area of the house. It gave space on the ground floor, of which approximately half was available for the covered entrance, garage and outside stair to a back door at first floor level, and of which the other half provided a playroom and covered space open to the garden for the children, and a small entrance hall and cloakroom. On the second floor approximately half was taken by bedrooms and bathroom for the children and for a possible children's maid, together with box-room, linen cupboards, etc. The children's four bedrooms, more over, could be used as two double spare rooms for guests by the provision of sliding partitions. The remaining half of the second floor was available for roof terrace opening straight off the top of the staircase and off the children's bedrooms. Thus all floors in the house were accessible to terraces in the open air.

It was particularly required that all heating and domestic supply of hot water should be by electricity on account of cleanliness and of the abolition of all stoking and of the carrying and storage of fuel. This requirement limited the possible areas in London for a site, as in many areas the cost of electricity is prohibitive for such extensive use.

This plan was conceived in anticipation that a site in London would only afford light and air on the front and back, and not on the sides. The site was found subsequently and although it proved to be a corner site the plan required no modification. The western boundary appeared to be obvious for the street front and the eastern outlook was more attractive than the southern. Moreover, in this position all trees on the site were preserved.

The plan of this house was formed without any preconceived idea of what the house would or should look like. I held a conviction that design was not a matter of erudition in style nor of aptitude for repeating the fine effects of other ages, but simply a matter of sensibility for structure, for the placing of masses and weights, and for materials. It seemed that reinforced concrete would be the most suitable structural material, in view of the open spaces required under the first floor, the desire for unbroken length of window and the freedom of placing internal partition walls without sacrificing precision of planning. Moreover, only a few designers in this country appeared to accept frankly reinforced concrete as a material and structural method different from that of any form of masonry and their work appealed to me as having that structural quality which personally, I find missing in nearly all other contemporary work with the exception of that of some engi-

neers. I felt confident, therefore that the plan in the right hands could be translated into a pleasing building. I may say frankly that in my opinion that confidence has been confirmed, and the experience has proved to be one of great interest. The plan was accepted and carried out without sacrificing one inch of my carefully measured detail requirements. The considered and deliberate placing and emphasis of line and surface, and the selection of variation in colour and texture, both externally and internally, followed sympathetically the structural forces of the separate entity of walls, fittings or other varying forms.

I can only regret that this building should offend the susceptibilities of some people and be beyond the comprehension of others. To me it has proved to be an experience of intense interest and delight.

**Talk at the Architectural Association
by Basil Ward,**
19 December 1956

A special issue of the *AAJ*:Architectural Association Journal, in 1956 on Connell Ward and Lucas heralded a new interest in the work of the partnership. Edited by AA student Brian Housden, it included contributions from AA teacher Arthur Korn and the American architectural historian Henry-Russell Hitchcock and Thomas (Sam) Stevens. To celebrate the publication, an AA Dinner meeting was held in the dining room on Wednesday 19 December 1956 under the chairmanship of Sir Kenneth Harper who introduced the speakers: Professor Bernard Ashmole, Peter Smithson and Basil Ward. The following is a transcription of Basil Ward's speech given that night and published in full from Ward's own annotated script. It has not been previously published.

'Poor Fred,
He's alive, he's dead,
There's no more to be said.'

Most of us, Mr Chairman, are 'Freds' and would view this modest epitaph with satisfaction – quiet satisfaction at that stage of existence! But in architecture there are those who leave behind them monuments a little more obtrusive, more material and this, in some cases, is obviously a pity. However, when one's own friends and colleagues, in one's own lifetime, take trouble to refer to one's own work and go to lengths to make kind remarks about it, then one can perhaps hope there may be more to be said in the case of Connell Ward and Lucas than there was for 'Poor Fred'.

On an occasion like this, it is of course inevitable that one would seem to speak egotistically, especially when one is puffed-up with pride at the very nice and interesting things said by you, Sir Kenneth, my very old and valued friend, by Professor Ashmole, the first of the few modern clients and by Peter Smithson, distinguished among the new generation. But the evening up till now has been a cheerful one and I must try to keep it so. A lot of personal reminiscence from me could cause the kind of damp cloud that always descends when someone talks too much about himself! In any case, the evening is in honour, not of one but of three individuals, Connell, Ward and Lucas. How nice it would be if Amyas and Colin were here! For my part our association together was an intensely interesting and absorbing experience. Amyas and I believed in the experiment of closest relationship towards gaining our end. You may be surprised to hear that we, with our families, shared a house together and this is perhaps more surprising, we shared a bank account! The strange experiment lasted longer than one could have hoped (until the war) and I am sure it was successful to a very high degree.

On this point of the Dinner, may I say, Mr Chairman, that when one or two of the more convivial of my friends saw in the Journal's publication a very good reason for a party, all that was thought of then was a small celebration dinner at which those present would no doubt have indulged in a little wine and in the very human exercise of scratching one-another's backs – always a pleasant process! Seriously however, when from a suggestion by my friend Tom Harper-Ellis, the idea grew to this larger one of embracing the name of the old firm, I was naturally delighted – delighted not only because of the added tribute to be paid to the work of Connell Ward and Lucas – a tribute most generous – but to the Honorary Editor, the Editor and the Editorial Board of the *AA Journal* and to their somewhat bold idea of promoting a publication of this kind, and to the work put into it by members particularly Brian Housden and Arthur Korn.

If Connell Ward and Lucas had still been in practice as a firm, the idea of a celebration dinner would, I am sure, have been inappropriate, but the three now exist only in the past. And enough in the past to be history and as their work is collected and made open to public discussion they, therefore, will not, I hope, become just legendary, adding to the many odd myths that have gone to make up the somewhat curious story of architects and architecture in modern times.

Of course, Mr Chairman, this occasion gives me a wonderful chance to air my views, particularly as it is, I believe, your intention to ask later if anyone would like to put a question or two about the work published in the Journal. It is an unusual opportunity given only to few, for example, Royal Academy Presidents and capable, much in-demand, after-dinner speakers and so on, but, at the risk of parading a few prejudices, I make bold to accept it.

'If I were again learning to be a modern architect, I'd eschew taste and design and all that stuff and learn engineering with plenty of mathematics and hard building experience.' Hardness, facts, experiments – that should be architecture, not taste Mr Chairman, I've quoted from a letter written not by a present-day protagonist for functionalism but by a man in 1907 who at one time was an avowed believer in the cult of traditionalism and the Arts and Crafts and who is still considered by some traditionalists, wrongly, I firmly believe, to be their champion. It is, of course, the English prophet of the modern movement whose centenary it is next year, WR Lethaby, but that is another story.

As I take my opportunity to air my views, may I say that I still, I strongly hope, hold to the position Connell and I took up twenty-five years ago. It is that of the functionalist and, as Thomas Stevens says, that of the constructivist. Supported by the views of Russell Hitchcock and of Thomas Stevens, perhaps I may claim that my attempts to rely upon what Phillip Webb called a 'basis in utility' in architecture have at least been consistent.

I confess, Mr Chairman, that, like Lethaby, I do not see architecture as a matter of taste, certainly not of purely personal and individual taste; and I do not see it as taste sanctioned by a select and specially informed few, a few who come to see themselves as self-appointed guardians of taste.

Exercise of the former kind of taste inevitably leads, I suggest, either to a preciousness that tends to ignore the utilitarian media of the art – function and structure – or it is a vehicle for the egoism, sometimes arrogant and unbridled, that has shown itself in architecture during the last hundred years.

Whereas exercise of the latter kind of taste, that is to say taste of the select few, at best leads to a somewhat ineffectual and rather boring academic eclectism, and, at worst to what Professor Sir Albert Richardson suggests is the sole duty of the artist namely 'improvement upon the past'! Neither of these attitudes, I would think, lend much of consequence to the timeless and universal qualities that go to make creative art at any level.

Someone has said that nowadays more smoke without fire is produced than in any other age! This may well be true. In the old days you certainly had to build a lot of large buildings, as did for example Gilbert Scott and William Burges, to come before the public eye. Today, Mr Chairman, the modern press, radio and television, make architectural Davy Crockett reputations overnight and without much reference to the horrid pains of building, thus underlying what Oscar Wilde once said, 'It is personalities not principles that move the age.'

There has been a fashion since the war to decry the functionalist and to dismiss the constructivism of the thirties, with references to the New Brutalism and the 'smell of concrete' and with the suggestion that the early work of the modern movement was moralist, puritanical, un-gay.

I speak without any particularly strong feeling about this kind of reaction except to think that it was an historic and post-war reflection, following years of war-time drabness and 'utility'. It did not influence everyone. On another aspect my friend Nikolaus Pevsner (I can never rid myself of my idea of him as a descendent, in the field of art criticism, of the Herr Muthesius who came over to study the English new architecture of the fin de siecle and turn of the century), Nikolaus Pevsner, generally so thorough in this scholarship and who has done so much to draw the attention of the English to their own ways of art, has suggested that there was something of *épater le bourgeois* in the early modern movement.

May I say that I think the publication in the Journal provides rather more substantial food for thought on the early modern movement than do these criticisms and that this may lead to conclusions historically a little more correct and a little less subjective?

The important and critical question of formalism as opposed to constructivism is taken up by Mr Stevens in his contribution to the Journal. I should like to touch on this question if I may. Firstly, I suggest that formalism could be defined as the doctrine of those who tend to design in the abstract, those who make shapes for the sake of shapes and for whom structure is a means to that end and for whom function is secondary. Formalism is the antithesis of constructivism.

I hold to the view, Mr Chairman, that 'form is function', therefore structure is not only a means to an end, but, by the very nature of man's creative work, it has its own aesthetic and is an artistic end in itself. This is an abiding truth for the constructivist and it enlivens his intellect and quickens his intuition. But the formalist, in order to achieve his abstract ends must inevitably compromise with this truth. What too often passes as intellect for him is, I suggest, knowledge, academic scholarship, and what passes as intuition is custom, convention and 'being in the swim'.

'It is not we who judge a work of art; rather it is the work of art that judges us' said John le Farge. Shall I be labelled moralist if I suggest that this rather penetrating thought be applied to formalism and to the formalist in his work?

'Style-mongering', as Lethaby called it, is at last on the way out, though monstrous building, dressed in historicist forms still go up about us. But eclectic formalism tends to take its place even including the choice of modern forms. However, one can be hopeful because the schools, once hot-beds of academicism, 'taste, design and all that stuff', begin to produce men for whom 'the basis of utility' is the only basis for architecture. Architects are now being 'trained to practical power' knowing that there is really no opposition between 'art and science' and who begin to realise that architecture is an art, 'whereby we show our science'.

Mr Chairman, I have only a few more words to say, but before turning to these may I undertake the very pleasant task of thanking my friends, who initiated and organised an evening that I shall never forget. Outstanding amongst these are Colonel Bassett of the Royal Marines, a Corps distinguished for its unconvention, a man whose self-effacing qualities are in direct but inverse ratio to the excitement and brilliance of his secret deeds; and Alec Nash, Master Builder, Master Painter-Stainer and very gentle Savage. I thank them as I thank my very patient friends Dick Wakelin, Reg Uren and Tom Harper-Ellis for this evening. And I thank you Sir Kenneth for your

very kindly chairmanship and Bernard Ashmole and Peter Smithson for your very interesting and too generous remarks and for toasting my health. Indeed, I thank you all for coming and I thank those who have sent messages. I am sure I speak for Connell and Lucas also. It is a great tribute to the work of the three.

I am particularly grateful to the original organisers of this evening for suggesting that my wife should be present tonight. If anyone deserves a tribute, may I say it is she. You would all understand this more if I were able and she were willing for me to describe the struggles to live in the terrible thirties.

The idea of the individual architect being entirely responsible in the architectural sense, for the work produced in his office, is a nice modern convention. It is a hangover from nineteenth-century individualism. He is indeed responsible in the legal and technical sense and unless he influences the work architecturally he is no longer a leader but all of us as principals rely upon our teams. I should like to mention one or two men, aside from my partners then and now who have greatly helped me: Ian Reynolds, a New Zealander, Maxwell Gregory, an Australian, Peter Stiles, George Buzuk and Alan Cordingley. There are others of course and they include my old friend and Quantity Surveyor Cyril Sweett and I am grateful to them.

Finally, may I be forgiven for quoting from the Epilogue to 'Architecture' (Incidentally if I refer to Lethaby a good deal it is because of the influence upon me of study of that remarkable man – study, opportunity for which I am most grateful to the Royal College of Art).

I quote: 'In the past, sections of the community – aristocracy and church – bestowed patronage upon the art of building. In exercise of their rights – assumed or otherwise does not matter – they acknowledged responsibilities towards architecture and by their acts were instruments of choice. Today, we are all of us patrons, we all have rights: do we know our responsibilities? Can we exercise choice?' 'Our great difficulty' – here I make direct reference to Lethaby's own words – 'is lack of spontaneous agreement; an expressive form of art is only reached by building out in one direction during a long time. No art that is ony one man deep is worth much; it should be a thousand men deep'.

'We cannot forget our historical knowledge, [I go on quoting] nor would we if we might. The important question is, can it be organised and directed, or must we continue to be betrayed by it? The only agreement that seems possible is agreement on a scientific basis, on an endeavour after perfect structural efficiency. If we could agree on this we need not trouble about beauty, for that would take care of itself.' Is this the champion of the Arts and Crafts?

'Our survey [Lethaby is referring to his book] should have shown us that there is not one absolute external form of beauty, but rather an endless series of changing modes in which the universal spirit of beauty may manifest itself; that, indeed, change of the form is one of the conditions of its continuance.' Mr Chairman – This was the modern position when Lethaby wrote nearly fifty years ago, and it is the modern position now.

Personal statement by Colin Lucas

This was Colin Lucas' submission to the book that accompanied the first Unit One exhibition at the Mayor Gallery. It appears in *Unit One: The Modern Movement in English Architecture, Painting and Sculpture*, edited by Herbert Read, London, 1934.

At one time I was interested in Aesthetics as a subject for discussion – nowadays I find arguments on Aesthetics as meaningless as they are endless: beauty and ugliness are things felt, and frankly, I cannot feel beauty and dissect it simultaneously.

I feel that a new thought process is needed, which will enable us to probe into the meaning of subjective phenomena without destroying them.

And I feel that we are all suffering from a muddle-headedness on the subject, which I attribute to the following basic cause: we have been taught for generations to believe that our minds are detachable from our bodies.

Now, human beings are not divisible into compartments of mind and body: no human being is a 'robot' and no human being is an abstract thought process. We are each a grouping together of many different elements, which work and interact as a single unit; and if one part of us is removed for examination, the rest of us will collapse and die.

And so it is with our work: a building designed by man is essentially a reflection of this unit human being: and there is no division in the reflection, just as there is no division in the source of light.

Someone seems to have broken the mirror badly, however, of late, for all our buildings are regarded from the two viewpoints of structure–economy–efficiency on the one side, and appearance–style–art on the other.

And needless to say, when dissected so ruthlessly from the unit, appearance becomes a sham, and economy expires, because appearance costs so much.

You will find, I believe, a growing tendency among modern architects to combat this muddle-headedness; but it is easily misunderstood: we are told by some that perfect efficiency is perfect beauty; by others that houses are machines or aeroplanes, or ships; but I believe those new viewpoints are just an indication that a few sensible people are struggling to see the problem of design as a reflection of the unit human being.

The reason why machines are given this undue attention in discussions on building design, is simply that engineers are free to design without being pestered by this strange duality of viewpoint, and so they are naturally and sensibly producing unified results. A 'clean-looking job' is the engineer's aesthetic, and an extremely successful one too: for the 'tidiness of design' as an aim, is a much more valuable criterion than all the aesthetic jargon, – simply because the expression implies a unity of viewpoint.

If only those in authority could clear their minds of this duality, and sanction only those buildings which are a true reflection of the unit human being I have described, there might be a chance of finding a sane viewpoint, and sooner or later an ordered layout of 'clean-looking' structures would replace this chaos in our architecture, which eats into our minds and hampers our every action.

Talk at the RIBA by Colin Lucas

Colin Lucas prepared this text for the RIBA Discussion 'Connell, Ward and Lucas' on 2 March 1976

Basil Ward has given you an amusing and interesting account of our environment in the early thirties – I would like to enlarge on some of the technical points he raised. As he hinted, the main inspiration in our work was reinforced concrete. The way in which we used reinforced concrete was actually quite unique. Many so-called modern houses of this period were partly built of reinforced concrete, but the walls were constructed of bricks or blocks. This to us was a sham. Our work was all in-situ concrete, with walls no more than 4 inches thick. The possibilities of architectural expression in this technique were immense. We used four inch walls as self-supporting beams over continuous window openings, and we supported the whole structure on the minimum number of freestanding columns. The whole house became a 'floating' structure in lightweight reinforced concrete.

When I first started as a builder in 1928 we had our own men. That was a great opportunity to experiment. Our first experiment was a single-storey house on the Thames (slide). This house was built entirely of concrete – concrete raft, concrete walls four inches thick, concrete roof slab. Steel window mullions supported the open portions. Walls were shuttered and poured in one lift, with insulating board inserted in the shuttering and left in when the shutters were struck. The external face was rendered and colour washed. It all worked very successfully, and the whole house only cost £1,300.

So we tried a two-storey version – a small house near Wrotham in Kent, in the corner of a field (slide). This little house was built on the same principle, all of in-situ concrete. Inside, the walls and ceilings were insulated with Celotex board, which was covered with stout lining paper and distempered. It was a delightful house to live in – nice and warm, no draughts, no creaking floorboards or leaking tiled roofs. (slide) Here is a view of the garden side. The flying staircase leads up to an open sleeping porch with big folding doors.

By this time the design possibilities were beginning to inspire me immensely. I began to dream about following in the footsteps of Auguste Perret, and becoming an 'architect-builder'. But I only got a few more houses to do, and most of our time was spent putting up shopfronts in the Old Kent Road. So when a mutual friend Philip Scholberg, introduced me to Amyas and Basil a year or two later it seemed a good idea to join forces. One of the strangest I could never explain was that we had both independently hit on the same technique. Amyas' house at Grayswood which you saw on the screen just now used four inch reinforced concrete walls on a lightweight frame. As far as I know we were alone in the field.

I am now going to show you where we had got to several years later (slide). This is a house in Roehampton for Philip Proudman. I wonder if you think it is more sophisticated, less naïve perhaps or do you prefer the first one? I wouldn't know – but certainly it is more advanced technically. The windows are double glazed and sliding-folding – a Swiss patent, all made of Austrian pine.

Here and there a little brickwork has appeared, and the exterior is finished with a scraped rendering – not too successful. Here is a photo of the living room, which as you see is on two levels (slide). As usual we made use of freestanding columns and even a freestanding chimney. This was a delightful room to live in, with views over Richmond Park. Actually,

this house now belongs to the G.L.C. and they are taking great care of it.

Here is a larger house, built on the golf course at Virginia Water. You will notice that the thinness of the reinforced concrete structure is emphasised by the treatment of flank walls and projecting canopies. Once again a little brickwork was used, but only for non-structural walls at ground level, to emphasise the floating character of the superstructure. This is the entrance side, with a curved porch and big staircase window (slide). You will notice that we used standard metal windows with large fixed lights between them. This was mainly for economy – in those days the aluminium window had not yet arrived. This house, by the way, was turned down flat by the estate people, and we had to go to arbitration. Fortunately we got the right arbitrator!

And finally, here is the last house we carried out together before the war ended our partnership – a house in Frognal, Hampstead, for Geoffrey Walford (slide). Before I show you other slides of Frognal I would like to read something that Geoffrey Walford wrote in the RIBA Journal at the time, explaining his reasons as a client for commissioning a house of this kind:

'I held a conviction', he said, 'that design was not a matter of erudition in style, nor of aptitude for repeating the fine effects of other ages, but simply a matter of sensibility for structure, for the placing of masses and weights, and for materials.

Only a few designers in this country appeared to accept frankly reinforced concrete as a material, and structural method, different from that of any form of masonry, and their work appealed to me as having that structural quality which, personally, I find missing in nearly all other contemporary work with the exception of that of some engineers.

I can only regret that this building should offend the susceptibilities of some people and be beyond the comprehension of others. To me it has proved an experience of intense interest and delight.'

Geoffrey Walford had a long and difficult fight to get his house built. It was turned down by the LCC Planning Committee, as Basil Ward has mentioned, and later refused permission by the Estate Surveyors. Finally he took it to the High Court and won his case. The house stands as a monument to his determination, and as a symbol of the modern movement... well, to carry on with the slides, (slide) this is a photo of the garden side – childrens' bedrooms up on the top floor, and a large terrace below, with a staircase down in the garden. (slide) Here is a view from the terrace of the big living room windows. In those days they had to be of steel, and they were a bit heavy to open. (slide) This is the interior of the living room – not a very good photo, but it was a magnificent room, with dining at the far end, sitting portion in the centre, and piano and books at this end. (slide) Then here is his dressing room, which was on the other side of the house. And here, believe it or not, is the invitation sent to members of the LCC Planning Committee after the house was finished. They all came along to see what the place was like – and, well, certainly they enjoyed the party!

Chronological list of projects

Ordered using the date the project began. Where the individual project architect is known, the name is picked out in **bold**.

Early buildings by Connell, Ward and Lucas

1927
Silver Birches, Burghclere, Hampshire, for Miss Madge-Porter
Lucas, Lloyd and Co.

1928
High and Over, Station Road, Highover Park, Amersham, Buckinghamshire, for Professor Bernard Ashmole, 1928–31
Connell and Thomson

1929
Garden design, Trent Park, Middlesex, for Sir P Sassoon
Amyas **Connell**

Garden design, Lyme Park, Cheshire
Amyas **Connell**

Noah's House and boathouse, Spade Oak Reach, Bourne End, Buckinghamshire, for Mr R Lucas, 1929–34
Lucas Lloyd and Co.

1930
The Sunlight House, Chelwood Gate, Forest Row, East Sussex, for Mr FR Lucas, 1930–31
Lucas Lloyd and Co.

1931
The Hopfield, Wrotham, Kent, for Colin Lucas, 1931–33
Lucas Lloyd and Co.

New Farm (now White House), Grayswood, Surrey, for Sir A Lowes-Dickinson, 1931–33
Connell and Ward

Ecole du Petit Cordon Bleu, cookery school and restaurant, 29 Sloane St, London, SW1, for D Lucas and R Hume
Colin **Lucas**

The Vitamin Café, 419 Oxford Street, London, W1
Connell and Hargroves

1932
Health Shop, 70-71 Welbeck Street, London, W1, for Edgar J Saxon Ltd
Connell, Ward and Hargroves

1933
Semi-detached houses, 97-101 Park Avenue, Parkwood Estate, Ruislip, Middlesex, with Walter Taylor (Builders) Ltd, 1933–35
Connell and **Ward** (and Lucas)

Saltings, 42 Sinah Lane, Hayling Island, Hampshire, for Dr RD Lawrence, 1933–34
Connell and Ward

44 Sinah Lane, Hayling Island, Hampshire, for Dr L Haydon, 1933–34
Connell and Ward

The Flat Roof House, Little Frieth, Buckinghamshire, for Margaret Sewell, 1933–35
Colin **Lucas**

The Sun Houses, 4,5,6 and 8 High and Over Estate, Station Road, Amersham, Buckinghamshire, for Mr C de Peyer and Mr J MacGibbon, 1933–35
Connell and Ward

1934
Usherwood, Sutton Abinger, Surrey, for Mr Usherwood, 1934–35
Connell and **Ward**

56, 62 and One Other, Wicklands Avenue, Saltdean, East Sussex, for Mr Snow, 1934–35
Connell and **Ward**

The Concrete House, 4 The Ridgeway, Westbury-on-Trym, Bristol, for Mr RH Gunn, 1934–35
Connell and Ward

Buildings and projects by the Connell Ward and Lucas Practice

1934
The Firs, 137 Brighton Road, Redhill, Surrey, for Miss EF Cooper, 1934–35
Connell **Ward** and Lucas

The Firkin, 4 Mill Street, Redhill, Surrey, for Mrs FM Unwin, 1934–35
Connell **Ward** and Lucas

House design, Frinton-on-Sea, Essex, for Frinton Park development scheme, 1934–35
Connell Ward and Lucas

Kent House, 13-17 Ferdinand Street, Camden, NW1, for St Pancras Home Improvement Society (Northern Group), 1934–35
Connell, Ward and Lucas

Plastic Bathroom (exhibit 71), Contemporary industrial design in the home exhibition, Dorland Hall, London
Connell Ward and Lucas

Sound City film producing and recording studios, Shepperton, Surrey, for Sound City, 1934–36
Connell Ward and Lucas

1935
95 Salisbury Road, Worcester Park, Surrey, for Mr EE Minion, 1935–36
Connell Ward and Lucas

6 Temple Gardens, Moor Park, Rickmansworth, Hertfordshire, for Mr HS Tanburn, 1935–37
Connell **Ward** and Lucas

Flats and Shops, Lord's Court, 32-36 St John's Wood Road, London, NW1, for Mr Bennett, 1935–38
Connell Ward and Lucas

Working-class domestic flats in reinforced concrete (competition entry)
Connell Ward and Lucas

Hertford Central Offices, Hertfordshire (competition entry)
Connell Ward and Lucas

Dragons, Woodmancote, West Sussex, for Dr DA Crow, 1935–36
Connell Ward and **Lucas**

The Edith Edwards Preventorium, Papworth, Cambridgeshire, for Mrs RG Edwards, 1935–39
Connell Ward and Lucas

Individual Health Centre, 1935–36
Connell Ward and Lucas

1936
Newport Civic Buildings, South Wales (competition entry)
Connell Ward and Lucas

66 Frognal, Hampstead, London, NW3, for Mr G Walford, 1936–38
Connell Ward and **Lucas**

Bracken or Greenside, Chestnut Avenue, Wentworth Estate, Virginia Water, Surrey, for Dr Williamson-Noble, 1936–37 (demolished 2004)
Connell Ward and **Lucas**

1937
Potcroft, Sutton, Pulborough, West Sussex, for Dr L Thomas, 1937–38
Connell Ward and **Lucas**

Design for St John Ambulance meeting hall, Surrey, for Miss A Stables, unbuilt
Connell Ward and **Lucas**

1938
Scheme for a community of unemployed (subsistence production), Llandegveth, Monmouthshire, for an Order of Friends
Connell **Ward** and Lucas

26 Bessborough Road, Roehampton, London, SW15, for Major PA Proudman, 1938–39
Connell Ward and **Lucas**

1939
St George's Hospital, London, SW1 (competition entry)
Connell Ward and Lucas

Later buildings by Amyas Connell from 1940, including principal works in East Africa

1940
Auckland Anglican Cathedral (competition entry) with H Thornley Dyer
1943
House at West Winterslow, Wiltshire
Housing scheme at Papworth, Cambridgeshire, for Papworth Village Settlement
1946
Crystal Palace Competition (with G Simonek and LC Cooper)
1947
Hospital, administrative offices, mosque and shops, Kanga village, nr. Tanga, Tanganyika (now Tanzania), for Bird & Co.
1949
Accountant's house, Raskajone, Tanga, for Barclays Bank
Manager's house, Raskajone, Tanga, for Barclays Bank
House, No.1, Ring Street, Tanga, for Charles Galanos
Manager's House (Dick Barker), Tanga, for Dalgety & Co.
Office, shops and flats, Tanga, for N Tzamburakis
Church for all denominations, Lushoto, Usambara Mountain, Tanganyika, for Lady William Lead
'Go-down', Tanga, for African Mercantile Co. Ltd.
1950
Manager's House, Raskajone, Tanga, for African Mercantile Co. Ltd.
Cinema, Tanga, for Novelty Talkies Co.
House, location unknown, for Daisy and Peter Roach
1951
Kenya legislative Council Building phase 1 (Parliament Buildings), Nairobi designed with H Thornley Dyer
1952
Offices, 3 King Street, Tanga, Tanganyika, for RG Vernon Ltd
House and studio, Mile Seven, Limuru Road, Roslyn, Nairobi, Kenya, for Amyas Connell
Extension of Lawns Hotel, Lushoto
1956
HH Aga Khan Platinum Jubilee Hospital for the Ismaili community of East Africa and nurses' home extension, Nairobi, Kenya (now the Aga Khan Memorial Hospital, Nairobi), 1956-62
1962
Metropolitan Competition for Cathedral of Christ the King, Liverpool (competition entry)
1963
Parliament buildings extension with new assembly chamber, designed with H Thornley Dyer, for the Ministry of Justice, Nairobi
c.1968
Hotel and catering training college, Karen, funded by the Danish Government
c.1970
The Netherlands Embassy and Dutch Ambassador's House, Muthaiga, Nairobi, Kenya
Other projects – dates unknown
House, Kitsuru, for Keble-White
Friends Community Centre, Ofafa
House on tea estate, Limuru
House, Kiambu, for Philip Coldman
House, Kiambu, for Cecily Pitt-Moore
Outpatients' clinics King George V Hospital, Nairobi
Law offices in Nairobi
Houses for Ginella & Co., Dar-es-Salaam
House for Felice Maggi, Dar-es-Salaam
Houses at Oyster Bay for Ralli Bros, Dar-es-Salaam
Hospital in Kuala Lumpur (competition entry)
Civic Centre in Johannesburg (competition entry)

Later buildings by Basil Ward from 1940

1953
Metabolic Research Unit at Hammersmith Hospital with Ramsay Murray White and Ward
Linear Accelerator and Cyclotron Building, Hammersmith Hospital with Murray, Ward and Partners
Provincial Insurance Building, Kendal, Cumbria with Murray, Ward and Partners
Laboratories, University of Oxford with Murray, Ward and Partners date?
Kai Tak airport, Hong Kong date?
1954
High altitude test facilities buildings, Derby, for Rolls Royce Ltd with Murray, Ward and Partners
East Molesey cricket pavilion

Later buildings by Colin Lucas from 1940

1949
Ackroydon Estate, Wimbledon, London, SW19, with the LCC
1951
Alton West Estate, Roehampton, London, with the LCC
1965 (-72)
Ferrier Estate, Kidbrooke. Greenwich, London, with the LCC

Bibliography

Books

Abercrombie, Patrick, *The Book of the Modern House: A Panoramic Survey of Contemporary Domestic Design*, Hodder and Stoughton, London, 1939

Allan, John, *Lubetkin – Architecture and the Tradition of Progress*, RIBA, London, 1992

Banham, *Reyner, Theory and Design in the first Machine Age*, Architectural Press, London, 1960 (see later editions)

Bauer, Catherine, *Modern Housing*, New York and London, 1935

Bertram, Anthony, *The House a Machine for Living In*, A & C Black Ltd, London, 1935

Bertram, Anthony, *Design*, Penguin, Harmondsworth, 1938

Bingham, Neil, *Christopher Nicholson*, Academy Editions, London, 1996

Blomfield, Sir Reginald, *Modernismus*, Macmillan, London, 1934

Bowness, Alan, *Barbara Hepworth: A Pictorial Autobiography*, The Tate Gallery, London, 1985

Brett, Lionel, *The Things we See: Houses*, Penguin, Harmondsworth, 1947

Bumpus, Judith, *Reginald Brill*, Scolar Press and Kingston University, London, 1999

Carter, Ella, *Seaside Houses and Bungalows*, Country Life Ltd, London, 1937

Carrington, Noel (ed.), *Design in the Home*, Country Life Ltd, London, 1933

Carrington, Noel, *The Shape of Things: An Introduction to Design in Everyday Life*, Nicholson and Watson, London, 1939

Cohn, Laura, *The Door to a Secret Room*, a Portrait of Wells Coates, Scolar Press, Aldershot, 1999

Collins, Peter, *Concrete – The Vision of a New Architecture*, Faber, London, 1959

Council for Research on Housing Construction, *Slum Clearance and Rehousing*, London, 1934

Country Life Ltd, *Recent English Architecture 1920–40*, selected by the Architecture Club, London, 1947

Curtis, William, *Modern Architecture since 1900*, Phaidon, Oxford, 1987; pb, 2006

Curtis, Wiliam, *Le Corbusier*, Phaidon, London; pb, 2007

Dean, David, *The Thirties: Recalling the English Architectural Scene*, Trefoil Books, London, 1983

Duncan, RA, *The Architecture of a New Era*, London, 1933

Elwall, Robert, *Erno Goldfinger*, Academy Editions, London, 1996

Fellows, Richard A, *Sir Reginald Blomfield: An Edwardian Architect*, London, 1985

Forty, Adrian, *Objects of Desire: Design and Society 1750–1980*, Cameron Books, London, 1986

Frampton, Kenneth, *Modern Architecture: A Critical History*, Thames and Hudson, London, 1980 (see latest edition)

Fry, E Maxwell, *Fine Building*, Faber and Faber, London, 1944

Garland, Madge, *The Indecisive Decade: The World of Fashion and Entertainment in the Thirties*, Macdonald, London, 1968

Gaudet, J, *Eléments et Théorie de l'Architecture. Cours professé a L'Ecole Nationale et Special des Beaux-Arts* (4 volumes), Librairie de la construction moderne, Paris, 1901–04`

Gibberd, Frederick, *The Architecture of England from the Norman Time to the Present-Day*, Architectural Press, London, 1947

Giedion, S, *Space, Time and Architecture*, Harvard University Press (1941), 1954

Giedion, S, *Walter Gropius, Work and Teamwork*, USA and London, 1954

Gloag, John, *Industrial Art Explained*, London, 1934

Gloag, John (ed.), *Design in Modern Life*, G. Allen and Unwin, London, 1934

Gould, Jeremy, *Modern Houses in Britain 1919–1939*, Society of Architectural Historians of Great Britain, 1977.

Grigson, Geoffrey, *Unit One, Herbert Read and the Mayor Gallery*, Bookman, 1933

Grigson, Geoffrey (ed.), *The Arts Today*, John Lane, The Bodley Head, London, 1935

Gropius, Walter, *The New Architecture and the Bauhaus*, translated by P Morton Shand, Faber, London, 1935

Gunn, Edwin, *Economy in House Design*, Architectural Press, London, 1932

Harrison, Charles, *English Art and Modernism 1900–1939*, Yale University Press, Yale, 1994

Hastings, Alan (ed.), *Weekend Houses, Cottages and Bungalows*, Architectural Press, London, 1939

Hill, Oliver, *Fair Horizons: Buildings of Today*, London, 1950

Hitchcock, H-R and Johnson, P, *The International Style: Architecture Since 1922*, New York, 1932

Hitchcock, H-R, Johnson, P and Mumford, L, *Modern Architecture*, to accompany the International Exhibition, New York, 1932

Hitchcock, Henry-Russell, *Modern Architecture in England*, Museum of Modern Art, New York, 1937

Holme, CG (ed.), *Industrial Architecture*, The Studio Ltd, London, 1935

Isaacs, Reginald, *Walter Gropius: An illustrated biography of the creator of the Bauhaus*, Little, Brown and Company, Canada, 1991

Jackson, Anthony, *The Politics of Architecture: A History of Modern Architecture in Britain*, Architectural Press, London and New York, 1970

Jordan, R Furneaux, *English House*, London, 1959

Kurtz, Donna (ed.), *Bernard Ashmole 1894–1988: An Autobiography*, Oxbow Books, Oxford, 1994

Lancaster, Osbert, *Progress in Pelvis Bay*, John Murray, London, 1936

Lancaster, Osbert, *Pillar to Post: The Pocket Lamp of Architecture*, John Murray, London, 1938

Lancaster, Osbert, *Homes Sweet Homes*, Butler & Tanner, London, 1939

LCC, *London Housing*, London, 1937

Leatheart, Julian, *Style in Architecture*, Thomas Nelson & Sons, London, 1940

Le Corbusier, *Towards a New Architecture*, translated by F Etchells, Rodker, London (several editions). First published as *Vers une Architecture* by Editions Crés, Paris, 1923

Lethaby, WR, *Form in Civilisation*, London, 1951

Lewison, Jeremy (ed.), *Circle: Constructive art in Britain 1934–40*, Kettles Yard Gallery, Cambridge, 1982

Lucas, Edgar, *The Builder's book of the House*, The Technical Press, London, 1938

Madge, John (ed.), *Tomorrow's Houses*, Pilot Press, London, 1946

MARS Group, Catalogue for New Burlington Gallery exhibition, London, 1938

Moholy-Nagy, L, *The New Vision*, London, 1933

McGrath, Raymond, *Twentieth Century Houses*, London, 1934

Martin, Leslie and Speight, Sadie, *The Flat Book*, London, 1939

Martin, Leslie, Nicholson, Ben and Gabo, Naum (eds), *Circle: International Survey of Constructive Art*, London, 1937

Miller, Duncan, *More colour schemes for the modern home*, The Studio Ltd, New York, 1938

Mills, Edward, *The New Architecture in Great Britain*, London, 1953

Muggeridge, Malcolm, *The Thirties: 1930–1940 in Great Britain*, Collins, London (1940), 1957

Myles Wright, H, *Small Houses £500-£2500*, The Architectural Press, London, 1937
Pearse, Innes H and Crocker, Lucy H, *The Peckham Experiment, A Study in the Living Structure of Society*, George Allen and Unwin, London, 1943

Pevsner, Nikolaus, *Pioneers of the Modern Movement from William Morris to Walter Gropius*, Faber, London, 1956

Pevsner, Nikolaus, *An Enquiry into Industrial Art in England*, Cambridge University Press, 1937

Pevsner, Nikolaus, *An Outline of European Architecture*, Pelican, London, 1960

Randal Phillips, R, *Houses for Moderate Means*, Country Life Ltd, London, 1936

Randal Phillips, R, *Small Family Homes of Today*, London, 1924?

Randal Phillips, R (ed.), *The Modern English House*, Country Life Ltd, London, 1928

Randal Phillips, R, *The £1,000 House*, Country Life Ltd, London, 1928

Read, Herbert (ed.), *Unit One: The Modern Movement in English Architecture, Painting and Sculpture*, London, 1934

Read, Herbert, *Art and Industry: The Principles of Industrial Design*, London, 1934 (and subsequent editions)

Reilly, CH, *Scaffolding in the Sky*, G Routledge and Sons, London, 1938

Richards, JM, *An Introduction to Modern Architecture*, Penguin, Harmondsworth, 1940 (and subsequent editions)

Richards, JM, *Memoirs of an Unjust Fella*, Weidenfeld and Nicolson, London, 1980

Richardson, HW and Aldcroft, D, *Building in the British Economy between the Wars*, Allen and Unwin, London, 1968

Robertson, Howard, *Modern Architectural Design*, London, 1932

Rothenstein, Sir John, *British Art since 1900*, London, 1962

Ruskin, John, *The Seven Lamps of Architecture*, Orpington, 1894

Sharp, Dennis (ed.), *Planning and Architecture - essays presented to Arthur Korn by the Architectural Association*, AA London, 1967

Sharp, Dennis, *Modern Architecture and Expressionism*, Longman, London, 1966

Sharp, Dennis, *Sources of Modern Architecture: A Critical Bibliography*, Granada, London, 1981

Sharp, Dennis, Connell Ward and Lucas, *Modern Movement Architects in England 1929–39*, Book Art, London, 1994

Sharp, Dennis, *Twentieth Century Architecture: A Visual History* (third revised edition), Images, Musgrove, 2002

Sharp, Thomas, *Town and Countryside*, Oxford University Press, 1932

Sharp, Thomas, *English Panorama*, .Pelican, London 1936

Shaw, Peter, *Louis Hay Architect*, Aukland, 1988

Simon, ED, *How to Abolish the Slums*, London, 1929

Simon, ED, *The Anti-slum Campaign*, London, 1933

Skelton, Robin, *Poetry of the Thirties*, Penguin, Harmondsworth, 1964

Smithells, Roger (ed), *Modern Small Country Houses*, Country Life Ltd, London, 1939

Smithells, Roger and Woods, S John, *The Modern home: its Decoration, Furnishing and Equipment*, F Lewis, Essex, 1936

Spender, Stephen, *The Thirties and After*, Fontana, London, 1978

Symonds, Julian, *The Thirties: A Dream Revealed*, Cresset Press, London, 1960

Taut, Bruno, *Modern Architecture* (English translation), The Studio Ltd, London, 1930

Taylor, GC, *The Modern Garden*, Country Life Ltd, London, 1937

Towndrow, FE, *Architecture in the Balance: an approach to the art of Scientific Humanism*, Chatto and Windus, London, 1933

Turnor, Reginald, *The Smaller English House (1500–1939)*, London, 1952

Wallace-Hadrill, Andrew, *The British School at Rome 100 years*, London, 2001

Walton, John K, *The British Seaside: Holidays and Resorts in the Twentieth Century*, Manchester, 2000

Williams-Ellis, Clough and Summerson, John, *Architecture Here and Now*, Thomas Nelson and Sons, 1934

Williams-Ellis, Clough and Ambel, *The Pleasure of Architecture*, London, 1934

Yorke, FRS, and Penn, Colin, *A Key to Modern Architecture*, London, 1939

Yorke, FRS, *The Modern House*, The Architectural Press, London, 1934 (and subsequent editions)

Yorke, FRS, *The Modern House In England*, The Architectural Press, London, 1937 (and subsequent editions)

Yorke, FRS and Gibberd, Frederick, *The Modern Flat*, The Architectural Press, London, 1937

Articles

Articles are here listed under the publications in which they appeared. Abbreviations used include:
AAJ: AA Journal
AAQ: AA Quarterly
A&BN: Architect and Building News
AJ: Architects' Journal
AR: Architectural Review
BD: Building Design
CQ: Concrete Quarterly

AAQ, Kenneth Frampton, 'MARS and Beyond: The British Contribution to Modern Architecture' (review of Jackson A, The Politics of Architecture, 1970), Vol.2, no.4, 1970, pp.51-55
AAQ, William Curtis, 'Berthold Lubetkin or Socialist Architecture in the Diaspora', Vol.8, no.3, London, 1976

AA Files, 'Polemic and Parody in the Battle for British Modernism', Helene Lipstadt, no.3, pp.68-79
AA Files, 'A History of Modern Architecture that still needs to be Written', Royston Landau, no.21, pp.49-53
AA Files, 'The Reconditioned Eye – Artists and Architects in English Modernism', Alan Powers, no.25, pp.54-62

AAJ, 'Connell, Ward and Lucas 1927–1939', Thomas Stevens, November 1956, pp.112-15
AAJ, 'England and the Outside World', H-R Hitchcock, November 1956
AAJ, 'Writing on Architecture', P Morton Shand, Special issue, January 1959

A&BN, 'Welsh Memorial Tuberculosis Hospital Competition', 20 November 1931
A&BN, 'Notes from the Information Bureau of The Building Research Station - XXVI', 19 August 1932, pp.228-29
A&BN, 'Planning-An Annual Notebook', E and OE, London, 1938, p.31
A&BN, 'The Ocean Hotel, Saltdean, Brighton', 12 August 1938, pp.175-81

AJ, 'Le Corbusier', Harold Tomlinson, July 1929, pp.433-34
AJ, 'Some new rules of Etiquette for Architects and Engineers', letter, 11 February 1931
AJ, 'Materials for Architecture', Wells Coates, 4 November 1931, pp.588-89
AJ, 'The White House Cambridge: George Checkley', 19 April 1933, pp.521-25
AJ, 'Correspondence between Robertson and Wells Coates on the MARS Group, 10 May 1933, p.623
AJ, 'The Intelligent Woman's Guide to the Exhibition of British Industrial Art in Relation to the Home', 29 June 1933, pp.865-72
AJ, 'Exhibition of Modern Living', 30 November 1933, pp.691-95
AJ, 'Sunspan House, Olympia', P Morton Shand, 26 April 1934, pp.607-10
AJ, 'Connell, Ward and Lucas, 10 March 1976, p.467
AJ, 'A Modern Briton', James Dunnett, 9 May 1984, pp.29-30
AJ, Obituary of Colin Lucas, James Dunnett, 5 September 1984, p.52

Architects Year Book, 'English Architecture from the Thirties', E. Maxwell Fry, No.8 pp.53-56, London 1957

Architectural Record, 'Cresta Shops', June 1931, pp.508-12

Architectural History Journal (Architectural Historians of Great Britain), 'A call to order – The Rome Prize', Louise Campbell, Vol.32, 1989, pp.131-51

Architecture North West, 'Things remembered: Heroic relics', Basil Ward, Vol. 29, June/July 1968, pp.12-16

AR, 'Ourselves and Europe', WG Newton, Vol.61, 1927, p1
AR, 'The House and the Town', Michael Rosenauer, July 1928, p.231
AR, 'Finella: A house for Mansfield Forbes by Raymond McGrath', AC Frost, December 1929, pp.265-68
AR, 'Modern English Furnishing', Paul Nash, January 1930, pp.43-48
AR, 'The Public and Art', Paul Nash, April 1930, pp.167-68
AR, 'Give the Public What it Wants', The Editor, April 1930, pp.223-25
AR, 'Progress – The Swedish Contribution', July 1930, p.52
AR, 'Stockholm 1930', S Giedion, July 1930, pp.67-72
AR, 'The architecture of the future', Gerald Heard, July 1932, p.1
AR, 'Furniture Today – Furniture Tomorrow', Wells Coates, July 1932, pp.29-38
AR, 'Responses to Tradition', Wells Coates, November 1932, pp.165-68
AR, 'Unit One', Herbert Read, 1933, pp.125-28
AR, 'Review of Unit One', Osbert Lancaster, June 1934, p.212
AR, 'What Price Progress', John Gloag, June 1934, p.133
AR, 'The Modern House', P Morton Shand, July 1934, pp.9-11
AR, 'The Small House of Today', E Maxwell Fry, July 1934, p.20
AR, 'Modern Flats at Hampstead: Wells Coates', August 1934, pp.77-82
AR, 'Walter Gropius', JM Richards, August 1935, pp.45-46
AR, 'Mansfield Forbes', Raymond McGrath, 1936
AR, 'Colour and the English Tradition', Amedée Ozenfant, January 1937, pp.41-44
AR, 'Colour and Method', Amedée Ozenfant, February 1937, pp.89-92
AR, A series by Amedée Ozenfant: 'Colour – Experiments, Rules, Facts', April 1937, pp.195-98; 'Colour Solidity', May 1937, pp.245-46; 'Colour in the Town', July 1937, pp.41-44; 'Colour pro domo', August 1937, pp.77-80
AR, 'Planning in Section', Wells Coates, August 1937, pp.51-58
AR, 'The Gospel of Constructivism, Circle: International Survey of Constructive Art, Review of the book', JE Barton, January 1938, pp.43-44
AR, 'Review of The Modern House in England by FRS Yorke', April 1938, p.90
AR, 'House near Henley-on-Thames by Christopher Nicholson', Vol. 83, June 1938, p.305
AR, 'Nine Swallows, No Summer', N Pevsner, May 1942, pp.109-12
AR, 'Walter Gropius', March 1955, pp.155-57
AR, 'Wells Coates 1893-1958', JM Richards, December 1958, pp. 357-60
AR, 'FRS Yorke', E Maxwell Fry, October 1962, pp.278-80
AR, 'Dudok and Repercussion of his European Influence', R Furneaux Jordan

Bauen & Wohnen, 'Zehn Jahre Bauen in Grossbritannien1924–34', Nikolaus Pevsner, Dec 1967

Building, 'Modern Shops and Modern Materials', Wells Coates, December 1932, pp.364-65
Building, 'E Maxwell Fry: Personal Portrait', September 1950, pp.337-39
BD, 'Heroes of the Modern Movement, Connell and

Menzies', 27 February 1976, pp.12-13
BD, Obituary of Colin Lucas, John Partridge, 7 September 1984, p.10

The Builder, 'Welsh Memorial Tuberculosis Hospital Competition', 20 November 1931

Bystander, 'Wells Coates', November 1937, pp.178-79

Commercial Art, 'Designing the Shop-Front', Howard Robertson, October 1931

CQ, Basil Ward, 'House of the Thirties', no 85, April/May 1970, pp.11-15

Contractor's Record and Municipal Engineer, 'Colour and texture in Concrete surfaces', 22 February 1950, pp.21-24

Design, 'Wells Coates', Richard Freeth, 1936, pp.455-58
Design, 'People: Jack Pritchard', September 1962

Design for Today, 'The English Living Room Today', Wells Coates, May 1933, pp.12-13
Design for Today, 'Minimum Flat', Wells Coates, July 1933, pp.96-97

Evening Standard, London, 'New Era of Flat life is at Hampstead', Winifred Lewis, 29 July 1934

Journal of Architecture, Vol.2, 'Connell, Ward and Lucas: Towards a Complex Critique', E Heeley and D Thistlewood, spring 1997, pp.83-103

New American, 'The Foundation of Arts', Amedée Ozenfant, New York, 1952

RIBAJ, 'The architect and housing by the speculative builder', 28 April 1934, pp.649-53
RIBAJ, 'Connell, Ward and Lucas', Vol.83, no.3, March 1976, p.93

RIBA Transactions, 'The Mars Group', Louise Campbell, Vol.4, no.2, 1984-5, pp.68-79

Conservation of Modern Architecture, a special edition of the Journal of Architectural Conservation, Dennis Sharp, 'Another One Bites the Dust: The Greenside Case', Donhead 2007, pp.117-31

Journal of the Twentieth Century Society, No. 2, 'The Modern House Revisited', London, 1996

The Listener, 'When Shall we be Civilised?' JE Barton, 16 March 1932, pp.378-80
The Listener, 'The Artist in the Home', Paul Nash, 16 March 1932, p.381
The Listener, Wells Coates correspondence, 12 July 1933, p.68
The Listener, 'Is Modern Architecture on the Right Track?' Various, 26 July 1933, pp.123-32
The Listener, 'The Architect's Dilemma I', E Maxwell Fry, 17 May 1955, pp.281-82
The Listener, 'The Architect's Dilemma II', E Maxwell Fry, 24 May 1955, pp.331-32

The Times, Obituary of Amyas Connell, 6 August 1976
The Times, Obituary of Colin Lucas, 29 August 1984

Weekend Review, 'Going Modern and Being British', 12 March 1932, p.643

Unpublished material

Elgohary, F, 'The Development of Modern Architecture in Western Europe and its influence on Public Architecture in Great Britain', Liverpool University School of Architecture, M Arch thesis, 1963

Elgohary, F, 'Wells Coates and his position at the beginning of the Modern Movement in England', Bartlett School of Architecture, UCL, Ph D thesis, 1966

Esau, Robert, 'Early Modern and Low Income Housing in England', 1994

Figueiredo, Peter de, 'Connell, Ward and Lucas 1927–1939', student thesis, 1970-71

Godwin, Sally, 'An examination of the early career of Colin Lucas with particular reference to the flat roofed house at Frieth', Cambridge Diploma thesis, 1998

Lucas, Mark, 'Colin Lucas – a view of a creative life', notes

Morrissey, Martin, 'Colin Lucas – Architect. A British Modernist in the Nineteen Thirties', University of London, Master of Science in Architecture, 1995

Reading, Malcolm, 'A History of the MARS. Group 1933–1945', Bristol, 1986

Roth, Peter, 'The Houses of Connell, Ward and Lucas 1927–1939', PLC dissertation

Zara, Paul, 'Connell, Ward and Lucas Works 1927–1939', Bartlett School of Architecture, UCL, dissertation, 1994

Exhibition catalogues

Modern Architecture in England, reprint of the catalogue to coincide with the exhibition of the same name at MOMA, New York, 1937, Greenwood Press, Connecticut, 1970

Modern Architecture International Exhibition, reprint of the catalogue to accompany the exhibition 10 February to 23 March 1932, New York, 1969

MARS Group, *New Architecture*, New Burlington Gallery, London, 1938

Unit One, The Portsmouth Festival Exhibition, Portsmouth City Museum and Art Gallery, 1978

Connell Ward Lucas: Modern Movement Architects in England 1929–1939, Dennis Sharp (ed.), Book Art, London, 1994

Photography takes command – The camera and British Architecture 1890–1939, Robert Elwall, RIBA, 1994

A Different World: Emigrés Architects in Britain 1928–1958, with contributions from Elain Harwood and David Elliott, RIBA Heinz Gallery, London, 1995

Project bibliographies

Articles are listed first followed by books and any unpublished works such as theses.

Private houses

Silver Birches, Burghclere, Hampshire, 1927
AAJ, Stevens, Thomas, 'Connell, Ward and Lucas 1927–1939', November 1956, pp.114-15

High and Over, Amersham, Buckinghamshire, 1928–31
A&BN, 'The first round – Amenities: local authority versus an architect', 29 November 1929, pp.666-69
A&BN, Robertson, Howard, 'An experiment with time, a house at Amersham', 3 January 1930, pp.12-13
A&BN, Robertson, Howard, 'Aoemenitas "High and Over" at Amersham', 26 June 1931, pp.428-35
A&BN, Robertson, Howard, 'Aoemenitas 'High and Over' at Amersham', 3 July 1931, pp.6-13
A&BN, Supplement no.147 'High and Over Amersham Bucks – I: A kitchen', 23 October 1931
A&BN, Supplement no.148 'High and Over Amersham Bucks – II: A private library', 30 October 1931
A&BN, Supplement no.149, 'High and Over Amersham Bucks – III: A drawing room', 6 November 1931
A&BN, Supplement no.151, 'High and Over Amersham Bucks – V: A concrete frame house', 20 November 1931
AAJ, Hitchcock, Henry-Russell and Stevens, Thomas, 'Connell, Ward and Lucas', November 1956, pp.94, 98-99
AR, Goodesmith, Walter, 'The evolution of design in steel and concrete', November 1932, p.192
Art New Zealand, Findlay, Michael, 'Amyas Connell: High and Over and the modern movement', no.52, spring 1989, pp.94-98
BD magazine, Winter, John, 'Living the high life', May 2007, pp.28-30
Country Life, Hussey, Christopher, 'Country houses and gardens old and new', Vol. LXX, no.1809, 19 September 1931, pp.302-07
Ideal Home, 'A modern English home: High and Over', December 1931, pp.443-47
Pleasing homogeneity, dull times and animated cocktails: New Zealand architecture in the 1930s (ed. McCarthy, Christine). Findlay, Michael, 'So high you can't get over it: neo-classicism, modernism and colonial practice in the forming of a twentieth century landmark', one day symposium, Victoria University, Wellington, 2006
Wasmuths Monatshefte Baukunst und Städtebau, 'Ein Englisches landhaus', issue 10, October 1931, pp.466-70

Dawe, Nick and Powell, Kenneth, *The Modern House Today*, Black Dog, London, 2001, pp.24-29
Gould, Jeremy, *Modern Houses in Britain 1919–39*, Society of Architectural Historians of Great Britain, London, 1977, p.13
McGrath, Raymond, *Twentieth Century Houses*, 1934, p.96
Nairn, Ian, *Modern Buildings in London*, 1964, p.100
Pevsner, Nikolaus, *The Buildings of England: Buckinghamshire*, London, 1960, p.50
Powers, Alan, *Modern – the modern movement in Britain*, Merrell, London, 2005, pp.88-89
Tinniswood, Adrian, *The Art Deco House*, Mitchell Beazley, 2002, pp.114-15
Turnor, Reginald, *The smaller English house, 1500–1939*, London, 1952, p.202

Noah's House, Boathouse and Outhouses, Bourne End, Buckinghamshire, 1929–34
A&BN, 'A bungalow and boathouse at Bourne End, Bucks', 19 August 1932, pp.223-27

AAJ, Hitchcock, Henry-Russell and Stevens, Thomas, 'Connell, Ward and Lucas', November 1956, p.100
AR, Goodesmith, Walter, 'The evolution of design in steel and concrete', November 1932, p.192
Morning Post, 'A Garden Room Paris Fashions', 22 August 1936
National Builder, supplement June 1936

Museum of Modern Art (New York), *Modern Architecture in England*, Greenwood Press, Connecticut, 1937, plate 16
Randall Phillips, R, *Houses for Moderate Means*, Country Life Ltd, London, 1936, p.9
Read, Herbert, *Unit One: The Modern Movement in English Architecture, Painting and Sculpture*, London, 1934, pp.122-24
Wright, Myles, *Small houses £500–2500*, Architectural Press, 1937, p.53

The Sunlight House, Chelwood Gate, East Sussex, 1930–31
AAJ, Hitchcock, Henry-Russell and Stevens, Thomas, 'Connell, Ward and Lucas, November 1956, p.102

Nairn, Ian and Pevsner, Nikolaus, *The Buildings of England: Sussex*, Penguin, Harmondsworth, first printed 1965, 1985 edition, p.506

The Hopfield, Wrotham, Kent, 1931–33
AAJ, Hitchcock, Henry-Russell and Stevens, Thomas, 'Connell, Ward and Lucas', November 1956, p.102
AJ, 'The Hopfield St Mary's Platt Kent', 20 July 1933, p.88
Decoration of the House Beautiful, 'The Ideal Home exhibition illustrated', no.2, vol. 4, April-June 1934, p.82
Christian Science Monitor, 30 April 1935
Vogue, 'A modern sports cottage in the heart of Kent', 14 June 1933, pp.66-67

Brett, Lionel, *The Things we see: Houses*, Penguin, Harmondsworth, 1947, p.26
Museum of Modern Art (New York), *Modern Architecture in England*, Greenwood Press, Connecticut, 1937, plate 15
Read, Herbert, *Unit One: The Modern Movement in English Architecture, Painting and Sculpture*, London, 1934, pp.120-21
Yorke, FRS, *The Modern House*, Surrey, 1944 edition, p.166

New Farm or The White House, Haslemere, Surrey, 1931–33
A&BN, 'A House near Haslemere', 10 March 1933, pp.314-16
AAJ, Hitchcock, Henry-Russell and Stevens, Thomas, 'Connell, Ward and Lucas', November 1956, pp.96, 101
AJ, Mead, Andrew, 'Balancing conservation with improved performance', Perspective, 16 February 1994, pp.18-20
AR, 'A House at Grayswood', March 1933, pp.118-19
AR, Connell, Amyas, 'RSVP', December 1977, p.326
Country Life, Powers, Alan, 'England's White House', Vol.200, no.15, 13 April 2006, pp.72-77
Design for To-day, Butt, Baseden, 'Advantages and Costs of Concrete Experimentation in Domestic Architecture', October 1933, pp.220-23
Independent on Sunday, 'Homes for a new age: the thirties house', 4 October 1992
Review of the Reinforced Concrete Association, Kaylor, H, 'Reinforced Concrete Buildings – their Heat Insulation', no.10, March 1935 (also published in Building, 1934)
RIBAJ, reader enquiry no. 203, June 1994, p.84
Telegraph, property section, Powell, Kenneth, 'Houses for third programme types', 12 October 1996, p.9

Dawe, Nick and Powell, Kenneth, *The Modern House*

Today, Black Dog, London, 2001, pp.30-33
Gould, Jeremy, *Modern Houses in Britain 1919–1939*, Society of Architectural Historians of Great Britain, London, 1977, pp.13-14
Jackson, Anthony, *The Politics of Architecture*, The Architectural Press, 1970, p.69
Powers, Alan, *Modern – the modern movement in Britain*, Merrell, London, 2005, pp.90-91
Mace, PMH, 'New Farm, Grayswood, nr Haslemere', Open University thesis, 1978
McGrath, Raymond, *Twentieth Century Houses*, 1934, pp.96-97
Tinniswood, Adrian, *The Art Deco House*, Mitchell Beazley, 2002, pp.118-19
Yorke, FRS, *The Modern House*, Surrey, 1944 edition, pp.124-25

42 and 44 Sinah Lane, 'Saltings', Hayling Island, Hampshire, 1933–34
AJ, Russell, Barry, 'Mending the Modern Movement', Vol.165, no.13, 30 March 1977, pp.582-83
Daily Mail, Property Mail supplement, Stuart, Malcolm, 'Presenting the most unlikely historic home', 6 May 1976

Balfour, Alan, *Portsmouth*, City Buildings Series, Essex, 1970, pp.77-78

Usherwood House, Sutton Abinger, Surrey, 1934–35
The Journal of Architecture, Heeley, E and Thistlewood, D, 'Connell Ward and Lucas: towards a complex critique', Vol. 2, spring 1997, pp.83-103

The Flat Roof House, Little Frieth, Buckinghamshire, 1933–35
AAJ, Stevens, Thomas, 'Connell, Ward and Lucas 1927–1939', November 1956, pp.114-15
AR, Alden, E, 'Unknown Lucas', no. 994, December 1979, pp.336-37
RIBAJ, Winter, John, 'The White Stuff', March 2001, pp.62-66

The Concrete House, 4 The Ridgeway, Westbury-on-Trym, Bristol, 1934–35
AAJ, Hitchcock, Henry-Russell and Stevens, Thomas, 'Connell, Ward and Lucas', November 1956, p.113
AR, April 1936, pp.170-71
Homefinder, 'Planning a traditional house in the modern way', October 1936, pp.76-77
Decoration, Butt, Baseden, 'The house of the month: concrete – a modern house in Bristol', December 1935, pp.18-19

Dawe, Nick and Powell, Kenneth, *The Modern House Today*, Black Dog, London, 2001, pp.34-37
Decorative Art – The Studio Yearbook 1938, The Studio Ltd, London/NY, p.49
Gould, Jeremy, *Modern Houses in Britain 1919–1939*, Society of Architectural Historians of Great Britain, London, 1977, p.16

The Firs and Firkin, Redhill, Surrey, 1934–35
A&BN, 'An addition to a house at Redhill', 7 June 1935, pp.280-81
AJ, 'Cuckoo', 27 October 1960, p.594
National House Builder, Lander, Susan, 'A reinforced concrete house for under £600 – weekend homes in the modern manner', date unknown, pp.20-21

Brett, Lionel, *The Things we see: Houses*, Penguin, Harmondsworth, 1947, p.22
Carter, Ella (ed.), *Seaside Houses and Bungalows*, Country Life Ltd, London, 1937, p.84
Nairn, Ian, *Modern Buildings in London*, LT, 1964, p.110
Yorke, FRS, *The Modern House in England*, Architectural Press, 1937, pp.130, 134-35

Dragons, Brighton Road, Woodmancote, West Sussex, 1935–36
A&BN, 'A Concrete house in Sussex', 17 April 1936, pp.69-73
AAJ, Hitchcock, Henry-Russell and Stevens, Thomas, 'Connell, Ward and Lucas', November 1956, pp.107, 110
AJ, 'House at Henfield, Sussex', 30 April 1936, pp.659-63
AR, 'House at Woodmancote', December 1936, pp.291-94
National Builder, Bentham, Ernest, 'Rural England and the modern style', supplement 8, 8 June 1936

Carter, Ella (ed.), *Seaside Houses and Bungalows*, Country Life Ltd, London, 1937, dustjacket
Nairn, Ian and Pevsner, Nikolaus, *The Buildings of England: Sussex*, Penguin, Great Britain, 1985 edition, pp.384-85
Yorke, FRS, *The Modern House in England*, Architectural Press, London, 1937, pp.89-91

95 Salisbury Road, Worcester Park, Surrey, 1935–36
AAJ, Stevens, Thomas, 'Connell, Ward and Lucas 1927–1939', November 1956, pp.114-15

6 Temple Gardens, Moor Park, Rickmansworth, Hertfordshire, 1935–37
A&BN, 'A House at Moor Park', 18 February 1938, pp.214-16
AAJ, Hitchcock, Henry-Russell and Stevens, Thomas, 'Connell, Ward and Lucas', November 1956, pp.97, 106
AJ, Culamix rendering advertisement, 4 November 1937, p.xxxix
All England Homefinder, Lander, Susan, 'A reinforced concrete house at Moor Park', October 1937, pp.12-15
Country Life, Randal Philips, R, 'A Modern House at Moor Park', 2 April 1938, pp.358-59
RIBAJ, 'Reinforced Concrete Houses', 17 July 1937, pp.901-9

Brett, Lionel, *The Things we see: Houses*, Penguin, Harmondsworth, 1947, p.17
Yorke, FRS, *The Modern House in England*, Architectural Press, 1937, pp.138-42
Decorative Art – The Studio Yearbook 1938, The Studio Ltd, London/NY, pp.21, 49, 87, 97
Turnor, Reginald, *The Smaller English House 1500–1939*, London, 1952, p.202

Bracken or Greenside, Wentworth, Virginia Water, Surrey, 1936–37
A&BN, 'House at Wentworth, Surrey', 3 December 1937, pp.284-85
AAJ, Hitchcock, Henry-Russell and Stevens, Thomas, 'Connell, Ward and Lucas', November 1956, pp.103, 112
BD and AJ covered the demolition of Greenside in many articles 2002-2006
Daily Telegraph, Clark, Ross, 'Modernist maverick on the seventeenth green', 22 July 2000, p.9
Docomomo Yearbook, Sharp, Dennis, 'A modern house bites the dust', no.30, March 2004, pp.47-49
Conservation of Modern Architecture, a special edition of the *Journal of Architectural Conservation*, Sharp, Dennis, 'Another One Bites the Dust: The Greenside Case ', Donhead, 2007, pp.117-31
Guardian, architecture section, Glancey, Jonathan, 'Pain in the grass', 4 November 2002, pp.12-14
RIBAJ, 'Reinforced Concrete Houses', 17 July 1937, pp.901-9

Twentieth Century Society Newsletter, Croft, Catherine, 'The fight for Greenside', winter 2002/3, p.2
Twentieth Century Society Newsletter, Bennett, Leslie, 'Greenside Update', spring 2005, p.6
Twentieth Century Society Newsletter, Mirwitch, Joseph, 'Greenside Update', autumn 2005, p.9

Decorative Art – The Studio Yearbook 1938, The Studio Ltd, London/NY, p.21
Yorke, FRS, *The Modern House in England*, Architectural Press, 1937, pp.101-3

66 Frognal, Hampstead, London, NW3, 1936–38
A&BN, '66 Frognal, Hampstead', 28 October 1938, pp.100-2
A&BN, 'Unhappy Hampstead', date unknown, p.236
AAJ, Hitchcock, Henry-Russell and Stevens, Thomas, 'Connell, Ward and Lucas', November 1956, pp.108, 110-11
AJ, 'New and old', 30 July 1936
AJ, 'House in Frognal, Hampstead', 11 June 1936, pp.696-98
AJ, Connell, Ward and Lucas, 'The Hampstead case', 27 October 1938, pp.696-98
AJ, Mead, Andrew and Allan, John, 'In the modern world', Vol.221, no.11, 24 March 2005, pp.24-33
AR, 'A house in Frognal, Hampstead', no. 503, October 1938, pp.155-58
BD, Howard, Alvin, 'Developing a Lifestyle', no.320, 22 October 1976, pp.20-21
Evening Standard, 'Hampstead critics of a concrete house', 21 May 1936
Evening Standard, 'Reply to the critics of a concrete house', 22 May 1936
Evening Standard, 'Artist shows what concrete house will look like', 26 July 1937, p.5
Evening Standard, 'Architects attack the concrete house of Hampstead', 31 July 1937
Hampstead Express, 'Building development in Hampstead', 12 August 1936
Manchester Guardian, 'Concrete in Frognal', 29 August 1937
News Chronicle, 'Vandalism in Hampstead', 14 July 1938
Otago Daily Times, 'London controversy: building of modern house', 5 September 1938
RIBAJ, Walford, Geoffrey, 'A client on his house: no. 66 Frognal Hampstead', 19 December 1938, pp.180-85
The Times, 'Vandalism in Hampstead, 22 July 1936
The Times, 'A modern house in Frognal', 9 August 1938

Dawe, Nick and Powell, Kenneth, *The Modern House Today*, Black Dog, London, 2001, p95
Powers, Alan, *Modern – the modern movement in Britain*, Merrell, London, 2005, pp.92-93
Pevsner, Nikolaus, *The Buildings of England: London volume 2*, Penguin, Harmondsworth, first published 1952, 1974 ed., p.199

Potcroft, Sutton, Pulborough, West Sussex, 1937–38
AAJ, Stevens, Thomas, 'Connell, Ward and Lucas 1927-39', November 1956, pp.114-15
Focus, Beardsmore, A C, 'Timber house at Sutton', number 2, winter 1938, Percy Lund Humphries and Co. Ltd, pp.28-34
Wood, Musman, RV, 'Timber house at Sutton', September 1939, pp.394-96

26 Bessborough Road, Roehampton, London, SW15, 1938–39
AAJ, Hitchcock, Henry-Russell and Stevens, Thomas, 'Connell, Ward and Lucas', November 1956, pp.108-9, 111

Dawe, Nick and Powell, Kenneth, *The Modern House Today*, Black Dog, London, 2001, p.95

Speculative houses

Parkwood Estate, Ruislip, Middlesex, 1933–35
AAJ, Hitchcock, Henry-Russell and Stevens, Thomas, 'Connell, Ward and Lucas', November 1956, p.105
AJ, 'Proposed Houses at Ruislip, Middlesex', 1 February 1934, pp.171-73
AJ, 'The Ruislip Case', 24 May 1934, pp.746-47
AJ, 'The Ruislip Case – latest', 21 June, 1934, p.891
AJ, 'Pair of houses at Ruislip, Middlesex', 23 May 1935, pp.812-13
AJ, 'Working details: 277, 278', 13 June 1935
AJ, 'Working details: 341, 342', 10 October 1935
AJ, 'The Ruislip case final correspondence', 27 September 1934, pp.455-57
American Architect and Architecture, 'Semi-detached houses at Ruislip', February 1937, p.41
The Observer & Gazette, 'Sun trap concrete houses', 27 April 1934

Dawe, Nick and Powell, Kenneth, *The Modern House Today*, Black Dog, London, 2001, p95
Yorke, FRS, *The Modern House in England*, Architectural Press, 1937, p.121

The Sun Houses, 4,5,6 and 8 High and Over Estate, Amersham, Buckinghamshire, 1933–35
AAJ, Hitchcock, Henry-Russell and Stevens, Thomas, 'Connell, Ward and Lucas', November 1956, p.104
A&BN, 'A house on the "High and Over" estate, Amersham, Bucks', 11 January 1935, p.75
Architecture Illustrated, 'Houses on the High and Over Estate, Amersham', August 1942, pp.99-100

56, 62 and 'One Other', Wicklands Avenue, **Saltdean**, East Sussex, 1934–35
AAJ, Hitchcock, Henry-Russell and Stevens, Thomas, 'Connell, Ward and Lucas', November 1956, p.104
AJ, 'Houses at Saltdean, near Brighton', 7 February 1935, pp.226-27

Turnor, Reginald, *The Smaller English House 1500-1939*, London, 1952, p.202

House Design for Frinton Park Development Scheme, Frinton-on-Sea, Essex, 1934–35
Building, 'Britain's first Modernist Town', December 1934, pp.482-87
Country Life, 'A planned Seaside Resort', 17 August 1935, p.182
Design for To-day, August 1935
RIBAJ, Lever, Jill, 'Deauville in Essex', November 1979, pp.496-99
The Builder, illustrations of 'Frinton park', 7 September 1934, p.386

Powers, Alan, *Oliver Hill: Architect and lover of life*, Mouton publications, 1989
Storey, Simon, 'Frinton Park Estate: A work of art and a social organism?' Loughborough University of Technology, 1992

Flats and Shops, Lord's Court, 32-36 St John's Wood Road, London, NW8, 1935–38
AAJ, Stevens, Thomas, 'Connell, Ward and Lucas 1927–1939', November 1956, pp.114-15

Social Housing

Kent House, 13–17 Ferdinand Street, Camden, NW1, 1934–35
A&BN, 'Model for new reinforced concrete flats', 8 January 1935
AAJ, Hitchcock, Henry-Russell and Stevens, Thomas, 'Connell, Ward and Lucas', November 1956, p.105
AJ, 'Proposed flats in chalk farm', 6 February 1934
AJ, 'Working Class flats for St Pancras work to start immediately', 21 June 1934, p.885
AJ, 'Kent House, Ferdinand Street', 19 December 1935, pp.909-15
AJ, 'Working Details: 388 – services', 9 January 1936, p.53-54
AJ, 'Working Details: 394 – balconies', 23 January 1936, pp.163-64
Daily Telegraph, New Zealand, 'Brighter Homes – New Zealand architects in England', 18 March 1936
Design for Today, 'the contemporary house', January 1936, pp.3-4
Design (London), 'Block of flats Ferdinand Street', no.312, December 1974, p.71
Evening News, 'Flats on stilts light and air for all. The Duke of Kent interested in an experiment', 29 November 1935
Housing Happenings, Scott, Nigel, (ed.), 'The North and South-West Groups', no.21, summer 1936, pp.39-40
The Builder, 'Model for new reinforced concrete flats for the St Pancras Housing Improvement Society', 15 February 1935, pp.317, 327
The Times, 'Flats on stilts', 2 February 1935
The Times, 'Blocks of Flats at Chalk Farm', 3 December 1935
The Times, 'Housing in St Pancras', 4 December 1935

White, Mildred (ed.), *Working details 1: Domestic*, Architectural Press, London, 1939

Competition for working class flats in reinforced concrete, 1935
A&BN, 'Competition for working-class flats in reinforced concrete – a review of unpremiated designs', 29 March 1935, p.406

Other projects

Ecole du Petit Cordon Bleu, 29 Sloane St, London, SW1, 1931
Lucas, Dione, and Hume, Rosemary, *Au Petit Cordon Bleu*, London, 1936

The Vitamin Café, 419 Oxford Street, London, W1, 1931
A&BN, 'Design in Metal Faced Plywood', 14 August 1931, pp.194-95
AR, Gibberd, Frederick, 'Some Wall Sheathings', January 1934, p.34
AR, 'The Craftsman's portfolio Number 67: Modern Light Fittings', March 1932, p.113

Health Shop, 70-71 Welbeck Street, London, W1, 1932
AJ, 'A Health Shop in Welbeck Street', 17 August 1932, pp.193-96

The Edith Edwards Preventorium, Papworth, Cambridgeshire, 1935–39
Daily Telegraph, New Zealand, 'Brilliant Career – former Napier Boy', 25 September 1935

Individual Health Centre, 1935–36
AAJ, Hitchcock, Henry-Russell and Stevens, Thomas, 'Connell, Ward and Lucas', November 1956, p.106
Architecture North-West, Ward, Basil, 'Things remembered: Heroic relics', Vol. 29, June/July 1968, pp.12-16

Sound City film production and recording studios, Shepperton, Surrey, 1934–36
A&BN, 'Studios for Messrs. Sound City (Films), Ltd, Shepperton', 4 September 1936. pp.273-77
A&BN, 'The architect portfolio – Film Studios at Sound City, Shepperton', supplement 18, September 1936
AJ, anon. 'Analysis of a Building: 6 – film studios at Shepperton', 27 August 1936, pp.267-71
Architecture d'aujourd'hui, April 1938, p.32
Cinema and Theatre Construction, 'Sound City Shepperton', July 1936, pp.25-30
Daily Telegraph, New Zealand, 25 September 1935
Kinematograph Weekly, 'Extensions at Sound City', 13 May 1937

Competition for Hertford County Buildings, Hertfordshire, 1935
A&BN, 'Hertford County Buildings Competition', 1 November 1935, pp.124-32
AJ, 'The Hertford Competition', 31 October 1935, pp.621-26

Competition for Newport Civic Buildings, South Wales, 1936
AJ, 'The Newport Competition', 17 December 1936, pp.836-39

Competition for St George's Hospital, London, SW1, 1939
AJ, 'St George's Hospital', 23 February 1939, pp.314-19

Later years of Connell, Ward and Lucas

Amyas Connell
Habitat International, Dennis Sharp, 'The Modern Movement in East Africa: The work of Amyas Connell in Tanganyika and Kenya…'. Vol.7, no.5/6, 1983, pp 311-26

Basil Ward
A&BN, 'Metabolic Unit, Hammersmith Hospital', 6 January 1955, pp.7-12
AR, 'Hospital Extension, Hammersmith', January 1954, pp.17-18
AR, 'Provincial Insurance Building', January 1954, pp.68-69
The Builder, 'On a Good Wicket', 18 March 1955, p.459

Colin Lucas
A&BN, 'LCC New Type Housing: Scheme for sites, Princes Way and Wimbledon Park Side, Wandsworth', 8 December 1950, pp.618-22
AR, Alton Estate, Roehampton, SW15', November 1956, pp.307-09
AR, 'Roehampton', N Pevsner, July 1959, pp.21-35

Index

Page numbers in *italic* refer to illustrations. Page numbers with a 'c' refer to information in captions.

Acknowledgements

It is difficult to know where to start in recording thanks for a project that germinated some 50 years ago. In a way this study began in 1956 at the AA School after a special issue of the AA Journal on Connell Ward and Lucas was published in June. Edited by Brian Housden, it included a contribution from Arthur Korn who praised the work of the trio comparing it to the best of European Modernism. That year Arthur Korn became my tutor and often referred to examples of Connell Ward and Lucas domestic work as benchmarks in careers that had spanned the 1930s.

Korn may well have pushed me off the starting block but contact and friendship with both Connell and Ward fuelled the race to find out more inclusive and reliable information. Others who helped at the early stage include architects who worked with Lucas, among them another AA tutor, John Killick, who with Bill Howell and John Partridge formed an important team at the LCC, and, in the 1970s, the AA's peripatetic and omniscient scholar Thomas (Sam) Stevens, who had also contributed to the AAJ special issue.

I was able to commission a major article on Connell Ward and Lucas from Basil Ward for an AA Festschrift (1966) for Arthur Korn and later to broadcast an interview for the Open University A305 series. Later still I got to know Ward well when he was head of the Manchester Polytechnic school of architecture (now Manchester Metropolitan University) when I was teaching down the Oxford Road at the University. Some of Basil Ward's papers that had been left to Lancaster University's Arts Centre and which were no longer required by the University were passed on to me for safe keeping by the late Dr Geoffrey Beard, director of the Arts Centre. They proved to be invaluable primary source material.

The work involved in collecting material, taking photographs, interviewing subjects and archival investigation has been supported by a number of bodies who have made awards and grants. These include two RIBA modern architecture research fund grants and a special award from the Arts Council of Great Britain, as well as a small writers' award from the Society of Authors. More recently the Paul Mellon Centre for Studies in British Art provided a research support grant in 2002 and a further author's publication grant in 2004. Additionally, a publication grant was allocated to Frances Lincoln the publisher. The Building Centre Trust generously underwrote the main costs of the 1994 exhibition 'Connell Ward and Lucas: Modern Movement Architects in England 1929–1939' and the subsequent tours and catalogue (Book Art, 1994).

Sally Rendel and I are most grateful for the continuous encouragement, help and shared memories of Amyas Connell's sons James and Graham Connell and Colin Lucas' son Mark Lucas, all of whom have been most generous in providing family history, drawings, papers, prints and panels. James was prepared to raid the family albums for photographs of his father's work in Tanzania and Kenya.
Tim Vaulkard of TRIAD Nairobi office allowed us to use archive photographs and also provided lists of buildings designed by Connell. Through correspondence Graham McCullough (TRIAD) shared his memories of Connell in Africa. My wife and partner, the architect Yasmin Shariff, who is from Kenya and worked with Connell in his London office, has offered unstinting encouragement, support, criticism and patience during the production of this book, despite the fact that it has often interfered with the smooth running of Dennis Sharp Architects. I cannot thank her enough for her tremendous support. Another Kenyan, the late architect and planner Erica Mann provided copies of the local architects' year books and journals which occasionally featured the work of Connell and colleagues in the Kenya Architects' Association. Supplementary information has come from the East African architect Mr Joginder Chudha and the Goan-born Tanzanian architect Anthony Almeida, no mean modernist himself.

To all these I should add the name of Jan Hemsing, a former close colleague of Connell's first in England and then as an assistant architect in East Africa, who provided me with information on their lives in Tange and Nairobi including personal photographs. Her recently completed biographical manuscript, so far unpublished, 'Amyas Connell: A Giant of a Man' brilliantly encapsulates the man, his moods and missions, as well as his personal foibles and unremitting commitment to architecture.

The work of Connell Ward and Lucas has been a favourite thesis topic for architecture and design students and our thanks go to the following former students for sight of their dissertations or project submissions. The first was Paul Zara, now of Conran Associates, who generously provided his own photographs and collected research material gathered for his UCL Bartlett dissertation on Connell Ward and Lucas, 1994. We also thank Robert Esau, Peter Roth (PCL 1982); Martin Morrissey (UCL 1995), Peter Figueredo (Liverpool 1970-1) and Nobuyuki Ogura (UCL, DPU 1985) for copies of their submissions and the OU projects on Connell Ward and Lucas by PMH Mace (1987) and Edward Alden (OU 1979) on the Flat Roof House at Little Frieth. This was also the subject that brought in Sally Rendel (née Godwin) when she sent me a copy of her Cambridge University dissertation on the same house in 1998.

DSA were commissioned to renovate the Flat Roof House and Sally joined me as a part-time researcher for the book on the partnership. Her work – enthusiastic, consistent and thorough to a commendable degree – has really made this publication possible. For all the support there has been from other people and other sources, it has been Sally's persistence, her research ability, her skills as a writer and editor of material for this book – as well as her appetite for forcing out gems of previously obscured information – that has, I believe, turned what might have been a catalogue raisonné into an enthralling narrative. No thanks are enough.

I must also acknowledge the hard work of Dennis Sharp Architects staff over many years for their work on this book, including Anna Golzari (research for the 1994 exhibition), Rachel Doragh (research work in New Zealand), secretary Sarah Tiffin and most recently DSA architecture student Rai Nakamura who produced seemingly endless scans for our designer Malcolm Frost to use. Malcolm's own contribution – along with that of Graeme Martin of Igma Imaging – has as usual been invaluable. My debt of gratitude to Malcolm goes back to the production of the Building Centre catalogue. His modern graphic work is of a very high standard and he has, as ever, been indefatigable. He gets things right. Particular thanks are also due to Jane Crawley, the book's commissioning editor, for her remarkable editorial skills, patient manner and strong encouragement to complete the task.

Much helpful support and encouragement was had from John Allan and Justin De Syllas of Avanti Architects, while other architects and colleagues who have given advice over many years include Jake Brown, HT Cadbury-Brown, the late Catherine Cooke, Dean Clark, Trevor Dannatt, Michael Findlay, Graham Francis, Tony Fretton, Maxwell Fry, Denys Lasdun, Alan Powers, Jack Pritchard, Patricia Pearson, Roy Stout and John Winter.

Material for this project was gathered at research centres and archives including the Architectural Association Library, Bristol Record Office, The British School in Rome, City of Westminster Archives Centre, East Sussex Record Office, Epsom and Ewell Borough Council, Essex County Council Archive, Hampshire County Council Record Office, Hertfordshire County Council Record Office, National Monument Record Centre, Wycombe District Council, Reigate and Banstead Borough Council, Royal Institute of British Architects Library, Surrey County Council Records, West Sussex County Council Record Office and Shepperton Studios.

The enthusiasm of the current owners of the buildings has given us access to the vast majority of them and a plethora of original material. Our thanks go to Mr Greenstein, Mr and Mrs Halley, Mr and Mrs Heffernan, Terry Hylton, Mr and Mrs Jankel, Mr Jones, Mr and Mrs Lawrence, Mr and Mrs Newbound, Mr Park, Mr and Mrs Putman, Mrs Rolfe, the late Phillada Sewell, Mr and Mrs Sharp, Mr and Mrs Stevenson, Mrs Tomkins and Mrs Vine. Members of the families who originally commissioned the buildings or architects who have since worked on them have given memories and photographs that have enriched the book; Anthony Proudman, Adam Lawrence, James Ley, Barry and Jean Russell and Annabel Veneto.

Sally Rendel would particularly like to thank Giles Oliver, Gregory Penoyre, Alan Powers, Sunand Prasad and Andrew Saint for their support and Sandy Rendel, without whom this project would not have come to fruition.

I would particularly like to thank the Editorial Director of the *Architectural Review* Paul Finch for his generous gesture in granting permission to use selected material from the *AR* and the *AJ*. Thanks also for the use of photographs from the publisher Rail Romances book on Basset-Lowke and James Gorst for Reginald Brill's painting of Bernard Ashmole.

Dennis Sharp

Picture Credits

All the original contemporary personal and professional photographs (including copies) used in this book came from the collection of material on Connell Ward and Lucas courtesy of James and Graham Connell and the TRIAD office in Nairobi. A number of personal photographs were supplied by Justin De Syllas, Mark Lucas, Adam Lawrence, James Ley, Jean Russell and Annabel Veneto. James Connell and Graham Connell retain the copyright on all their material including the Connell Ward and Lucas working drawings on pp. 14, 48, 54, 100, 104, 112, 116, 142.

Photographers and copyright holders names are followed by page numbers and shown as t-top, c-centre, b-bottom, l-left, m-middle and r-right.

Architectural Press, 17cb, 18, 32, 35b, 40, 137tcbr
Associated Press, 155
Bernard Ashmole, courtesy of John Allan, 44, 45b, 47t
BookART and Architecture Picture Library, 20, 21, 22t, 23tcb, 24tb, 25tc, 26b, 27tc, 34b, 35t, 67t, 70b, 95c, 134, 138br
British School at Rome, 10b, 13
Paul Barnfather, 140tr, br
Reginald Brill, courtesy of James Gorst, 12t
Tim Crocker, 42, 82, 84, 85, 87, 123, 124, 126 and 127tr
Christopher Dean, 59br
Jan Hemsing, 182, 183tc
Wessel de Jonge, 173
National Monuments Record, 28, 51
Adam Lawrence, courtesy of, 75m, b
Mark Lucas, courtesy of, 16b, 17t, 58br, 195b
Peter Lucas, courtesy of Mark Lucas, 197
Murray White and Ward, 152tb
Rail Romances Publishing, 22clr
Sally Rendel, 59br, 75t, 76t, 77, 79t, 80, 81ml, 135, 149m
Aaron Schuman/RIBA Journal, 78, 81tr, mr
Phillada Sewell, courtesy of James Ley, 79b
Morley von Sternberg, 52, 66
Bill Toomey, courtesy of Jean Russell, 72, 74t
TRIAD, Nairobi, courtesy of Tim Vaulkhard, 180, 185, 187b
Annabel Veneto, courtesy of, 119t

The photographers who were commissioned by Connell Ward and Lucas for the contemporary journals in which their work was featured included Herbert Felton, Hugh Francis, Sydney Newbery, de Burgh Galwey, Cracknell and Humphrey Spender. Other photographs, sketches and drawings, not among the CWL archival material, are by the authors.

The authors would like to thank Tim Crocker for photographing Potcroft, Frognal and the Concrete House for the book. They are most grateful for the helpful co-operation of a number of magazine and publications editors who have kindly loaned material either commissioned for their journals or in their possession. This material has been used in good faith and acknowledged if and as requested. It shall not be the subject of any outside claim. In the event that any other material has been used that is subject to copyright and this has inadvertently not been cleared notification should be made to the authors who will be pleased to correct any errors and add credits if required in any subsequent editions.